Mastering
UML with Rational Rose 2002

Mastering™
UML with Rational Rose® 2002

Wendy Boggs

Michael Boggs

SYBEX®   San Francisco   London

Associate Publisher: Richard Mills

Acquisitions Editor: Peter Arnold

Developmental Editor: Tom Cirtin

Editor: Donna Crossman

Production Editor: Mae Lum

Technical Editor: Eric Aker

Graphic Illustrator: Tony Jonick

Electronic Publishing Specialist: Jill Niles

Proofreaders: Emily Hsuan, Nelson Kim, Yariv Rabinovitch, Nancy Riddiough

Indexer: Nancy Guenther

CD Coordinator: Christine Detlefs

CD Technician: Kevin Ly

Book Designer: Maureen Forys, Happenstance Type-O-Rama

Cover Designer: Design Site

Cover Illustrator: Tania Kac, Design Site

An earlier version of this book was published under the title *Mastering UML with Rational Rose*, © 1999, SYBEX Inc.

Library of Congress Card Number: 2001096976

ISBN: 0-7821-4017-3

SYBEX and the SYBEX logo are either registered trademarks or trademarks of SYBEX Inc. in the United States and/or other countries.

Mastering is a trademark of SYBEX Inc.

Screen reproductions produced with FullShot 99. FullShot 99 © 1991-1999 Inbit Incorporated. All rights reserved. FullShot is a trademark of Inbit Incorporated.

The CD interface was created using Macromedia Director, COPYRIGHT 1994, 1997–1999 Macromedia Inc. For more information on Macromedia and Macromedia Director, visit www.macromedia.com.

TRADEMARKS: SYBEX has attempted throughout this book to distinguish proprietary trademarks from descriptive terms by following the capitalization style used by the manufacturer.

The author and publisher have made their best efforts to prepare this book, and the content is based upon final release software whenever possible. Portions of the manuscript may be based upon pre-release versions supplied by software manufacturer(s). The author and the publisher make no representation or warranties of any kind with regard to the completeness or accuracy of the contents herein and accept no liability of any kind including but not limited to performance, merchantability, fitness for any particular purpose, or any losses or damages of any kind caused or alleged to be caused directly or indirectly from this book.

Manufactured in the United States of America

10 9 8 7 6 5 4 3 2 1

For Andrew

Acknowledgments

A great deal of effort goes into writing a book. While some of this work is done by the authors, a lot of it is done by a whole team of people. We would like to thank everyone involved in this book. Thanks to Richard Mills and Jordan Gold at Sybex for making it possible, and to Tom Cirtin, who was instrumental in getting the book ready for publication. Thanks to Eric Aker for performing the technical review. Thanks to the editorial and production team at Sybex: Mae Lum, Donna Crossman, Jill Niles, Christine Detlefs, Kevin Ly, and Tony Jonick. Thanks to indexer Nancy Guenther and thanks to the proofreaders: Emily Hsuan, Nelson Kim, Yariv Rabinovitch, and Nancy Riddiough. We couldn't have done it without all of you.

Contents at a Glance

Contents

Introduction

IN THIS EVER-CHANGING WORLD of object-oriented application development, it has been getting harder and harder to develop and manage high-quality applications in a reasonable amount of time. As a result of this challenge, and out of a need for a universal object-modeling language every company could use, the Unified Modeling Language (UML) was born. UML is the information technology industry's version of a blueprint. It is a method for describing the system's architecture in detail. Using this blueprint, it becomes much easier to build or maintain a system and to ensure that the system will hold up to requirement changes.

A lot of wonderful books out there discuss the processes of rapid application development, object-oriented analysis and design, object modeling, and UML. This book focuses specifically on designing systems with UML and Rational Rose 2001, 2001A and 2002. Rose is one of a handful of tools that supports rapid application development using UML. It supports Use Case diagrams, Activity diagrams, Sequence diagrams, Collaboration diagrams, Statechart diagrams, Component diagrams, and Deployment diagrams. Through forward- and reverse-engineering features, it supports the code generation and reverse engineering of C++, Java, Visual Basic, and XML DTDs. Add-ins are available for a number of other object-oriented languages to further extend the functionality provided by Rose.

What's New

The object-oriented world has evolved quite a bit over the past few years. We've seen the proliferation of web-based systems, new innovations in object-oriented tools and languages, and the increased globalization of development efforts. And, of course, we've seen the evolution of UML. UML is becoming a comprehensive language that can be used to model all of the different aspects of a system design. It can be used to model constructs in XML, J2EE, and numerous programming languages; design a database; and even model the business surrounding a computerized system.

As UML has evolved, so has Rose. Rational Rose 2001, 2001A and 2002 include new functionality, such as support for web application development, that helps make the design process better than ever. Some of the new features of Rational Rose 2001, 2001A and 2002 include:

◆ Business modeling

◆ Activity diagrams

◆ Web modeling

◆ Increased Java and J2EE support

◆ Increased EJB support

◆ XML DTD support

◆ Data modeling

- ◆ ANSI C++ language support

- ◆ SQL Server 2000 support

- ◆ Support for Sun Java Server Pages and Microsoft Active Server Pages

Who Should Read This Book

This book is designed for programmers, software architects, and analysts who need comprehensive coverage of Rose—beginning, intermediate, and advanced topics—especially those who don't have much experience with UML. As we developed the book, we tried to answer three questions: what are the diagrams and constructs of UML, why is each type of diagram used, and how do you model each diagram and each construct using Rose?

This book covers the fundamentals of Rose:

- ◆ How to model business processes

- ◆ How to create actors, use cases, and Use Case diagrams

- ◆ How to create Sequence and Collaboration diagrams

- ◆ How to create classes, attributes, operations, relationships, and Class diagrams

- ◆ How to create Statechart diagrams

- ◆ How to create components and Component diagrams

- ◆ How to create Deployment diagrams

- ◆ How to use UML and Rose to create a complete, detailed blueprint of your system

- ◆ How to use the new features provided by Rose 2001, 2001A, and 2002

- ◆ How to generate code from Rose into C++, Java, and Visual Basic

- ◆ How to reverse engineer C++, Java, and Visual Basic code into Rose

- ◆ How to generate and reverse engineer an XML DTD

- ◆ How to model a database structure using Rose

- ◆ How to model a web application

This book does not need to be read sequentially. Each chapter was designed to give you a detailed understanding of one piece of Rational Rose. There are exercises provided at the end of most chapters to give you some practice using Rose and UML.

While the book explains the fundamentals of UML and its modeling elements, it focuses on the portions of UML that are supported by Rational Rose, and does not cover every aspect of UML.

If you are new to Rose or UML, you may want to read chapters 1 through 11 sequentially and complete all of the exercises. The exercises in these chapters will walk you through the steps for modeling a sample system. If you are familiar with Rose and UML, this book may be used as a reference for specific Rose or UML questions.

How This Book is Organized

This book is organized into 19 chapters and an appendix. Chapters 1 and 2 provide an overview of UML, the object-modeling process, and the Rational Rose tool. In Chapter 1, we cover the fundamentals of UML and introduce you to Rational Rose. We discuss the different types of UML diagrams, what each diagram is used for, and how it is built. In Chapter 2, we take a tour of Rose, introducing you to the pieces of the Rose user interface and the functionality that Rose provides.

Chapters 3 through 11 cover all of the basics of Rose. These chapters cover creating and updating diagrams, adding classes and class details, and generating reports. Through the creation of the different types of diagrams discussed in these chapters, a system development team can gain a complete understanding of the structure and behavior of the system being built.

Chapters 12 through 17 cover the C++, Java, Visual Basic, and XML code-generation and reverse-engineering features of Rose. In these chapters, we examine how each UML construct maps to a particular programming language. You'll see a number of code examples that were generated from Rose and modeling elements that were reverse engineered from source code.

Chapter 18 covers the Data Modeler feature of Rose. This is a robust tool that supports the modeling of database tables, joins, stored procedures, triggers, and other elements. You can create your data model automatically from an object model, or reverse engineer an object model from your data model. The Data Modeler also includes a code-generation feature, which will create and optionally run the DDL (data definition language) needed to create or update your database structure. The database structure can also be reverse engineered into your Rose model.

Chapter 19 provides an overview of the web-modeling process. This includes the different stereotypes you can use to model a web application, the generation of code from a model for a web application, and the reverse engineering of a web application.

Finally, for those who need an easy primer for UML, the appendix, "Getting Started with UML," should be all you need to get up and running.

About the CD-ROM

In the book, as we explore the features of Rose, we'll build some Rose models for a sample system. On the CD-ROM that is packaged with this book, you will find sample UML models for this system and examples of the code that was generated using Rational Rose. You'll also find some sample Rose scripts, which are examples of macros written in the script language that comes packaged with Rose. A link to the Rational website is also included so that you can find all sorts of information about Rational partners and products, UML, and object modeling.

How to Contact the Authors

If you have any questions at all about Rose or UML, please feel free to contact us. You can contact Wendy at wboggs@attbi.com or Mike at mboggs@attbi.com. Please also visit the Sybex website at www.sybex.com.

Chapter 1

Introduction to UML

THE PACE OF BUSINESS is getting faster and faster, with a greater need to compete and sustain a market. In this age of e-commerce, e-business, e-tailing, and other e's, "traditional" system development just doesn't cut it anymore. Systems now must be developed in "Internet time." Also, this faster pace has increased the need for flexible systems. Before, a user could send a request to the data-processing center and wait two years for a change. Now a user sends a request for change to the IT department and demands it in two weeks! Six-week development cycles, demanding managers, demanding users, and even the concept of XP (extreme programming) drive this point: System changes must happen fast!

This is where the Unified Modeling Language (UML) enters the picture. UML is the industry-standard modeling notation for object-oriented systems, and is the premiere platform for rapid application development. In this chapter, we describe how UML came into being, introduce the concepts of object-oriented programming, and show you how to use UML to structure your applications.

- ◆ Learning about the object-oriented paradigm and visual modeling
- ◆ Exploring types of graphical notation
- ◆ Looking at types of UML diagrams
- ◆ Developing software using visual modeling

Introduction to the Object-Oriented Paradigm

Structured programming was the mainstream in the earlier days of software engineering. Programmers began developing standard blocks of code to perform operations like printing, and then copied and pasted that code into every application they wrote. While this reduced the development time for new applications, it was difficult if a change was needed in that block of code, because the developer had to make the change everywhere that code had been copied. Structured programming presented some challenges for which *object-oriented* programming was designed to solve.

With object-oriented programming, developers create blocks of code, called *objects*. These objects are then used by the various applications. Should one of the objects require modification, a developer needs to make the change only once. Companies are rushing out to adopt this technology and integrate it into their existing applications. In fact, most applications being developed today are object-oriented. Some languages, such as Java, require an object-oriented structure. But what does it mean?

The object-oriented paradigm is a different way of viewing applications. With the object-oriented approach, you divide an application into many small chunks, or objects, that are fairly independent of one another. You can then build the application by piecing all of these objects together. Think of it as building a castle out of blocks. The first step is to make or buy some basic objects, the different types of blocks. Once you have these building blocks, you can put them together to make your castle. Once you build or buy some basic objects in the computer world, you can simply put them together to create new applications.

In the world of structured programming, to create a form with a list box, for example, you would need to write voluminous code: the code to create the form itself, the code to create and populate the list box, and the code to create an OK button that will accept the value in the list box. With object-oriented programming, on the other hand, you simply need to use three (typically prebuilt) objects: a form, a list box, and an OK button. The exercise of coding used to be along the lines of "create from scratch, but copy whatever you can find from old programs to save some time." The newer paradigm is "put together a bunch of objects, and then just focus on what's *unique* to this particular application."

One of the primary advantages of the object-oriented paradigm is the ability to build components once and then use them over and over again. Just as you can reuse a toy building block in a castle or a house, you can reuse a basic piece of object-oriented design and code in an accounting system, an inventory system, or an order-processing system.

So, how is this object-oriented paradigm different from the traditional approach to development? Traditionally, the approach to development has been to concern ourselves with the information that the system will maintain. With this approach, we ask the users what information they will need, design databases to hold the information, provide screens to input the information, and print reports to display the information. In other words, we focus on the information and pay less attention to what is done with the information or the behavior of the system. This approach is called *data-centric* and has been used to create thousands of systems over the years.

Data-centric modeling is great for database design and capturing information, but taking this approach when designing business applications presents some problems. One major challenge is that the requirements for the system will change over time. A system that is data-centric can handle a change to the database very easily, but a change to the business rules or to the behavior of the system is not so easy to implement.

The object-oriented paradigm has been developed in response to this problem. With the object-oriented approach, we focus on both information *and* behavior. Accordingly, we now can develop systems that are resilient and flexible to changes in information and/or behavior.

The benefit of flexibility can be realized only by designing an object-oriented system well. This requires knowledge of some principles of object orientation: encapsulation, inheritance, and polymorphism.

Encapsulation

In object-oriented systems, we combine a piece of information with the specific behavior that acts upon that information. Then we package these into an object. This is referred to as *encapsulation*.

Another way to look at encapsulation is that we divide the application into small parts of related functionality. For example, we have information relating to a bank account, such as the account number, balance, customer name, address, account type, interest rate, and opening date. We also have behavior for a bank account: open, close, deposit, withdraw, change type, change customer, and change address. We encapsulate this information and behavior together into an *account* object. As a result, any changes to the banking system regarding accounts can simply be implemented in the account object. It works like a one-stop shop for all account information and behavior.

Another benefit of encapsulation is that it limits the effects of changes to the system. Think of a system as a body of water and the requirement change as a big rock. You drop the rock into the water and—SPLASH!—big waves are created in all directions. They travel throughout the lake, bounce off the shore, reverberate, and collide with other waves. In fact, some of the water may even splash over the shore and out of the lake. In other words, the rock hitting the water caused a huge ripple effect. But if we encapsulate our lake by dividing it into smaller bodies of water with barriers between them, then the requirement change hits the system—SPLASH! As before, waves are created in all directions. But the waves can only go as far as one of the barriers, and then they stop. So, by encapsulating the lake, we have limited the ripple effect of dropping the rock in, as shown in Figure 1.1.

FIGURE 1.1

Encapsulation:
Lake model

Let's apply this idea of encapsulation to the banking system. Recently, the bank management decided that if the customer has a credit account at the bank, the credit account could be used as an overdraft for their checking account. In a nonencapsulated system, we begin with a shotgun approach to impact analysis. Basically, we do not know where all of the uses of withdraw functionality are in the system, so we have to look everywhere. When we find it, we have to make some changes to incorporate this new requirement. If we're really good, we probably found about 80 percent of the uses of withdraw within the system. With an encapsulated system, we do not need to use the shotgun approach to analysis. We look at a model of our system and simply find where the withdrawal behavior was encapsulated. After locating the functionality in the account, we make our requirement change once, only in that object, and our task is complete! As you can see in Figure 1.2, only the Account class needs to change.

A concept similar to encapsulation is *information hiding*. Information hiding is the ability to hide the murky details of an object from the outside world. To an object, the outside world means anything outside of itself, even though that outside world includes the rest of the system. Information hiding provides the same benefit as encapsulation: flexibility. We will explore this concept more in Chapter 6, "Classes and Packages."

FIGURE 1.2

Encapsulation:
Banking model

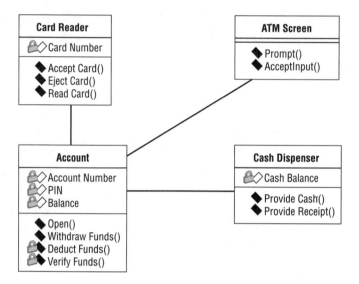

Inheritance

Inheritance is the second of the fundamental object-oriented concepts. No, it has nothing to do with the million dollars you're leaving for little Johnny. It has more to do with the nose you got from your father or mother. In object-oriented systems, inheritance is a mechanism that lets you create new objects based on old ones: The *child* object inherits the qualities of a *parent* object.

You can see examples of inheritance in the natural world. There are hundreds of different types of mammals: dogs, cats, humans, whales, and so on. Each of these has certain characteristics that are unique and certain characteristics that are common to the whole group, such as having hair, being warm-blooded, and nurturing their young. In object-oriented terms, there is a *mammal* object that holds the common characteristics. This object is the parent of the child objects cat, dog, human, whale, etc. The dog object inherits the characteristics of the mammal object, and has some additional *dog* characteristics of its own, such as running in circles and slobbering. The object-oriented paradigm has borrowed this idea of inheritance from the natural world, as shown in Figure 1.3, so we can apply the same concept to our systems.

One of the major benefits of inheritance is ease of maintenance. When something changes that affects all mammals, only the parent object needs to change—the child objects will automatically inherit the changes. If mammals were suddenly to become cold-blooded, only the mammal object would need to change. The cat, dog, human, whale, and other child objects would automatically inherit the new, cold-blooded characteristic of mammals.

In an object-oriented system, an example of inheritance might be in the windows. Say we have a large system with 125 windows. One day, a customer requests a disclaimer message on all of the windows. In a system without inheritance, we now have the rather tedious task of going into each one of the 125 windows and making the change. If our system were object-oriented, we would have inherited all of the windows from a common parent. Now, all we need to do is go into the parent and make the change once. All of the windows will automatically inherit the change, as shown in Figure 1.4.

FIGURE 1.3

Inheritance: Natural model

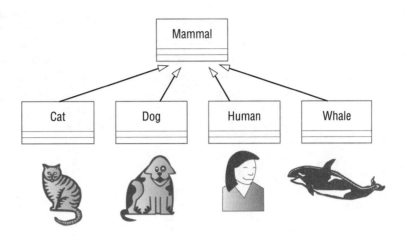

FIGURE 1.4

Inheritance: Window model

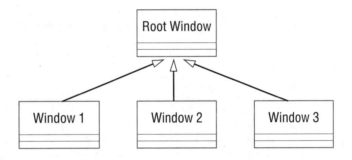

In a banking system, we might use inheritance for the different types of accounts we have. Our hypothetical bank has four different types of accounts: checking, savings, credit card, and certificates of deposit. These different types of accounts have some similarities. Each one has an account number, interest rate, and owner. So, we can create a parent object called account to hold the common characteristics of all the accounts. The child objects can have their own unique characteristics in addition to the inherited ones. The credit account, for example, will also have a credit limit and minimum payment amount. The certificate of deposit will also have a maturity date. Changes to the parent will affect all children, but the children are free to adapt without disturbing each other or their parents.

Polymorphism

The third principle of object orientation is *polymorphism*. The dictionary defines it as the occurrence of different forms, stages, or types. Polymorphism means having many forms or implementations of a particular functionality. As with inheritance, polymorphism can be seen in the natural world. Given the command, or function, of "Speak!" a human may reply, "How do you do?" The dog may reply "Woof!" The cat may reply "Meow!" but will probably just ignore you.

In terms of an object-oriented system, this means that we can have many implementations of a particular functionality. For example, we might be building a graphic drawing system. When the user wants to draw something, be it a line, circle, or rectangle, the system issues a draw command. The system is comprised of many types of shapes, each of which contains the behavior to draw itself. So, when the user wants to draw a circle, the circle object's draw command is invoked. By using polymorphism, the system figures out as it is running which type of shape is being drawn. Without polymorphism, the code for the draw function might look like this:

```
Function Shape.drawMe()
{
SWITCH Shape.Type
Case "Circle"
Shape.drawCircle();
Case "Rectangle"
Shape.drawRectangle();
Case "Line"
Shape.drawLine();
END SWITCH
}
```

With polymorphism, the code for draw would just call a `drawMe()` function for the object being drawn, as in this example:

```
Function draw()
{
Shape.drawMe();
}
```

Each shape (circle, line, rectangle, etc.) would then have a `drawMe()` function to draw the particular shape.

One of the benefits of polymorphism, as with the other principles of object orientation, is ease of maintenance. What happens, for example, when the application now needs to draw a triangle? In the nonpolymorphic case, a new `drawTriangle()` function has to be added to the shape object. Also, the `drawMe()` function of the shape object has to be changed to accommodate the new type of shape. With polymorphism, we create a new triangle object with a `drawMe()` function to draw itself. The `draw()` function that initiates the drawing operation does not have to change at all.

What Is Visual Modeling?

If you were building a new addition to your house, you probably wouldn't start by just buying a bunch of wood and nailing it together until it looks about right. Similarly, you'd be more than a little concerned if the contractor doing the job decided to "wing it" and work without plans. You'd want some blueprints to follow so you can plan and structure the addition before you start working. Odds are, the addition will last longer this way. You wouldn't want the whole thing to come crashing down with the slightest rain.

Models do the same thing for us in the software world. They are the blueprints for systems. A blueprint helps you plan an addition before you build it; a model helps you plan a system before you build it. It can help you be sure the design is sound, the requirements have been met, and the system can withstand even a hurricane of requirement changes.

As you gather requirements for your system, you'll take the business needs of the users and map them into requirements that your team can use and understand. Eventually, you'll want to take these requirements and generate code from them. By formally mapping the requirements to the code, you can ensure that the requirements are actually met by the code, and that the code can easily be traced back to the requirements. This process is called *modeling*. The result of the modeling process is the ability to trace the business needs to the requirements to the model to the code, and back again, without getting lost along the way.

Visual modeling is the process of taking the information from the model and displaying it graphically using a standard set of graphical elements. A standard is vital to realizing one of the benefits of visual modeling: communication. Communication between users, developers, analysts, testers, managers, and anyone else involved with a project is the primary purpose of visual modeling. You could accomplish this communication using nonvisual (textual) information, but on the whole, humans are visual creatures. We seem to be able to understand complexity better when it is displayed to us visually as opposed to written textually. By producing visual models of a system, we can show how the system works on several levels. We can model the interactions between the users and a system. We can model the interactions of objects within a system. We can even model the interactions between systems, if we so desire.

After creating these models, we can show them to all interested parties, and those parties can glean the information they find valuable from the model. For example, users can visualize the interactions they will make with the system from looking at a model. Analysts can visualize the interactions between objects from the models. Developers can visualize the objects that need to be developed and what each one needs to accomplish. Testers can visualize the interactions between objects and prepare test cases based on these interactions. Project managers can see the whole system and how the parts interact. And chief information officers can look at high-level models and see how systems in their organization interact with one another. All in all, visual models provide a powerful tool for showing the proposed system to all of the interested parties.

Systems of Graphical Notation

One important consideration in visual modeling is what graphical notation to use to represent various aspects of a system. This notation needs to be conveyed to all interested parties or the model will not be very useful. Many people have proposed notations for visual modeling. Some of the popular notations that have strong support are Booch, Object Modeling Technology (OMT), and UML.

Rational Rose supports these three notations; however, UML is a standard that has been adopted by the majority of the industry as well as the standards' governing boards such as ANSI and the Object Management Group (OMG).

Booch Notation

The *Booch* method is named for its inventor, Grady Booch, at Rational Software Corporation. He has written several books discussing the needs and benefits of visual modeling, and has developed a notation of graphical symbols to represent various aspects of a model. For example, objects in this notation are represented by clouds, illustrating the fact that objects can be almost anything. Booch's notation also includes various arrows to represent the types of relationships between objects. We will discuss these types of objects and relationships in Chapter 4, "Use Cases and Actors." Figure 1.5 is a sampling of the objects and relationships represented in the Booch notation.

FIGURE 1.5

Examples of symbols in the Booch notation

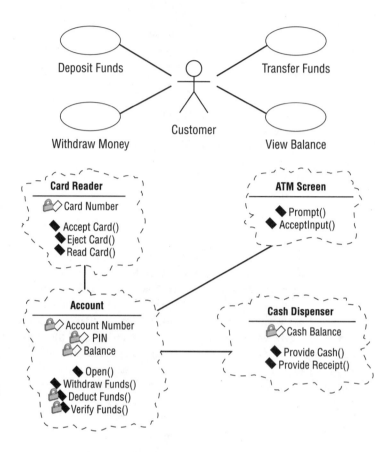

Object Management Technology (OMT)

The *OMT* notation comes from Dr. James Rumbaugh, who has written several books about systems analysis and design. In an aptly titled book, *Object-Oriented Modeling and Design* (Prentice Hall, 1990), Rumbaugh discusses the importance of modeling systems in real-world components called objects. OMT uses simpler graphics than Booch to illustrate systems. A sampling of the objects and relationships represented in the OMT notation follows in Figure 1.6.

FIGURE 1.6

Examples of
symbols in the
OMT notation

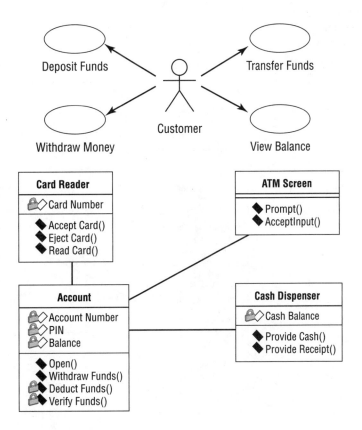

Unified Modeling Language (UML)

UML notation comes from a collaborative effort of Grady Booch, Dr. James Rumbaugh, Ivar Jacobson,
Rebecca Wirfs-Brock, Peter Yourdon, and many others. Jacobson is a scholar who has written about
capturing system requirements in packages of transactions called *use cases*. We will discuss use cases in
detail in Chapter 4. Jacobson also developed a method for system design called *Object-Oriented Software
Engineering (OOSE)* that focused on analysis. Booch, Rumbaugh, and Jacobson, commonly referred to as
the "three amigos," all work at Rational Software Corporation and focus on the standardization and
refinement of UML. UML symbols closely match those of the Booch and OMT notations, and also
include elements from other notations. Figure 1.7 shows a sample of UML notation.

FIGURE 1.7

Examples of
symbols in UML
notation

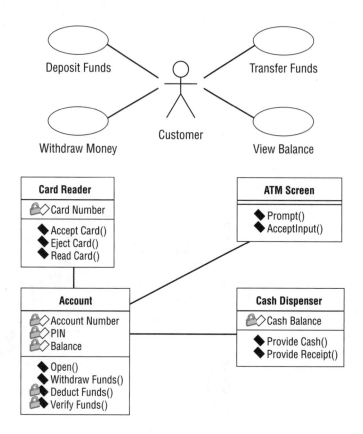

The consolidation of methods that became UML started in 1993. Each of the three amigos of UML began to incorporate ideas from the other methodologies. Official unification of the methodologies continued until late 1995, when version 0.8 of the Unified Method was introduced. The Unified Method was refined and changed to the Unified Modeling Language in 1996. UML 1.0 was ratified and given to the Object Technology Group in 1997, and many major software development companies began adopting it. In 1997, OMG released UML 1.1 as an industry standard.

Over the past years, UML has evolved to incorporate new ideas such as web-based systems and data modeling. The latest release is UML 1.3, which was ratified in 2000. The specification for UML 1.3 can be found at the Object Management Group's website, www.omg.org. UML 1.3 is the version used in this book.

Understanding UML Diagrams

UML allows people to develop several different types of visual diagrams that represent various aspects of the system. Rational Rose supports the development of the majority of these models, as follows:

- ◆ Business Use Case diagram
- ◆ Use Case diagram

- Activity diagram

- Sequence diagram

- Collaboration diagram

- Class diagram

- Statechart diagram

- Component diagram

- Deployment diagram

These model diagrams illustrate different aspects of the system. For example, the Collaboration diagram shows the required interaction between the objects in order to perform some functionality of the system. Each diagram has a purpose and an intended audience.

Business Use Case Diagrams

Business Use Case diagrams are used to represent the functionality provided by an organization as a whole. They answer the questions "What does the business do?" and "Why are we building the system?" They are used extensively during business modeling activities to set the context for the system and to form a foundation for creating the use cases. An example of a simplified Business Use Case diagram for a financial institution is shown in Figure 1.8.

FIGURE 1.8

Business Use Case
diagram for a
financial institution

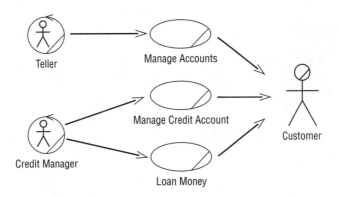

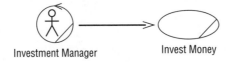

Business Use Case diagrams are drawn from the organizational perspective. They do not differentiate between manual and automated processes. (Use Case diagrams, which will be discussed next, focus on the automated processes.) Business Use Case diagrams show the interactions between business use cases and business actors. Business use cases represent the processes that a business performs, and business actors represent roles with which the business interacts, such as customers or vendors. In other words, business actors represent anyone or anything outside the business that interacts with the business; they do not represent roles or workers within a business. Workers within a business are represented by business workers, which are discussed in Chapter 3, "Business Modeling."

Use Case Diagrams

Use Case diagrams show the interactions between use cases and actors. Use cases represent system functionality, the requirements of the system from the user's perspective. Actors represent the people or systems that provide or receive information from the system; they are among the stakeholders of a system. Use Case diagrams, therefore, show which actors initiate use cases; they also illustrate that an actor receives information from a use case. In essence, a Use Case diagram can illustrate the requirements of the system.

While Business Use Case diagrams are not concerned with what is automated, Use Case diagrams focus on just the automated processes. There is not a one-to-one relationship between business use cases and use cases. A single business use case may require 30 use cases, for example, to implement the process. An example of a Use Case diagram for an Automated Teller Machine (ATM) system is shown in Figure 1.9.

FIGURE 1.9

Use Case diagram for an Automated Teller Machine (ATM) system

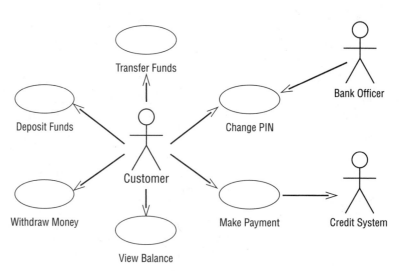

This Use Case diagram shows the interactions between the use cases and actors of an ATM system. In this example, the bank's customer initiates a number of use cases: Withdraw Money, Deposit Funds, Transfer Funds, Make Payment, View Balance, and Change PIN. A few of the relationships are worthy of further mention. The bank officer can also initiate the Change PIN use case. The Make Payment use case shows an arrow going to the credit system. External systems may be actors and, in this case, the credit system is shown as an actor because it is external to the ATM system. The arrow going from a use case to an actor illustrates that the use case produces some information that an actor uses. In this case, the Make Payment use case provides credit card payment information to the credit system.

Much information can be gleaned from viewing Use Case diagrams. This one diagram shows the overall functionality of the system. Users, project managers, analysts, developers, quality assurance engineers, and anyone else interested in the system as a whole can view these diagrams and understand what the system is supposed to accomplish.

Activity Diagrams

Activity diagrams illustrate the flow of functionality in a system. They may be used in business modeling to show the business workflow. They may be used in requirements gathering to illustrate the flow of events through a use case. These diagrams define where the workflow starts, where it ends, what activities occur during the workflow, and in what order the activities occur. An activity is a task that is performed during the workflow.

The structure of an activity diagram is similar to a Statechart diagram, which we will discuss later in this chapter. An example of an activity diagram is shown in Figure 1.10. The activities in the diagram are represented by rounded rectangles. These are the steps that occur as you progress through the workflow. Objects that are affected by the workflow are represented by squares. There is a start state, which represents the beginning of the workflow, and an end state, which represents the end. Decision points are represented by diamonds.

You can see the object flow through the diagram by examining the dashed lines. The object flow shows you which objects are used or created by an activity and how the object changes state as it progresses through the workflow. The solid lines, known as transitions, show how one activity leads to another in the process. If needed, you can place greater detail on the transitions, describing the circumstances under which the transition may or may not occur and what actions will be taken during the transition.

The activity diagram may be divided into vertical *swimlanes*. Each swimlane represents a different role within the workflow. By looking at the activities within a given swimlane, you can find out the responsibility of that role. By looking at the transitions between activities in different swimlanes, you can find out who needs to communicate with whom. All of this is very valuable information when trying to model or understand the business process.

Activity diagrams do not need to be created for every workflow, but they are powerful communication tools, especially with large and complex workflows.

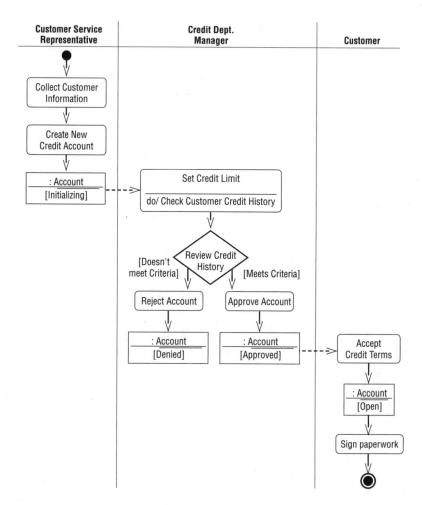

FIGURE 1.10

Activity diagram for opening an account

Sequence Diagrams

Sequence diagrams are used to show the flow of functionality through a use case. For example, the Withdraw Money use case has several possible sequences, such as withdrawing money, attempting to withdraw without available funds, attempting to withdraw with the wrong PIN, and several others. The normal scenario of withdrawing $20 (without any problems such as entering the wrong PIN or insufficient funds in the account) is shown in Figure 1.11.

This Sequence diagram shows the flow of processing through the Withdraw Money use case. Any actors involved are shown at the top of the diagram; the customer actor is shown in the above example. The objects that the system needs in order to perform the Withdraw Money use case are also shown at the top of the diagram. Each arrow represents a message passed between actor and object or object and object to perform the needed functionality. One other note about Sequence diagrams—they display objects, not classes. Classes represent types of objects, as we'll discuss later in Chapter 5, "Object Interaction." Objects are specific; instead of just *customer*, the Sequence diagram shows Joe.

FIGURE 1.11

Sequence diagram for
Joe withdrawing $20

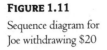

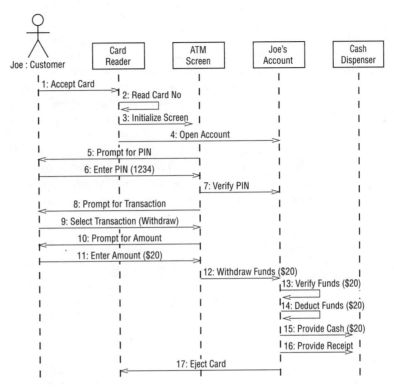

The use case starts with the customer inserting his card into the card reader, an object indicated by the rectangle at the top of the diagram. Then, the card reader reads the card number, opens Joe's account object, and initializes the ATM screen. The screen prompts Joe for his PIN. He enters 1234. The screen verifies the PIN with the account object and they match. The screen presents Joe with his options, and he chooses *withdraw*. The screen then prompts Joe for the amount to withdraw. He chooses $20. Then, the screen withdraws the funds from the account. This initiates a series of processes that the account object performs. First, Joe's account verifies that the account contains at least $20. Then, it deducts the funds from the account. Next, it instructs the cash dispenser to provide $20 in cash. Joe's account also instructs the dispenser to provide a receipt. Lastly, it instructs the card reader to eject the card.

This Sequence diagram illustrated the entire flow of processing for the Withdraw Money use case by showing a specific example of Joe withdrawing $20 from his account. Users can look at these diagrams to see the specifics of their business processing. Analysts see the flow of processing in the Sequence diagrams. Developers see objects that need to be developed and operations for those objects. Quality assurance engineers can see the details of the process and develop test cases based on the processing. Sequence diagrams are therefore useful for all stakeholders in the project.

Collaboration Diagrams

Collaboration diagrams show exactly the same information as the Sequence diagrams. However, Collaboration diagrams show this information in a different way and with a different purpose. The Sequence diagram illustrated in Figure 1.11 is shown in Figure 1.12 as a Collaboration diagram.

In this Collaboration diagram, the objects are represented as rectangles and the actors are stick figures, as before. Whereas the Sequence diagram illustrates the objects and actor interactions over time, the Collaboration diagram shows the objects and actor interactions without reference to time. For example, in this diagram, we see that the card reader instructs Joe's account to open and Joe's account instructs the card reader to eject the card. Also, objects that directly communicate with each other are shown with lines drawn between them. If the ATM screen and cash dispenser directly communicated with one another, a line would be drawn between them. The absence of a line means that no communication occurs directly between those two objects.

FIGURE 1.12

Collaboration diagram for Joe withdrawing $20

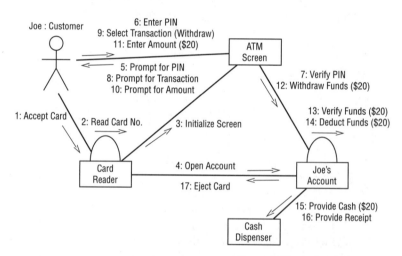

Collaboration diagrams, therefore, show the same information as Sequence diagrams, but people look at Collaboration diagrams for different reasons. Quality assurance engineers and system architects look at these to see the distribution of processing between objects. Suppose that the Collaboration diagram was shaped like a star, with several objects communicating with a central object. A system architect may conclude that the system is too dependent on the central object and redesign the objects to distribute the processing power more evenly. This type of interaction would have been difficult to see in a Sequence diagram.

Class Diagrams

Class diagrams show the interactions between classes in the system. Classes can be seen as the blueprint for objects, as we'll discuss in Chapter 5. Joe's account, for example, is an object. An account is a blueprint for Joe's checking account; an account is a class. Classes contain information and behavior that acts on that information. The Account class contains the customer's PIN and behavior to check the PIN. A class on a Class diagram is created for each type of object in a Sequence or Collaboration diagram. The Class diagram for the system's Withdraw Money use case is illustrated in Figure 1.13.

FIGURE 1.13

Class diagram for the ATM system's Withdraw Money use case

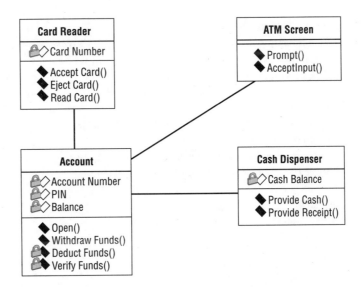

The Class diagram above shows the relationships between the classes that implement the Withdraw Money use case. This is done with four classes: Card Reader, Account, ATM Screen, and Cash Dispenser. Each class on a Class diagram is represented by a rectangle divided into three sections. The first section shows the class name. The second section shows the *attributes* the class contains. An attribute is a piece of information that is associated with a class. For example, the Account class contains three attributes: Account Number, PIN, and Balance. The last section contains the *operations* of the class. An operation is some behavior that the class will provide. The Account class contains four operations: Open, Withdraw Funds, Deduct Funds, and Verify Funds.

The lines connecting classes show the communication relationships between the classes. For instance, the Account class is connected with the ATM Screen class because the two directly communicate with each other. The Card Reader is not connected to the Cash Dispenser because the two do not communicate. Another point of interest is that some attributes and operations have small padlocks to the left of them. The padlock indicates a private attribute or operation. Private attributes and operations can only be accessed from within the class that contains them. The Account Number, PIN, and Balance are all private attributes of the Account class. In addition, the Deduct Funds and Verify Funds operations are private to the Account class.

Developers use Class diagrams to actually develop the classes. Tools such as Rose generate skeletal code for classes, then developers flesh out the details in the language of their choice. Analysts use Class diagrams to show the details of the system. Architects also look at Class diagrams to see the design of the system. If one class contains too much functionality, an architect can see this in the Class diagram and split out the functionality into multiple classes. Should no relationship exist between classes that communicate with each other, an architect or developer can see this too. Class diagrams should be created to show the classes that work together in each use case, and comprehensive diagrams containing whole systems or subsystems can be created as well.

Statechart Diagrams

Statechart diagrams provide a way to model the various states in which an object can exist. While the Class diagrams show a static picture of the classes and their relationships, Statechart diagrams are used to model the more dynamic behavior of a system. These types of diagrams are extensively used in building real-time systems. Rose can even generate the full code for a real-time system from the Statechart diagrams.

A Statechart diagram shows the behavior of an object. For example, a bank account can exist in several different states. It can be open, closed, or overdrawn. An account may behave differently when it is in each of these states. Statechart diagrams are used to show this information. Figure 1.14 shows an example of a Statechart diagram for a bank account.

FIGURE 1.14

Statechart diagram for the Account class

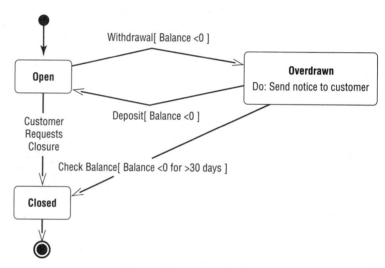

In this diagram, we can see the states in which an account can exist. We can also see how an account moves from one state to another. For example, when an account is open and the customer requests the account's closure, the account moves to the closed state. The customer's request is called the *event* and the event is what causes a transition from one state to another.

If the account is open and the customer makes a withdrawal, the account may move to the overdrawn state. This will only happen if the balance of the account is less than zero. We show this by placing [Balance < 0] on the diagram. A condition enclosed in square brackets is called a *guard condition*, and controls when a transition can or cannot occur.

There are two special states—the *start state* and the *stop state*. The start state is represented by a black dot on the diagram, and indicates what state the object is in when it is first created. The stop state is represented by a bull's-eye, and shows what state the object is in just before it is destroyed. On a Statechart diagram, there is one and only one start state. On the other hand, you can have no stop state, or there can be as many stop states as you need.

Certain things may happen when the object is inside a particular state. In our example, when an account is overdrawn, a notice is sent to the customer. Processes that occur while an object is in a certain state are called *actions*.

Statechart diagrams aren't created for every class; they are used only for very complex classes. If an object of the class can exist in several states, and behaves very differently in each of the states, you may want to create a Statechart diagram for it. Many projects won't need these diagrams at all. If they are created, developers will use them when developing the classes.

Statechart diagrams are created for documentation only. When you generate code from your Rose model, no code will be generated from the information on the Statechart diagrams. However, Rose add-ins are available for real-time systems that can generate executable code based on Statechart diagrams.

Component Diagrams

Component diagrams show you a physical view of your model, as well as the software components in your system and the relationships between them. There are two types of components on the diagram: executable components and code libraries.

In Rose, each of the classes in the model is mapped to a source code component. Once the components have been created, they are added to the Component diagram. Dependencies are then drawn between the components. Component dependencies show the compile-time and run-time dependencies between the components. Figure 1.15 illustrates one of the Component diagrams for the ATM system.

FIGURE 1.15

Component diagram for the ATM client

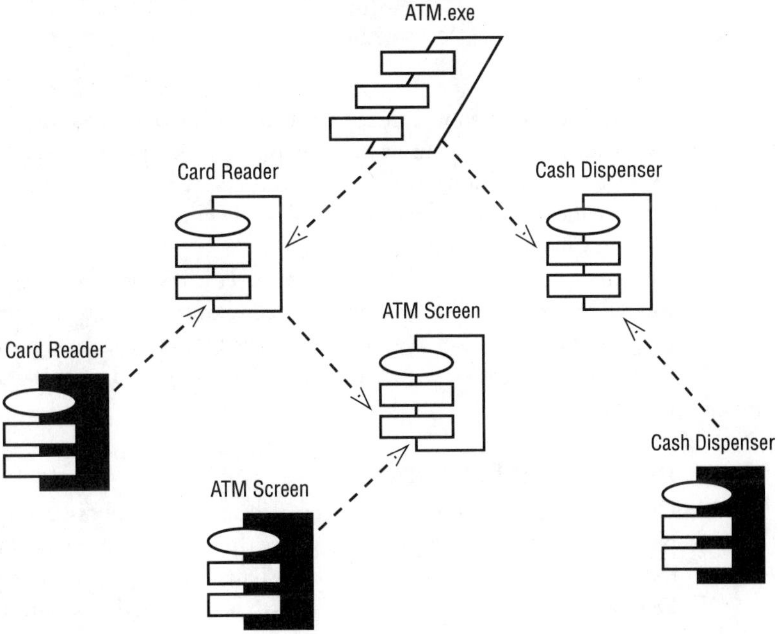

This Component diagram shows the client components in the ATM system. In this case, the team decided to build the system using C++. Each class has its own header and body file, so each class is mapped to its own components in the diagram. For example, the ATM Screen class is mapped to the ATM Screen component. The ATM Screen class is also mapped to a second ATM Screen component. These two components represent the header and body of the ATM Screen class. The shaded component is called a *package body*. It represents the body file (.cpp) of the ATM Screen class in C++. The unshaded component is called a *package specification*. The package specification represents the header (.h) file of the C++ class. The component called ATM.exe is a task specification and represents a thread of processing. In this case, the thread of processing is the executable program.

Components are connected by dashed lines showing the dependency relationships between them. For example, the Card Reader class is dependent upon the ATM Screen class. This means that the ATM Screen class must be available in order for the Card Reader class to compile. Once all of the classes have been compiled, then the executable called ATMClient.exe can be created.

The ATM example has two threads of processing and therefore two executables. One executable comprises the ATM client, including the Cash Dispenser, Card Reader, and ATM Screen. The second executable comprises the ATM server, including the Account component. The Component diagram for the ATM server is shown in Figure 1.16.

FIGURE 1.16

Component diagram for the ATM server

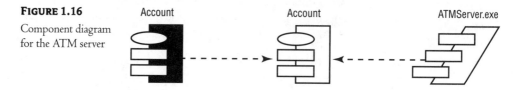

As this example shows, there can be multiple Component diagrams for a system, depending on the number of subsystems or executables. Each subsystem is a package of components. In general, packages are collections of objects. In this case, packages are collections of components. The ATM example includes two packages: the ATM client and the ATM server. Packages will be discussed more in Chapter 3.

Component diagrams are used by whoever is responsible for compiling the system. The diagrams will tell this individual in what order the components need to be compiled. The diagrams will also show what run-time components will be created as a result of the compilation. Component diagrams show the mapping of classes to implementation components. These diagrams are also where code generation is initiated.

Deployment Diagrams

Deployment diagrams are the last type of diagram we will discuss. The Deployment diagram shows the physical layout of the network and where the various components will reside. In our ATM example, the ATM system comprises many subsystems running on separate physical devices, or nodes. The Deployment diagram for the ATM system is illustrated in Figure 1.17.

FIGURE 1.17

Deployment diagram
for the ATM system

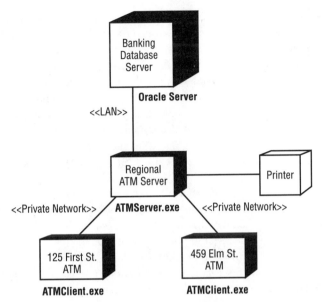

This Deployment diagram tells us much about the layout of the system. The ATM client executable will run on multiple ATMs located at different sites. The ATM client will communicate over a private network with the regional ATM server. The ATM server executable will run on the regional ATM server. The regional ATM server will, in turn, communicate over the local area network (LAN) with the banking database server running Oracle. Lastly, a printer is connected to the regional ATM server.

So, this one diagram shows us the physical setup for the system. Our ATM system will be following a three-tier architecture with one tier each for the database, regional server, and client.

The Deployment diagram is used by the project manager, users, architect, and deployment staff to understand the physical layout of the system and where the various subsystems will reside. This diagram helps the project manager communicate what the system will be like to the users. It also helps the staff responsible for deployment to plan their deployment efforts.

All of these diagrams together describe the system from several different perspectives. In Chapter 3, we will discuss each of these diagrams more closely and show how they are generated in Rational Rose. You will also be given the opportunity to try creating and using these diagrams in Rational Rose. But before we get into the details of Rose, another aspect of software development projects deserves some attention—the process. While this is not a methodology or process book, we do want to familiarize you with a process for development using UML diagrams we have discussed.

Visual Modeling and the Software Development Process

Software development can be done in many ways. There are several different types of development processes that projects follow, including everything from the waterfall model to object-oriented processes. Each has its benefits and disadvantages. In this section, we do not plan to tell you which one to use, but we will present an overview of a process that focuses on visual modeling. Again, this is just an overview.

For a long time, software development followed the waterfall model. In this model, we analyzed the requirements, designed a system, developed the system, tested the system, and deployed the system. As its name suggests, we didn't flow back up this chain—water cannot go up. This method has been the documented methodology used on thousands of projects, but we contend that it has not been used as purely as we would like to think. One of the main shortcomings of the waterfall model is that it is necessary to backtrack through the steps. At the outset of a project following the waterfall model, we take on the daunting task of determining *all* of the system requirements. We do this through detailed discussions with the users and detailed examination of business processes. After we're done, we make sure the users sign off on the voluminous requirements we have written, even if they haven't read them yet. If we're really lucky, we might get about 80 percent of the requirements of the system during this analysis stage.

Then, it's on to design. We sit down and determine the architecture of our system. We address issues such as where programs will reside and what hardware is necessary for acceptable performance. While doing this, we may find out that some new issues have arisen. We then go back to the users and talk about the issues. These result in new requirements. So, we're back in analysis. After going back and forth a few times, we move to development and begin coding the system.

While coding, we discover that a certain design decision is impossible to implement, so we go back to design and revisit the issue. After coding is done, testing begins. While testing, we learn that a requirement was not detailed enough and the interpretation was incorrect. Now we have to go back to the analysis phase and revisit the requirement.

After some time, we finally finish the system and deliver it to the users. Since it took quite awhile and the business has probably changed while we were building the system, the users respond less than enthusiastically with, "That's just what I asked for, but not what I want!" This incantation by the users is a powerful spell that causes the entire project team to age 10 years immediately!

So, after looking at this dismal scenario and wondering if you are in the right industry, what can you do to make it better? Is the problem that the business changes so quickly? Is it that the users don't communicate what they want? Is it that the users don't understand the project team? Is it that the team didn't follow a process? The answers are yes, yes, yes, and no. The business changes very rapidly, and as software professionals we need to keep up. The users do not always communicate what they want because what they do is second nature to them. Asking an accounting clerk who has been on the job for 30 years is roughly like asking someone how you breathe. It becomes so second nature that it is difficult to describe. Another problem is that the users don't always understand the project team. The team shows them flowcharts and produces volumes of requirements text, but the users don't always understand what is being given to them. Can you think of a way around this problem? Visual modeling can help. Lastly, the team did follow a process: the waterfall method (illustrated in Figure 1.18). Unfortunately, the plan and the execution of the method were two different things.

One of the problems is that the team planned to use the waterfall method, with its neat and orderly passage through the stages of the project, but they had to backtrack throughout the project. Is this due to poor planning? Probably not. Software development is a complex process and trying to do everything in neat stages doesn't always work. If the need for backtracking had been ignored, then the system would have design flaws, missing requirements, and possibly worse.

But over the years we have learned to plan the backtracking. With this insight comes *iterative development*. Iterative development just means that we are going to do things over and over. In the object-oriented process, we will go through the steps of analysis, design, development, testing, and deployment in small stages many times (illustrated in Figure 1.19). There are many different implementations of iterative lifecycles. One such implementation is the Rational Unified Process (RUP), which we will discuss briefly here. Please note that this book does not explore the details of RUP. For more details, please see Rational's website at `www.rational.com`.

FIGURE 1.18

Waterfall method

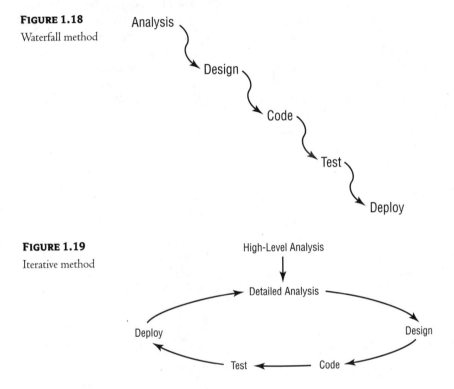

FIGURE 1.19

Iterative method

It is impossible to learn all of the requirements during the early part of the project. New things are bound to come out, so we plan for them by planning the project in iterations. With this concept, a project can be seen as a series of small waterfalls. Each one is designed to be big enough to mark the completion of an important part of the project, but small enough to minimize the need for backtracking.

In the project, we go through four phases: inception, elaboration, construction, and transition. Inception is the beginning of the project. We gather information and do proofs-of-concept. At the end of inception is a go/no-go decision for the project. (A tenet of the Unified Process is a go/no-go decision at the end of each phase.) In elaboration, use cases are detailed and architectural decisions are made. Elaboration includes some analysis, design, coding, and test planning. Construction is where the bulk of the coding is done. Transition is the final preparation and deployment of the system to the users. Next, we will discuss what each of these phases means in an object-oriented project.

Inception

The inception phase is the beginning of the project. Inception begins when someone says, "Gee, wouldn't it be great if we had a system to do...?" Then, someone researches the idea and management asks how long it would take, how much it will cost, or how feasible the project is. Finding out the answers to these questions is what the inception phase is all about.

We begin this phase with business modeling. During this process, we analyze the business around the proposed system. We discover what the high-level features of the system are and document them. We create business use cases, business actors, and Business Use Case diagrams. (We do not go into details about the use cases here, but provide just a sentence or two.) We may also create activity diagrams to model the workflow. Armed with this information, we then move on to analyze the system to be developed. We also provide estimates to upper management. So, using Rose to support our project, we will create actors and use cases and produce Use Case diagrams. Inception ends when the research is done and management commits the resources to work on the elaboration phase.

One more task remains in inception—the development of an iteration plan. An iteration plan is a plan describing which use cases will be implemented during which iterations. If we find 10 use cases during inception, we may draw up an iteration plan like this:

Iteration One	Use Cases 1, 5, 6
Iteration Two	Use Cases 7, 9
Iteration Three	Use Cases 2, 4, 8
Iteration Four	Use Cases 3, 10

The plan tells us which use cases will be done first. Determining this plan requires looking at dependencies between use cases and planning accordingly. If Use Case 3 is required in order for Use Case 5 to work, then the plan described above is not feasible because Use Case 3 would be implemented during the fourth iteration, far after Use Case 5 is in the first iteration. We may have to adjust our plan to accommodate the dependencies.

USING ROSE IN INCEPTION

The inception phase begins with business modeling. Rose can be used to build the Business Use Case model, including business use cases, business actors, and business workers. The next step involves determining what use cases and actors are needed. Rose can be used to document these use cases and actors, and to create the diagrams to show their relationships. The Use Case diagrams can be presented to the users to validate that the diagrams are a comprehensive view of the system features.

Elaboration

The elaboration phase of the project includes some planning, analysis, and architectural design. Following the iteration plan, elaboration is done for each use case in the current iteration. Elaboration includes several aspects of a project, such as coding proofs-of-concept, developing test cases, and making design decisions. The elaboration phase focuses on setting the architectural foundation for the project.

The major tasks in the elaboration phase are detailing the use cases. In Chapter 4, we will discuss what the details of a use case include. The low-level requirements of a use case include the flow of processing through the use case; what actors are involved with the use case; Sequence and Collaboration diagrams to show the flow of processing graphically; and Statechart diagrams to show any state changes that may occur during the use case. The requirements, in the form of detailed use cases, are gathered into a document called a Software Requirement Specification (SRS). The SRS contains all of the details of the system requirements.

Other tasks are done in elaboration, such as refining the initial estimates, reviewing the SRS and use case model for quality, and investigating risks. Rational Rose can help with refining the use case model and creating the Sequence and Collaboration diagrams to show the graphical flow of processing. Class diagrams showing the objects to be built are also designed during the elaboration phase.

The elaboration phase is over when the high-risk and architecturally significant use cases have been fully detailed and accepted by the users, proofs-of-concept have been completed to mitigate risks, and the initial Class diagrams are complete. In other words, this phase is complete when the system architecture has been finalized.

USING ROSE IN ELABORATION

The elaboration phase presents several opportunities to use Rational Rose. Since elaboration includes the detailing of many of the system requirements, the use case model might require updating. Rational Rose may be used to create activity diagrams to illustrate the flow of events. As the flow of processing is detailed, Sequence and Collaboration diagrams help illustrate the flow. They also help design the objects that will be required for the system. Elaboration also involves preparing the initial design for the system so the developers can begin its construction. This can be accomplished by creating Class diagrams and Statechart diagrams in Rose. Finally, many of the system components will be identified during elaboration. Rose is used to create a Component diagram to show these components and their relationships.

Construction

During the construction phase, the remainder of the system is analyzed, designed, and built. Using the architecture from the elaboration phase as a foundation, the team will build the remainder of the system during construction. Tasks in the construction phase include determining any remaining requirements, developing the software, and testing the software.

As the design is completed, Rational Rose can generate skeletal code for the system. In order to use this feature for some languages, you need to create components and a Component diagram as an early part of construction. Once you have created components and diagrammed their dependencies, code generation can begin. Code generation will provide as much code as possible based on the design. This does not mean that you will get any business-specific code out of Rose. What you will get depends greatly on the language that is chosen, but generally includes class declarations, attribute declarations, scope declarations (public, private, and protected), function prototypes, and inheritance statements. This saves time because this is tedious code to write. After generating code, the developers can focus on the business-specific aspects of the project. As code is completed, it should be reviewed by a peer group of developers to ensure that it meets standards, design conventions, and is functional. After code review, the objects should be subjected to quality assurance review. If any new attributes or functions are added during construction, or if any interactions between objects are altered, then the new code should be updated in the Rose model through reverse engineering. We will cover this topic further in Chapters 12 through 15 of this book.

Construction is over when the software is complete and tested. It's important to make sure that the model and software are synchronized; the model will be extremely valuable once the software enters maintenance mode.

USING ROSE IN CONSTRUCTION

As in the elaboration phase, Rose is used to create Sequence, Collaboration, Class, Statechart, and Component diagrams during construction. Rose is used to create components according to the object design. Component diagrams are created to show the compile-time dependencies between the components. After languages have been selected for each component, the generation of skeletal code can be done. After code has been created by the developers, the model can be synchronized with the code through reverse engineering. Rose is also used in construction to create Deployment diagrams, which describe how the components are to be deployed.

Transition

The transition phase is when the completed software product is turned over to the user community. Tasks in this phase include completing the final software product, completing final acceptance testing, completing user documentation, and preparing for user training. The Software Requirements Specification, Use Case diagrams, Class diagrams, Component diagrams, and Deployment diagrams must be updated to reflect any final changes. It is important to keep these models synchronized with the software product because the models will be used once the software product goes into maintenance mode. Several months after the completion of the project, the models will be priceless in helping to make enhancements to the software.

Rose is used in the transition phase primarily to update the models as the software product is completed. In particular, updates to the Component and Deployment diagrams are common during the transition phase.

Summary

Visual modeling and Rational Rose are useful at several different stages of the software development process. Toward the beginning of the project, in inception, Rose is used to produce the business model and the use case model. During elaboration and construction, Rose is used extensively to develop activity diagrams showing the flow of events. Sequence and Collaboration diagrams show the objects that will be developed and how they interact with one another. Class diagrams are also developed in Rose, showing how the objects relate to each other. Component diagrams are created using Rose to show the dependencies of the components in the system and to allow you to generate skeletal code for the system.

Throughout construction, we use Rose to reverse engineer newly developed code back into the model to incorporate any changes that arise during development. After construction, we move into transition, where Rose is used to update any of the models created during the project.

In the next chapter, we'll take a short tour of Rose. We'll examine the different features and capabilities of the Rose tool, and talk about how to create and save a Rose model or elements of the model. We'll discuss how to navigate Rose, the four views of the model that Rose provides, and how to publish your Rose model on the Web.

Chapter 2

A Tour of Rose

THIS CHAPTER CONCLUDES OUR introduction to UML and Rose. After reading this chapter, you will be armed with enough information to embark on learning the fundamentals of designing systems with Rose. In this chapter, we discuss what Rational Rose is and what a Rational Rose model includes, and then take you on a visual tour, discussing the various parts of the screen and how to navigate through the product. We'll discuss the four views of a system that are available through Rose and how to work with Rose. Finally, we'll look at how to publish a Rose model to the Web, and how to manage versions of a Rose model.

◆ Getting around in Rose

◆ Exploring four views in a Rose model

◆ Working with Rose

◆ Web Publisher

◆ Version control with Rose

◆ Setting global options

What Is Rose?

Rational Rose is a powerful visual modeling tool to aid in the analysis and design of object-oriented software systems. It is used to model your system *before* you write any code, so you can be sure that the system is architecturally sound from the beginning. Using the model, you can catch design flaws early, while they are still inexpensive to fix.

Rational Rose supports business modeling, helping you to understand the business around the system. It helps with systems analysis by enabling you to design use cases and Use Case diagrams to show the system functionality. It will let you design Interaction diagrams to show how the objects work together to provide the needed functionality. Class diagrams can be created to show the classes in a system and how they relate to each other. Component diagrams can be developed to illustrate how the classes map to implementation components. Finally, a Deployment diagram can be produced to show the network design for the system.

A Rose *model* is a picture of a system from various perspectives. It includes all of the UML diagrams, actors, use cases, objects, classes, components, and deployment nodes in a system. It describes in great detail what the system will include and how it will work, so developers can use the model as a blueprint for the system being built.

A blueprint is a good analogy for a Rose model. Just as a house has a set of blueprints that let different members of the construction crew see it from different perspectives (plumbing, electrical, and so on), a Rose model contains a number of different diagrams that let the project team see the system from different perspectives (customer, designer, project manager, tester, and so on).

Having a blueprint ahead of time helps alleviate an age-old problem. The team has talked to the customers and documented the requirements. Now the developers are ready to code. One developer (we'll call him Bob) takes some of the requirements, makes certain design decisions, and writes some code. Jane, another developer, takes some requirements, makes completely different design decisions, and writes some more code.

This difference in programming style is perfectly natural; 20 developers given the same requirements may code 20 different systems. The problem comes about when someone needs to understand or maintain the system. Without conducting detailed interviews with each of the developers, it's hard for anyone to see what design decisions were made, what the pieces of the system are, or what the overall structure of the system is. Without a documented design, it's hard to be sure that the system you built is actually the system the users had in mind.

Traditionally, we follow a process that looks like this:

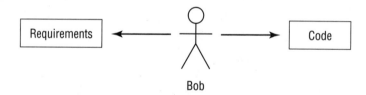

The requirements are documented, but the design is inside Bob's brain, so no one other than Bob has a good idea of the system structure. If Bob leaves, that information leaves with him. If you've ever been the one taking over for Bob, you can appreciate how difficult it can be to understand a system with little documentation.

A Rose model gives us a process that looks like this:

Now the design is documented. We get rid of Bob (figuratively speaking, of course!) and replace our dependency on him with a documented design. The developers can all gather to discuss the design decisions *before* the code is written. You don't have to worry about everyone going off in a separate direction with the system design.

But the developers aren't the only ones to use the model:

♦ The entire team will use the Business Use Case diagrams to get an understanding of the business surrounding the system.

- Customers and project managers will use the Use Case diagrams to get a high-level view of the system and to agree on the project scope.

- Project managers will use the Use Case diagrams and documentation to break the project down into manageable pieces.

- Analysts and customers will look at the use case documentation to see what functionality the system will provide.

- Technical writers will look at the use case documentation to begin to write the user manual and training plans.

- Analysts and developers will look at Sequence and Collaboration diagrams to see how the logic in the system will flow, the objects in the system, and the messages between the objects.

- Quality assurance staff will use the use case documentation and the Sequence and Collaboration diagrams to get the information they need for testing scripts.

- Developers will use the Class diagrams and Statechart diagrams to get a detailed view of the pieces of the system and how they relate.

- Deployment staff will use the Component and Deployment diagrams to see what executable files, DLL files, or other components will be created, and where these components will be deployed on the network.

- The whole team will use the model to be sure the requirements are traced to the code, and that the code can be traced back to the requirements.

Rose, therefore, is a tool meant to be used by the entire project team. It is a repository of scope, analysis, and design information that each team member can use to get the information they need.

In addition to the above, Rational Rose will help developers by generating skeletal code. It can do this for a number of different languages available on the market, including C++, Ada, CORBA, Java, COM objects, Visual Basic, and XML. Further, Rose can reverse engineer code and create a model based on an existing system. Having a model in Rose for an existing application is very beneficial. When a change occurs to the model, Rose can modify the code to incorporate the change. Similarly, when a change occurs in the code, you can incorporate that change into the model automatically. These features help you keep the model and the code synchronized, reducing the risk of having an outdated model.

Rose can also be extended using RoseScript, a programming language packaged with Rose. Using this programming language, you can write code to automatically make changes to your model, create a report, or perform other tasks with your Rose model.

There are three different versions of Rose currently available:

- Rose Modeler, which allows you to create a model for your system, but will not support code generation or reverse engineering.

- Rose Professional, which allows you to generate code in one language.

- Rose Enterprise, which allows you to generate code for C++, Java, Ada, CORBA, Visual Basic, COM, Oracle8, and XML. A model can have components that are generated in different languages.

WHAT'S NEW IN ROSE 2002

In the last several years, Rose has been enhanced to accommodate some of the newer UML notation and diagrams. The following list includes the newest of the enhanced Rose features at the time of this writing:

◆   A main diagram for each package can now be selected.

◆   Items on a diagram can now be moved around using the arrow keys.

◆   The Page Up and Page Down keys can now be used to scroll through a diagram.

◆   Default C++ component styles can be set.

◆   Directories and file extensions for C++ code generation can be specified.

◆   It includes support for Microsoft Interface Definition Library (MIDL) round-trip engineering.

◆   It includes support for J2EE deployment.

◆   It includes additional support for the reverse engineering of Enterprise JavaBeans (EJBs).

WHAT'S NEW IN ROSE 2001A

Some other new Rose features include:

◆   Business modeling, which was discussed briefly in Chapter 1, "Introduction to UML," focuses on the world around the system, and helps to set the context for the use case model.

◆   Activity diagrams, which can be used to describe the workflow through a business use case or the flow of events through a use case.

◆   Support for ANSI C++, which will be discussed in detail in the code generation and reverse engineering section of this book. A model converter can be used to convert older Rose C++ models to Rose ANSI C++ models.

◆   Tighter integration with Rational's ClearCase tool, which is used for version control.

◆   Enhanced data-modeling capabilities.

◆   Modeling, code generation, and reverse engineering of Enterprise Java Beans.

Getting Around in Rose

In the next few sections of this chapter, we'll describe each part of the Rose interface. Rose is largely a menu-driven application, with toolbars to help with commonly used features. Rose supports eight different types of UML diagrams: Use Case diagrams, Activity diagrams, Sequence diagrams, Collaboration diagrams, Class diagrams, Statechart diagrams, Component diagrams, and Deployment diagrams. Rose will present you with a different toolbar for each of these diagrams. In the next nine chapters, we'll show you how to create all of these types of diagrams.

In addition to the toolbars and menus, Rose includes context-sensitive shortcut menus, visible by right-clicking an item. For example, right-clicking a class on a Class diagram will display a menu that includes options for adding attributes or operations to the class, viewing or editing the class specifications, generating code for the class, or viewing the generated code. When in doubt, right-click! Rose will almost always give you helpful menu options.

One of the easiest ways to get around in Rose is to use the browser, which is the treeview on the left side of the screen. With the browser, you can quickly and easily get to the diagrams and other elements of the model. If you run into trouble while using Rose, press F1 at any time to access the extensive online help file.

Parts of the Screen

The five primary pieces of the Rose interface are the browser, the documentation window, the toolbars, the diagram window, and the log. In this section, we'll look at each of these. Briefly, their purposes are:

Browser Used to quickly navigate through the model

Documentation window Used to view or update documentation of model elements

Toolbars Used for quick access to commonly used commands

Diagram window Used to display and edit one or more UML diagrams

Log Used to view errors and report the results of various commands

Figure 2.1 illustrates the various parts of the Rose interface.

FIGURE 2.1

The Rose interface

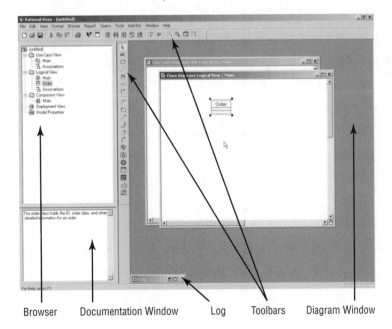

Browser   Documentation Window   Log   Toolbars   Diagram Window

BROWSER

The browser is a hierarchical structure you can use to easily navigate through your Rose model. Anything you add to the model—actors, use cases, classes, components, and so on—will display in the browser. The browser is shown in Figure 2.2.

Using the browser, you can

◆ Add model elements (use cases, actors, classes, components, diagrams, etc.)

◆ View existing model elements

◆ View existing relationships between model elements

◆ Move model elements

◆ Rename model elements

◆ Add a model element to a diagram

◆ Attach a file or URL to an element

◆ Group elements into packages

◆ Access the detailed specifications of an element

◆ Open a diagram

FIGURE 2.2

Rose browser

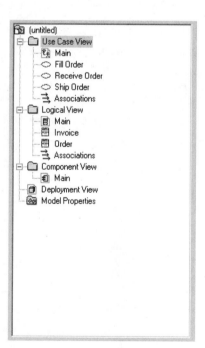

There are four views in the browser: the Use Case view, the Logical view, the Component view, and the Deployment view. Table 2.1 lists each of these views and the model elements found in the views.

TABLE 2.1: VIEWS IN RATIONAL ROSE

VIEW	CONTENTS
Use Case view	Business actors
	Business workers
	Business use cases
	Business Use Case diagrams
	Business Use Case realizations
	Actors
	Use cases
	Associations
	Use case documentation
	Use Case diagrams
	Activity diagrams
	Sequence diagrams
	Collaboration diagrams
	Packages
Logical view	Classes
	Class diagrams
	Associations
	Interfaces
	Sequence diagrams
	Collaboration diagrams
	Statechart diagrams
	Packages
Component view	Components
	Interfaces
	Component diagrams
	Packages
Deployment view	Processes
	Processors
	Connectors
	Devices
	Deployment diagram

Using the browser, you can view the model elements in each of these four views, move or edit elements, or add new elements. By right-clicking an element in the browser, you can attach files or URLs to the element, access the detailed specifications of the element, delete the element, or rename the element.

The browser is organized in a treeview style. Each model element may contain other elements beneath it in the hierarchy.

By default, the browser will appear in the upper-left area of the screen. You can move the browser to another location or hide the browser altogether.

To show or hide the browser:

1. Right-click in the browser window.

2. Select Hide from the shortcut menu. Rose will show or hide the browser.

   OR

   Select View ➤ Browser. Rose will show or hide the browser.

DOCUMENTATION WINDOW

The documentation window is used to document the elements of your Rose model. For example, you may want to write a short definition for each of your actors. You can enter this definition using the documentation window, as shown in Figure 2.3.

FIGURE 2.3

The documentation window

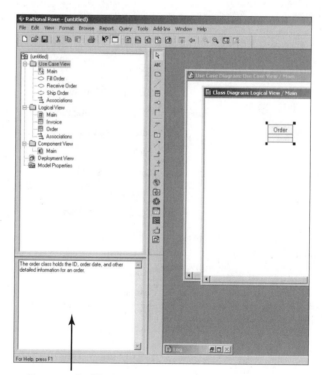

Documentation Window

When you add documentation to a class, anything you type in the documentation window will appear as a comment in the generated code, reducing the need to go in later and comment on the system's code. The documentation will also appear in the reports you can generate from Rose.

As you select different elements from the browser or on a diagram, the documentation window will automatically be updated to display the documentation for the selected element.

TOOLBARS

Rose toolbars provide you with quick access to commonly used commands. There are two toolbars in Rose: the Standard toolbar and the Diagram toolbar, which is called the *toolbox*. The Standard toolbar contains options you can use in any diagram. These options are shown in Table 2.2. The toolbox changes for each type of UML diagram. The different Diagram toolbars will be discussed in detail in the remainder of this book.

TABLE 2.2: ICONS IN STANDARD TOOLBAR

ICON	BUTTON	PURPOSE
	Create New Model	Creates a new Rose model (.mdl) file.
	Open Existing Model	Opens an existing Rose model (.mdl) file.
	Save Model or Log	Saves the Rose model (.mdl) file or the log for the current model.
	Cut	Moves text to the clipboard.
	Copy	Copies text to the clipboard.
	Paste	Pastes text from the clipboard.
	Print Diagrams	Prints one or more diagrams from the current model.
	Context Sensitive Help	Accesses the help file.
	View Documentation	Views the documentation window.
	Browse Class Diagram	Locates and opens a Class diagram.
	Browse Interaction Diagram	Locates and opens a Sequence or Collaboration diagram.
	Browse Component Diagram	Locates and opens a Component diagram.
	Browse State Machine Diagram	Locates and opens a Statechart diagram.
	Browse Deployment Diagram	Opens the Deployment diagram for the model.
	Browse Parent	Opens a diagram's parent diagram.

Continued on next page

TABLE 2.2: ICONS IN STANDARD TOOLBAR *(continued)*

ICON	BUTTON	PURPOSE
	Browse Previous Diagram	Opens the diagram you were most recently viewing.
	Zoom In	Increases the zoom.
	Zoom Out	Decreases the zoom.
	Fit in Window	Sets the zoom so the entire diagram fits within the window.
	Undo Fit in Window	Undoes the Fit in Window command.

All of the toolbars can be customized. To customize a toolbar, select Tools ➤ Options, then select the Toolbars tab.

To show or hide the Standard toolbar:

1. Select Tools ➤ Options.

2. Select the Toolbars tab.

3. Use the Show Standard Toolbar check box to show or hide the Standard toolbar.

To show or hide the Diagram toolbar:

1. Select Tools ➤ Options.

2. Select the Toolbars tab.

3. Use the Show Diagram Toolbar check box to show or hide the Diagram toolbar (toolbox).

To customize a toolbar:

1. Right-click the desired toolbar.

2. Select the Customize option.

3. Add or remove buttons to customize the toolbar by selecting the appropriate button and then clicking the Add or Remove button, as shown in Figure 2.4.

FIGURE 2.4

Customizing a toolbar

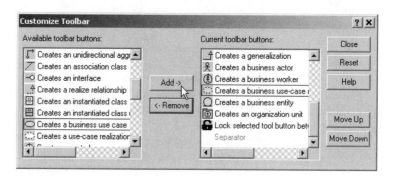

DIAGRAM WINDOW

In the diagram window shown in Figure 2.5, you can view UML diagrams in your model. As you make changes to elements in a diagram, Rose will automatically update the browser as necessary. Similarly, when you make changes to an element using the browser, Rose will automatically update the appropriate diagrams. By doing so, Rose helps you maintain a consistent model.

FIGURE 2.5

Diagram window

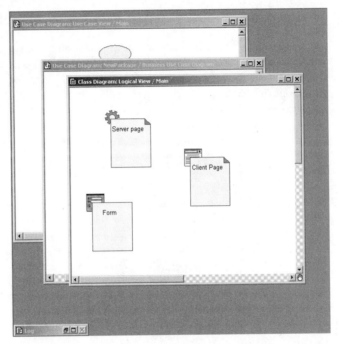

LOG

As you work on your Rose model, certain information will be posted to the log window. For example, when you generate code, any errors that are generated are posted in the log window, shown in Figure 2.6.

FIGURE 2.6

Log window

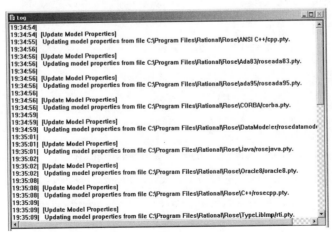

Exploring Four Views in a Rose Model

There are four views in a Rose model: the Use Case view, the Logical view, the Component view, and the Deployment view. Each of these four views addresses a different audience and purpose. In the following sections, we'll take a brief look at each of these views. In the remainder of this book, we'll discuss the detailed model elements that appear in each of these views.

Use Case View

The Use Case view includes all of the actors, use cases, and Use Case diagrams in the system. It may also include some Sequence and Collaboration diagrams. The Use Case view is an implementation-independent look at the system. It focuses on a high-level picture of *what* the system will do, without worrying about the details of *how* the system will do it. Figure 2.7 illustrates the Use Case view in the Rose browser.

FIGURE 2.7

Use Case view

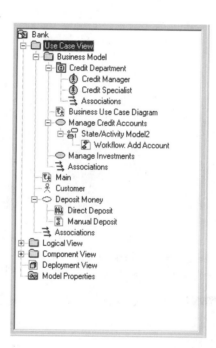

The Use Case view includes:

 Business use cases, which are workflows within the organization.

 Business actors, which are people, companies, or other entities outside the organization who interact with the business.

 Business workers, which are roles within the organization.

 Organizational units, which are groups of business use cases and/or business workers.

 Activity diagrams, which are used to describe the workflow within a business use case or a flow of events through a use case.

Actors, which are external entities that interact with the system being built.

Use cases, which are high-level pieces of functionality the system will provide.

Use case documentation, which details the flow through the use case, including any error handling. This icon represents an external file that has been attached to your Rose model. The icon used will depend upon the application you used to document the flow of events. Here, we used Microsoft Word.

Use Case diagrams, which show the actors, the use cases, and the interactions between them. There are typically several Use Case diagrams per system, each showing a subset of the actors and/or use cases.

Interaction diagrams, which display the objects or classes involved in one flow through a use case. There may be many Interaction diagrams for each use case. Interaction diagrams can be created in either the Use Case view or the Logical view. Any Interaction diagrams that are implementation-independent are typically created in the Use Case view. Any Interaction diagrams that are language-specific are located in the Logical view.

Packages, which are groups of use cases, actors, or other modeling elements. A package is a UML mechanism that helps you to group related items together. In most cases, there are few enough use cases and actors that packaging is not essential. However, it's a tool that is always available to help you organize the Use Case view. In particular, it can be convenient to package these elements for configuration management.

When the project first begins, the team may optionally produce a business model in the Use Case view. If this task is undertaken, the team members that will be needed include the customer, the project manager, and analysts who focus on business processes (frequently termed *business analysts*). The rest of the team—including designers, coders, testers, and so on—will refer to the business model throughout the project to gain an understanding of the overall business and how the new system fits into its organizational structure. We will discuss the business model in more detail in Chapter 3, "Business Modeling."

Once the business model has been completed, the team moves on to the use case model. Customers, analysts, and project managers will work with the use cases, Use Case diagrams, and use case documentation to agree on a high-level view of the system.

NOTE   *This view focuses only on what the system will do. Implementation details should be left for future discussions. In an object-oriented system, use cases are the system requirements.*

As the project goes along, all members of the team can look at the Use Case view to get a high-level understanding of the system being built. The use case documentation will describe the flow of events through a use case. With this information, quality assurance staff can begin to write testing scripts. Technical writers can begin the user documentation. Analysts and customers can help ensure that all requirements were captured. Developers can see what high-level pieces of the system will be created, and how the system logic should flow.

Once the customer has agreed to the use cases and actors, they have agreed to the system scope. The development can then continue to the Logical view, which focuses more on how the system will implement the behavior spelled out in the use cases.

Logical View

The Logical view, shown in Figure 2.8, focuses on how the system will implement the behavior in the use cases. It provides a detailed picture of the pieces of the system, and describes how the pieces interrelate. The Logical view includes, among other things, the specific classes that will be needed, the Class diagrams, and the Statechart diagrams. With these detailed elements, developers can construct a detailed design for the system.

FIGURE 2.8

Logical view

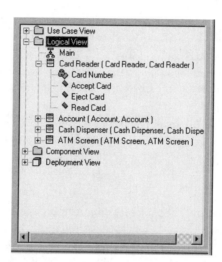

The Logical view includes:

Classes, which are the building blocks for a system. A class consists of a little bit of information (its attributes) and a little bit of behavior (its operations), grouped together. For example, an Employee class might store information about the employee's name, address, and social security number, and might include behavior such as hiring or firing an employee. There are different types of icons that are used for different types of classes. We will discuss these further in Chapter 6, "Classes and Packages."

Class diagrams, which are used to view the classes in the system, their attributes and operations, and their relationships to each other. Typically, a system will have several Class diagrams, each showing a subset of all the classes.

Interaction diagrams, which include Sequence and Collaboration diagrams, are used to display the classes that participate in one flow of events through a use case. As we mentioned above, Interaction diagrams can be created in either the Use Case view or the Logical view. Interaction diagrams in the Use Case view tend to be high-level and implementation-independent, while Interaction diagrams in the Logical view are more detailed.

Statechart diagrams, which show the dynamic behavior of an object. A Statechart diagram includes all of the states in which a particular object can exist. It also illustrates how the object moves from one state to another, what state the object is in when it is first created, and what state the object is in when it is destroyed. A Statechart diagram can be useful in detailing business rules.

Packages, which are groups of related classes or other modeling elements. Packaging isn't required, but it is certainly recommended. A typical system may have a hundred classes or more. Packaging your classes can help reduce the complexity of your model. To get a general picture of the system, you can look at the packages. To see a more detailed view, you can go into any of the packages and view the classes inside.

Frequently, teams take a two-pass approach to the Logical view. In the first approach, they identify *analysis classes*. Analysis classes are language-independent classes. By focusing first on analysis classes, the team can begin to see the structure of the system without getting bogged down in the implementation-specific details. In UML, analysis classes can be represented using the following icons:

Boundary   Control   Entity

The analysis classes might also appear on some Interaction diagrams in the Use Case view. Once the analysis classes have been identified, the team can change each one to a *design class*. A design class is a class that has language-specific details. For example, we may have an analysis class that's responsible for talking to another system. We don't worry about what language the class will be written in—we focus only on what information and behavior it will have. When we turn it into a design class, however, we look at the language-specific details. We may decide that now we have a Java class. We might even decide that we need two Java classes to actually implement what we uncovered in analysis—there isn't necessarily a one-to-one mapping between analysis classes and design classes. Design classes are shown on the Interaction diagrams that appear in the Logical view.

The focus of the Logical view is on the logical structure of the system. In this view, you identify the pieces of the system, examine the information and behavior of the system, and examine the relationships between the pieces. Reuse is one of the main considerations here. By carefully assigning information and behavior to classes, grouping your classes together, and examining the relationships between the classes and the packages, you can identify classes and packages that can be reused. As you complete more and more projects, you can add new classes and packages to a reuse library. Future projects then become more of a process of assembling what you already have, rather than building everything from scratch.

Nearly everyone on the team will use information from the Logical view, but the primary users will be the developers and architect. The developers will be concerned with what classes are created, what information and behavior each class should have, and what relationships exist between the classes. The architect, who is more concerned with the structure of the overall system, is responsible for ensuring that the system has a stable architecture, that reuse has been considered, and that the system will be flexible enough to change as requirements change. Analysts will look at the classes and Class diagrams to help ensure that the business requirements will be implemented in the code. Quality assurance staff will look at the classes, packages, and Class diagrams to see what pieces of the system exist and need to be tested. They will also use the Statechart diagrams to see how a particular class should behave. The project manager will look at the classes and diagrams to ensure that the system is well structured, and to get an estimate of how complex the system is.

Once you've identified the classes and diagrammed them, you can move on to the Component view, which focuses more on the physical structure.

Component View

The Component view contains information about the code libraries, executable files, run-time libraries, and other components in your model. A *component* is a physical module of code.

In Rose, components and Component diagrams are displayed in the Component view, as shown in Figure 2.9. The Component view of the system allows you to see the relationships between the modules of code.

FIGURE 2.9

Component view

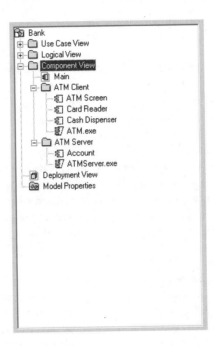

The Component view includes:

Components, which are physical modules of code.

Component diagrams, which show the components and their relationships to each other. Relationships between the components let you know what the compilation dependencies are. With this information, you can determine the compilation order of the components.

Packages, which are groups of related components. As with packaging classes, reuse is one of the considerations when packaging components. A group of related components may be very easy to pick up and reuse in other applications, so long as the relationships between the group and other groups are carefully monitored. We'll discuss these issues in detail later.

The main users of the Component view are those people responsible for controlling the code and compiling and deploying the application. Some of the components will be code libraries. Others will be run-time components, such as executable files or dynamic link library (DLL) files. Developers will also use the Component view to see what code libraries have been created and which classes are contained in each code library.

Deployment View

The final view in Rose is the Deployment view. The Deployment view is concerned with the physical deployment of the system, which may differ from the logical architecture of the system.

For example, the system may have a logical three-tier architecture. In other words, the interface may be separated from the business logic, which is separated from the database logic. However, the deployment may be two-tiered. The interface may be placed on one machine, while the business and database logic are located on another machine.

Other issues, such as fault tolerance, network bandwidth, disaster recovery, and response time, are also handled using the Deployment view. The Deployment view is shown in Figure 2.10.

FIGURE 2.10

Deployment view

The Deployment view includes:

Processes, which are threads that execute in their own memory space.

Processors, which include any machines with processing power. Each process will run on one or more processors.

Devices, which include any hardware without processing power. Examples are dumb terminals and printers.

A Deployment diagram shows the processes and devices on the network and the physical connections between them. The Deployment diagram will also display the processes, and show which processes run on which machines.

Again, the whole team will use the information in the Deployment view to understand how the system will be deployed. However, the primary users will be the staff responsible for distributing the application.

Working with Rose

Everything you do in Rose relates to a model. In this section, we will discuss how to use models. We will first look at how to create and save Rose models. Then, we will discuss team design considerations by using controlled units, and show you how to publish a Rose model to the Web.

Creating Models

The first step in working with Rose is to create a model. Models can be either created from scratch or made using an existing framework model. A Rose model and all diagrams, objects, and other model elements are saved in a single file with the extension .md1 (model).

To create a model:

1. Select File ➤ New from the menu, or press the New button on the Standard toolbar.

2. If the Framework Wizard is installed, then the list of available frameworks will be displayed, as in Figure 2.11. Select the framework you want to use and click OK, or click Cancel to use no framework.

FIGURE 2.11

Framework Wizard

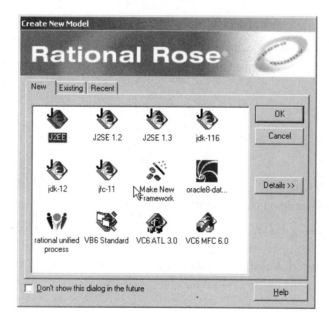

If you select a framework, Rose will automatically load the default packages, classes, and components that come with that framework. For example, loading the J2EE framework provides default applet, beans, and other classes, as can be seen in Figure 2.12.

FIGURE 2.12

J2EE foundation

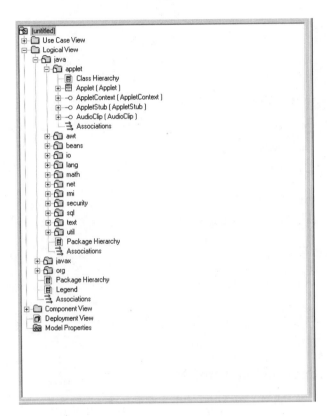

Although they cannot all be seen in the figure, the J2EE framework provides classes and interfaces within each of the packages. Each one has the appropriate attributes and operations, so the team does not need to manually enter them.

There are two benefits to using a framework:

♦ The team does not need to spend unnecessary time modeling elements that already exist. The focus of the modeling effort is on what's unique to a project, not reinventing existing components (although reusing them is fine!).

♦ A framework helps provide consistency across projects. As we mentioned in Chapter 1, a primary benefit of modeling is ensuring consistency between team members or even between entire teams. Using the same framework in different projects ensures that both teams are building from the same foundation.

Rose even gives you the option of creating your own framework. Using this approach, you collect and model the classes and components that form your organization's architectural foundation. Upon this foundation, you can design and build multiple systems.

Saving Models

As with any other application, it is good practice to save the file periodically. Rose is no exception. As mentioned above, the entire model is saved in one file. In addition, you can save the log to a file.

To save a model:

Select File ➤ Save from the menu.

> **OR**

Click the Save button on the Standard toolbar.

To save the log:

1. Select the log window.

2. Select File ➤ Save Log As from the menu.

3. Enter the filename of the log.

> **OR**

1. Select the log window.

2. Click the Save button on the Standard toolbar.

3. Enter the filename of the log.

Exporting and Importing Models

One of the main benefits of the object-oriented paradigm is reuse. Reuse can apply not only to the code but to the models as well. To fully take advantage of reuse, Rose supports exporting and importing models and model elements. You can export a model or a portion of a model and import it into other models.

To export a model:

1. Select File ➤ Export Model from the menu.

2. Enter the name of the export file.

To export a package of classes:

1. Select the package to export from a Class diagram.

2. Select File ➤ Export <package> from the menu.

3. Enter the name of the export file.

To export a class:

1. Select the class to export from a Class diagram.

2. Select File ➤ Export <class> from the menu.

3. Enter the name of the export file.

To import a model, package, or class:

1. Select File ➤ Import Model from the menu.

2. Select the file to import. Allowable file types are model (`.mdl`), petal (`.ptl`), category (`.cat`), or subsystem (`.sub`).

Publishing Models to the Web

You can easily publish all or any part of your Rose model to the Web—either to an intranet, the Internet, or a filesystem site—using Rational Rose 2001A or 2002. This way, users who may need to view the model can do so without having Rose installed and without printing a ream of model documentation. A model published to the Web is shown in Figure 2.13.

FIGURE 2.13

ATM model on the Web

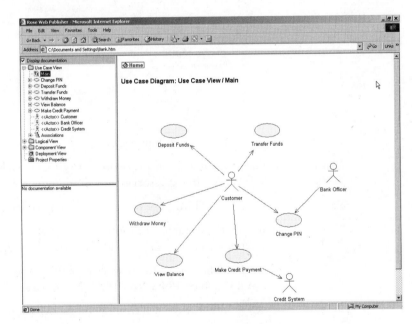

To publish a model to the Web:

1. Select Tools ➤ Web Publisher from the menu.

2. Select the model views and packages to publish from the Web Publisher window, as shown in the Selections field in Figure 2.14.

3. In the Level of Detail field, select the desired level of detail. The Documentation Only option includes only high-level information; none of the properties of the model elements are displayed. The Intermediate option displays the properties found on the General tab on model element specifications. The Full option publishes all properties, including those listed on the Detail tab on model element specifications.

4. Select the notation to use while publishing. Notation will default to the default notation in Rose.

5. Choose whether or not to publish inherited items.

FIGURE 2.14

Web Publisher window

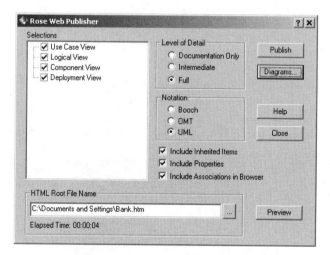

6. Choose whether or not to publish properties.

7. Choose whether or not to publish associations, which are the relationships between model elements. If this box is selected, associations will appear in the browser treeview.

8. Enter the name of the HTML root filename where the model will be published.

9. If you want to choose the graphic file format for the diagrams, select the Diagrams button. The Diagram Options window will be displayed, as in Figure 2.15.

   Select the type of graphic format to use while publishing diagrams: Windows bitmaps, Portable Network Graphics (PNGs), or JPEGs. You can also select to not publish diagrams.

10. When ready, click Publish. Rose will create all of the web pages to publish your model.

11. If desired, click Preview to see the published model.

FIGURE 2.15

Diagram Options window

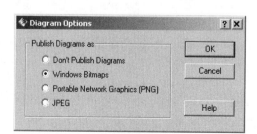

Working with Controlled Units

Rose supports multiuser, parallel development through the use of controlled units. A *controlled unit* in Rose can be any package within the Use Case view, Logical view, or Component view. In addition, the Deployment view and the Model Properties units can also be placed under control. When a unit is controlled, all of the model elements inside it are stored in a separate file from the rest of the model. This way, the separate file can be controlled through the use of an SCC-compliant version control tool, such as Rational ClearCase or Microsoft SourceSafe, or minimally within Rose directly. To create or manage a controlled unit, right-click the package to control and select the Units option, as shown in Figure 2.16.

FIGURE 2.16

Managing units

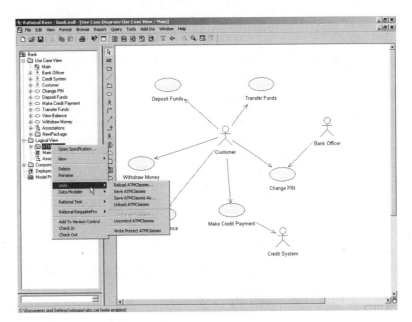

Follow these steps to create a controlled unit:

1. In the browser, right-click the package to be placed under control.

2. Select Units ➤ Control <package> from the menu.

3. Enter the filename for the controlled unit. Notice that the icon in the browser now has a page symbol on the folder to symbolize that the package is controlled.

In a parallel development environment, you may need to unload a package so that others can work on the package. You may only modify a loaded package. An unloaded package is available for others to load and modify. To unload a controlled unit:

1. Right-click the package to be unloaded.

2. Select Units ➤ Unload <package> from the menu. Notice that the items in the package are removed from the browser because they have been removed from the model.

To unload all controlled units in a view:

1. Right-click the view.

2. Select Units ➤ Unload Subunits of <view> from the menu.

Periodically, you may want to reload a package that has just been updated by another development team. To load a controlled unit:

1. Right-click the package to be reloaded.

2. Select Units ➤ Reload <package> from the menu.

To uncontrol a controlled unit:

1. Make sure the controlled unit is loaded.

2. Right-click the package to be uncontrolled.

3. Select Units ➤ Uncontrol <package> from the menu. Note that the controlled unit's file is not deleted from your computer.

At times, you may want to view certain items without modifying them. To protect from modifying controlled units, mark the unit as write-protected.

To write-protect a controlled unit:

1. Right-click the package to be write-protected.

2. Select Units ➤ Write Protect <package> from the menu.

To write-enable a controlled unit:

1. Right-click the package to be write-enabled.

2. Select Units ➤ Write Enable <package> from the menu.

Using the Model Integrator

The Model Integrator in Rose is a way to compare and merge up to seven Rose models. This feature is especially useful in situations with multiple designers. Each can work individually, and then all models can be integrated into one.

When comparing models, Rose will show you the differences between them. To begin, select Tools ➤ Model Integrator from the menu. You will see the screen shown in Figure 2.17. If you do not see a Model Integrator option on the Tools menu, select Add Ins ➤ Add In Manager, and then select the Model Integrator.

To compare two or more Rose models:

1. Select File ➤ Contributors from the menu.

2. Press the […] button to select the first model to compare.

3. Press the New button to add additional Rose models.

4. Select additional files as needed, until all files you wish to compare have been selected.

5. Press the Compare button. The differences will be displayed, as shown in Figure 2.18.

FIGURE 2.17

The Model
Integrator

FIGURE 2.18

Model differences

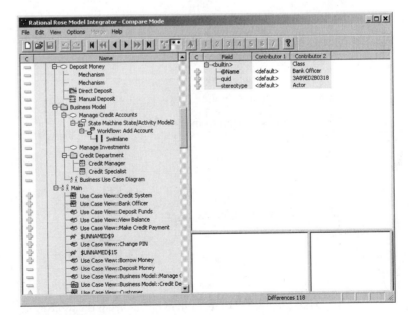

6. Press the Merge button to merge rather than compare models. The Model Integrator will attempt to merge the files for you. If there are any conflicts, you will see a message in the lower-right corner of the window informing you of the number of unresolved items. Use the Previous Conflict and Next Conflict toolbar buttons to navigate to the conflicts and resolve them.

7. Once all conflicts are resolved, you may save the new model.

Working with Notes

A note is simply a small amount of text that you would like to add to a diagram. It can be related to the overall diagram or to a particular element on the diagram. If it is related to a particular element, it is attached to that element, as shown in Figure 2.19.

FIGURE 2.19

Notes

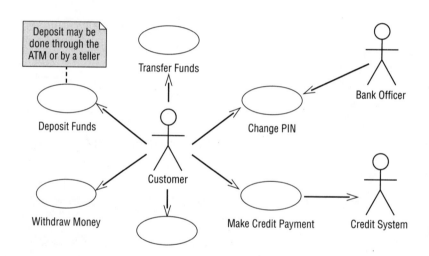

To add a note to a diagram:

1. Select the Note icon from the toolbar.

2. Click anywhere inside the diagram to place the note.

3. Select the Anchor Note to Item button from the toolbar.

4. Drag and drop from the note to the item.

To remove a note from a diagram, simply select it and press the Delete key.

Working with Packages

A package is a UML construct that is used to group model elements together. You can create a package of use cases, actors, classes, or any other type of model element.

Packages are mainly used to organize the model. In the Use Case view, packages simply group the use cases and actors into more manageable views. In the Logical view, packages are used for two purposes:

◆ They can be used to group the classes and other model elements into logical groupings (i.e., all of the classes that deal with orders, all of the classes that deal with customers, etc.).

◆ They can be used to show the physical deconstruction of the system into architectural layers. For example, one package may hold the user interface elements, while another holds the business logic, and still another holds the database connection classes. The team can then model and analyze the dependencies between the packages to evaluate the system's architecture.

Packages are a powerful UML tool in this respect. Analyzing the dependencies can show the team how reusable a particular package is, what other packages may need to change if a particular package changes, what the effect would be if a package were to change, and which architectural layers communicate directly with which other architectural layers. A dependency indicates that a class in one package has a relationship to a class in another package.

In general, dependencies between architectural layers should flow from the user interface layer to the business logic layer to the database communications layer to the database itself, as shown in Figure 2.20.

FIGURE 2.20

Dependencies in architectural layers

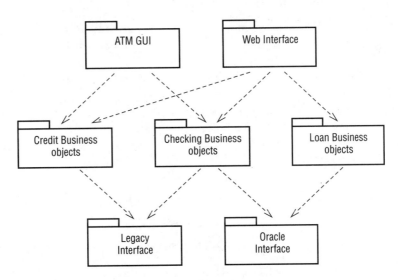

Also, as a general guideline, dependencies should not "skip" layers. For example, the user interface should not depend directly upon the database. The team may decide not to follow these guidelines, which is fine, but modeling the architecture through packages is a great way of seeing the implications of these types of architectural decisions. We will discuss this topic further in Chapter 6.

In the Component view, packages are again used to model the different layers, or tiers, of the system architecture, but in this case the packages focus on components rather than classes. In the Deployment view, they can be used to separate different categories of processors or devices.

Packages can be created within packages to further organize the model. This can be especially helpful when modeling very large, complex systems or when modeling applications that communicate with a number of other applications. While it is not necessary to use packages at all, they do help to keep the model organized.

A second use for packages that is specific to Rational Rose is in version control, especially in a multiuser environment. Packages can be used to split the Rose model into separate files, which can then be checked in and out using version control software such as Rational's ClearCase.

To add a package in Rose:

1. Right-click in the model hierarchy shown in the browser. You can create a package directly under one of the four views (Use Case, Logical, Component, or Deployment) by right-clicking either the Use Case View option, the Logical View option, or the Component View option. Alternatively, you can create a package underneath any existing package by right-clicking the existing package and selecting New ➤ Package.

2. The new package will appear in the browser. Single-click it to assign it a name.

To remove a package in Rose:

1. Right-click the package in the browser and select Delete. You will be prompted for confirmation before the package is deleted.

2. The package will be removed from the model. Please note that any classes, diagrams, or other model elements within the package will be deleted.

Adding Files and URLs to Rose Model Elements

While the Rose model contains a great deal of information about the system, there are other documents, such as the requirements document, vision statement, test scripts, and so on, that are located outside the Rose model. It can be helpful to attach these files to specific elements within the Rose model. Once a Word file, for example, has been attached to the hierarchy in the browser window, you can launch Word and load that file by simply double-clicking the filename in the browser.

To attach a file or URL to a model element:

1. Right-click the model element in the browser.

2. Select New ➤ File or New ➤ URL.

3. Select the appropriate file or URL in the files window.

4. Once the file or URL has been attached, double-click it in the browser to open it.

5. To delete the file or URL, right-click it in the browser and select Delete. Note that this operation will simply remove the attachment between the Rose model and the file; it will not delete the file from your system.

Adding and Deleting Diagrams

A Rose model can contain many diagrams, each of which shows a slightly different view of the system. As a collection, these diagrams should give the team a thorough understanding of the system from many different perspectives. The eight types of diagrams supported by Rational Rose are:

- Use Case diagrams
- Activity diagrams
- Sequence diagrams
- Collaboration diagrams
- Statechart diagrams
- Class diagrams
- Component diagrams
- Deployment diagrams

The Use Case view typically includes Use Case diagrams, Activity diagrams, Sequence diagrams, and Collaboration diagrams. When you create a new Rose model, one Use Case diagram called "Main" is automatically created in the Use Case view. This diagram cannot be removed.

The Logical view typically contains Sequence diagrams, Collaboration diagrams, Class diagrams, and Statechart diagrams. In a new Rose model, one Class diagram called "Main" is automatically created for you in the Logical view. The Component view contains one or more Component diagrams, while the Deployment view contains a Deployment diagram. There is only one Deployment diagram per system.

To add a new diagram:

1. Right-click a package in the browser. The new diagram will be added underneath the package you have right-clicked.

2. Select New ➤ <diagram type>.

3. Type the name of the new diagram.

4. Double-click the new diagram to open it.

5. To delete a diagram, right-click it in the browser and select Delete. Note that although the diagram is deleted, the model elements, such as classes or use cases that were on the diagram, are not deleted.

Setting Global Options

Options such as the font and color are used for all model objects, including classes, use cases, interfaces, packages, and so on. In this section, you will learn how to change the fonts and colors for model objects. You can set the default fonts and colors by using the Tools ➤ Options menu item.

Working with Fonts

In Rose, you can change the font of individual objects on a diagram, which can improve the readability of your model. Fonts and font sizes are set using the Font window shown in Figure 2.21.

To set the font or font size of an object on a diagram:

1. Select the desired object or objects.

2. Select Format ➤ Font from the menu.

3. Select the desired font, style, and size.

FIGURE 2.21

Font Selection window

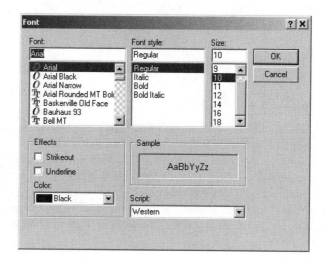

Working with Colors

In addition to changing the fonts, the colors of objects can be individually changed. You can change the line color and fill color for an object by using the Color window in Figure 2.22.

To change the line color of an object:

1. Select the desired object or objects.

2. Select Format ➤ Line Color from the menu.

3. Select the desired line color.

To change the fill color of an object:

1. Select the desired object or objects.

2. Select Format ➤ Fill Color from the menu.

3. Select the desired fill color.

FIGURE 2.22

Color Selection

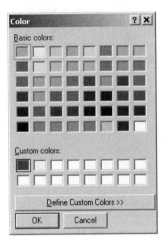

Summary

At this point, you should be familiar enough with the basics of Rose to follow the Rose examples and instructions in the remainder of this book.

There are four views within a Rose model:

- The Use Case view, which describes the system from the stakeholders' perspective

- The Logical view, which includes the classes, packages of classes, and other logical constructs within the system

- The Component view, which focuses on the physical layout of the files

- The Deployment view, which is concerned with the structure of the network on which the system will be deployed

Through these four views, the members of a project team should have a complete picture of the system, from a high level to a very detailed level. As we progress through this book, we will fill in the details of each of these four views.

Chapter 3

Business Modeling

WHILE THE REST OF UML focuses on a system that will be built, *business modeling* instead concentrates on the business around the system. In this chapter, we will examine the business itself, the entities that interact with it, and the workflows within it to truly understand the business environment before designing the system. We can then be sure that the system will work to meet the unique goals of the unique business in which it exists.

We'll begin by introducing the concept of business modeling and then discuss some of the reasons you may want to model your business. Not every project requires business modeling. However, there are many situations where business modeling adds a great deal of value. We'll discuss some of these situations.

We will then get into the specific elements within business modeling. Some of these elements are business actors, business use cases, and business workers. We will discuss each of these and show you how to model them using Rose.

- ◆ Introduction to business modeling
- ◆ Business modeling concepts
- ◆ Reasons for modeling a business
- ◆ Working with business use cases, business actors, and business workers

Introduction to Business Modeling

Business modeling is the study of an organization. During the business-modeling process, you examine the organization's structure and look at the roles within the company and how they interrelate. You also examine the organization's workflows, the major processes within the company, how they work, how effective they are, and whether there are any bottlenecks. You'll examine the outside entities, either individuals or other companies, which interact with the business, and look at the implications of that interaction.

In short, you try to understand what is inside and outside the business, and how the inside and outside talk to each other. In UML, you'll document this information in the business model.

Why Model the Business?

There are many reasons to do business modeling. These reasons include gaining an understanding of your organization and its software system, helping in a business process–re-engineering effort, and building a powerful training tool, as explained in the following sections.

UNDERSTANDING THE ORGANIZATIONAL VISION

Even if you are not building a software system, you can use business modeling to understand and document what your organization does. This is a wonderful way to develop a vision statement for your organization; the diagrams in business modeling will help you understand what the outside world gains from its relationship with your organization, as well as how your organization goes about accomplishing these goals. The business modeling does not apply only to the organizational level. A particular division within an organization may want to go through the business-modeling process to develop its own division charter or mission statement.

BUSINESS PROCESS RE-ENGINEERING

Business modeling is also very helpful in a business process–re-engineering effort. One of the chief artifacts of the business-modeling process is the workflow diagram. These diagrams depict how a particular process flows within the organization. It shows the individuals involved in the process, the steps within the process, and the business entities that are involved in the process. A business process–re-engineering team will start by documenting the current process with workflow diagrams. They can then analyze these diagrams to look for inefficiencies or other problems within the workflow. For example, they may discover that a particular document goes from an analyst, to a manager for approval, back to the analyst for additional information, and then back to the manager. The process may be able to be improved by having the analyst fill out all of the required information up front. This is just one example of how workflow diagrams can be analyzed.

The business process–re-engineering team will also use workflow diagrams to analyze possible future workflows. By designing a number of potential processes, the team will be better able to view and discuss the pros and cons of each approach and to select the new process that is most appropriate for the organization.

TRAINING

Whether a new process has just been developed or a new staff member has just joined the team, the results of business modeling can be a powerful training tool. The workflow diagrams illustrate who is involved in the process, what the steps are, and what the artifacts are. Any member of the team can review these diagrams to understand how they fit into the process, what artifacts they are responsible for producing or receiving, and with whom they need to communicate. These simple diagrams can save a great deal of organizational headaches by clearly stating what each person's responsibilities are within a workflow. They help ensure that everyone has a common understanding of the business processes and the roles within them.

CONTEXT FOR A SOFTWARE SOLUTION

Of course, many of us who are using UML are using it to build software. In this situation, business modeling can help us understand the context of the system we are building. While this may sound trivial, it can have serious consequences on the success or failure of a software project. If we fail to understand the business, we may make faulty assumptions about what the software should do and how it can best be used by the business community.

The "world around the system" is an important consideration when building software. Over the past several years, as companies were using UML without business modeling, one of the concerns that arose was the inability to understand how the system fit into the organization around it.

Enter business modeling. This solves the hole in the process by giving the team a view of the business itself, the workflows within it, and the way the new system will help automate portions of the workflow.

Do I Need to Do Business Modeling?

Without the help of some gifted psychics, we can't give you a definite answer to that question. However, we can give you some guidelines:

You may need to do business modeling if:

◆ You and your workgroup are new to the organization.

◆ The organization has undergone some recent business process re-engineering.

◆ The organization is planning to go through business process re-engineering.

◆ You are building software that will be used by a significant portion of the organization.

◆ There are large and complex workflows within the organization that are not well documented.

◆ You are a consultant in an organization you have not worked with before.

You may not need to do business modeling if:

◆ You have a thorough understanding of the organization's structure, goals, business vision, and stakeholders.

◆ You are building software that will be used by only a small part of the organization, and will not have an effect on the rest of the business.

◆ The workflows within the organization are fairly straightforward and are well documented.

◆ There simply isn't time. Let's be realistic; not all projects have the time needed to do a complete business analysis. But be careful! Don't let lack of time be an excuse. Fight for the time if you feel that business modeling would help ensure the success of your project.

Business Modeling in an Iterative Process

In an iterative process, the team goes through a series of steps multiple times, each time focusing on a different part of the business or system. There are two approaches to business modeling in an iterative environment. First, you can complete all of the business modeling up front, and then iterate through the analysis, design, coding, testing, and deployment steps. Alternatively, you can include the business modeling in the iterations. We'll discuss a few of the pros and cons of each approach, but first let's discuss where business modeling falls in relation to the other steps in the lifecycle.

The typical sequence of steps in developing software is as follows (note that these are not all of the steps in the lifecycle):

◆ Business modeling
  ◆ Business Use Case diagrams
  ◆ Activity diagrams (workflows)
  ◆ Analysis-level Class diagrams (business entities)
◆ System use case modeling
  ◆ Actors
  ◆ Use cases
  ◆ Use Case diagrams
◆ Analysis
  ◆ Use case flow of events
  ◆ Supplementary specifications
  ◆ Analysis-level Sequence and Collaboration diagrams
  ◆ Analysis-level Class diagrams
◆ Design
  ◆ Design-level Sequence and Collaboration diagrams
  ◆ Design-level Class diagrams
  ◆ Statechart diagrams (if needed)
  ◆ Component diagrams
  ◆ Deployment diagrams
◆ Coding
◆ Testing
◆ Deployment

As you can see, business modeling is the first step in the process. It is the first step whether you are using an iterative lifecycle or a waterfall approach. The reason for this is that business modeling sets the context for the rest of the project. As you go through the system's design, the business modeling will help you keep in mind why you are building the system in the first place.

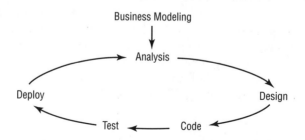

Completing the business modeling up front, as opposed to iteratively, gives you the advantage of fully understanding the business process before beginning to scope the system at all. Thus, you can determine from the beginning the areas of the workflow that most need to be automated and the areas in which the system can most effectively help the organization. All of this leads to the ability to build a system that can have a greater positive impact on the company.

The disadvantage to this approach is that, as projects are often time-constrained, it can be unrealistic. Unfortunately, it can lead to the cutting out of business modeling altogether. Your end users or customers may want to get to the system quickly and may not be willing to wait for you to analyze the business first.

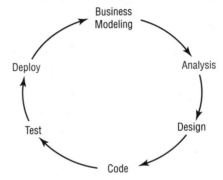

Alternatively, you can complete the business modeling in iterations. This has the advantage of letting you study the organization without delaying the building of the software system. You do, of course, run the risk of misunderstanding the company and building a software system that doesn't quite meet its needs. Or, you may discover a previously unknown business process later in the game that has a significant impact on the system. These types of risks can typically be controlled, but they are the downfalls of using this type of approach with business modeling.

Business-Modeling Concepts

In this section, we will discuss some of the fundamental concepts of business modeling. Ideas such as business actors, business workers, and activity diagrams will help us understand the organization itself. In this section, we will cover the following concepts:

- Business actors
- Business workers
- Business use cases
- Business Use Case diagrams
- Communication relationships between business use cases and business actors
- Business entities
- Activity diagrams

Again, it is important to remember that business modeling does not focus on what will and will not be automated (although that information can be found in the workflows). Instead, it focuses on two areas. First, what are the boundaries of the organization and with whom does it need to communicate? And second, what are the workflows within the organization and how can they be optimized?

Business Actors

A business actor is anyone or anything that is *external* to the organization but interacts with it. For example, a business actor for your organization might be its customers, its creditors, its investors, or its suppliers. Each of these actors has an interest in the actions of the company.

In UML, a business actor is modeled using the following icon:

Customer

Although the icon looks like a person, a business actor does not need to be an individual. It could represent a group of people or a company. We model business actors to understand who and what needs to interact with the business and how they interact with the business. When we are re-engineering processes or building new systems, we must always keep in mind that the organization must still meet the needs of these external entities. What good would it be to a grocery store to streamline its processes by getting rid of the cash registers? An extreme example, of course, but the idea is the same: We must keep in mind why the business is there in the first place. Modeling business actors helps with this effort.

Business Workers

A business worker is a role *within* the organization. Notice that business workers are roles, not positions. A single person may play many roles but hold only one position. The benefit of being role-based rather than position-based is that positions tend to change over time, while roles remain fairly constant.

In UML, a business worker is modeled using the following icon:

Salesperson

We model business workers to understand the roles within the business and how these roles interact. By describing each business worker, we can understand what the responsibilities of that role include, what skills are required for that role, and other details. At a minimum, think about the following for a business worker:

- What are the worker's responsibilities?

- What skills does the worker need to carry out those responsibilities?

- ◆ With what other workers does it interact?

- ◆ In what workflows does it participate?

- ◆ What are the worker's responsibilities within each workflow?

Business Use Cases

A business use case is a group of related workflows within the organization that provide value to the business actors. In other words, the business use cases tell the reader what the organization *does*. More specifically, they tell someone what the organization does that provides value to the businesses and individuals that interact with it. The set of all business use cases for an organization should completely describe what the business does.

Examples of business use cases for a retail store might include "Restock Inventory," "Price Products," "Sell Products," "Refund Money," or "Deliver Products." For an e-business, they might include "Register New User," "Create/Modify Order," "Fill Order," "Restock Inventory," or "Cancel Order." An investment house might have "Buy Stock" and "Sell Stock," among others.

A company does not even have to be highly automated to use business modeling. A cattle rancher might have business use cases like "Buy Cattle," "Sell Cattle," "Bottle Milk," or "Replenish Feed."

In UML, we use the following icon for business use cases:

Restock Inventory

The business use cases are typically named in the format "<verb><noun>," as in "Price Products." This is a good standard to follow for several reasons. It keeps the business use cases consistent, even if multiple analysts are defining them. Also, it makes the use cases easier for the end user to understand. "Price" alone doesn't tell the user much about the business, nor would "Products." Finally, and perhaps most importantly, it keeps the focus on what the business is *doing*—what it's accomplishing—not just what entities it uses.

Of course, even "Price Products" doesn't tell us much without some details. For each business use case, you will want to create some type of report that lets people know specifically what goes on within the use case. Does a clerk use historical prices to set the current price? Do they use surveys to determine what the customers are willing to pay? Do they do an in-depth study of the prices of each product in Egypt and Turkey and then average the two? Or do they just make up product prices as they go along? We won't know for sure unless the specific workflow is documented somewhere.

The workflow can be documented in a couple of ways. The simplest in some situations is just to create a numbered, step-by-step list of what happens as the use case progresses:

1. The clerk talks to the manager to obtain a list of all new products to be priced.

2. The clerk checks the store's purchase records to see how much the store paid for each new item.

3. The clerk adds 10% to the purchase price to find the item's price.

4. The clerk gives the new prices to the manager for approval.

5. If the manager does not approve, the clerk and manager decide upon new prices.

6. The clerk creates price tags for each new item.

7. The clerk places price tags on each new item.

The problem with this approach is that if there is a lot of conditional logic, it can confuse the reader. In the simple example above, the condition is fairly straightforward. Unfortunately, though, the real business world isn't always so simple. A business worker may perform some actions if condition A occurs, others if condition B occurs, and still others if condition C occurs. In this situation, it might be more beneficial to use an activity diagram.

An activity diagram shows in graphical form what the steps are in a workflow, the sequence of the steps, and who is responsible for performing each step. A sample activity diagram for the workflow described above would look like Figure 3.1.

FIGURE 3.1

Activity diagram

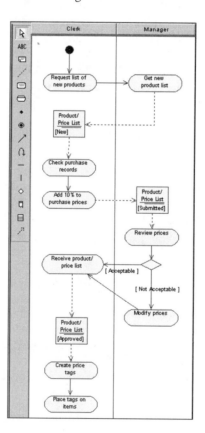

We'll discuss activity diagrams, including the different symbols that appear on the diagram, later in this chapter. For now, just look at the message the diagram is conveying. As before, we can see what the steps are in pricing products, but the graphical representation helps in making these steps easier to read and understand. The difference is even more striking with large and complex workflows.

Business Use Case Diagrams

A Business Use Case diagram shows you the business use cases, business actors, and business workers for an organization and the interactions between them. It gives you a complete model of what the company does, who is inside the company, and who is outside the company. It gives you the scope of the organization, so you can see what it encompasses and where its borders are.

An example of a Business Use Case diagram is shown in Figure 3.2.

FIGURE 3.2

Business Use Case diagram

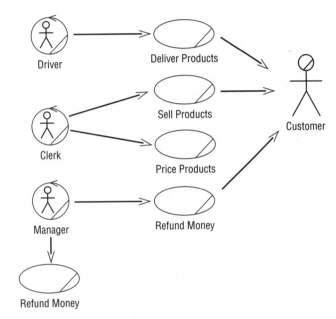

This diagram is simple by design. It is intended to quickly convey high-level information about the business without getting into all the details or confusing the reader with too much notation. If you have a large number of business use cases, simply create multiple diagrams with each containing a subset of the use cases.

An arrow from a business actor or a business worker to a use case suggests that the actor or worker initiates the use case. In this example, the clerk begins the process of pricing products. An arrow from a business use case to a business actor suggests that the organization initiates communication with the business actor. In this example, while the Deliver Products workflow is occurring, the organization (in this case, the driver) communicates with the customer.

Activity Diagrams

An activity diagram is a way to model the workflow of a use case in graphical form. The diagram shows the steps in the workflow, the decision points in the workflow, who is responsible for completing each step, and the objects that are affected by the workflow.

An example of an activity diagram is shown in Figure 3.3. In this example, a customer has received a defective product and is asking for a refund.

FIGURE 3.3

Activity diagram

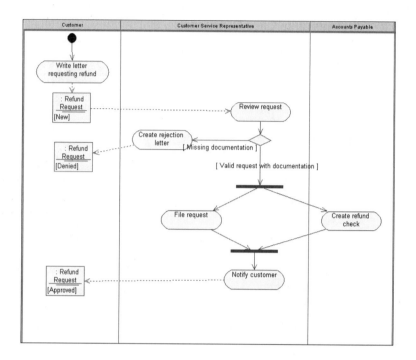

We can read the diagram as follows: The customer begins the process by writing a letter asking for a refund. The customer service representative reviews the letter. If the required documentation is missing, the customer service representative writes a rejection notice and sends it to the customer, who now has a request that has been denied. If the documentation is present, the customer service representative files the request at the same time as the accounts payable clerk writes a check. Once these two steps are completed, the customer service representative notifies the customer, who now has a request that has been approved.

Let's examine the notation in this diagram. The first piece is the start state, which is the solid dot in the upper-left portion of the diagram. This symbol lets you know where the process begins.

The rounded rectangles in the diagram are known as activities. An activity is simply a step in the workflow. It is a task that a business worker performs. Notice that the diagram is divided into three vertical sections, known as swimlanes. Along the top of the swimlanes, we can see the role that performs all of the activities in the swimlane.

Within an activity, you can list the actions that occur for that activity. Actions are simply steps within the activity. For example, if you have an activity called "create purchase order," the actions that make up that step might include: "get the supplier's name and address," "enter the item(s) to be ordered with price and quantity," "calculate the total," and "print the purchase order." These are steps that are too small to be shown as their own activities on a high-level business activity diagram but that add information about the process.

There are four types of actions:

- Those that occur when you enter an activity. These are marked with the word *entry*.

- Those that occur while an activity is occurring. These are the steps within the activity. These are marked with the word *do*.

- Those that occur when you leave an activity. These are marked with the word *exit*.

- Those that occur when a specific event happens. These are marked with the word *event*.

The arrows connecting the activities are known as transitions. A transition lets you know which activity is performed once the current activity has completed.

In this example, as soon as the clerk finishes checking the purchase prices of the items, he or she begins the process of adding 10% to those prices.

We can place guard conditions on the transitions to show when the transition occurs. Guard conditions are placed in square brackets. In this example, the activity "create rejection letter" is only performed if the guard condition "missing documentation" is true.

The horizontal bars are called synchronizations. They let you know that two or more activities occur simultaneously. The upper synchronization shows a fork in which the control of the workflow is split into two branches. Once those activities are complete, another synchronization, called a join, occurs. After the join, the workflow again has only one thread of control. Synchronization bars may be either horizontal or vertical. In the example shown previously in Figure 3.3, the customer service representative files the request at the same time the accounts payable clerk creates a refund check. Only after those two activities have completed does the customer service representative notify the customer.

Finally, the square symbols represent objects. These objects are affected by the workflow, and change state as the workflow goes along. In this example, a request could be new, denied, or accepted. Dashed lines are used to show which activities affect the state of an object. For example, the creation of a rejection letter sets the state of the request to "denied."

Business Entities

A business entity is an object that the organization uses to conduct its business or produces during the course of its business. A business entity is, as its name implies, an entity that the business uses. Entities include the things that the business workers deal with day to day. Examples might be sales order, account, shipping box, contract, small blue thumbtack—whatever is relevant to the business.

Look at that last statement carefully. You want to list the major items the business deals with, but without getting carried away. If you are in the business of producing thumbtacks, a small blue thumbtack might actually be a valid business entity. If not, it probably isn't worth worrying about. Ask questions like:

What products does the company produce?

What services does the company provide?

What items does the company purchase to do its work?

What are the items it delivers to/receives from its customers?

What items are passed from business worker to business worker for processing?

Another trick is to look at the nouns in the names of the business use cases you've defined. For the most part, each noun is a business entity. We use the following icon for a business entity:

Account

You can refine the business entities by adding attributes. An attribute is a piece of information that describes the entity. For example, an entity called account might have attributes such as account number, account type (checking or savings), balance, date opened, date closed, and status.

WARNING *It can be very easy to get carried away with attribute modeling. Remember that the purpose here is to elaborate on the business. You don't want to start designing a database yet! Include only those attributes that will help someone more fully understand the business.*

If you have defined attributes for the entity, they are displayed below the entity name, as shown here:

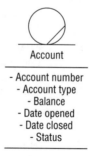

Account

- Account number
- Account type
- Balance
- Date opened
- Date closed
- Status

Organization Unit

An organization unit is simply a collection of business workers, business entities, or other business-modeling elements. It is a mechanism that can be used to organize the business model.

Many companies are organized into divisions, groups, or units. Each of these can be modeled as an organization unit. The organization unit will contain all of the business workers within that division, group, or unit. In UML, the following icon is used to represent an organization unit:

Marketing

Where Do I Start?

To begin, define the boundaries of your business-modeling effort. Are you modeling the entire organization or just one division? Which workflows within the business are relevant to your current project? It might be nice to analyze all the business workflows, but that could be quite an undertaking.

Once you have a clear definition of the scope of the project, it's very important to assemble the right team. You will need individuals with business knowledge, as well as individuals with business-modeling knowledge. In general, the people on the team do not need to be technical at all, and in fact it is sometimes better if they are not. Technical teams might dive too quickly into the solution space—the system design.

Some of the important roles to consider include the following:

Team lead   This person should have both business knowledge and modeling knowledge. He or she will be responsible for coordinating the efforts of the other members of the team and for keeping discussions focused.

Business representative(s)   These people are representatives from different parts of the organization to be modeled. They should be very familiar with the workflows of the business, including the current problems and benefits of those workflows. They should be able to see both their workflows in detail and the organization at a high level.

Business process re-engineer(s)   These individuals should be familiar with current workflows, and they should have an eye for finding efficiency problems and coming up with creative solutions. Ideally, they would have been involved in business process–re-engineering efforts in the past. They should be inquisitive but not belligerent, be excellent communicators (both written and verbal), and have the ability to decompose problems into manageable pieces. This is an optional role, used for business process–re-engineering efforts.

Business modeler(s) or business process analyst(s)   This role is very similar to that of a business process re-engineer, but in this case the business processes will not change. In this role, you need someone who understands the business workflows, who communicates extremely well, and has good analysis skills.

Management representative(s)   Someone must have the authority to decide what pieces of the business will be covered by the business-modeling effort. This person can also help the team understand the workflows from a manager's perspective.

Identifying the Business Actors

After the team has been assembled, begin identifying the business actors, business use cases, and business workers. This can be done in any order. To find the business actors, look at the scope of the project you are undertaking and ask yourself what lies outside that scope. If you are modeling the entire business and you ask what lies outside the business boundaries, your answer would be a whole world of people, companies, and other entities! You should therefore narrow the focus a little—for example, what lies *just* outside the business? In other words, who or what communicates with the business? These are your business actors.

It can be very helpful to hold brainstorming sessions to find some initial business actors. You can also review the project vision statement if one exists, the organization's marketing and other public relations materials, business goals, and business vision. Each of these might help you determine the outside entities that are important to the business.

Let's look at the example of an airline. Looking at the marketing materials for a particular airline, we find two types: those trying to win new customers, and those trying to win new employees. We can therefore identify two business actors: customers and potential employees (actual employees are business workers, because they lie within the scope of the organization). Reviewing some public relations materials, we find that they largely focus on the needs and concerns of the shareholders, so we add another business actor called shareholder. Knowing that this is an airline, there are certain federal regulations they must adhere to. The Federal Aviation Administration (FAA) is concerned with whether these rules are followed, so it is an actor as well. The airline buys its planes and many of its parts from a large plane manufacturer, which also is an actor. It buys the meals and drinks for its passengers from an outside catering company. These are just a few examples, but there are frequently a number of business actors for an organization, especially a large organization. Figure 3.4 shows examples of some of the business actors for an airline.

FIGURE 3.4

Business actors for
an airline

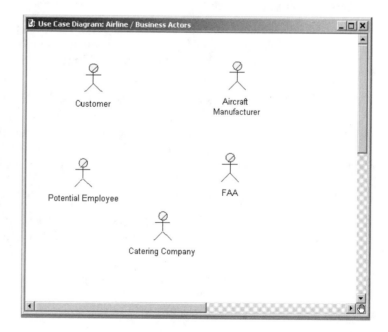

Identifying the Business Workers

To identify business workers, again look first at the scope of your project. If you are modeling the entire business, an organizational chart is a good place to start. Consider each *role* within the chart rather than each *position* to define the business workers. Remember that a single person may fill multiple roles. Once you have listed the business workers, begin detailing them. Document their responsibilities within the organization, their required skills, and their interactions with other business workers and with business actors.

In the airline example, the business workers are all of the different roles within the company. If we were modeling the entire organization, business workers would include, among others, pilots, co-pilots, navigators, stewards and stewardesses, mechanics, ticket sales staff, luggage handlers, and security guards. Figure 3.5 shows some of the business workers for an airline.

FIGURE 3.5

Business workers for an airline

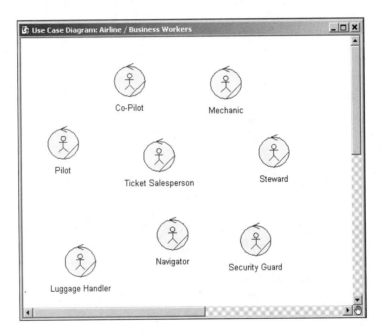

Identifying the Business Use Cases

To identify business use cases, you can start with the vision or mission statement for the organization. These should say, at a high level, what the business accomplishes that is of value to the outside world. An airline's main service is flying a customer from one city to another, so let's begin with that idea.

You then ask what needs to happen in order to transport that customer from Los Angeles to New York. First, the airline needs to have a mechanism for the customer to purchase a ticket. It then must check in the customer and their luggage; load the aircraft with fuel, luggage, and people; perform a safety check on the plane flying from L.A. to New York; land; and unload the aircraft. Some business use cases might include "Issue Ticket," "Check In Passengers," "Check In Luggage," "Perform Safety Check," "Load Aircraft," "Land Aircraft," and "Unload Aircraft." Of course, these represent only the core workflow of the business. If you are modeling the entire organization, you will need to think also about sales, marketing, accounting, and the other areas of the business.

Other ways to find business use cases might include brainstorming sessions, reviews of the organization's processes and procedures, interviews with customers and other stakeholders, or your own business knowledge. Be patient if this is time-consuming; this process is a little bit of art and a little bit of science.

Showing the Interactions

The next step is to draw one or more Business Use Case diagrams that show the interactions between the business workers, business actors, and business use cases. An arrow from a business worker to a business use case suggests that the worker initiates the process represented by the use case. In the following example, the safety coordinator initiates the process of performing a pre-flight safety check:

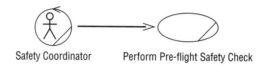

Safety Coordinator   Perform Pre-flight Safety Check

An arrow from a business actor to a business use case suggests that the actor initiates the process. For example, a customer may initiate the "Issue Airline Ticket" process:

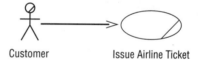

Customer   Issue Airline Ticket

If you have a large number of business use cases, actors, and workers, you may want to group them into organizational units. This can help organize the model and make it easier for the reader to understand. If you take this approach, create a separate Business Use Case diagram for each organization unit.

An example of a Use Case diagram for an airline is shown in Figure 3.6.

Once the initial Use Case diagrams have been constructed, distribute them for feedback and finally for approval.

Documenting the Details

This process will give you a high-level view of what is inside and outside the organization. What it will not do yet is give you any of the workflow details behind any of the use cases. Therefore, the next step in the process is to dive into those details.

For each business use case, document the workflow through the use case. As we discussed above, the workflow could be documented using numbered steps, flowcharts, or activity diagrams. Remember to document the primary flow, which is the normal course of events, and any alternate flows. If it is a complex process or there are many alternate flows, an activity diagram may be the best way to document the workflow.

If you are working with the Rational Unified Process, another artifact to create is a business use case report, which includes details about the use case such as the description, goals, workflow, relationships, and special requirements.

After these details have been documented for all business use cases, you have a great picture of the organization. The use cases tell you what the organization does. The workflows give you the details of how each use case is accomplished. The actors tell you what is outside the organization that interacts with it. The business workers tell you the roles within the organization. The organization units tell you how the company is structured. The business use case reports give you additional information about each use case. Finally, the Business Use Case diagrams tell you what the relationships are between all of those elements.

FIGURE 3.6

Business Use Case Diagram for an airline

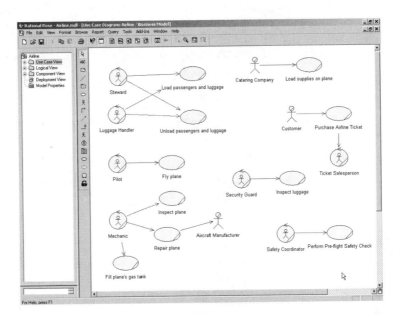

Next, let's take a look at how to model these UML concepts in Rational Rose.

Creating Business Use Case Diagrams

Business Use Case diagrams are created in the Use Case view within Rose. After they are created, they will appear in the browser hierarchy under Use Case view. A Business Use Case diagram will show some or all of the business actors, business workers, and business use cases in the model and the relationships between them. You can place a specific business actor, worker, or use case on as many Use Case diagrams as you'd like.

Although you can create Business Use Case diagrams directly under the Use Case view, keep in mind that your system use cases, system actors, and System Use Case diagrams will also be placed in the Use Case view. It can be helpful to begin by creating a separate area for the business modeling. This is accomplished by adding a package, which will contain all of your business use cases, business actors, and other business-modeling elements. Of course, you can create packages within this package to further organize your business model.

To create a Business Model package (optional):

1. Right-click the Use Case View entry in the browser.

2. Select New ➤ Package.

3. Enter the name of the new package, such as Business Model.

An example of a model that was organized using this method is shown in Figure 3.7. The Business Model package contains all business use cases, business workers, business actors, and Business Activity diagrams, while the System Model package contains all of the technical details for the system itself.

FIGURE 3.7

Business Model package

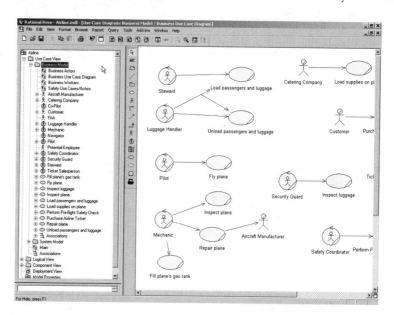

To create a new Business Use Case diagram:

1. Right-click the Business Model package in the Use Case view in the browser. If you did not create a business-modeling package within the Use Case view, right-click the Use Case View entry.

2. Select New ➤ Use Case Diagram from the shortcut menu.

3. With the new diagram selected, type in the name of your new diagram.

4. Double-click the name of the new diagram in the browser to open it.

To open an existing Business Use Case diagram:

1. Locate the Business Use Case diagram in the Use Case view in the browser.

2. Double-click the Business Use Case diagram's name to open it.

OR

1. Select Browse ➤ Use Case Diagram.

2. In the Package list box, select the package that contains the diagram you want to open.

3. In the Use Case Diagrams list box, select the diagram you want to open.

4. Press OK.

Deleting Business Use Case Diagrams

If you need to delete a Business Use Case diagram, you can do so in the browser. The business use cases, business actors, and other model elements on the diagram will not be deleted from the model. To delete a diagram, simply right-click it in the browser and select the Delete option from the shortcut menu.

WARNING *Rose does not allow you to undo a deletion of a diagram or to delete the Use Case diagram called Main.*

The Use Case Diagram Toolbar

When creating a Business Use Case diagram, the toolbar that will display shows the icons that are typically used for a System Use Case diagram. We will need to customize the toolbar to include the business-modeling icons.

To customize the Use Case toolbar:

1. Right-click the Use Case toolbar and select the Customize option. The window displayed in Figure 3.8 will appear.

FIGURE 3.8

Customizing the Use Case toolbar

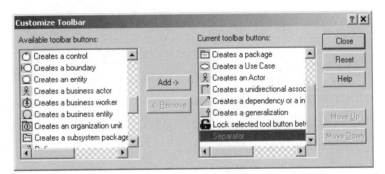

2. Find the business-modeling toolbar buttons in the Available Toolbar Buttons list box and press the Add key to add them to the toolbar.

Table 3.1 lists the business-modeling icons that are available to add to the Use Case Diagram toolbar. Note that there are other icons available on the toolbar. Table 3.1, however, lists only the business-modeling icons. We will discuss the other icons in Chapter 4, "Use Cases and Actors."

NOTE *In Rose, all of the business-modeling icons will be displayed in yellow.*

TABLE 3.1: BUSINESS-MODELING ICONS IN THE USE CASE DIAGRAM TOOLBAR

ICON	BUTTON	PURPOSE
	Business Actor	Adds a new business actor, who is external to the organization
	Business Worker	Adds a new business worker, who is internal to the organization
	Organization Unit	Adds a new organization unit, which is used to group business workers and other business-modeling elements
	Business Use Case	Adds a new business use case
	Business Use Case Realization	Adds a new business use case realization
	Business Entity	Adds a new business entity

Adding Business Use Cases

To add a business use case, first create or open a Use Case diagram and then add the new business use case to the diagram. When you create the business use case with this method, it is automatically added to the browser.

To add a new business use case:

1. Select the Business Use Case button from the toolbar.

2. Click anywhere inside the Use Case diagram. The new use case will be named NewUseCase by default.

3. With the new use case selected, type in the name of the new use case.

4. Note that the new use case has been automatically added to the browser under the Use Case view.

To add an existing business use case to a Use Case diagram:

1. Drag the business use case from the browser to the open Use Case diagram and drop it any-where in the diagram.

   OR

   Select Query ➤ Add Use Cases. A dialog box will display, as in Figure 3.9, which will allow you to select and add existing use cases.

2. In the Package drop-down list box, select the package that contains the business use case(s) you want to add.

3. Move the business use case(s) you want to add from the Use Cases list box to the Selected Use Cases list box.

4. Press OK to add the business use cases to the diagram.

FIGURE 3.9

Adding existing
business use cases to
a Use Case diagram

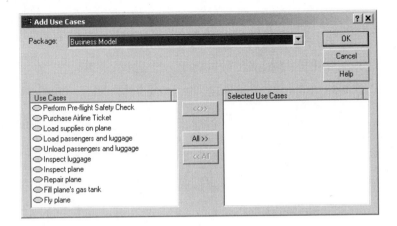

Business Use Case Specifications

In Rose, you can specify the name, priority, and other details for each business use case through the use case specification window, shown in Figure 3.10.

FIGURE 3.10

Use case specification
window

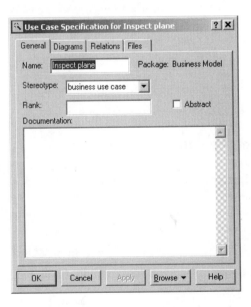

In the following sections, we'll take a look at each of the specifications available on the tabs of this window. But first, you should know the methods to use for viewing the specifications.

To open the business use case specifications:

1. Right-click the business use case on a Use Case diagram.

2. Select Open Specification from the shortcut menu.

OR

1. Right-click the use case in the browser.

2. Select Open Specification from the shortcut menu.

OR

1. Select the use case on a Use Case diagram.

2. Select Browse ➤ Specification.

OR

1. Select the use case on a Use Case diagram.

2. Press Ctrl+B.

Assigning a Priority to a Business Use Case

To help you manage the project, you may want to prioritize the business use cases. You could use the priority, for example, to determine in what order the business use cases will be analyzed and documented. The Rose specifications window provides a field called Rank, which can be used to prioritize the business use cases. It does not set up a numbering scheme for you, but you can use letters, numbers, or any other way of prioritizing the use cases.

To assign a priority to a business use case:

1. Right-click the business use case in the browser or on the Use Case diagram.

2. Select Open Specification from the shortcut menu.

3. On the General tab, enter the priority in the Rank field.

Viewing Diagrams for a Business Use Case

As you analyze a business use case, you may create a number of activity diagrams to document the workflow. Using the specification window or the browser, you can see a list of all of the diagrams for this particular business use case. Note that this list does not show you on which diagrams the use case resides; instead it shows you which diagrams contain some details for the use case.

To view the diagrams for a business use case:

1. Right-click the business use case in the browser or on a Use Case diagram.

2. Select Open Specification from the shortcut menu.

3. The diagrams will be listed on the Diagrams tab of the specification window, as shown in Figure 3.11. In this example, the use case has five activity diagrams.

FIGURE 3.11

Diagrams tab of a
use case specification
window

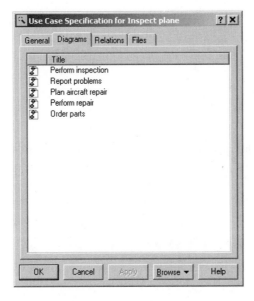

OR

Look through the browser. The diagrams for the use case will appear underneath the business use
case in the browser, as shown in Figure 3.12.

FIGURE 3.12

Diagrams for a
use case

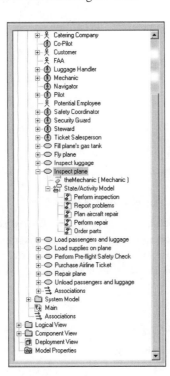

To open a diagram for a use case:

Double-click the diagram name on the Diagrams tab of the use case specification window.

OR

Right-click the diagram name on the Diagrams tab of the use case specification window and select Open Diagram from the shortcut menu.

OR

Double-click the diagram in the browser.

To add a diagram to a use case:

1. Right-click anywhere inside the Diagrams tab of the use case specification window.

2. From the shortcut menu, select the type of diagram (Use Case, Sequence, Collaboration, Statechart, Activity, or Class) you want to add.

3. Enter the name of the new diagram.

OR

1. Right-click the use case in the browser.

2. Select New ➤ (Collaboration Diagram, Sequence Diagram, Class Diagram, Use Case Diagram, Statechart Diagram, Activity Diagram) from the shortcut menu.

3. Enter the name of the new diagram.

To delete a diagram for a use case:

1. Right-click the diagram name on the Diagrams tab of the use case specification window.

2. Select Delete from the shortcut menu.

OR

1. Right-click the diagram name in the browser.

2. Select Delete from the shortcut menu.

Viewing Relationships for a Business Use Case

A relationship is a link between the business use case and a business actor or worker. It shows which business actor or worker initiates the business use case. As with diagrams, you can view the relationships for a particular business use case either through the specifications window or directly in the Rose browser. In the specifications window, the relationships are listed in the Relations tab, as shown in Figure 3.13.

To view the relationships for a use case:

1. Right-click the use case in the browser or on a Use Case diagram.

2. Select Open Specification from the shortcut menu.

3. The relationships will be listed on the Relations tab. The actor or worker who initiates the use case (or who is a client of the use case's functionality) will be listed in the Client column. The business use case itself (which supplies the functionality) is listed in the Supplier column.

FIGURE 3.13

Relations tab of a
use case specification
window

OR

1. Select the use case on a Use Case diagram.

2. Select Report ➤ Show Usage.

OR

Simply look at the hierarchy in the browser. The relationships for the business use case will be in the treeview below the use case itself.

To view the relationship specifications:

1. Double-click the relationship in the list.

2. The relationship specification window will appear. See the section "Working with Relationships" later in this chapter for a detailed description of relationship specifications.

OR

1. Right-click the relationship in the list.

2. Select Specification from the shortcut menu.

3. The relationship specification window will appear. See the section "Working with Relationships" later in this chapter for a detailed description of relationship specifications.

To delete a relationship:

1. Right-click the relationship in the list.

2. Select Delete from the shortcut menu.

Working with Business Actors

As you now know, a business actor is anyone or anything outside the business that interacts with it. Once you identify the business actors for your organization, the next step is to add them to the Rose model and create relationships between the business actors and business use cases.

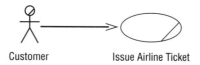

Customer   Issue Airline Ticket

Adding Business Actors

Like business use cases, business actors are added to the Rose model by adding them to a Use Case diagram. The first step in the process is to create or open a Use Case diagram. Once you have, you can add business actors using the toolbar.

To add a business actor to a Use Case diagram:

1. Select the Business Actor button from the toolbar (the yellow actor icon is a business actor).

2. Click anywhere inside the Use Case diagram. The new business actor will be named NewClass by default.

3. With the new actor selected, type in its name. Note that the new business actor has been automatically added to the browser under the Use Case view.

Adding Actor Specifications

Details about the business actor, such as the name, relationships, and attributes, are controlled through the business actor specifications window, shown in Figure 3.14.

As you work with classes later in this book, you may note that the actor specification window and the class specification window are very similar. This is because Rose treats an actor as a specialized form of a class. The actor specification window includes the same fields as the class specification window, but some of these fields are disabled for actors.

To open the business actor specifications:

1. Right-click the business actor on the Use Case diagram.

2. Select Open Specification from the shortcut menu.

OR

1. Right-click the actor in the browser.

2. Select Open Specification from the shortcut menu.

OR

1. Select the actor on the Use Case diagram.

2. Select Browse Specification.

OR

1. Select the actor on the Use Case diagram.

2. Press Ctrl+B.

FIGURE 3.14

Business actor specification window

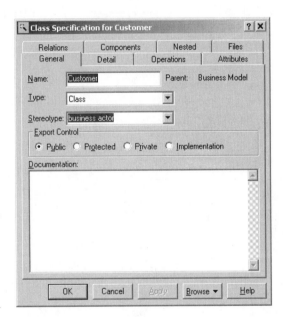

Assigning an Actor Stereotype

A stereotype is a way to categorize model elements in UML. Stereotypes are used when you have many different types of one element. For example, Visual Basic has a number of different types of classes: interface, form, control, collection, and so on. Each of these is represented in UML as a different stereotype.

The same concept applies to business actors. You may have several different types of business actors: those from supplier companies, those from government agencies, those from customer companies, and so on. If you would like, you can create your own stereotypes to categorize your business actors. You assign a stereotype to a business actor in the specifications window.

To assign a business actor stereotype:

1. Right-click the business actor in the browser or on a Use Case diagram.

2. Select Open Specification from the shortcut menu.

3. In the Stereotype field, enter the business actor stereotype.

WARNING *If you change the stereotype of a business actor, Rose will no longer display the actor using the UML actor symbol. It will display it as a box instead. This won't affect the rest of your model, but may make the Use Case diagram harder to understand.*

Setting Business Actor Multiplicity

Multiplicity refers to the number of instances you expect to have for a particular business actor. For example, you may expect to have 300,000 people play the role of customer. You can capture this information in the specifications window.

Rose provides you with several multiplicity options:

Multiplicity	Meaning
0..0	Zero
0..1	Zero or one
0..n	Zero or more
1..1	Exactly one
1..n	One or more
n (default)	Many

Or, you can enter your own multiplicity, using one of the following formats:

Format	Meaning	Example
\<number\>	Exactly \<number\>	3
\<number 1\>..\<number 2\>	Between \<number 1\> and \<number 2\>	3..7
\<number\>..n	\<number\> or more	3..n
\<number 1\>,\<number 2\>	\<number 1\> or \<number 2\>	3, 7
\<number 1\>, \<number 2\>..\<number 3\>	Exactly \<number 1\> or between \<number 2\> and \<number 3\>	3, 7–9
\<number 1\>..\<number 2\>, \<number 3\>..\<number 4\>	Between \<number 1\> and \<number 2\> or between \<number 3\> and \<number 4\>	3–5, 7–10

To set business actor multiplicity:

1. Right-click the business actor in the browser or on a Use Case diagram.

2. Select Open Specification from the shortcut menu.

3. Select the Detail tab.

4. Select from the Multiplicity drop-down list box, or type in the business actor's multiplicity using one of the formats listed above.

Viewing Relationships for a Business Actor

As with business use cases, you can view all of the relationships for a business actor either by using the Relations tab in the specification window or by going through the browser.

To view the relationships for a business actor:

1. Right-click the business actor in the browser or on a Use Case diagram.

2. Select Open Specification from the shortcut menu. The relationships will be listed on the Relations tab.

OR

Look at the browser window. All of the business actor's relationships will be listed under it in the treeview.

To view the relationship specifications:

1. Double-click the relationship in the list.

2. The relationship specification window will appear. See the upcoming section "Working with Relationships" for a detailed description of relationship specifications.

OR

1. Right-click the relationship in the list.

2. Select Specification from the shortcut menu.

3. The relationship specification window will appear. See the upcoming section "Working with Relationships" for a detailed description of relationship specifications.

To delete a relationship:

1. Right-click the relationship in the list.

2. Select Delete from the shortcut menu.

Working with Relationships

In business modeling, there are two types of relationships that are used: association relationships and generalization relationships. Association relationships are links between business actors and business use cases or between business workers and business use cases. Generalization relationships show an inheritance structure among business-modeling elements. In this section, we will discuss these two types of relationships and how to model them in Rose.

Association Relationship

An association relationship is a relationship between a business actor or business worker and a business use case. It indicates that a particular business actor or business worker initiates the functionality provided by the use case. The relationship is shown as an arrow:

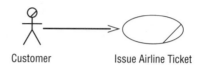

Customer   Issue Airline Ticket

The direction of the arrow indicates who initiates the communication. In the example above, the customer initiates the Issue Airline Ticket transaction. In the following example, after the pilot initiates the "Cancel Flight" business use case, the organization initiates communication with the customer.

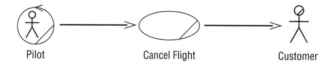

Pilot   Cancel Flight   Customer

We can see from the direction of the arrows that the pilot begins the process and that during the cancellation of the flight, the organization is responsible for notifying the customer.

To add a communicates relationship:

1. Select the Unidirectional Association toolbar button.

2. Drag the mouse from the business actor or business worker to the business use case (or from the business use case to the business actor or worker if the organization initiates the communication).

3. Rose will draw a relationship between the business use case and the business actor or worker.

To delete a communicates relationship:

1. Select the relationship on the Use Case diagram.

2. Select Edit ➤ Delete from Model, or press Ctrl+D.

Generalization Relationship

A generalization relationship is used when there are two or more business actors, business workers, or business use cases that are very similar. As an example, there may be two different groups of people selling airline tickets: phone representatives and staff who work at the airport counter for in-person sales. For the most part, these two groups of people do the same job, but there are some differences in their responsibilities.

In UML, you can model this situation through a generalization relationship. We create a generic business worker called ticket salesperson, and then create two more business workers, one for each type of salesperson. You can see this example modeled in Figure 3.15.

FIGURE 3.15

Generalization
relationship

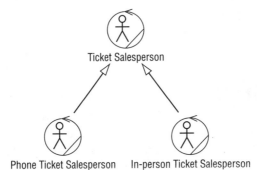

In a generalization relationship, the arrow points from the specific actor to the generic actor. Someone reading this diagram would say that there are two types of ticket salespeople: phone salesperson and counter salesperson.

The generic actor may actually be an *abstract* actor. An abstract actor is one that is never directly instantiated. In this example, no one ever plays the role of a ticket salesperson; they are always either a phone salesperson or a counter salesperson. The ticket salesperson actor is just there to hold the commonality between phone and counter salespeople. Because no one ever directly plays that role, ticket salesperson is an abstract business actor. Phone salesperson and counter salesperson, on the other hand, are examples of *concrete* business actors because people do directly play those roles.

A fairly recent evolution of UML is in generalization relationships between use cases. You can use this type of relationship when you have two or more use cases that are very similar but that still have some differences. First, you create an abstract use case, much the same as we did for business actors. This abstract use case holds the elements that are common between the other business use cases. You then inherit the other business use cases from the abstract business use case with a generalization relationship.

To add a generalization relationship:

1. Add the business actors, business workers, or business use cases to the Use Case diagram.

2. Select the Generalization button from the toolbar.

3. Drag from the concrete business actor, worker, or use case to the abstract business actor, worker, or use case.

4. Open the specification window for the abstract business actor, worker, or use case.

5. Select the Detail tab.

6. Check the Abstract check box.

To delete a generalization relationship:

1. Select the relationship on the Use Case diagram.

2. Select Edit ➤ Delete from Model, or press Ctrl+D.

WARNING *Be careful of using too many generalization relationships. Unless the reader is familiar with generalizations, they may make the diagram very difficult to understand.*

Working with Organization Units

As we discussed above, an organization unit is a UML construct used to group business actors, business workers, and business use cases together. Typically, a UML organization unit corresponds to a division or group within the organization. We might have organization units called Sales, Finance, Manufacturing, and Human Resources for those divisions within the company. Each organization unit would hold the business actors, workers, and use cases appropriate for that division. It can also be helpful to create a Use Case diagram specific to that organization unit, which shows only the business actors, workers, and use cases for that unit.

As you know from earlier in this chapter, an organization unit is represented by the following symbol:

Marketing

Adding Organization Units

In Rose, you can add organization units through a Use Case diagram. Once the units have been created, you can create new business actors, workers, or use cases inside them, or move existing business actors, workers, or use cases into the new unit. You can create as many organization units as you need, and create organization units within organization units to further organize the business model.

To add an organization unit:

1. Open a Use Case diagram.

2. Use the Organization Unit toolbar button to add a new unit. It will be named NewPackage by default, and will be automatically added to the browser.

3. Type in the name of the new organization unit.

To move an item into an organization unit, go to the browser and drag and drop the item from its existing location to the new organization unit.

Deleting Organization Units

Organization units can be deleted from the model using either the browser or a Use Case diagram. When you delete an organization unit, all business actors, business workers, business use cases, activity diagrams, and all other model elements within it will also be deleted from the model.

To remove an organization unit from a diagram without deleting it from the model:

1. Select the organization unit on a Use Case diagram.

2. Press the Delete key.

3. Note that the unit has been removed from the Use Case diagram, but it still exists in the browser and on other Use Case diagrams.

To delete an organization unit from the model:

1. Right-click the unit in the browser.

2. Select Delete from the shortcut menu.

OR

1. Select the organization on a Use Case diagram.

2. Select Edit ➤ Delete from Model, or press Ctrl+D.

WARNING *When you delete an organization unit from the model, all business use cases, business actors, and other items in the unit will also be deleted from the model.*

Activity Diagrams

In Rose, you can use an activity diagram to model the workflow through a particular business use case. The main elements on an activity diagram are:

◆ *Swimlanes*, which show who is responsible for performing the tasks on the diagram.

◆ *Activities*, which are steps in the workflow.

◆ *Actions*, which are steps within an activity. Actions may occur when entering the activity, exiting the activity, while inside the activity, or upon a specific event.

◆ *Business objects*, which are entities affected by the workflow.

◆ *Transitions*, which show how the workflow moves from one activity to another.

◆ *Decision points*, which show where a decision needs to be made during the workflow.

◆ *Synchronizations*, which show when two or more steps in the workflow occur simultaneously.

◆ *The start state*, which shows where the workflow begins.

◆ *The end state*, which shows where the workflow ends.

In this section, we'll take a look at how to model these different parts of the activity diagram using Rose.

Adding an Activity Diagram

You can create as many activity diagrams as you need for a particular business use case. The activity diagrams for a business use case will appear in the State/Activity Model area under the business use case in the browser.

To add an activity diagram:

1. Right-click the business use case in the browser.

2. Select New ➤ Activity Diagram from the menu.

3. Rose will create an entry in the browser called State/Activity Model under the business use case, as shown in Figure 3.16. The new activity diagram will appear under the State/Activity Model entry.

FIGURE 3.16

Adding an activity diagram

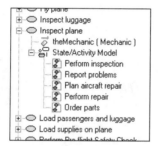

4. Name the new activity diagram.

5. Double-click the diagram to open it.

Adding Details to an Activity Diagram

Once the diagram has been created, the next step is to add the swimlanes, activities, and other details to it. This is accomplished using the Activity Diagram toolbar. Table 3.2 lists the icons available on the Activity Diagram toolbar and the purpose of each.

TABLE 3.2: ICONS ON THE ACTIVITY DIAGRAM TOOLBAR

ICON	BUTTON	PURPOSE
⤢	Selection Tool	Returns the cursor to an arrow to select a toolbar button
ABC	Text Box	Adds a text box to the diagram
▭	Note	Adds a note to the diagram

Continued on next page

TABLE 3.2: ICONS ON THE ACTIVITY DIAGRAM TOOLBAR *(continued)*

ICON	BUTTON	PURPOSE
	Anchor Note to Item	Connects a note to an item in the diagram
	State	Adds a state to the diagram
	Activity	Adds an activity to the diagram
	Start State	Adds a start state to the diagram
	End State	Adds an end state to the diagram
	State Transition	Transitions from one activity or state to another
	Transition to Self	Transitions to the current activity or state
	Horizontal Synchronization	Shows where two or more activities occur simultaneously
	Vertical Synchronization	Shows where two or more activities occur simultaneously
	Decision	Shows decision points in the workflow
	Swimlane	Shows who is responsible for completing activities
	Object	Shows an object that is affected by the workflow
	Object Flow	Shows what activities change the state of the object

To add a swimlane to the diagram:

1. Select the Swimlane toolbar button.

2. Click inside the diagram. A new swimlane will appear, and will be titled NewSwimlane by default, as shown in Figure 3.17.

3. Name the new swimlane, using the name of a business worker or organization unit.

To add a start state to the diagram:

1. Select the Start State toolbar button.

2. Click inside the diagram within the swimlane for the worker or unit who will start the workflow.

To add activities to the diagram:

1. Select the Activity toolbar button.

2. Click inside the diagram within the swimlane for the worker or unit who is responsible for performing the activity.

3. Name the new activity.

FIGURE 3.17

Swimlane in an activity diagram

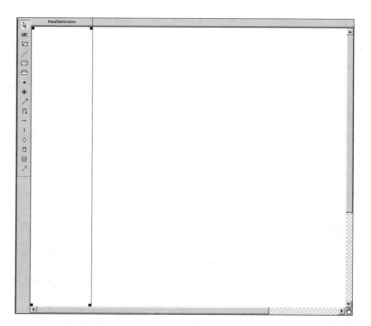

To add actions to the activities:

1. Right-click the activity.

2. Select the Open Specification option. The activity specification window will appear.

3. Select the Actions tab.

4. Right-click inside the tab and select Insert. The default action type, called Entry, will appear in the Type column, as shown in Figure 3.18.

5. Double-click the new action. The action specification window will appear.

6. In the When drop-down list box, select the appropriate option:

- ◆ On Entry for actions that occur when entering the activity

- ◆ On Exit for actions that occur when leaving the activity

- ◆ Do for actions that occur within the activity

- ◆ On Event for actions that occur when a specific event happens

7. Enter the action's name, as shown in Figure 3.19.

FIGURE 3.18

Adding actions to
an activity

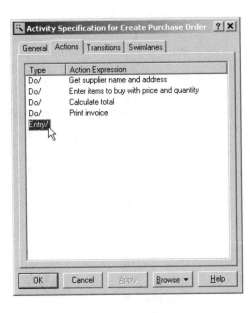

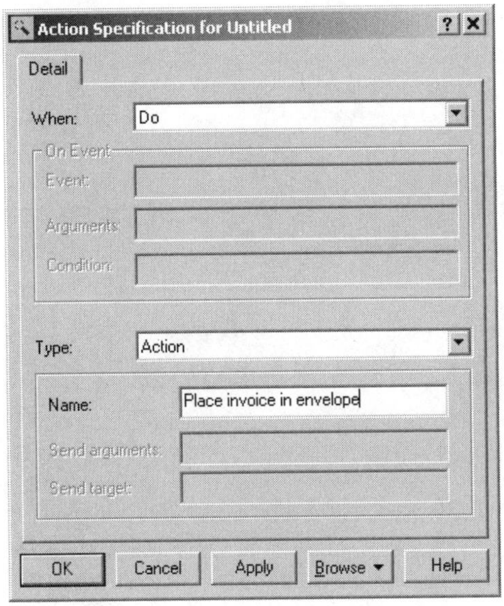

FIGURE 3.19

Action specification
window

8. If the action was on an event, enter the event that triggers the action, any arguments to the event, and any guard conditions. A guard condition must be true for the action to occur.

9. Click OK to close the action specification.

10. Click OK to close the activity specification.

To add a business object:

1. Select the Object toolbar button.

NOTE *The Object button does not appear by default when you install Rose. You may need to customize the toolbar to see it.*

2. Click inside the diagram within the swimlane for the worker or unit responsible for performing the activity that will affect the object.

3. Name the new object.

To draw transitions between activities:

1. Select the State Transition toolbar button.

2. Drag and drop from one activity to another.

To set a condition on the transition:

1. Right-click the transition.

2. Select the Open Specification option.

3. Select the Detail tab.

4. Type the condition in the Guard Condition field. When the condition is displayed on the diagram, it will be surrounded by square brackets to indicate that it is a guard condition, as shown in Figure 3.20. You can also type the guard condition directly on the transition by enclosing it in square brackets.

FIGURE 3.20

Guard conditions on transitions

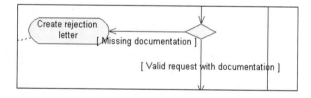

To add a decision point:

1. Select the Decision toolbar button.

2. Click inside the diagram to place the decision.

3. Draw two or more transitions from the decision, one for each decision possibility.

To add a synchronization:

1. Select the Horizontal or Vertical Synchronization toolbar button.

2. Click inside the diagram to place the synchronization.

3. Draw two or more transitions from the synchronization, one to each activity that will occur simultaneously, as shown in Figure 3.21.

FIGURE 3.21

Synchronization in an activity diagram

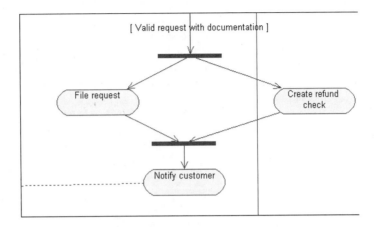

To show which activities affect a business object:

1. Select the Object Flow toolbar button.

2. Drag and drop from the activity that changes the state of the object to the object itself. A dashed arrow will appear between the two. Figure 3.22 shows an example of how creating a rejection letter sets the state of the request object to Denied.

FIGURE 3.22

Object flow in an activity diagram

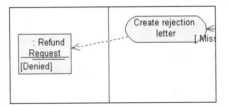

Summary

In this chapter we discussed business modeling. We began by examining why we would want to do business modeling in the first place. It is not right for all projects, but there are many times when business modeling can add a great deal of value to a project. We then moved on to discuss some of the fundamental elements of business modeling, including business actors, business use cases, business workers, and organization units, and how you would find some of these things in your organization.

From there, we moved into a discussion of the details of a business use case. You model the flow through a use case either by using text or via an activity diagram. Activity diagrams have the advantage of clarity and ease of use, especially when considering a workflow that is large and complex. We examined the different pieces of an activity diagram, including swimlanes, activities, actions, objects, transitions, and synchronizations.

Once we examined the business-modeling ideas, we moved on to how these items can be modeled using Rational Rose. We walked through the Rose toolbars and specification windows to examine the details of the elements that can be added to a Rose model.

In the next chapter, we'll begin the process of system modeling. Business modeling isn't as concerned with what is automated by a particular system. System modeling, in contrast, is focused on the implementation of a particular software project. Business modeling helps us set the context for the system model.

Chapter 4

Use Cases and Actors

USE CASES AND ACTORS define the scope of the system you are building. Use cases include anything that is within the system; actors include anything that is external to the system. We'll start this chapter by discussing some of the fundamental concepts of use case, or system, modeling: use case, actor, association relationship, includes relationship, extends relationship, generalization relationship, flow of events, activity diagram, and Use Case diagram. Then, we'll look at how to model each of these in Rose.

At the end of the chapter, we provide an exercise that builds on the business case of Chapter 3, "Business Modeling," by adding use cases, actors, and Use Case diagrams to a Rose model.

◆ Using the Use Case view and Use Case diagrams

◆ Working with use cases, actors, and relationships

◆ Using notes

◆ Adding and deleting Use Case packages

Use Case Modeling Concepts

In this section, we'll discuss some of the fundamental concepts of use case modeling: use cases, actors, relationships, activity diagrams, and Use Case diagrams. If you have gone through the business modeling process, you will notice the similarities between what we will discuss here and business modeling. Business modeling also works with actors, use cases, relationships, activity diagrams, and Use Case diagrams. The difference is that business modeling focuses on the organization, while system modeling focuses on the system being built. The terms system use case or system actor are sometimes used to differentiate them from business use cases or business actors.

Item	Business Modeling	System Modeling
Use case	Describes what the business does	Describes what a system within the business does
Actor	External to the organization	External to the system (may be internal to the organization)
Business worker	Internal to the organization	Not used

In the last chapter, we went through the business modeling process for an airline. During that example, we focused on the business of being an airline, not on what systems we would build. Now, we focus in on a particular system. Assume that we are building a ticket reservation system for the airline. It will eventually let people call in or go online to order plane tickets and to change or cancel a reservation.

Actors

An *actor* is anyone or anything that interacts with the system being built. As we will see shortly, use cases describe anything that is inside the system's scope. Actors are anything that is outside the system's scope. In UML, actors are represented with stick figures:

Customer

There are three primary types of actors: users of the system, other systems that will interact with the system being built, and time.

The first type of actor is a physical person, or a user. These are the most common actors, and are present in just about every system. For our flight reservation system, actors are the people who will be *directly* using the system. Because we know some of the functionality will be available over the Internet, customers can directly use the system. We also know that customers can call in to a customer service representative to make a reservation. The customer service representative will directly use the system, so this role is an actor as well.

When naming actors, remember to use role names rather than position names. A given individual will play many roles. John Doe may be a customer service representative, but if he goes online to buy a ticket for himself, he is playing the role of a customer. Using role names rather than position names will give you a more stable picture of your actors. Position names change over time, as roles and responsibilities are moved from one position to another. By using roles, you won't need to update your model every time a new position is added or a position changes.

The second type of actor is another system. For example, the airline's reservation system may need to interface with an external application to validate credit cards for purchases. In this example, the external credit application is an actor. It is another system that we won't be changing at all, so it is outside the scope of the current project, but it does need to interface with our new system. Any systems like this, which lie just beyond the boundaries of our application, are actors.

The third type of actor that is commonly used is time. Time becomes an actor when the passing of a certain amount of time triggers some event in the system. For example, part of our airline's promotions may be the chance to win a free ticket. Every day at 3:00 p.m. the system may automatically select a random customer to give a free ticket to. Because time is outside of our control, it is an actor.

Use Cases

A *use case* is a high-level piece of functionality that the system will provide. In other words, a use case illustrates how someone might use the system. Let's begin by looking at an example.

Along with our actors, we need to define the use cases for the airline reservation system. It really doesn't matter if you identify the use cases or the actors first. In fact, these two steps are usually done together. To identify the use cases, we answer the question: What will the system do that provides value to the outside world? We can see from our brief vision statement above that it will let users purchase tickets, change a reservation, or cancel a reservation. These are all good candidates for use cases; each is some piece of functionality the system will provide that is of value to the end user. Notice that we didn't include a use case, such as "Get Flight Information" from the legacy system. This is a behind-the-scenes piece of logic that the end user really doesn't care about, so it doesn't qualify as a use case. "Purchase Ticket," "Change Reservation," or "Cancel Reservation," on the other hand, are things that the end user would care about and high-level pieces of functionality the system will provide, so they are good use cases. In UML, a use case is represented by the following symbol:

Purchase Ticket

The advantage of looking at a system with use cases is the ability to dissociate the implementation of the system from the reason the system is there in the first place. It helps you focus on what is truly important—meeting the customer's needs and expectations without being instantly overwhelmed by implementation details. By looking at the use cases, the customer can see what functionality will be provided, and can agree to the system scope before the project goes any further.

Use cases take a different approach than traditional methods. Splitting the project into use cases is a process-oriented, not an implementation-oriented, way of looking at the system. It is therefore different from the functional decomposition approach that is so often taken. While functional decomposition focuses on how to break the problem down further and further into pieces that the system will handle, the use case approach focuses first on what the user expects from the system.

When you are beginning a project, a natural question is: How do I go about finding the use cases? A good way to begin is to examine any documentation the customers have provided. For example, a high-level scope or vision document can frequently help you identify the use cases. Consider also each of the stakeholders of the project. Ask yourself what functionality each stakeholder expects from the system. For each stakeholder, ask questions such as:

◆ What will the stakeholder need to do with the system?

◆ Will the stakeholder need to maintain any information (create, read, update, delete)?

◆ Does the stakeholder need to inform the system about any external events?

◆ Does the system need to notify the stakeholder about certain changes or events?

As we mentioned before, use cases are an implementation-independent, high-level view of what the user expects from the system. Let's examine each piece of this definition separately.

First, the use cases are implementation-independent. As you are defining the use cases, assume you are building a manual system. Your use cases should be able to be built in Java, C++, Visual Basic, or on paper. Use cases focus on *what* the system should do, not *how* the system will do it. We'll get into the *how* later on in the process.

Secondly, the use cases are a high-level view of the system. Your collection of use cases should let the customers easily see, at a very high level, your entire system. There should not be so many use cases that the customer is forced to wade through pages and pages of documentation just to see what the system will do. At the same time, there should be enough use cases to completely describe what the system will do. A typical system will have somewhere between 20 and 70 use cases. (If your system has 3000 use cases, you've lost the benefit of simplicity.) You can use different types of relationships, called includes and extends relationships, to break down the use cases a little if you need to. You can also package the use cases together to form groups of use cases to help you organize them better. We'll explore these topics later in this chapter.

Finally, the use cases should be focused on what the user will get out of the system. Each use case should represent a complete transaction between the user and the system that results in something of value to the user. The use cases should be named in user terms, not technical terms, and should be meaningful to the customer. We wouldn't have a use case, for example, called "Interface with the Bank's Credit System to Validate the Credit Card Number." The customer is trying to purchase a ticket, so that's what we call the use case: "Purchase Ticket." Use cases are typically named with verbs or short verb phrases in the format "<verb> <noun>," and describe what the customer sees as the end result. The customer doesn't care how many other systems you have to interface with, what specific steps need to be taken, or how many lines of code you need to confirm a Visa card. That customer cares only that a ticket was purchased. Again, you focus on the result the user expects from the system, not the steps that were taken to achieve the result.

So, when you have the final list of use cases, how do you know if you've found them all? Some questions to ask are:

◆ Is each functional requirement in at least one use case? If a requirement is not in a use case, it will not be implemented.

◆ Have you considered how each stakeholder will be using the system?

◆ What information will each stakeholder be providing for the system?

◆ What information will each stakeholder be receiving from the system?

◆ Have you considered maintenance issues? Someone will need to start the system and shut it down.

◆ Have you identified all of the external systems with which the system will need to interact?

◆ What information will each external system be providing to the system and receiving from the system?

Traceability

As with business modeling, a very important concept to consider at this point is traceability. Each of the system use cases should be able to be traced back to a business use case. The system use case is what implements part of the functionality in the business use case.

This is not a one-to-one mapping. Business use cases tend to be very high level, so many system use cases may be needed to support a single business use case. For example, an airline has a business use case called "Repair Plane." If we build a system to support this use case, it will have a lot of system use cases in it, such as "Enter Problem," "Check Inventory for Available Parts," "Receive Part from Inventory,"

"Order Part," "Schedule Maintenance," and so on. Each of these system use cases would be traced to the business use case called "Repair Plane."

Every system use case must be traced back to a business use case, but not all business use cases will be supported by system use cases. Hypothetically, if the business use case called "Unload Passengers and Luggage" is a completely manual process, then it would not have any supporting system use cases at all. Here is an example of how system use cases might map to business use cases:

Business Use Case	System Use Cases
Repair Plane	Enter Problem; Check Inventory for Parts; Receive Part from Inventory; Order Part; Schedule Maintenance
Load Supplies on Plane	Determine Needed Supplies; Check Supply Availability; Reserve Supplies; Receive Supplies
Perform Preflight Safety Check	Confirm Luggage Inspection; Confirm Passenger Check-In; Inspect Plane Exterior; Check Status of Emergency Equipment

If you are using a requirements management tool, such as Rational's Requisite Pro, you can map the system use cases to business use cases directly in the tool. If not, it is important to set up a process, even in a simple spreadsheet or database, to ensure that the system use cases are mapped to business use cases. The real purpose of traceability is ensuring that, at the end of the day when the system is built and implemented, all of the requirements are met and all of the code can be traced back to a requirement.

After the system use cases are traced to business use cases, the next step is to trace the requirements to the system use cases. Each functional requirement *must* be traced to a system use case, because the system use cases describe the functionality that will be provided by the system. The system design is driven by the use cases, so if a requirement is not traced to a use case, it will not be considered in the design and may not end up in the final system.

NOTE   *Notice that we said* functional *requirements. There are non-functional requirements, such as system response time or the number of concurrent users supported that do not need to be traced to system use cases. These are typically maintained in a Supplementary Specification document.*

Again, if you are using a tool such as Requisite Pro, you can trace the requirements to use cases in the tool. If not, set up a method to ensure that each requirement is traced to a use case. As we go through the whole process, traceability should be shown as in Figure 4.1.

FIGURE 4.1

Traceability through the life cycle

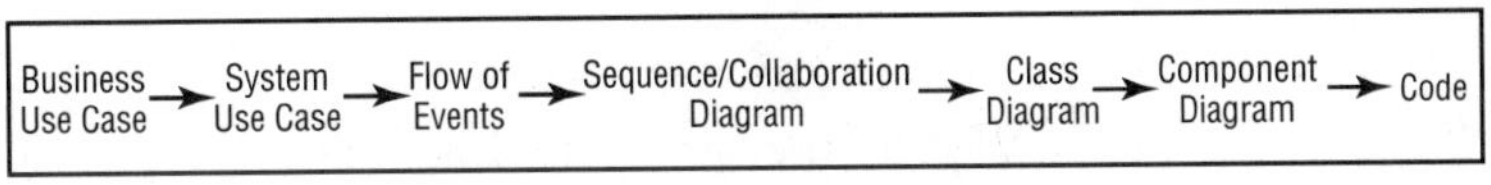

Business Use Case → System Use Case → Flow of Events → Sequence/Collaboration Diagram → Class Diagram → Component Diagram → Code

Flow of Events

The use cases begin to describe what your system will do. To actually build the system, though, you'll need more specific details. These details are written as the *flow of events*. The purpose of the flow of events is to document the flow of logic through the use case. This document will describe in detail what the user of the system will do and what the system itself will do.

Although it is detailed, the flow of events is still implementation-independent. You can assume as you are writing the flow that there will be an automated system. However, you shouldn't yet be concerned with whether the system will be built in C++, PowerBuilder, or Java. The goal here is describing *what* the system will do, not *how* the system will do it. The flow of events typically includes:

- A brief description
- Preconditions
- Primary flow of events
- Alternate flow of events
- Postconditions

Let's look at these items one at a time.

DESCRIPTION

Each use case should include a short description that explains what the use case will do. The Purchase Ticket use case from our airline example might have a description like the following: The Purchase Ticket use case will allow a customer to view available flight information, check availability, and purchase a ticket with a credit card.

The description should be short and to the point, but should include the different types of users who will be executing the use case and the end result the user expects to achieve through the use case. As the project progresses (especially with a very long project), these use case definitions will help the whole team remember why each use case is included in the project and what the use case is intended to do. They also help reduce confusion among the team members by documenting a clear purpose for the use case.

PRECONDITIONS

The *preconditions* for a use case list any conditions that have to be met before the use case can start at all. For example, a precondition might be that another use case has been executed or that the user has the necessary access rights to run the current use case. Not all use cases will have preconditions.

Use Case diagrams aren't intended to show in which order the use cases are executed. Preconditions, however, can be used to document some of this type of information. For example, the precondition for one use case may be that another use case has run.

PRIMARY AND ALTERNATE FLOW OF EVENTS

The specific details of the use case are described in the primary and alternate flow of events. The flow of events describes, step-by-step, what will happen to execute the functionality in the use case. The flow of events focuses on *what* the system will do, not *how* it will do it, and is written from the user's perspective. The primary and alternate flow of events include:

- How the use case starts
- The various paths through the use case

- The normal, or primary, flow through the use case

- Any deviations from the primary flow, known as alternate flows, through the use case

- Any error flows

- How the use case ends

Along with the flow of events in text form, activity diagrams are frequently used. In this section, we'll talk about the option of using text. We'll go over activity diagrams later in this chapter.

There are three types of flows: the primary, alternate, and error flows. The primary flow is the "happy day" scenario, or most frequently used path through the use case. When purchasing a ticket, the primary flow is a successful ticket purchase. Alternate flows are deviations from the primary flow that do not suggest an error condition. For example, a customer may purchase a ticket using frequent-flyer miles, the customer's credit card may not be valid, or the requested flight may not be available. Each of these is a legitimate scenario that the system will be expected to handle, but doesn't suggest that something has gone wrong with the system itself. Finally, error flows are deviations from the primary or alternate flows that suggest some sort of error condition. For example, the system may be unable to verify the credit card or the flight availability. Error flows suggest that there is a problem with the system itself.

Using our "Purchase Ticket" use case example, the flow of events might look like the steps in the following sections.

Primary Flow

The steps for the primary flow of events include:

1. The use case begins when the customer selects the option to view flight information.

2. The system prompts for the departure and destination cities and the departure and return dates.

3. The user enters the departure and destination city, departure date, and return date.

4. The system displays a list of available flights, including the fare.

    A1: There are no available flights.

5. The user selects the flight they would like to reserve.

6. The system displays all available fare options for that flight.

7. The user selects the fare option they would like to reserve.

    A2: The user selects a free ticket through frequent-flyer membership.

8. The system displays the fare that the user will pay.

9. The user confirms the rate.

10. The system prompts for a credit card type, number, name, and expiration date.

11. The user enters the card type, number, name, and expiration date.

12. The system submits the credit purchase.

> A6: Account not found
>
> A7: Insufficient funds
>
> E1: Credit system not accessible

13. The system reserves a seat on the plane for the user.

14. The system generates and displays a confirmation code to the user.

15. The user confirms receipt of the code.

16. The use case ends.

Alternate Flows

A1: No available flights

1. The system displays a message that there are no available flights for the departure and destination cities, departure date, and return date entered.

2. The user confirms the message.

3. The flow returns to the primary flow, step 2.

A2: Free ticket through frequent-flyer membership

1. The system prompts for the frequent-flyer number.

2. The user enters the number.

3. The system confirms the validity of the number.

> A3: Invalid number

4. The system confirms that there are enough miles on this membership to qualify for the free ticket.

> A4: Not enough miles to qualify for a free ticket
>
> A5: No frequent-flyer tickets available

5. The ticket fare is set to $0.

6. The flow returns to the primary flow, step 8.

A3: Invalid frequent-flyer number

1. The system displays a message that the frequent-flyer number is invalid.

2. The user reenters the number or selects the option to cancel the frequent-flyer request.

3. If the user reenters the number, the flow returns to step 1 of alternate flow A2.

4. If the user cancels the frequent-flyer request, the flow returns to step 6 of the primary flow.

A4: Not enough frequent-flyer miles to qualify for free ticket

1. The system displays a message that there are not enough miles to qualify. The message contains the required number of miles and the number of miles available.

2. The flow returns to step 6 of the primary flow.

A5: No frequent-flyer tickets available

1. The system displays a message that there are no frequent-flyer tickets available for the selected flight.

2. The flow returns to step 6 of the primary flow.

    A6: Credit account not found

3. The system displays a message that the credit account was not found.

4. The flow returns to step 10 of the primary flow.

A7: Insufficient funds

1. The system displays a message that there were not enough funds on the card to complete the transaction.

2. The flow returns to step 10 of the primary flow.

Error Flows

E1: Credit system not available

1. The system displays a message that the credit system is not available.

2. The flow returns to step 10 of the primary flow.

Notice the pattern in the flow of events: the user does something, then the system does something in response, then the user does something, then the system responds, and so on. Keeping to this pattern as much as possible helps you ensure that you have a complete understanding of how the conversation between the user and the system should flow. When documenting the flow of events, you can use numbered lists as we have done here, text in paragraph form, bulleted lists, or even flowcharts. With the user/system pattern, another way to document the flow is by using a table:

User Action	System Response
Select option to view flight information	Prompt for departure and destination cities, departure and arrival dates
Enter departure and destination cities, departure and arrival dates	Display flight number, departure time, and arrival time for available flights
. . .	. . .
. . .	. . .
. . .	. . .
. . .	. . .

How Detailed Does This Need to Be?

The classic question when documenting a flow of events is how detailed should it be? To answer that question, keep in mind the reviewers of the document. There are three primary users of the flow of events:

1. The customers will be reviewing this document to make sure it accurately reflects their expectations. The flow of events must be detailed enough so that both you and the customer have the same understanding of the system. The more gaps you leave in the details, the greater the potential for disconnects in expectations. At the same time, you don't want to get into implementation details that the customers won't understand or won't care about. A short answer for most customers is: get as detailed as you can without getting into the implementation. Try to avoid phrases such as "The system will take frequent flyers into account." What does "into account" mean? You want to be sure that both you and the customer understand what that phrase means in that situation.

2. The system designers will be using it to create the system design and eventually to build the system. The flow of events must give them enough information to understand the sequence of events that needs to occur through the use case. Although the flow of events isn't implementation-specific (try to avoid words like "menu," "window," "treeview," or other phrases that will tie the developers to a particular implementation), it does have a lot of information about how the system is supposed to behave. Be sure there is no ambiguity about what the users want, so that the designers will understand the users' needs.

3. The quality assurance team will use the flow of events to create test scripts. Because the flow of events lists step-by-step what the system *should* do, the testing team can use it as a basis for comparison against what the system *does* do when all is said and done. The flow of events won't be a test script by itself, but it can serve as great input into a test case.

As you are writing the flow, focus on *what* and be sure to avoid detailed discussions of *how*. Think of writing a recipe. In a recipe, you would say "Add two eggs." You wouldn't say "Go to the refrigerator. Get two eggs from the door. Pick up the first egg. Crack the egg against the side of the bowl...." In a flow of events, you might say "Validate the user ID," but you wouldn't specify that this is done by looking at a particular table in a database. Focus on the information that is exchanged between the user and the system, not on the details of how the system will be implemented.

POSTCONDITIONS

Postconditions are conditions that must always be true after the use case has finished executing. Like preconditions, postconditions can be used to add information about the order in which the use cases are run. If, for example, one use case must always be run after another use case, you can document this in the postconditions. Not every use case will have postconditions.

Relationships

So far, we have taken a look at use cases and actors individually. Now we'll explore the relationships between use cases and actors to get a full picture of our system.

The association relationship is used to show the relationship between a use case and an actor.

There are three types of relationships between use cases: an includes relationship, an extends relationship, and a generalization relationship. These relationships are used when there is a certain amount of commonality between the use cases.

There is only one relationship allowed between actors. This is a generalization relationship.

ASSOCIATION RELATIONSHIP

The relationship between an actor and a use case is an *association relationship*. In UML, association relationships are diagrammed using an arrow:

Customer   Purchase Ticket

In this example, the use case initiates communication with the credit system actor. As the "Purchase Ticket" use case is being run, the reservation system initiates communication with the credit system to check the card and complete the transaction. Although information flows in both directions—from the reservation system to the credit system and back again—the arrow indicates only who initiated the communication.

Customer   Purchase Ticket   Credit System

With the exception of use cases in includes and extends relationships, every use case must be initiated by an actor.

INCLUDES RELATIONSHIP

An *includes relationship* allows one use case to use the functionality provided by another use case. This relationship can be used in one of two cases.

First, if two or more use cases have a large piece of functionality that is identical, this functionality can be split into its own use case. Each of the other use cases can then have an includes relationship with this new use case.

The second case where an includes relationship is helpful is a situation in which a single use case has an unusually large amount of functionality. An includes relationship can be used to model two smaller use cases instead.

Includes relationships are shown in Rose with dashed arrows and the word <<include>>, as in Figure 4.2.

FIGURE 4.2

An includes
relationship

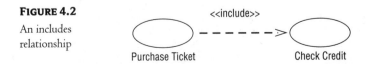

<<include>>

Purchase Ticket   Check Credit

In this example, the "Check Credit" use case will check that a valid card number was entered and that the credit account has sufficient funds to complete the transaction. Because this functionality is used during the Purchase Ticket process, there is an includes relationship between them.

An includes relationship suggests that one use case *always* uses the functionality provided by another. No matter how you proceed through the Purchase Ticket use case, the "Check Credit" use case is always run.

EXTENDS RELATIONSHIP

In contrast, an *extends relationship* allows one use case the option to extend the functionality provided by another use case. It is very similar to an includes relationship, because in both of these types of relationships, you separate some common functionality into its own use case.

In UML, the extends relationship is shown as a dashed arrow with the word <<extend>>, as in Figure 4.3.

FIGURE 4.3

An extends relationship

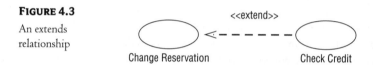

In this example, the "Check Credit" use case extends the "Change Reservation" use case. While the "Change Reservation" use case is running, "Check Credit" runs *if and only if* the amount of the reservation has changed. If the amount has not changed, "Check Credit" does not need to run.

Because "Check Credit" is optionally run, there is an extends relationship between the use cases. The arrow is drawn from the use case that is optionally run ("Check Credit") to the use case that is being extended ("Change Reservation").

GENERALIZATION RELATIONSHIP

A *generalization* relationship is used to show that several actors or use cases have some commonality. For example, you may have two types of customers: corporate customers and individual customers. You can model this relationship using the notation displayed in Figure 4.4.

FIGURE 4.4

Actor generalization relationship

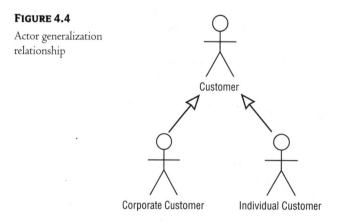

This diagram shows our two types of customers: individual and corporate. Because the individual and corporate actors will be directly instantiated, they are called *concrete* actors. Because the customer actor is never directly instantiated, it is an *abstract* actor. It exists only to show that there are two types of customers.

We can break down things even further if we need to. Say there are two types of corporate customers: government agencies and private companies. We can modify the diagram to look like Figure 4.5.

FIGURE 4.5

Modified actor
generalization
relationship

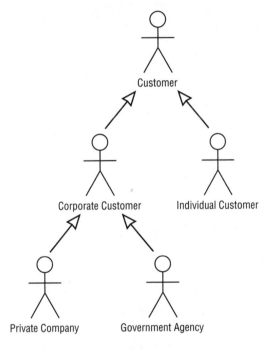

It isn't always necessary to create these types of relationships. In general, they are needed only if one type of actor behaves differently than another type, *as far as the system is concerned*. If the corporate customers will be initiating some use cases that individual customers will not, it's probably worth including the actor generalizations. If both types of customers use the same use cases, it's probably not necessary to show an actor generalization. If both types use the same use cases, but slightly differently, it still isn't worth including the generalization. The slight differences are documented in the flow of events for the use cases.

TIP   The point of these diagrams is communication. If including an actor generalization would give the team some useful information, then include it. Otherwise, don't clutter up the diagrams with them.

The same concept is true for use cases. If you have a base set of functionality that one or more use cases expand upon, you can create a generic use case and then inherit the other use cases from it with a generalization relationship.

Use Case Diagrams

A *Use Case diagram* shows you some of the use cases in your system, some of the actors in your system, and the relationships between them. As you know, a *use case* is a high-level piece of functionality that the system will provide. An actor is anyone or anything that interacts with the system being built. An example of a Use Case diagram is shown in Figure 4.6.

FIGURE 4.6

Sample Use Case diagram

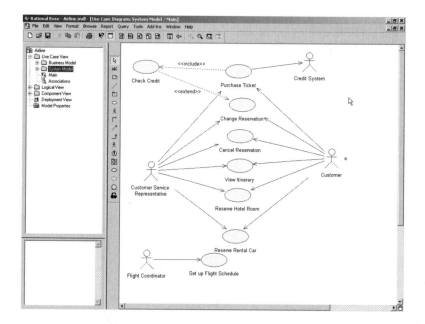

In this diagram, we see the system actors, the system use cases, and the relationships between them. Because the system will be available both online and over the phone, the customer and customer service representative can initiate the same use cases. We have one extends relationship and one includes relationship. There are eight major pieces of functionality the system will provide: purchasing tickets, changing a reservation, checking credit, canceling a reservation, viewing a customer itinerary, reserving a hotel room, reserving a rental car, and setting up the flight schedule.

One of the major benefits of Use Case diagrams is communication. Your customers can look at this diagram and receive a great deal of information. By looking at the use cases, they will know what functionality will be included in the system. By looking at the actors, they will know exactly who will be interfacing with the system. By looking at the set of use cases and actors, they will know exactly what the scope of the project will be. This can help them identify up front any missing functionality. For example, someone could look at the diagram above and say, "That's great, but I also need the ability to check my frequent-flyer membership to see how many miles I have." If so, all we need to do is add another use case called "View Frequent-Flyer Information."

Frequently, you will want to create several Use Case diagrams for a single system. A high-level diagram, usually called Main in Rational Rose, will show you just the packages, or groupings, of use cases. Other diagrams will show you sets of use cases and actors. You may also want to create a single diagram with all of the use cases and all of the actors. How many Use Case diagrams you create and what you name them is entirely up to you. Be sure that the diagrams have enough information to be useful, but are not so crowded as to be confusing.

TIP *Rational Rose can automatically create diagrams with all modeling elements in a package. In the* `rose.ini`, *set the AutoConstructMainDiagrams=Yes flag to enable this feature and a main diagram will be automatically created for each package with all modeling elements of the package.*

Use Case diagrams fulfill a specific purpose: to document the actors (everything outside the system scope), the use cases (everything inside the system scope), and their relationships. Some things to keep in mind as you are creating Use Case diagrams include:

♦ Do not model actor-to-actor associations (although generalizations are OK). By definition, the actors are outside the scope of the current project. The communication between the actors, therefore, is also outside the scope of what you're building. You can use a workflow diagram to examine the actor associations.

♦ Do not draw an association directly between two use cases (although includes or extends relationships are OK). The diagrams show what use cases are available, but don't show in which order the use cases will be executed, so there shouldn't be an association between use cases.

♦ Every use case must be initiated by an actor. That is, there should be an arrow starting with an actor and ending with the use case. Again, the exception here is an includes or extends relationship.

♦ Think of the database as a layer underneath the entire Use Case diagram. You can enter information in the database using one use case, and then access that information from the database in another use case. You don't have to draw associations from one use case to another to show information flow.

Activity Diagrams

An activity diagram is another way to model the flow of events. Using text, as we did in the example above, is useful, but it can be difficult to read and understand if the logic is complex, if there are a lot of alternate flows, or if your customers simply prefer diagrams over text.

An activity diagram shows you the same information as a textual flow of events would. We use activity diagrams in business modeling to depict the workflow through a business process. Here, we will use them to depict the flow through a piece of the system.

Figure 4.7 is the activity diagram that corresponds to the flow of events for purchasing an airline ticket from earlier in this chapter.

As you can see, the activity diagram can be an easier way to communicate the steps in the flow. Let's look at the different pieces of notation in this diagram.

FIGURE 4.7

Activity diagram

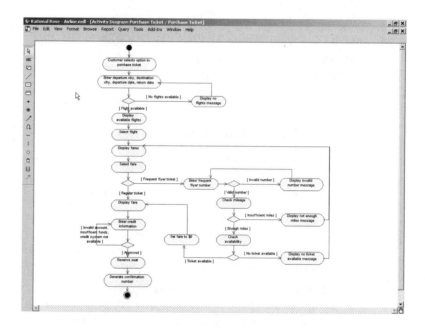

Activity

As the name implies, an activity is one of the essential pieces of an activity diagram. An activity is simply a step in the process. The steps we outlined in the text above become our activities here. An activity is modeled using the following symbol:

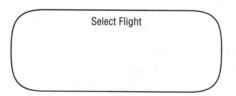

We can add more detailed steps to the activity by using actions. Actions are smaller steps that take place within an activity. They may occur at one of four times:

◆ Upon entering the activity. An entry action occurs as soon as the activity begins, and is marked with the word "entry."

◆ When exiting the activity. An exit action occurs as you are leaving the activity, and is marked with the word "exit."

◆ While performing the activity. These actions occur while in the activity and continue until you leave the activity. They are marked with the word "do."

♦ Upon a specific event. These actions happen if and only if a specific event occurs. They are marked by the word "event," followed by the event name.

Actions are optional, but they can give us detailed information that will help us complete the system design later. If actions are included, they are displayed inside the activity, regardless of which of the above four categories they fall into. Here is an example of an activity with actions:

```
                Display Available Flights
    ─────────────────────────────────────────────
    entry/ Find all flights for selected cities/dates
    entry/ Determine flights with available seats
    do/ Display list of flights with available seats
    do/ Highlight flight with lowest fare
    event/ User requests fare information/ Display fare information
```

In this example, the actions show the steps within the "display available flights" activity. When the activity first begins, the system will find all flights for the selected cities and dates, and then determine which of these flights has available seats. While inside the activity, the system displays a list of flights and highlights the one with the lowest fare. Finally, upon the event that the user wishes to see fare information, the system will display the fare information.

Start and End States

The start and end states let you know where the flow begins and ends. Each activity diagram must have a start state, which is drawn as a solid dot, to signify where the flow begins.

End states are optional on the diagram. They show you where the flow ends, and are represented by a bull's-eye. You can have more than one end state on the diagram, but only a single start state.

Objects and Object Flows

An object is an entity that is affected by the flow. It may be used or changed by an activity in the flow. On an activity diagram, you can display the object and its state so that you can understand where and how the object's state changes.

Objects are linked to activities through object flows. An object flow is a dashed arrow drawn from an activity to the object it changes, or from the object to the activity that needs to use it.

In this example, once the user enters their credit information, a ticket is created with a status of "unconfirmed." Once the credit processing is complete and the credit is approved, the "reserve seat" activity occurs, which sets the state of the ticket to "purchased." These are both examples of how an activity can change an object.

An object can also serve as input into an activity. In this example, in order to generate a confirmation number, the system must have a purchased ticket. The ticket is therefore input into the "generate confirmation number" activity. In either case, the relationships between the activities and the objects are drawn as dashed arrows and are known as an object flow.

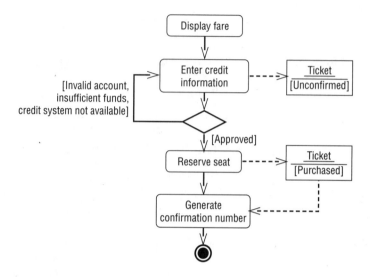

Transitions

A transition shows how the flow of control moves from one activity to another. In the simplest situation, a transition is simply an arrow from one activity to another:

In this simple situation, we can assume that as soon as one activity ends, the next begins.

We can, however, set limitations on the transition to control when the transition occurs. This can be done either by using an event or a guard condition. If an event is specified for a transition, the event must happen in order for the transition to occur. The transition arrow is labeled with the event name, along with any arguments in parenthesis.

Here we can see that if the user changes their mind and performs a cancel event, the purchase price will be refunded and the ticket will be canceled.

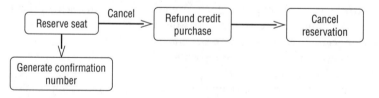

While an event triggers a transition, a guard condition controls whether or not the transition can occur. If a guard condition is present, it must be true in order for the transition to occur. The guard condition is listed along the transition arrow, following any event, and is enclosed in square brackets:

In this example, a new confirmation number is needed only if there is a new reservation made. If we are changing an existing reservation, the old confirmation number will remain. Because we need to generate a confirmation number only if this is a new reservation, "New reservation" becomes our guard condition.

Synchronization

A synchronization is a way to show that two or more branches of a flow occur in parallel. In our example, if we want to show that the system would—at the same time—reserve a seat, generate a confirmation number, generate a receipt, and e-mail a receipt before displaying the confirmation number, the diagram would look like this:

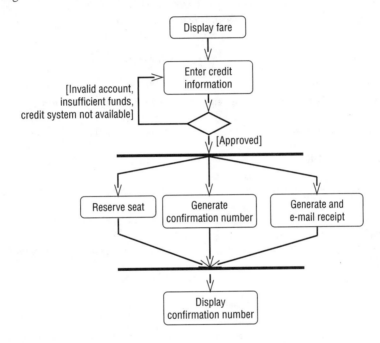

The synchronizations are displayed as solid bars, and show where the logic forks and where it comes back together. A synchronization can be either horizontal or vertical.

Working with Use Cases in Rational Rose

In this section, we'll review how to create, update, and delete use cases and Use Case diagrams in Rose. We'll look at the Use Case Diagram toolbar, which can be used to add use cases, actors, relationships, and other elements to the Use Case diagrams. Then, we'll discuss creating, deleting, and setting the specifications of a use case in Rose.

It's not unusual to create a number of Use Case diagrams for a given project. Each would show a different subset of the use cases and actors. Rose provides you with one default Use Case diagram called Main, which can be used to show just the packages of use cases and actors, or show all the use cases and actors if you prefer. You can create as many Use Case diagrams as you need in a Rose model.

The Use Case Diagram Toolbar

When a Use Case diagram is opened, the Diagram toolbar changes to show icons used in Use Case diagrams. In the toolbar, Rose provides shortcuts for all of the commonly used functions for a Use Case diagram. Some of the buttons you will have available are shown in Table 4.1. In the remainder of this chapter, we'll discuss how to use each of these toolbar buttons to add use cases, actors, and other details to your Use Case diagrams.

TIP   *The buttons below are the defaults for the toolbar. As with any other toolbar, Rose toolbars can be customized. If you do not see all of the buttons listed, right-click the toolbar and select Customize.*

TABLE 4.1: ICONS IN THE USE CASE DIAGRAM TOOLBAR

ICON	BUTTON	PURPOSE
	Selects/Deselects an Item	Returns the cursor to an arrow so you can select an item.
ABC	Text Box	Adds a text box to the diagram.
	Note	Adds a note to the diagram.
	Anchor Note to Item	Connects a note to a use case or actor on the diagram.
	Package	Adds a new package to the diagram.
	Use Case	Adds a new use case to the diagram.
	Actor	Adds a new actor to the diagram.
	Unidirectional Association	Draws a relationship between an actor and a use case.
	Dependency or Instantiates	Draws a dependency between items on the diagram.
	Generalization	Draws a includes or an extends relationship between use cases, or draws an inheritance relationship between actors.

Creating Use Case Diagrams

In Rose, Use Case diagrams are created in the Use Case view. The Use Case view contains all of the following:

◆ Use cases

◆ Actors

- Communication relationships between use cases and actors

- Includes and extends relationships between use cases

- Actor generalization relationships

- Use Case diagrams

- Activity diagrams

- Use Case realizations

- Sequence and Collaboration diagrams

We'll talk about all of the above except Sequence and Collaboration diagrams, which we'll cover in Chapter 5, "Object Interaction." The Use Case view is largely implementation-independent. The use cases and actors describe the project scope without getting into implementation details like the programming language that will be used. We will add implementation details starting with the Sequence diagrams in Chapter 5.

Rose provides you with one default Use Case diagram called Main. You can create as many additional diagrams as you need to model your system.

To access the Main Use Case diagram, do the following:

1. Click the + (plus sign) next to the Use Case view in the browser to open it.

2. The Main Use Case diagram will be visible. Note that Use Case diagrams in Rose have the following icon on their left:

3. Double-click the Main diagram to open it. The title bar will change to include [Use Case Diagram: Use Case View / Main].

To create a new Use Case diagram:

1. Right-click the package Use Case view in the browser.

2. Select New ➤ Use Case Diagram from the shortcut menu, as shown in Figure 4.8.

3. With the new diagram selected, type in the name of your new diagram.

4. Double-click the name of your new diagram in the browser to open it.

To open an existing Use Case diagram:

1. Locate the Use Case diagram in the Use Case view in the browser.

2. Double-click the Use Case diagram's name to open it.

OR

1. Select Browse ➤ Use Case Diagram. The window displayed in Figure 4.9 will appear.

2. In the Package list box, select the package that contains the diagram you want to open.

3. In the Use Case Diagrams list box, select the diagram you want to open.

4. Press OK.

FIGURE 4.8

Adding a new Use Case diagram

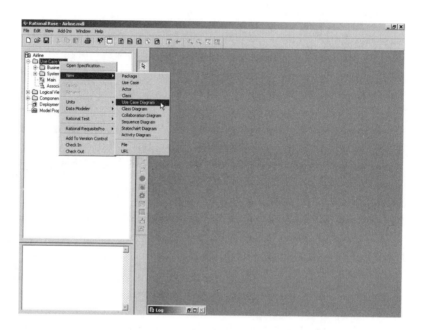

FIGURE 4.9

Opening an existing Use Case diagram

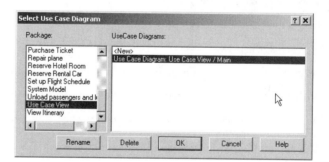

To add an item to a Use Case diagram, use the toolbar buttons as described in the sections later in this chapter to add use cases, actors, and relationships to the diagram.

There are two ways to remove an item from a Use Case diagram. The first will remove the item from the open diagram, but will leave the item in the browser and on other diagrams. To remove an item from the current diagram only, highlight the item in the diagram and press the Delete key. The second method will delete the item from the entire model—from all diagrams as well as the browser. To remove an item from the entire model, highlight the item in the browser, right-click to see the shortcut menu, and select Delete from the shortcut menu. Or you can highlight the item in the diagram and press Ctrl+D.

Deleting Use Case Diagrams

You may need to delete some of the Use Case diagrams you've created. Toward the beginning of a project, it's not uncommon to create many Use Case diagrams as you brainstorm the scope. Some of the diagrams may contain the use cases, others will show the actors, and still others will show a subset of the use cases and the actors. As the project goes along, you may find the need to clean up some of these old diagrams. You can delete a Use Case diagram directly in the browser. Be careful, though— once you've deleted a diagram, you cannot undo the deletion.

To delete a Use Case diagram:

1. Right-click the diagram in the browser.

2. Select Delete from the shortcut menu.

WARNING   *Rose does not allow you to undo a deletion of a diagram or to delete the Main Use Case diagram.*

Deleting a Use Case diagram will not delete the model elements that were on it. Those will stay in the browser and on any other diagrams.

Adding Use Cases

There are two ways to add a use case to the model. You can add the use case to the active Use Case diagram. Or you can add the new use case directly into the browser, and then add it to a Use Case diagram from the browser.

To add a new use case to a Use Case diagram:

1. Select the Use Case button from the toolbar.

2. Click anywhere inside the Use Case diagram. The new use case will be named NewUseCase by default.

3. With the new use case selected, type in the name of the new use case.

4. Note that the new use case has been automatically added to the browser, under the Use Case view.

OR

1. Select Tools ➤ Create ➤ Use Case, as shown in Figure 4.10.

2. Click anywhere inside the Use Case diagram to place the new use case. The new use case will be called NewUseCase by default.

3. With the new use case selected, type in the name of the new use case.

4. Note that the new use case has been automatically added to the browser, under the Use Case view.

FIGURE 4.10

Adding a use case to
a Use Case diagram

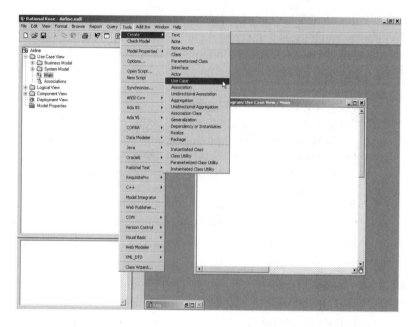

To add an existing use case to a Use Case diagram:

Drag the use case from the browser to the open Use Case diagram.

OR

1. Select Query ➢ Add Use Cases. A dialog box will display, as in Figure 4.11, that will allow you to select and add existing use cases.

2. In the Package drop-down list box, select the package that contains the use case(s) you want to add.

3. Move the use case(s) you want to add from the Use Cases list box to the Selected Use Cases list box.

4. Press OK to add the use cases to the diagram.

To add a use case to the browser:

1. Right-click the Use Case view package in the browser.

2. From the shortcut menu, select New ➢ Use Case.

3. The new use case, called NewUseCase by default, will appear in the browser. To the left of the new use case will be the Use Case icon.

4. With the new use case selected, type in the name of the new use case.

5. To then add the use case to the diagram, drag the new use case from the browser to the diagram.

FIGURE 4.11

Adding existing use cases to a Use Case diagram

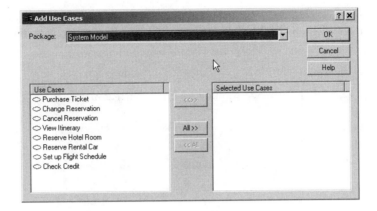

Deleting Use Cases

There are two ways to delete a use case. It can be removed from a single diagram or removed from the entire model and all diagrams. As with Use Case diagrams, it's not uncommon to have many extra use cases toward the beginning of a project. They can be very useful for brainstorming the scope of the project. Once the final set of use cases has been agreed upon, however, you will need to go in and delete any extraneous use cases.

To remove a use case from a Use Case diagram:

1. Select the use case on the diagram.

2. Press Delete.

3. Note that the use case has been removed from the Use Case diagram, but still exists in the browser and on other Use Case diagrams.

To remove a use case from the model:

1. Select the use case on the diagram.

2. Select Edit ➤ Delete from Model, or press Ctrl+D.

3. Rose will remove the use case from all Use Case diagrams, as well as the browser.

OR

1. Right-click the use case in the browser.

2. Select Delete from the shortcut menu.

3. Rose will remove the use case from all Use Case diagrams, as well as the browser.

Use Case Specifications

Rose provides detailed specifications for each use case. These specifications can help you document the specific attributes of the use case, such as the use case name, priority, and stereotype. Figure 4.12

shows the use case specification window, which is used to set the use case specifications. In the following sections, we'll take a look at each of the specifications available on the tabs of this window.

To open the use case specifications:

1. Right-click the use case on a Use Case diagram.

2. Select Open Specification from the shortcut menu.

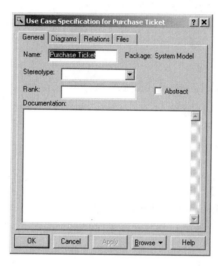

OR

1. Right-click the use case in the browser.

2. Select Open Specification from the shortcut menu.

OR

1. Select the use case on a Use Case diagram.

2. Select Browse ➤ Specification, or press Ctrl+B.

Naming a Use Case

Each use case in the model should be given a unique name. The use case should be named from the perspective of your customer, as the use cases will help determine the project scope. The use case name should also be implementation-independent. Try to avoid phrases, such as *Internet*, that tie the use case to a specific implementation. Use cases are typically named with verbs or short verb phrases.

There are two ways to name a use case. You can use the use case specification window or name the use case directly on the diagram.

To name a use case:

1. Select the use case in the browser or on the Use Case diagram.

2. Type the use case name.

OR

1. Right-click the use case in the Use Case diagram or browser.

2. Select Open Specification from the shortcut menu.

3. In the Name field, enter the use case name.

To add documentation to a use case:

1. Select the use case in the browser.

2. In the documentation window, type the use case description.

OR

1. Right-click the use case in the browser or on the Use Case diagram.

2. From the shortcut menu, select Open Specification.

3. In the specification window, type the use case description in the Documentation area.

Viewing Participants of a Use Case

You may want to see a listing of all of the classes and operations that participate in a particular use case. As the project progresses and you add or change requirements, it can be very helpful to know what classes might be affected by the change. In our airline example, we will need to know which classes are used by which use case as the requirements evolve and the use cases change.

Even after the system is complete, you may need an inventory of which classes are included in each use case. As the system moves into maintenance mode, you will need to control the scope of upgrades and changes. In Rose, you can view the use case participants using the Report menu.

To view the classes and operations participating in a use case:

1. Select the use case on a Use Case diagram.

2. Select Report ➤ Show Participants in UC.

3. The Participants window will appear, as shown in Figure 4.13.

FIGURE 4.13

Use case Participants window

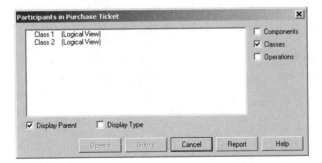

Checking the Display Parent check box will display the package that owns each of the classes participating in the use case. The parent appears in parentheses after the class or operation name.

Checking the Display Type check box will add a notation next to each item in the list box to let you know whether the item is a class or an operation. The type appears in parentheses after the class or operation name.

Use the Components, Classes, and Operations check boxes to control whether components, classes, operations, or all three appear in the list box. Use the Open It button to view the specifications for an item in the list, and use the Goto It button to select the item in the browser.

Assigning a Use Case Stereotype

In UML, *stereotypes* are used to help you categorize your model elements. Say, for example, you had two primary types of use cases, type A and type B. You can create two new use case stereotypes, A and B. Stereotypes aren't used very often for use cases; they are used more for other model elements, such as classes and relationships. However, you do have the option of adding a use case stereotype if you'd like.

To assign a use case stereotype:

1. Right-click the use case in the browser or on the Use Case diagram.

2. Select Open Specification from the shortcut menu.

3. Enter the stereotype in the Stereotype field.

Assigning a Priority to a Use Case

As you define your use cases, you might want to assign a priority to each. By adding priorities, you'll know in what order you'll be working on the use cases as the project progresses. In the use case specification in Rose, you can enter the use case priority description using the Rank field.

To assign a priority to a use case:

1. Right-click the use case in the browser or on the Use Case diagram.

2. Select Open Specification from the shortcut menu.

3. On the General tab, enter the priority in the Rank field.

Creating an Abstract Use Case

An *abstract use case* is one that is not started directly by an actor. Instead, an abstract use case provides some additional functionality that can be used by other use cases. Abstract use cases are the use cases that participate in an includes or extends relationship. Figure 4.14 includes examples of abstract use cases.

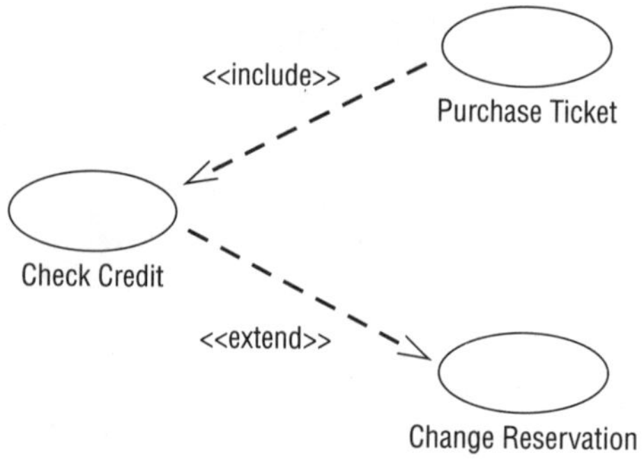

FIGURE 4.14

Abstract use cases

In this example, "Check Credit" is an abstract use case. The actor will run either the "Purchase Ticket" or "Change Reservation" use case, but not the "Check Credit" use case directly. See the section later in this chapter titled "Working with Relationships" for a description of how to draw the arrows between the use cases.

To create an abstract use case:

1. Create the use case in the browser or on a Use Case diagram.

2. Right-click the use case in the browser or on the diagram.

3. Select Open Specification from the shortcut menu.

4. Check the Abstract check box.

Viewing Diagrams for a Use Case

In the use case specifications, you can see all of the activity diagrams, Sequence diagrams, Collaboration diagrams, Class diagrams, Use Case diagrams, and Statechart diagrams that have been defined under the use case in the browser. Figure 4.15 shows the Diagrams tab in the use case specification window. On this tab, you will see the Rose icons that indicate the type of diagram, as well as the diagram name. Double-clicking any of the diagrams will open the diagram in the diagram window.

To view the diagrams for a use case:

1. Right-click the use case in the browser or on a Use Case diagram.

2. Select Open Specification from the shortcut menu.

3. The diagrams will be listed on the Diagrams tab of the specification window.

FIGURE 4.15

Use case specification window's Diagrams tab

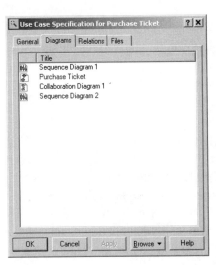

OR

Look through the browser. The diagrams for the use case will appear underneath the use case in the browser.

To open a diagram for a use case:

Double-click the diagram name on the Diagrams tab of the use case specification window.

OR

1. Right-click the diagram name on the Diagrams tab of the use case specification window.

2. Select Open Diagram from the shortcut menu.

OR

Double-click the diagram in the browser.

To add a diagram to a use case:

1. Right-click anywhere inside the Diagrams tab of the use case specification window.

2. From the shortcut menu, select the type of diagram (Use Case, Sequence, Collaboration, State, or Class) you want to add.

3. Enter the name of the new diagram.

OR

1. Right-click the use case in the browser.

2. Select New ➤ (Activity Diagram, Collaboration Diagram, Sequence Diagram, Class Diagram, Use Case Diagram) from the shortcut menu.

3. Enter the name of the new diagram.

To delete a diagram from a use case:

1. Right-click the diagram name on the Diagrams tab of the use case specification window.

2. Select Delete from the shortcut menu.

OR

1. Right-click the diagram name in the browser.

2. Select Delete from the shortcut menu.

Viewing Relationships for a Use Case

The Relations tab in the use case specification window will list all of the relationships the use case participates in, either to other use cases or to actors, as shown in Figure 4.16. The list includes the relationship name and the names of the items joined by the relationship. The relationship name will include any role names or relationship names you have added to the relationship.

To view the relationships for a use case:

1. Right-click the use case in the browser or on a Use Case diagram.

2. Select Open Specification from the shortcut menu.

3. The relationships will be listed on the Relations tab.

FIGURE 4.16

Use case specification
Relations tab

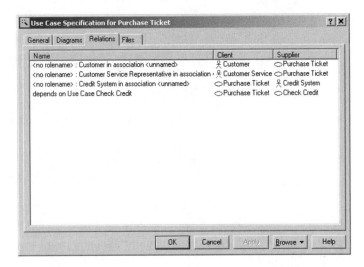

OR

1. Select the use case on a Use Case diagram.

2. Select Report ➤ Show Usage.

To view the relationship specifications:

1. Double-click the relationship in the list.

2. The relationship specification window will appear. (See the upcoming "Working with Relationships" section for a detailed description of relationship specifications.)

OR

1. Right-click the relationship in the list.

2. Select Specification from the shortcut menu.

3. The relationship specification window will appear. (See the upcoming section titled "Working with Relationships" for a detailed description of relationship specifications.)

To delete a relationship:

1. Right-click the relationship in the list.

2. Select Delete from the shortcut menu.

Working with Actors

In this section, we'll take a look at how to model actors using Rational Rose. As with use cases, you can keep a lot of details—name, stereotype, relationships, multiplicity, and so on—about an actor in a Rose model. We maintain these details in the actor specification window. Rose uses the same specification window for actors and classes, so we'll see some fields that don't apply to actors.

Adding Actors

As with use cases, there are two ways to add an actor: to an open Use Case diagram or directly into the browser. An actor in the browser can then be added to one or more Use Case diagrams.

To add an actor to a Use Case diagram:

1. Select the Actor button from the toolbar.

2. Click anywhere inside the Use Case diagram. The new actor will be named NewClass by default.

3. With the new actor selected, type in the name of the new actor. Note that the new actor has been automatically added to the browser, under the Use Case view.

OR

1. Select Tools ➤ Create ➤ Actor, as shown in Figure 4.17.

2. Click anywhere inside the Use Case diagram to place the new actor. The new actor will be called NewClass by default.

3. With the new actor selected, type in the name of the new actor. Note that the new actor has been automatically added to the browser, under the Use Case view.

FIGURE 4.17

Adding an actor to a Use Case diagram

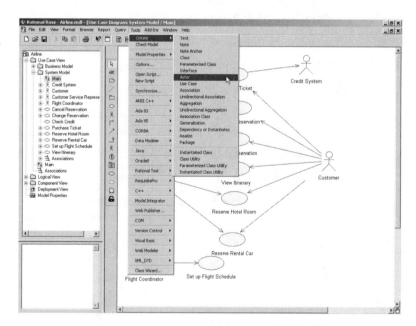

To add an actor to the browser:

1. Right-click the Use Case view package in the browser.

2. Select New ➤ Actor.

3. The new actor, called NewClass by default, will appear in the browser. To the left of the actor's name will be the Actor icon.

4. With the new actor selected, type in the name of the new actor.

5. To then add the actor to the diagram, drag the new actor from the browser to the diagram.

Deleting Actors

As with use cases, there are two ways to delete an actor: from a single diagram or from the entire model. If you delete an actor from the entire model, it will be removed from the browser as well as all Use Case diagrams. If you delete an actor from a single diagram, it will remain in the browser and on other Use Case diagrams.

To remove an actor from a Use Case diagram:

1. Select the actor on the diagram.

2. Press Delete.

To remove an actor from the model:

1. Select the actor on the diagram.

2. Select Edit ➤ Delete from Model, or press Ctrl+D.

OR

1. Right-click the actor in the browser.

2. Select Delete from the shortcut menu.

Rose will remove the actor from all Use Case diagrams as well as the browser. All relationships the deleted actor has with other modeling elements will also be removed.

Actor Specifications

Like a use case, each actor has certain detailed specifications in Rose. In the actor specification window, as shown in Figure 4.18, you can specify the actor's name, stereotype, multiplicity, and other details. In the next several sections, we'll take a look at each of the specifications you can set for an actor.

As you work with classes later in this book, you may note that the actor specification window and the class specification window are very similar. This is because Rose treats an actor as a specialized form of a class. The actor specification window includes the same fields as the class specification window, but some of these fields are disabled for actors.

To open the actor specifications:

1. Right-click the actor on the Use Case diagram.

   OR

   Right-click the actor in the browser.

2. Select Open Specification from the shortcut menu. The actor specification window will appear.

OR

1. Select the actor on the Use Case diagram.

2. Select Browse Specification, or press Ctrl+B. The actor specification window will appear.

FIGURE 4.18

Actor specification window

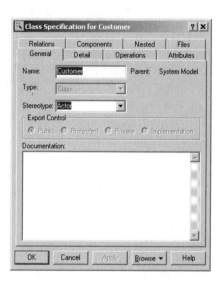

Most of the tab pages in the actor specification will apply to classes, but will not apply to actors. The tab pages that include information about actors are the General tab, the Detail tab, the Relations tab, and the Files tab. Some of the options on these tabs apply only to classes. The options that are available for actors are described below.

Naming Actors

Each actor should be given a unique name. You can name an actor by using the actor specification window or by typing the name directly onto a Use Case diagram or into the browser.

To name an actor:

1. Right-click the actor in the Use Case diagram or browser.

2. Select Open Specification from the shortcut menu.

3. In the Name field, enter the actor name.

OR

1. Select the actor in the browser or on the Use Case diagram.

2. Type in the actor name.

To add documentation to an actor:

1. Select the actor in the browser.

2. In the documentation window, type the actor description.

OR

1. Right-click the actor in the browser or on the Use Case diagram.

2. From the shortcut menu, select Open Specification.

3. In the specification window, type the actor description in the Documentation area.

Assigning an Actor Stereotype

As with use cases, you can assign a stereotype to an actor in the specifications window. However, if you change the stereotype of an actor, Rose will change the icon used to represent the actor on a Use Case diagram. Rather than using the actor symbol, Rose will use the standard rectangle that is used to represent a class.

Other than "Actor," there are no stereotypes provided for an actor. You can, however, define your own actor stereotypes and use these in your Rose model.

To assign an actor stereotype:

1. Right-click the actor in the browser or on a Use Case diagram.

2. Select Open Specification from the shortcut menu.

3. In the Stereotype field, enter the actor stereotype.

WARNING *If you change the stereotype of an actor, Rose will no longer display the actor using the UML actor symbol. Rose will treat the actor like any other class.*

Setting Actor Multiplicity

You can specify in Rose how many instances of a particular actor you expect to have. For example, you may want to know that there are many people playing the role of the customer actor, but only one person playing the role of the manager actor. You can use the Multiplicity field to note this.

Rose provides you with several multiplicity options:

Multiplicity	Meaning
0..0	Zero
0..1	Zero or one
0..n	Zero or more
1..1	Exactly one
1..n	One or more
n (default)	Many

Or, you can enter your own multiplicity options, using one of the following formats:

Format	Meaning
<number>	Exactly <number>
<number 1>..<number 2>	Between <number 1> and <number 2>
<number>..n	<number> or more
<number 1>,<number 2>	<number 1> or <number 2>
<number 1>, <number 2>.. <number 3>	Exactly <number 1> or between <number 2> and <number 3>
<number 1>..<number 2>, <number 3>..<number 4>	Between <number 1> and <number 2> or between <number 3> and <number 4>

To set actor multiplicity:

1. Right-click the actor in the browser or on a Use Case diagram.

2. Select Open Specification from the shortcut menu.

3. Select the Detail tab.

4. Select from the Multiplicity drop-down list box, or type in the actor's multiplicity using one of the formats listed above.

Creating an Abstract Actor

An *abstract actor* is an actor that has no instances. In other words, the actor's multiplicity is exactly zero. For example, you may have several actors: hourly employee, salaried employee, and temporary employee. All of these are types of a fourth actor, employee. However, no one in the company is just an employee—everyone is either hourly, salaried, or temporary. The employee actor just exists to show that there is some commonality between hourly, salaried, and temporary employees. There are no instances of an employee actor, so it is an abstract actor. Figure 4.19 shows an example of an abstract actor called "employee."

FIGURE 4.19

Abstract actor

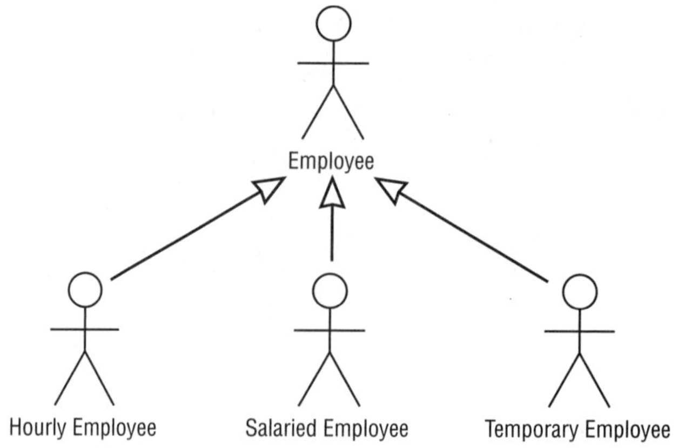

To create an abstract actor:

1. Create the actor in the browser or on a Use Case diagram.

2. Right-click the actor in the browser or on the diagram.

3. Select Open Specification from the shortcut menu.

4. Select the Detail tab.

5. Check the Abstract check box.

Viewing Relationships for an Actor

The Relations tab in the actor specification window lists all of the relationships in which the actor participates. Figure 4.20 shows the Relations tab of the window. This tab includes all relationships the actor has with use cases, as well as the relationships to other actors. The list includes the relationship name and the actors or use cases that participate in the relationship. From this tab, you can view, add, or delete relationships.

FIGURE 4.20

Actor specification window's Relations tab

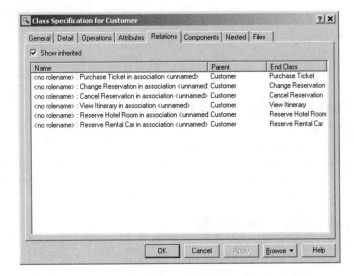

To view the relationships for an actor:

1. Right-click the actor in the browser or on a Use Case diagram.

2. Select Open Specification from the shortcut menu. The relationships will be listed on the Relations tab.

To view the relationship specifications:

1. Double-click the relationship in the list.

2. The relationship specification window will appear. (See the upcoming "Working with Relationships" section for a detailed description of relationship specifications.)

OR

1. Right-click the relationship in the list.

2. Select Specification from the shortcut menu.

3. The relationship specification window will appear. (See the upcoming "Working with Relationships" section for a detailed description of relationship specifications.)

To delete a relationship:

1. Right-click the relationship in the list.

2. Select Delete from the shortcut menu.

Viewing an Actor's Instances

As you are modeling the system, you may want to know on which Sequence and Collaboration diagrams a particular actor resides. Rose provides this ability through the Report menu.

To view all Sequence and Collaboration diagrams containing the actor:

1. Select the actor on a Use Case diagram.

2. Select Report ➤ Show Instances.

3. Rose will display a list of all Sequence and Collaboration diagrams that contain the actor. To open a diagram, double-click it in the list box or press the Browse button.

Working with Relationships

UML supports several types of relationships for use cases and actors. These include association relationships, includes relationships, extends relationships, and generalization relationships. Association relationships describe the relationships between the actors and the use cases. Includes and extends relationships describe the relationships between the use cases. Generalization relationships describe inheritance relationships among use cases or actors.

Association Relationship

An association relationship, as we discussed in the "Use Case Modeling Concepts" section earlier in this chapter, is a relationship between an actor and a use case. The direction of the relationship shows whether the system or the actor initiates the communication. Once communication is established, information can flow in both directions.

To add an association relationship:

1. Select the Unidirectional Association toolbar button.

2. Drag the mouse from the actor to the use case (or from the use case to the actor).

3. Rose will draw a relationship between the use case and the actor.

To delete an association relationship:

1. Select the relationship on the Use Case diagram.

2. Select Edit ➤ Delete from Model, or press Ctrl+D.

Includes Relationship

An includes relationship is used whenever one use case needs to use the functionality provided by another. This relationship implies that one use case *always* uses the other.

To add an includes relationship:

1. Select the Dependency toolbar button.

2. Drag from one use case to the use case being used (from the concrete use case to the abstract use case).

3. Rose will draw a dependency between the two use cases.

4. Right-click the relationship's line and select Open Specification.

5. Rose will open the dependency specification, as shown in Figure 4.21.

6. In the Stereotype drop-down list box, select include.

FIGURE 4.21

Dependency
specification

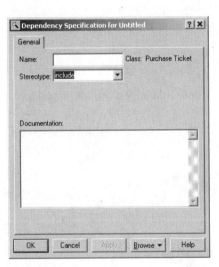

7. Click OK to close the specification window.

8. The word <<include>> should appear over the dependency arrow. If it does not, right-click on the relationship's line and be sure there is a check mark next to the Stereotype Label field.

9. Open the use case specification window of the abstract use case.

10. Check the Abstract check box.

NOTE   You can also customize the toolbar to provide a button for an includes relationship. Right-click the toolbar and select Customize, then add the Includes Relationship icon.

To delete an includes relationship:

1. Select the relationship on the Use Case diagram.

2. Select Edit ➤ Delete from Model, or press Ctrl+D.

Extends Relationship

In an extends relationship, one use case optionally extends the functionality provided by another. In Rose, extends relationships are modeled much the same as includes relationships.

To add an extends relationship:

1. Select the Dependency toolbar button.

2. Drag from the use case providing the extending functionality to the use case being extended (from the abstract use case to the concrete use case).

3. Rose will draw a dependency between the two use cases.

4. Right-click on the relationship's line and select Open Specification.

5. Rose will open the dependency specification.

6. In the Stereotype drop-down list box, select extend.

7. Click OK to close the specification window.

8. The word <<extend>> should appear over the dependency arrow. If it does not, right-click on the relationship's line and be sure there is a check mark next to the Stereotype Label field.

9. Open the use case specification window of the Abstract use case.

10. Check the Abstract check box.

To delete an extends relationship:

1. Select the relationship on the Use Case diagram.

2. Select Edit ➤ Delete from Model, or press Ctrl+D.

Generalization Relationship

As we discussed above, a generalization relationship is used to show an inheritance among actors or use cases. An inheritance relationship suggests that one actor or use case, for example, has some base characteristics that are shared by other actors or use cases. All actors or use cases that have a generalization relationship with it will "inherit" those base characteristics.

To add a generalization:

1. Add the actors or use cases to the Use Case diagram.

2. Select the Generalization button from the toolbar.

3. Drag from the actor or use case to the generalized actor or use case.

To delete a generalization relationship:

1. Select the relationship on the Use Case diagram.

2. Select Edit ➤ Delete from Model, or press Ctrl+D.

Working with Activity Diagrams

With Rose, you can create one or more activity diagrams for a use case. Activity diagrams are typically used to model the flow of events through the use case. Any activity diagrams for a use case will appear in the browser, underneath the appropriate use case.

The Activity Diagram Toolbar

The Activity Diagram toolbar is used to add activities, transitions, objects, and other elements to an activity diagram. Table 4.2 lists the icons in the Activity Diagram toolbar and explains their meaning.

TABLE 4.2: ICONS IN THE USE CASE DIAGRAM TOOLBAR

ICON	BUTTON	PURPOSE
	Selects/Deselects an Item	Returns the cursor to an arrow so you can select an item.
	Text Box	Adds a text box to the diagram.
	Note	Adds a note to the diagram.
	Anchor Note to Item	Connects a note to a use case or actor on the diagram.
	State	Adds a state for an object.
	Activity	Adds a new activity to the diagram.
	Start State	Shows where the workflow begins.
	End State	Shows where the workflow ends.
	State Transition	Adds a transition from one activity to another.
	Transition to Self	Adds a transition from one activity to itself.
	Horizontal Synchronization	Adds a horizontal synchronization.
	Vertical Synchronization	Adds a vertical synchronization.
	Decision	Adds a decision point in the workflow.
	Swimlane	Adds a swimlane (usually used in business modeling).
	Object	Adds an object to the diagram.
	Object Flow	Connects an object to an activity.

Creating Activity Diagrams

To add an activity diagram, we use the browser window. Once the diagram is created, we can add activities, transitions, and other activity diagram elements. In this section, we'll discuss the different pieces of an activity diagram and how to add them.

To add an activity diagram:

1. Right-click the use case in the browser.

2. Select New ➤ Activity Diagram.

3. If this is the first activity diagram for a use case, Rose will create an entry titled State/Activity Model under the use case in the browser. The new activity diagram, and any other activity diagrams for this use case, will be placed under this State/Activity Model entry.

4. Type the name of the new diagram.

ADDING ACTIVITIES AND ACTIONS

An activity is a step in the flow. Activities are shown on the diagrams as rounded rectangles. We can also add actions to the activity to show any detailed steps within the activity. There are four types of actions: those that occur when entering the activity, those that occur while exiting the activity, those that occur while inside the activity, and those that occur upon a specific event.

To add an activity:

1. Select the Activity icon from the toolbar.

2. Click anywhere inside the diagram to place the activity.

3. Type in the activity name.

To add an action:

1. Right-click the activity.

2. Select Open Specification.

3. Select the Actions tab.

4. Right-click anywhere in the whitespace within the tab and select Insert.

5. A new action will be added to the list. Its default type will be Entry.

6. Double-click the new action (the word Entry). The action specification window will open.

7. In the When drop-down list box, select the On Entry, On Exit, Do, or On Event option.

8. If you selected On Event, enter the event, any arguments, and the condition in the appropriate fields.

9. Enter the name of the action in the Name field.

10. Press OK to return to the activity specification window.

11. To delete an action, right-click it on the Actions tab of the activity specification window and select Delete.

12. Right-click to enter another action, or press OK to close the activity specification window.

ADDING OBJECTS AND OBJECT FLOWS

An object is an entity that is affected by or used by the workflow. We can model both the object and the state that the object is in. We can also show how an object is affected by or used by a workflow through object flows. A dashed arrow between an object and an activity represents an object flow.

To add an object:

1. Select the Object icon from the toolbar.

2. Click anywhere inside the diagram to place the object.

3. Type the object's name.

4. Right-click and select Open Specification.

5. If you have defined a class for the object, select that class in the Class field.

6. If you would like to mark the object's state, select a state from the drop-down list box in the State field. If there are no available states or if you'd like to add one, select <new>. The State Specification window will open. Enter the name of the new state and press OK.

To add an object flow:

1. Select the Object Flow icon from the toolbar.

2. Drag and drop from the activity that changes the object to the object itself, or from the object to the activity that uses it.

3. Rose will draw an object flow (dashed arrow).

ADDING TRANSITIONS AND GUARD CONDITIONS

A transition shows the movement from one activity to another. We can add an event to the transition that shows what event triggers the transition. We can also add a guard condition, which controls whether or not the transition can occur.

To add a transition:

1. Select the Transition icon from the toolbar.

2. Drag and drop from one activity to another.

3. Rose will draw a transition between the two activities.

To add an event:

1. Right-click the transition.

2. Select Open Specification. The transition specification window will appear.

3. Type the event in the Event field. If there are any arguments for the event, enter them in the Arguments field.

To add a guard condition:

1. Right-click the transition.

2. Select Open Specification. The transition specification window will appear.

3. Select the Detail tab.

4. Type the guard condition in the Guard Condition field.

NOTE *You can also add guard conditions directly on the transition arrow. Enclose the guard condition within square brackets.*

ADDING SYNCHRONIZATIONS AND DECISIONS

Finally, we can show synchronous activity and conditions in the logic of the flow by using of horizontal synchronizations, vertical synchronizations, and decision points.

To add a synchronization:

1. Select the Horizontal or Vertical Synchronization icon from the toolbar.

2. Click anywhere inside the diagram to place the synchronization.

3. Draw transitions from activities to the synchronization or from the synchronization to one or more activities.

To add a decision:

1. Select the Decision icon from the toolbar.

2. Click anywhere inside the diagram to place the decision.

3. Draw transitions from activities to the decision, or from the decision to one or more activities. Place guard conditions on *all* transitions leaving the decision, so the reader can know under what conditions each path is followed.

Deleting Activity Diagrams

To delete an activity diagram, simply right-click it in the browser and select Delete. Note that, although the diagram has been deleted, all of the activities and other elements on the diagram are still in the Rose model. You can see these elements in the browser.

To delete all of the elements that were on the diagram, right-click each element one at a time in the browser and select Delete. Or, you can right-click the State/Activity Model listing for the use case in the browser and select Delete. All activity diagrams, along with all activities and other items on the diagrams for that use case, will be deleted from the model.

NOTE *The activity diagram must stay where it was created. You cannot move an activity diagram from one use case, class, or package to another. Also remember that you cannot copy a state or other element from one activity diagram to another.*

Exercise

In this exercise, we'll create the Use Case diagram for the order-processing system.

Problem Statement

After Andy and April got the business model done, Andy started working on the Use Case diagram for the e-business system. Andy started by looking at each of the business use cases and deciding which ones would be best automated with the e-business system. He decided that the "Purchase Items," "Purchase Inventory," "Stock Inventory," "Determine Items to Sell," and "Fulfill Order" business use cases would be best automated in the system. Andy started working out the system use cases and system actors based on the business use cases and actors involved. He then developed the system use case model based on this information and interviews with others in the firm.

Create a Use Case Diagram

Create the Use Case diagram for the order-processing system. The steps for creating the diagram are outlined below. Your final Use Case diagram should look like Figure 4.22.

FIGURE 4.22

E-Business System Use Case diagram

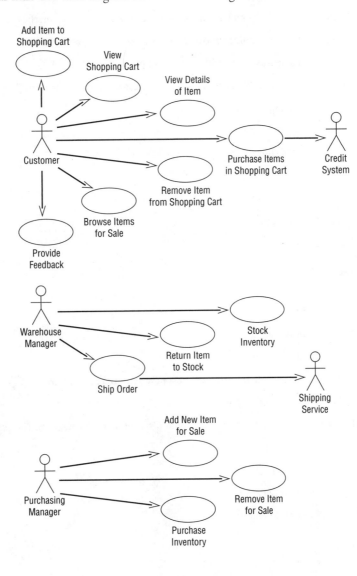

EXERCISE STEPS:

ADD THE SYSTEM USE CASE MODEL PACKAGE, USE CASE DIAGRAM, USE CASES, AND ACTORS

1. Right-click the Use Case View package in the browser and select New ➢ Package.

2. Name the new package **System Use Case Model**.

3. Right-click the System Use Case Model package and select New ➢ Use Case Diagram.

4. Name the new diagram **Main**.

5. Double-click the Main Use Case diagram in the browser to open the diagram.

6. Use the Use Case toolbar button to add a new use case to the diagram.

7. Name this new use case **Add Item to Shopping Cart**.

8. Repeat steps 6 and 7 to add the remaining use cases to the diagram. The use cases are:

   View Shopping Cart

   View Details of Items

   Purchase Items in Shopping Cart

   Remove Item from Shopping Cart

   Browse Items for Sale

   Provide Feedback

   Stock Inventory

   Return Item to Stock

   Ship Order

   Add New Item for Sale

   Remove Item for Sale

   Purchase Inventory

9. Use the Actor toolbar button to add a new actor to the diagram.

10. Name this new actor **Customer**.

11. Repeat steps 9 and 10 to add the remaining actors to the diagram. The actors are:

    Credit System

    Warehouse Manager

    Shipping Service

    Purchasing Manager

Continued on next page

ADD ASSOCIATIONS

1. Use the Unidirectional Association toolbar button to draw the association between the customer actor and the "Add Item to Shopping Cart" use case.

2. Repeat step 1 to add the rest of the associations to the diagram.

ADD USE CASE DESCRIPTIONS

1. Select the "Add Item to Shopping Cart" use case in the browser.

2. Using the documentation window, add the following description to the "Enter New Order" use case: **This use case allows the customer to add an item for sale to their shopping cart for purchase**.

3. Using the documentation window, add descriptions to the remaining use cases.

ADD ACTOR DESCRIPTIONS

1. Select the customer actor in the browser.

2. Using the documentation window, add the following description to the salesperson actor: **The customer is the individual who is purchasing items from the organization.**

3. Using the documentation window, add descriptions to the remaining actors.

Summary

In this chapter, we discussed how to work with use cases, actors, and Use Case diagrams. The requirements of the system to be built are the set of all use cases and actors. You begin by creating a Main Use Case diagram to show the overall view of the system. Then, you can create additional diagrams to illustrate the interactions between actors and use cases. Use cases can include or extend other use cases. Otherwise, they cannot directly communicate with each other. One use case includes another when the functionality will always be needed. One use case extends another when the functionality is optionally needed. If a use case is included by or extends another use case, that use case is abstract. Use cases in which actors directly participate are concrete.

Actors can communicate with use cases, illustrating which actors participate in which use cases. Actors can also inherit from one another. For example, a student may be an actor in the system. We may need to further refine the role of student into full-time student and part-time student. We do this by inheriting the full-time and part-time students from the student actor.

Use cases and Use Case diagrams are useful ways to describe system functionality. In the next chapter, we will discuss the use of Sequence and Collaboration diagrams, which are used to show the interactions between objects and actors.

Chapter 5

Object Interaction

IN THIS CHAPTER, WE will discuss how to model the interactions between the objects in the system. The two types of Interaction diagrams we'll take a look at in this chapter are Sequence diagrams and Collaboration diagrams. Both show the objects participating in a flow through a use case and the messages that are sent between the objects. Sequence diagrams are ordered by time; Collaboration diagrams are organized around the objects themselves.

In the exercise at the end of the chapter, we will build a sample Sequence diagram.

◆ Looking at Sequence and Collaboration diagrams

◆ Adding objects to Sequence and Collaboration diagrams

◆ Using messages with Sequence and Collaboration diagrams

◆ Switching between Sequence and Collaboration diagrams

◆ Using the two-pass approach to create Interaction diagrams

Interaction Diagrams

An *Interaction diagram* shows you, step-by-step, one of the flows through a use case: what objects are needed for the flow, what messages the objects send to each other, what actor initiates the flow, and what order the messages are sent. In our airline example, we have several alternate flows through the "Purchase Ticket" use case. Therefore, we will have several Interaction diagrams for this use case. We'll have the "happy day" Interaction diagram, which shows what happens when all goes well. And we'll have additional diagrams showing what happens with the alternate flows, such as what happens when someone requests a frequent-flyer ticket, what happens when someone's credit card is denied, and so on. All of the different scenarios that our system will need to implement are documented in an Interaction diagram.

The two types of Interaction diagrams we'll talk about are Sequence diagrams and Collaboration diagrams. A Sequence diagram is ordered by time. Figure 5.1 is an example of a Sequence diagram.

FIGURE 5.1

Sequence
diagram

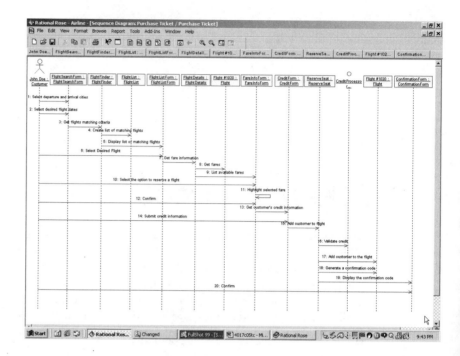

A Collaboration diagram shows the same information, but is organized differently. Figure 5.2 is an example of a Collaboration diagram.

FIGURE 5.2

Collaboration
diagram

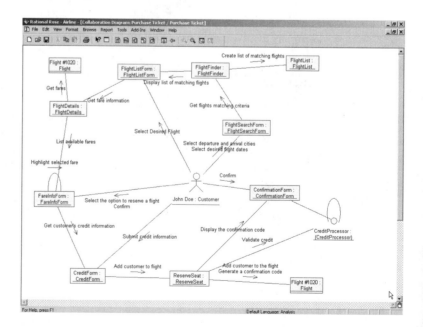

Although a Sequence diagram and a Collaboration diagram show you the same information, there are a couple of differences between these two diagrams. Sequence diagrams can show a focus of control; Collaboration diagrams can show a data flow. We'll talk about these differences when discussing messages below.

Interaction diagrams contain a lot of the same detail that is spelled out in the flow of events, but here the information is presented in a way that is more useful to the developers. While the flow of events focuses on *what* the system needs to do, Sequence and Collaboration diagrams help to define *how* the system will do it. These diagrams focus on the objects that will be created to implement the functionality spelled out in the use cases. Sequence and Collaboration diagrams can show objects, classes, or both.

Before we get into the details of Sequence and Collaboration diagrams, let's review the concept of an object and a class. If you are familiar with object-oriented concepts, skip to the section titled "Where Do I Start?"

What Is an Object?

We see objects all around us. The chair you're sitting in, the book you're reading, and the lightbulb that's helping you see are all examples of objects in the real world. An object in the software world is very much the same.

An *object* is something that encapsulates information and behavior. It's a term that represents some concrete, real-world thing. Examples of objects are:

◆ Flight #1020

◆ The house at 7638 Main Street

◆ The yellow flower just outside my kitchen window

In the airline example, some of the objects would include an airplane, a flight, a passenger, a piece of luggage, or a ticket.

Every object encapsulates some information and some behavior. There might be a flight #1020 object, for example, that has some information: The departure date is May 24, the departure time is 9:40 p.m., the flight number is 1020, and the departure city is Los Angeles. The flight object also has some behavior: It knows how to add a passenger to the flight, remove a passenger from the flight, and determine when it is full.

The pieces of information held by an object are known as its *attributes*. Although the values of the attributes will change over time (flight 1020 will have a departure date of May 25 the next day), the attributes themselves will not change. Flight 1020 will always have a departure date, a departure time, a flight number, and a departure city.

The behaviors an object has are known as its *operations*. In this case, the operations for the flight include adding a passenger, removing a passenger, and checking to see when the flight is full. In Rose, objects are added to the Interaction diagrams. When dragging an actor (which in Rose is a class stereotype) or some other class onto an Interaction diagram, an object instantiation of that class will automatically be created. Removing an object from a diagram in Rose will not delete the class from the model.

What Is a Class?

A *class* is something that provides a blueprint for an object. In other words, a class defines what information an object can hold and what behavior it can have. For example, classes for flight #1020, the house at 7638 Main Street, and the yellow flower just outside my kitchen window would be: Flight, House, and Flower. The House *class* would just specify that a house has a height, width, number of rooms, and square footage. The House at 7638 Main Street *object* might have a height of 40 feet, a width of 60 feet, 10 rooms, and 2000 square feet. A class is a more generic term that simply provides a template for objects.

```
┌─────────────────┐
│      Class      │
├─────────────────┤
│  – Attribute    │
├─────────────────┤
│  + Operation()  │
└─────────────────┘
```

Think of a class as a blueprint for a house, and the objects as the 25 houses that were all built from that blueprint. We'll talk more about classes in the next chapter.

Where Do I Start?

To create a Sequence or Collaboration diagram, we first go through the flow of events and determine how many of the flows will need an Interaction diagram. You can create a diagram for just the primary flow or for all the alternate flows and error flows as well. If two alternate or error flows are very similar, they may be combined onto one diagram. The more diagrams you create, the more thorough your exploration of how the system should be built and the easier the rest of the steps in the process will be. (Class diagrams, Component diagrams, and Deployment diagrams will be covered in the coming chapters.) The trade-off, of course, is time. It can take quite some time to build a detailed Sequence or Collaboration diagram, because great many design decisions need to be made at this point.

Patterns can come to the rescue here. You can build patterns for common logic. They include things such as retrieving data from the database, checking the user's security level, error handling and logging, interprocess communication, and so on. If you document these patterns in their own Sequence diagrams, it isn't necessary for every diagram to show how you check the user's security level; you can simply reference the security pattern. These types of patterns are also excellent candidates for reuse in other projects.

The steps involved in creating a Sequence or Collaboration diagram are:

◆ Find the objects.

◆ Find the actor.

◆ Add messages to the diagram.

We will discuss each of these steps in the next sections.

Finding Objects

A good way to find some initial objects is to examine the nouns in your flow of events. Another good place to look is in the scenario documents. A *scenario* is a specific instance of a flow of events.

The flow of events for the "Purchase Ticket" use case has several scenarios. For example, John Doe purchases a ticket for flight #1020; John requests and gets a frequent-flyer ticket for flight #1020; John requests a frequent-flyer ticket for flight #1020, but there are no seats available; John requests a frequent-flyer ticket for flight #1020, but he does not have enough frequent-flyer miles. More scenarios would be developed to explain exceptions, such as what happens if there's a problem with the credit card, if John is already booked for flight #1020, or if the credit system can't be accessed. Any exceptions like these that should be programmed into the system should be captured in the flow of events and on a Sequence or Collaboration diagram.

Most use cases will have a number of Sequence and Collaboration diagrams, one for each scenario through the flow of events. These diagrams can be built at a high level of abstraction, to show how systems communicate, or at a very detailed level, showing exactly what classes need to participate in a particular scenario.

As you look at the nouns in your scenarios, some of the nouns will be actors, some will be objects, and some will be attributes of an object. When you're building your Interaction diagrams, the nouns will tell you what the objects will be. If you're looking at a noun and wondering whether it's an object or an attribute, ask whether it has any behavior. If it's information only, it's probably an attribute. If it has some behaviors also, it may be an object. Another check is whether it has attributes of its own. Is a passenger an attribute of a flight or an object of its own? The answer to that question really depends on the application you are building. If all you need to store is the name of the passenger, then it can be modeled as an attribute of a flight. If, however, you also want to store the passenger's address, credit card information, and phone number, then it would be better modeled as a separate object.

Not all of the objects will be in the flow of events. Forms, for example, may not appear in the flow of events, but will have to appear on the diagram in order to allow the actor to enter or view information. Other objects that probably won't appear in the flow of events are control objects.

You should consider each of these categories as you identify objects:

Entity objects These are objects that hold information. They may eventually map to some of the tables and fields in the database. Many of the nouns in the flow of events will give you entity objects. Entity objects in our airline example might be flight #1020, passenger John Doe, or ticket #1347A. These are business entities that have meaning to the end user.

Boundary objects These are objects that lie on the boundary between the system and the outside world. In other words, these are the forms and windows of the application and the interfaces to other applications. Forms may appear in the flow of events, but interfaces probably won't. As you go through the logic in the flow of events, ask whether any other system will need to be involved to carry out the logic in the flow. If so, you may need one or more interface objects.

Control objects These are optional objects that control the flow through the use case. They don't carry out any business functionality in and of themselves. Instead, they coordinate the other objects and control the overall logic flow. For example, a control object would know that the user's security level should be checked before a particular report is run. The control object wouldn't check the security level or run the report, it simply holds the sequencing logic and the business rules for the scenario. It would first tell another object to check the security, and then tell the report to run. Control objects won't appear in the flow of events. Using them is, instead, a design decision; if you decide to use control objects, add one to your Sequence or Collaboration diagram.

Finding the Actor

Once you have identified the objects for your Interaction diagram, the next step is to identify the necessary actor. An actor on an Interaction diagram is the external stimulus that starts the workflow for a flow of events. You can identify the actor by looking at the flow of events and determining who or what starts the process.

There may be more than one actor for a given Interaction diagram. Each actor that receives a message from or sends a message to the system in a particular scenario should be shown on the diagram for that scenario.

Using Interaction Diagrams

From the diagrams, designers and developers can determine the classes they will need to develop, the relationships between the classes, and the operations or responsibilities of each class. The Interaction diagrams become the cornerstones upon which the rest of the design is built.

Sequence diagrams are ordered by time. They are useful if someone wants to review the flow of logic through a scenario. Although Collaboration diagrams include sequencing information, it is easier to see on a Sequence diagram.

Collaboration diagrams are useful if you want to assess the impact of a change. It's very easy to see on a Collaboration diagram which objects communicate with which other objects. If you need to change an object, you can easily see which other objects might be affected.

Interaction diagrams contain:

Objects   An Interaction diagram can use object names, class names, or both.

Messages   Through a message, one object or class can request that another carry out some specific function. For example, a form may ask a report object to print itself.

One thing to remember as you create the Interaction diagrams is that you are assigning responsibility to objects. When you add a message to an Interaction diagram, you are assigning a responsibility to the object receiving the message. Be sure to assign the appropriate responsibilities to the appropriate objects. In most applications, screens and forms shouldn't do any business processing. They should only allow the user to enter and view information. By separating the front-end from the business logic, you've created an architecture that reduces the ripple effect of changes. If the business logic needs to change, the interface shouldn't be affected. If you change the format of a screen or two, the business logic won't need to be changed. Other objects should be assigned appropriate responsibilities as well. For example, if you need to print a list of all flights in an airline's schedule, flight #1020 shouldn't be responsible for that. The responsibilities of the flight #1020 object should focus on just that flight. Another object can be responsible for looking at *all* of the flights in order to generate a report.

Another way to look at responsibilities is to consider the entity, boundary, and control categories we discussed earlier in the "Finding Objects" section. Entity objects should hold information and conduct business functionality. Boundary classes (forms and windows) should display and receive information, but should also do minimal business processing. Boundary classes (interfaces) should send information to another system or receive information from another system, but again do minimal business processing. Control classes should take care of the sequencing.

Sequence Diagrams

Let's begin by taking a look at Sequence diagrams. *Sequence diagrams* are Interaction diagrams that are ordered by time; you read the diagram from the top to the bottom. As we mentioned above, each use case will have a number of alternate flows. Each Sequence diagram represents one of the flows through a use case. For example, Figure 5.3 is the Sequence diagram that shows John Doe purchasing a ticket for flight #1020.

We can read this diagram by looking at the objects and messages. The objects that participate in the flow are shown in rectangles across the top of the diagram. In this example, there are a number of objects: the flight search form, flight list form, fare information form, credit form, and confirmation form are all client pages that are displayed to the end user. The remaining objects constitute the server-side logic and include server pages, interfaces, and other server-side objects. Notice that some of the objects have the same name as their classes. It is not necessary to name the objects differently from the classes.

FIGURE 5.3

Sequence diagram for purchasing a ticket

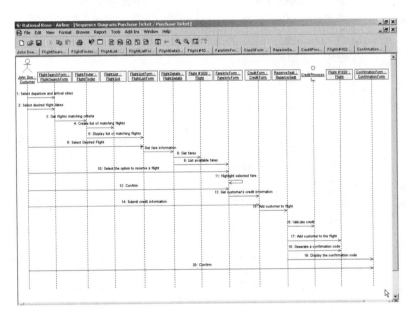

The process begins when John Doe selects his departure and destination cities and departure and return dates. The FlightFinder server-side object looks for flights that match the criteria and builds the FlightListForm, which displays all matching flights. John selects his flight, and the FlightDetails server-side object looks for fare information for that flight. Once fare information has been retrieved, it is displayed using the FareInfoForm. John confirms the rate, and the CreditForm is displayed. John enters his credit information, and the CreditProcessor object interfaces to the external credit system to confirm John's credit. Once the credit has been confirmed, a seat is reserved, the confirmation number is generated, and the confirmation is displayed to John.

Each object has a *lifeline*, drawn as a vertical dashed line below the object. The lifeline begins when the object is instantiated and ends when the object is destroyed. A message is drawn between the lifelines of two objects to show that the objects communicate. Each message represents one object making a function call of another. Later in the process, as we define operations for the classes, each message will become an operation. Messages can also be reflexive, showing that an object is calling one of its own operations.

The Sequence Diagram Toolbar

When a Sequence diagram is opened, the Diagram toolbar changes to let you add objects, messages, and other items to the diagram. Table 5.1 lists the buttons available in the Sequence Diagram toolbar and explains the purpose of each. In the following sections, we'll discuss adding each of these items.

TABLE 5.1: ICONS IN THE SEQUENCE DIAGRAM TOOLBAR

ICON	BUTTON	PURPOSE
	Selects or Deselects an Item	Returns the cursor to an arrow to select an item.
ABC	Text Box	Adds a text box to the diagram.
	Note	Adds a note to the diagram.
	Anchor Note to Item	Connects a note to an item in the diagram.
	Object	Adds a new object to the diagram.
→	Object Message	Draws a message between two objects.
	Message to Self	Draws a reflexive message.
	Return Message	Shows a return from a procedure call.
	Destruction Marker	Shows when an object is destroyed.
	Procedure Call	Draws a procedure call between two objects.
	Asynchronous Message	Draws an asynchronous message between two objects.

Collaboration Diagrams

Like Sequence diagrams, *Collaboration diagrams* are used to show the flow through a specific scenario of a use case. While Sequence diagrams are ordered by time, Collaboration diagrams focus more on the relationships between the objects. Figure 5.4 is the Collaboration diagram for John Doe purchasing a ticket for flight #1020.

FIGURE 5.4

Collaboration diagram for John purchasing a ticket

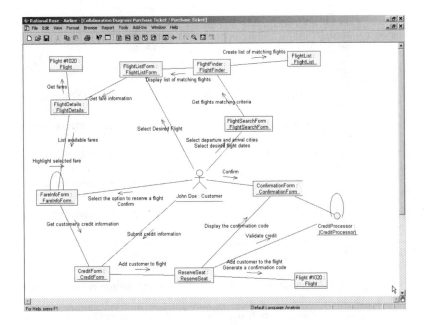

As you can see, the information that was in the Sequence diagram in Figure 5.3 is still here in the Collaboration diagram, but this diagram gives us a different view of the flow. In this diagram, it's easier to see the relationships between the objects. However, it's a little more difficult to see the sequencing information.

For this reason, you may want to create both a Sequence and a Collaboration diagram for a scenario. Although they serve the same purpose and contain the same information, each gives you a slightly different view. In Rose, you can create a Sequence diagram from a Collaboration diagram (or vice-versa) either by pressing F5 or selecting Browse ➤ Create (Sequence/Collaboration) Diagram.

The Collaboration Diagram Toolbar

The Collaboration diagram toolbar is very similar to the Sequence diagram toolbar. There are a few options available here that aren't available in a Sequence diagram, such as an object link and data flows. The following sections describe how to use each of these toolbar buttons to add items to the diagram. Table 5.2 shows the toolbar buttons available on the Collaboration diagram toolbar.

TABLE 5.2: ICONS IN THE COLLABORATION DIAGRAM TOOLBAR

ICON	BUTTON	PURPOSE
--→	Selects or Deselects an Item	Returns the cursor to an arrow to select an item.
✗	Text Box	Adds a text box to the diagram.
→	Note	Adds a note to the diagram.

Continued on next page

TABLE 5.2: ICONS IN THE COLLABORATION DIAGRAM TOOLBAR *(continued)*

ICON	BUTTON	PURPOSE
	Anchor Note to Item	Connects a note to an item on the diagram.
	Object	Adds a new object to the diagram.
ABC	Class Instance	Adds a new class instance to the diagram.
	Object Link	Creates a path for communication between two objects.
	Link to Self	Shows that an object can call its own operations.
	Link Message	Adds a message between two objects or from an object to itself.
	Reverse Link Message	Adds a message in the opposite direction between two objects or from an object to itself.
	Data Token	Shows information flow between two objects.
	Reverse Data Token	Shows information flow in the opposite direction between two objects.

Working with Actors on an Interaction Diagram

Most Sequence and Collaboration diagrams have an actor object. The actor object is the external stimulus that tells the system to run some functionality. The actor objects for the Interaction diagram will include the actors that interact with the use case on the Use Case diagram.

To create an actor object on an Interaction diagram:

1. Open the Interaction diagram.

2. Select the actor in the browser.

3. Drag the actor from the browser to the open diagram.

To remove an actor object from an Interaction diagram:

1. Select the actor on the Interaction diagram.

2. Select Edit ➤ Delete from Model, or press Ctrl+D.

NOTE   *Deleting an actor from the diagram does not delete the actor from the model.*

Working with Objects

The Sequence and Collaboration diagrams show you the objects that participate in one flow through a particular use case. Once the actor object has been added to the diagram, the next step is to add other objects. As we discussed above, you can find the objects that participate in a particular Sequence or Collaboration diagram by examining the nouns in the flow of events and scenario documents. After this step, we will go in and add the messages between the objects.

Adding Objects to an Interaction Diagram

One of the first steps in creating a Sequence or a Collaboration diagram is adding the objects. Look at the nouns from your flow of events and scenarios to start finding objects.

To add an object to a Sequence diagram:

1. Select the Object toolbar button.

2. Click in the location on the diagram where you want the object to reside. In a Sequence diagram, objects are arranged in a row near the top.

NOTE   *In Rose 2001A and 2002, you can move an object down from the top to the point at which it is created.*

3. Type the name of the new object.

4. Once you have added the objects, you can rearrange them by dragging and dropping. You can insert an object between two existing objects by clicking between the two existing objects in step two.

To add an object to a Collaboration diagram:

1. Select the Object toolbar button.

2. Click in the location on the diagram where you want the object to reside. In a Collaboration diagram, objects can be located anywhere.

3. Type the name of the new object.

Deleting Objects from an Interaction Diagram

As you build your Interaction diagrams, you may need to delete some of the objects. When you delete an object from the diagram, Rose will automatically delete any messages that start or end with that object and automatically renumber all of the remaining messages.

When you delete an object from a Sequence diagram, Rose will automatically delete the object from the Collaboration diagram but will not delete the corresponding class from the model. Similarly, when you delete an object from a Collaboration diagram, Rose will remove it from the Sequence diagram. If you change your mind, you can use the Undo option on the Edit menu.

To remove an object from a Sequence or Collaboration diagram:

1. Select the object in the Sequence or Collaboration diagram.

2. Select Edit ➤ Delete from Model, or press Ctrl+D.

NOTE   *Deleting an object from the diagram does not delete the corresponding class from the model.*

If you have several copies of an object on a single diagram and all copies have the same name and the same class, you can press Delete to remove one copy of the object. Pressing Ctrl+D or selecting Delete from Model will remove all copies.

Setting Object Specifications

There are a number of different fields that Rose provides to add some detail to the objects in your diagram. For example, you can set the object's name, its class, its persistence, and whether there are multiple instances of the object. You can also add documentation to the object in the object specification window, shown in Figure 5.5. Adding documentation to an object does not add the documentation to the class, and adding documentation to an object on one diagram does not add the documentation to the object on other diagrams. In the following sections, we'll take a look at each of the options available on the object specification window.

FIGURE 5.5

Object specification window

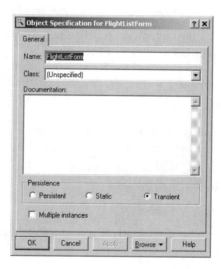

To open the object specifications:

1. Right-click the object in the Sequence or Collaboration diagram.

2. Select Open Specification from the shortcut menu.

OR

1. Select the object in the Sequence or Collaboration diagram.

2. Select Browse ➤ Specification, or press Ctrl+B.

Naming an Object

Each object on a Sequence or Collaboration diagram should be given a unique name. However, for readability you may have multiple copies of a single object on the diagram, and in this case each copy will have the same name. While class names are very generic (Employee and Company, for example), object names are very specific (John Doe and Rational Software Corporation). On an Interaction diagram, you may have two objects that are instances of the same class. For example, in an inventory system, you may have one instance of a Part class, called Engine, which communicates with another instance of Part, called Carburetor. You can enter the name of each object on the diagram in the object specification window, or directly on the diagram.

To name an object:

1. Right-click the object in the Sequence or Collaboration diagram.

2. Select Open Specification from the shortcut menu.

3. In the Name field, enter the object's name. You may also use this field to change the name of the object later on.

OR

1. Select the object in the Sequence or Collaboration diagram.

2. Right-click so that a cursor shows up in the object.

3. Type the object name.

To add documentation to an object:

1. Right-click the object in the Sequence or Collaboration diagram.

2. Select Open Specification from the shortcut menu.

3. In the Documentation field, you can enter documentation for the object.

OR

1. Select the object in the Sequence or Collaboration diagram.

2. Type the object documentation in the documentation window.

Mapping an Object to a Class

On a Sequence or Collaboration diagram, each object may be mapped to a class. For example, flight #1020 may be mapped to a class called Flight. In the object specification window, you can use the Class field to set the object's class. By default, the class will be set to (Unspecified).

When selecting a class for the object, you can either use an existing class from your model or create a new class for the object. In the procedures below, we describe both of these approaches.

By the time you are ready to generate code, all of the objects should be mapped to classes. To map an object to an existing class:

1. Right-click the object in the Interaction diagram.

2. Select Open Specification from the shortcut menu.

3. In the Class drop-down list box, type the class name or select an option from the drop-down list box.

4. Once you have mapped the object to a class, the class name will appear with the object name on the diagram, preceded by a colon. You can toggle the display of the class name by right-clicking the object and selecting Show Class.

OR

1. Select the class in the Logical view of the browser.

2. Drag the class from the browser to the object in the diagram.

3. Once you have mapped the object to a class, the class name will appear with the object name on the diagram, preceded by a colon:

To remove an object's class mapping:

1. Right-click the object in the Sequence or Collaboration diagram.

2. Select Open Specification from the shortcut menu.

3. In the Class drop-down list box, select (Unspecified).

To create a new class for the object:

1. Right-click the object in the Sequence or Collaboration diagram.

2. Select Open Specification from the shortcut menu.

3. Select <New> in the Class drop-down list box. Rose will take you to the specification window for the new class.

To ensure all objects have been mapped to classes:

1. Select Report ➤ Show Unresolved Objects.

2. Rose will display a list of all objects in the model that have not yet been mapped to a class.

To show only the object name on the diagram:

1. Right-click the object in the Sequence or Collaboration diagram.

2. De-select Show Class.

To show both the object and class name on the diagram:

1. Right-click the object in the Sequence or Collaboration diagram.

2. Select Show Class.

To show only the class name on the diagram:

1. If you would rather use only the class name, and not see the object's name at all on the diagram, right-click the object in the Sequence or Collaboration diagram.

2. Select Open Specification from the shortcut menu.

3. Delete the object name from the Name field. Rose will display the object using only the class name. Again, the class name is preceded by a colon.

Setting Object Persistence

In Rose, you can set the persistence option for each object in the diagram. Rose provides you with three options:

Persistent   A persistent object is one that will be saved to a database or to some other form of persistent storage. The implication here is that the object will continue to exist, even after the program has terminated.

Static   A static object is one that stays in memory until the program is terminated. It lives beyond the execution of this Sequence diagram, but is not saved to persistent storage. There is, at most, one instance of a static object in memory at any given time.

Transient   A transient object is one that stays in memory only for a short time (until the logic in the Sequence diagram has finished, for example).

To set the persistence of an object:

1. Right-click the object in the Sequence or Collaboration diagram.

2. Select Open Specification from the shortcut menu.

3. In the Persistence field, select the appropriate radio button: Persistent, Static, or Transient.

NOTE   If you have set the persistence of the object's class to Persistent, you may set the object's persistence to Persistent, Static, or Transient. If you have set the persistence of the object's class to Transient, you may set the object's persistence to Static or Transient.

Using Multiple Instances of an Object

Rose provides the option of using one icon to represent multiple instances of the same class. Say, for example, that you would like to represent a list of employees on a Sequence or Collaboration diagram. Rather than showing each employee as a separate object, you can use the multiple instances icon to show the employee list. The UML notation for multiple instances looks like this:

To use multiple instances of an object:

1. Right-click the object in the Sequence or Collaboration diagram.

2. Select Open Specification from the shortcut menu.

3. Set the Multiple Instances check box to on or off. Rose will use the appropriate icon (single instance or multiple instances) on a Collaboration diagram and use the single instance icon on a Sequence diagram.

Working with Messages

A *message* is a communication between objects in which one object (the client) asks another object (the supplier) to do something. By the time you generate code, a message will translate to a function call. In this example, one form is asking another to display itself:

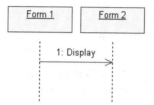

Adding Messages to an Interaction Diagram

Once you have placed the objects on your Sequence or Collaboration diagram, the next step is to add the messages sent between the objects. On a Sequence diagram, messages can be added by drawing an arrow between the lifelines of two objects. On a Collaboration diagram, you must first add a link between two objects. Then you can add messages to the link.

Adding Messages to a Sequence Diagram

In a Sequence diagram, messages are drawn between the lifelines of the objects or from an object's lifeline to itself. Messages are shown in chronological order, from the top of the diagram to the bottom.

To add a message to a Sequence diagram:

1. Select the Object Message button from the toolbar.

2. Drag the mouse from the lifeline of the object or actor sending the message to the object or actor receiving the message, as shown in Figure 5.6.

3. Type in the text of the message.

To add a reflexive message to a Sequence diagram:

1. Select the Message to Self toolbar button.

2. Click on the lifeline of the object sending and receiving the message, as shown in Figure 5.7.

3. With the new message still selected, type in the text of the message.

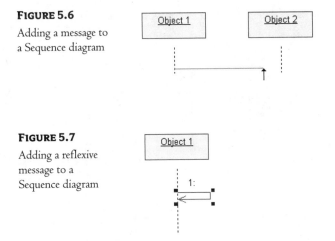

FIGURE 5.6

Adding a message to
a Sequence diagram

FIGURE 5.7

Adding a reflexive
message to a
Sequence diagram

Deleting Messages from a Sequence Diagram

As you work on your Sequence diagram, you may need to delete some of the messages that you've drawn. If you delete a message, Rose will automatically renumber all of the remaining messages.

To delete a message from a Sequence diagram:

1. Select the message to be deleted.

2. Select Edit ➤ Delete from Model, or press Ctrl+D.

Reordering Messages in a Sequence Diagram

At times, you may want to reorder the messages in your Sequence diagram. In Rose, reordering messages is very easy to do; you simply drag and drop the message into its new location. As the messages are reordered, they will automatically be renumbered.

To reorder the messages in a Sequence diagram:

1. Select the message to be moved (select the arrow, not the text).

2. Drag the message up or down in the diagram. Rose will automatically renumber the messages as you reorder them.

Message Numbering in a Sequence Diagram

Although you read the diagram from top to bottom, you have the option of using numbers on each message to display the message order, as shown in Figure 5.8. Message numbering is optional on Interaction diagrams. By default, numbering is disabled for Sequence diagrams.

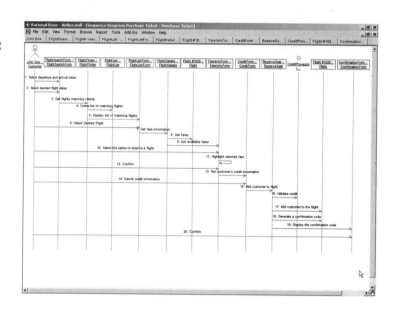

FIGURE 5.8

Message numbering on a Sequence diagram

To turn message numbering on or off:

1. Select Tools ➤ Options.

2. Select the Diagram tab.

3. Set the Sequence Numbering check box to on or off, as shown in Figure 5.9.

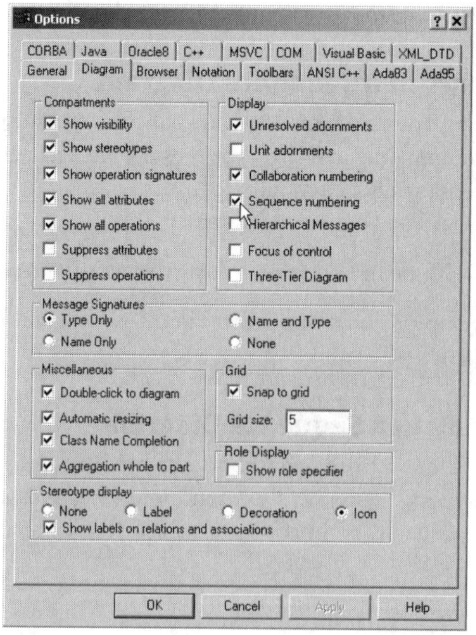

FIGURE 5.9

Message numbering check box

Viewing the Focus of Control in a Sequence Diagram

In a Sequence diagram, you have the option of showing the focus of control, which lets you know which object has control at a particular point in time. As shown in Figure 5.10, a small rectangle represents the focus of control. This is one of the differences between a Sequence and a Collaboration diagram; the focus of control is shown only on a Sequence diagram.

FIGURE 5.10

Focus of control on a Sequence diagram

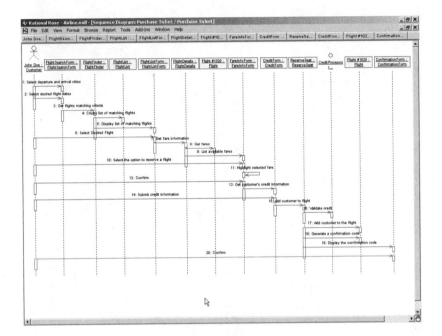

To turn the focus of control on or off:

1. Select Tools ➤ Options.

2. Select the Diagram tab.

3. Set the Focus of Control check box to on or off, as shown in Figure 5.11.

Adding Messages to a Collaboration Diagram

Before you can add messages to a Collaboration diagram, you have to establish a path of communication between two objects. This path is called a *link*, and is created using the Object Link toolbar button. Once the link has been added, you can add messages between the objects.

To add a message to a Collaboration diagram:

1. Select the Object Link toolbar button.

2. Drag from one object to the other to create the link.

3. Select the Link Message or Reverse Link Message toolbar button.

4. Click the link between the two objects. Rose will draw the message arrow, as shown in Figure 5.12.

5. With the new message selected, type the text of the message.

FIGURE 5.11

Focus of Control
check box

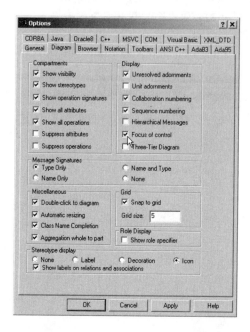

FIGURE 5.12

Adding a message
to a Collaboration
diagram

To add a reflexive message to a Collaboration diagram:

1. Select the Link to Self toolbar button.

2. Click the object sending and receiving the message. Rose will draw a reflexive link on the object. It will appear above the object and look like a half-circle.

3. Select the Link Message toolbar button.

4. Click the object's reflexive link. Rose will add the message arrow, as shown in Figure 5.13.

5. With the new message still selected, enter the text of the message.

NOTE *If you are adding more than one reflexive message to an object in a Collaboration diagram, skip steps one and two for each additional message.*

FIGURE 5.13

Adding a reflexive message to a Collaboration diagram

Deleting Messages from a Collaboration Diagram

As with Sequence diagrams, you can delete messages from a Collaboration diagram. When you delete a message, Rose will automatically renumber the remaining messages.

To delete a message from a Collaboration diagram:

1. Select the message to delete.

2. Select Edit ➤ Delete From Model, or press Ctrl+D.

Message Numbering in a Collaboration Diagram

With a Sequence diagram, you know that you read the diagram from top to bottom, so message numbering isn't necessary. A Collaboration diagram, however, loses its sequencing information if you remove the message numbering.

You do have the option in Rose of turning off message numbering in a Collaboration diagram. To turn message numbering on or off:

1. Select Tools ➤ Options.

2. Select the Diagram tab.

3. Set the Collaboration and Sequence Numbering check box to on or off.

Adding Data Flows to a Collaboration Diagram

We mentioned earlier that one of the differences between a Sequence and a Collaboration diagram is the use of the focus of control. The other difference is in the use of data flow. Collaboration diagrams show data flows; Sequence diagrams do not.

Data flows are used to show the information that is returned when one object sends a message to another. In general, you don't add data flows to every message on a Collaboration diagram, because it can clutter the diagram with information that's not really valuable. If a message just returns a comment such as "OK, the message was received and everything worked fine" or "Oops! There was an error in running the requested function," it's probably not worth showing on the diagram. But if a message returns a structure, say a list of employees working for the company, this may be significant enough to show on a diagram.

When you eventually map each message to an operation of a class, the information in the data flows will be added to the operation's details. As a general rule, don't waste too much time worrying about data flows now. Add them to the diagram if you think they're significant enough to help the developers. If not, leave them out.

To add a data flow to a Collaboration diagram:

1. Select the Data Token or Reverse Data Token toolbar button.

2. Click on the message that will be returning data. Rose will automatically add the data flow arrow to the diagram, as shown in Figure 5.14.

3. With the new data flow still selected, type in the data that will be returned.

FIGURE 5.14

Adding a data flow to a Collaboration diagram

Setting Message Specifications

In Rose, you can set a number of different options to add detail to each message. As with use cases and actors, you can add names and documentation to messages. You can also set synchronization and frequency options. In this section, we'll discuss each of the options you can set for a message.

To open the message specifications:

Double-click the message on the diagram. The message specification window will appear, as shown in Figure 5.15.

OR

1. Select the message on the diagram.

2. Select Browse ➤ Specification, or press Ctrl+B.

FIGURE 5.15

Message specification window

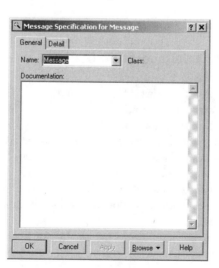

Naming a Message

In the message specification window, you can name the message or change the name, and add documentation. Each message should have a name that indicates the purpose of the message. Later, as you map each of the messages to operations, the message name will be replaced with the operation name.

To name a message:

1. Double-click the message on the Sequence or Collaboration diagram.

2. If you have mapped the receiving object to a class, the operations of that class will appear in the Name drop-down list box. Select an entry from the list or type in the name of the message.

OR

1. Select the message on the Sequence or Collaboration diagram.

2. Type the message name.

NOTE *If you have mapped the receiving object to a class, the name of the receiving class will appear next to the name, in the Class field. This field cannot be modified. To change the receiving class, map the object to another class in the object specification window.*

To add documentation to a message:

1. Double-click the message to open the message specification window.

2. In the Documentation area, enter comments for the message. You may, for example, want to enter a little bit of pseudocode that describes what the message will do.

OR

1. Select the message on the Sequence or Collaboration diagram.

2. Enter comments in the Documentation window.

Mapping a Message to an Operation

Before you generate code, each message on your Sequence and Collaboration diagrams should be mapped to an operation of a class. In this example, the message "Request Some Functionality" will be mapped to an operation of the Supplier class.

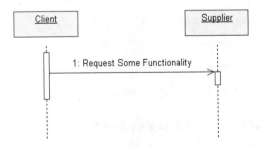

To map a message to an existing operation:

1. Be sure the receiving object (the supplier) has been mapped to a class.

2. Right-click the message in the Sequence or Collaboration diagram.

3. A list of the supplier's operations will appear.

4. Select the operation from the list, as shown in Figure 5.16.

To remove a message's operation mapping:

1. Double-click the message in the Sequence or Collaboration diagram.

2. In the Name field, delete the operation name and enter the new message name.

To create a new operation for the message:

1. Be sure the receiving object (the supplier) has been mapped to a class.

2. Right-click the message in the Sequence or Collaboration diagram.

3. Select <new operation>.

4. Enter the new operation's name and details. (The options available on the operation specification window are discussed in detail in Chapter 7, "Attributes and Operations.")

FIGURE 5.16

Mapping a message to an existing operation

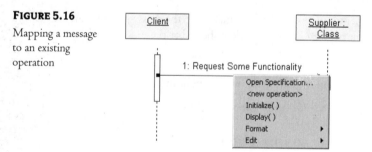

5. Click OK to close the operation specification window and add the new operation.

6. Right-click the message.

7. Select the new operation from the list that appears.

To ensure each message has been mapped to an operation:

1. Select Report ➤ Show Unresolved Messages.

2. Rose will display a list of all messages that have not yet been mapped to operations.

Setting Message Synchronization Options

In the Detail tab of the message specification window, as shown in Figure 5.17, you can specify the concurrency of the message being sent.

FIGURE 5.17

Setting
synchronization
options

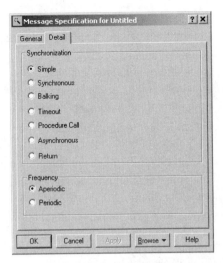

The arrows on the diagram will change if you set the concurrency to Balking, Timeout, or Asynchronous. You have seven synchronization options:

Simple This is the default value for messages. This option specifies that the message runs in a single thread of control. On the Sequence diagram, simple messages use this symbol:

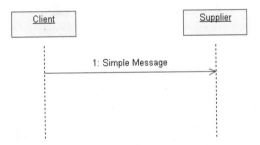

Synchronous Use this option when the client sends the message and waits until the supplier has acted upon the message. On the Sequence diagram, synchronous messages will appear this way:

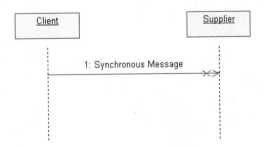

Balking   With this option, the client sends the message to the supplier. If the supplier is not immediately ready to accept the message, the client abandons the message. On the Sequence diagram, balking messages appear like this:

Timeout   Using this option, the client sends the message to the supplier and waits a specified amount of time. If the supplier isn't ready to receive the message in that time, the client abandons the message. On the Sequence diagram, timeout messages appear using this arrow:

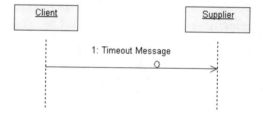

Asynchronous   With this option, the client sends the message to the supplier. The client then continues processing, without waiting to see if the message was received or not. On the Sequence diagram, asynchronous messages look like this:

Procedure Call   With this option, the client sends the message to the supplier. The client then must wait until the entire nested sequence of messages is processed before continuing. On the Sequence diagram, procedure call messages look like this:

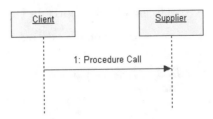

Return   This option indicates the return from a procedure call. On the Sequence diagram, return messages look like this:

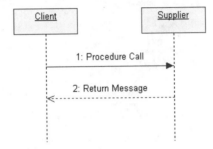

To set the message synchronization:

1. Double-click the message on the Sequence or Collaboration diagram.

2. In the message specification window, select the Detail tab.

3. Select the desired synchronization option from the radio buttons in the window.

Setting Message Frequency

Message frequency lets you mark a message to be sent at regular intervals. Say, for example, you have a message that should run once every 30 seconds. You can set that message to be periodic. The frequency options are available in the Detail tab of the message specification window, as shown in Figure 5.18.

There are two frequency options:

Periodic   This option suggests that the message is sent on a regular, periodic basis.

Aperiodic   This option suggests that the message is not sent on a regular basis. It may be sent only once or at irregular points in time.

NOTE   Message frequency will not change the appearance of the Sequence or Collaboration diagram.

To set the message frequency:

1. Double-click the message in the Sequence or Collaboration diagram.

2. In the message specification window, select the Detail tab.

3. Select the desired frequency option from the radio buttons in the lower part of the window.

FIGURE 5.18

Setting message frequency

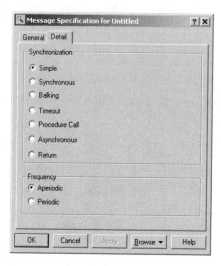

End of a Lifeline

Rose 2001A and 2002 give you greater control over the display of an object's lifeline on a Sequence diagram. Specifically, they give you the ability to position an object at the point at which it is instantiated and the ability to add a destruction marker to indicate when the object is destroyed.

Let's first look at the beginning of the lifeline. As a scenario progresses, objects will be created and destroyed. In Rose 2001A and 2002, you can move an object vertically to indicate where it is created:

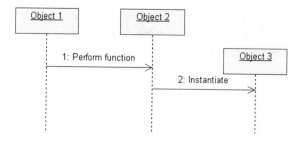

You can also indicate when an object is removed from memory. This can be especially helpful in optimizing a design, because it gives you a quick way to see when memory is "cleaned up" in a specific scenario.

The destruction marker is used to indicate the end of a lifeline. It appears as an "X" on the lifeline itself, and the lifeline will not extend beyond it:

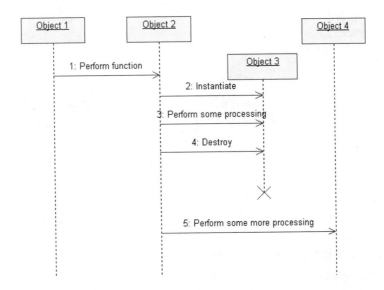

To add a lifeline:

1. Select the Destruction Marker icon from the toolbar.

2. Click on the object's lifeline, at the point where it is removed from memory.

Working with Scripts

In Rose, notes are typically used to add a comment to an object. Scripts, on the other hand, are usually used to add a comment to a message. Scripts are only used on Sequence diagrams. They are usually placed on the left side of the diagram, opposite the message they refer to.

You can use a script to clarify the meaning of a message. You may have a message that reads "Validate User." In the script, you can expand on the meaning: "Validate the ID to be sure that the user exists and that the password is correct."

You can also use scripts to enter some conditional logic in your diagram. Figure 5.19 illustrates some sample scripts in a Sequence diagram.

In general, try to avoid putting so much conditional logic on the diagram that the diagram loses its simplicity. By the time you add the details of a nested If statement inside a nested If statement inside a nested If statement, your diagram will probably be cluttered. On the other hand, there are times when you need to show a little bit of conditional logic. Just balance the two extremes. As long as the diagram is *easily* readable and understandable, you should be fine. If the conditional logic gets too complicated, just create additional Sequence diagrams: one to deal with the *if* part, one to deal with the *else* part, and so on.

Besides If statements, you can use scripts to show loops and other pseudocode on your diagram. Scripts won't generate any code, but they will let the developers know how the logic is intended to flow.

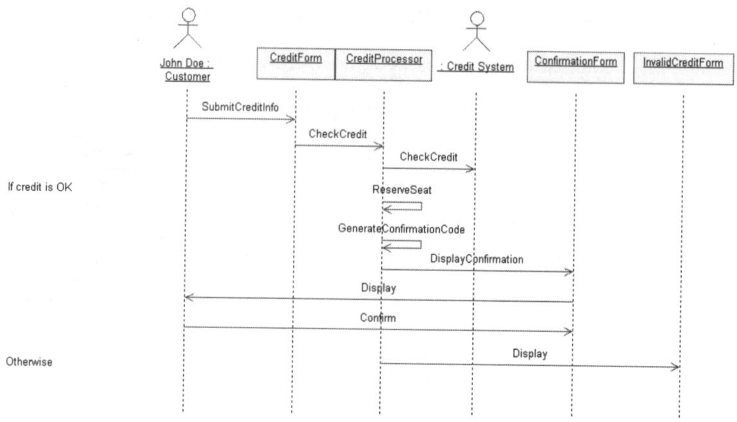

FIGURE 5.19

Using scripts in a
Sequence diagram

To add a script to a Sequence diagram:

1. Select the Text Box toolbar button.

2. Click in the location on the diagram where you want the script to reside. Usually this is near the left edge of the diagram.

3. With the text box selected, type the text of the script.

4. Select the text box. Press and hold down Shift and select the message.

5. Select Edit ➤ Attach Script.

6. Now, when you move the message up or down in the diagram, the script will move along with it.

To detach a script from a message:

1. Select the script.

2. Select Edit ➤ Detach Script.

Switching Between Sequence and Collaboration Diagrams

Typically, you create either a Sequence or a Collaboration diagram for a particular scenario. Without a modeling tool like Rose, it can be too time-consuming to create both, especially because both show you the same information.

In Rose, however, it's very easy to create a Sequence diagram from a Collaboration diagram, or to create a Collaboration diagram from a Sequence diagram. Once you have both a Sequence and a Collaboration diagram for a scenario, it's very easy to switch between the two.

To create a Collaboration diagram from a Sequence diagram:

1. Open the Sequence diagram.

2. Select Browse ➤ Create Collaboration diagram, or press F5.

3. Rose will create a Collaboration diagram with the same name as the open Sequence diagram.

To create a Sequence diagram from a Collaboration diagram:

1. Open the Collaboration diagram.

2. Select Browse ➤ Create Sequence diagram, or press F5.

3. Rose will create a Sequence diagram with the same name as the open Collaboration diagram.

To switch between Sequence and Collaboration diagrams:

1. Open the Sequence or Collaboration diagram.

2. Select Browse ➤ Go to (Sequence or Collaboration) Diagram, or press F5.

3. Rose will look for a Sequence or Collaboration diagram with the same name as the open diagram.

Two-Pass Approach to Interaction Diagrams

Frequently, people use a two-pass approach to creating Interaction diagrams. On the first pass, they focus on higher-level information that the customers will be concerned with. Messages aren't mapped to operations yet, and objects may not be mapped to classes. These diagrams let just the analysts, customers, and anyone else interested in the business flow see how the logic will flow in the system.

The first pass of a Sequence diagram might look like Figure 5.20.

FIGURE 5.20

First-pass Sequence diagram

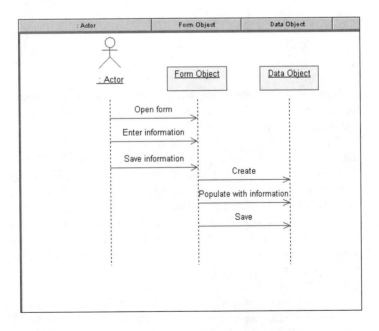

In the second pass, once the customers have agreed to the flow from the first-pass diagram, the team adds more of the detail. The diagram at this point may lose its usefulness to the customer, but will become very useful to the developers, testers, and other members of the project team.

To begin, some additional objects may be added to the diagram. Each Interaction diagram may have a control object, which is responsible for controlling the sequencing through a scenario. All of the Interaction diagrams for a use case may share the same control object, so you have one control object that handles all of the sequencing information for the use case.

If you add a control object, your Sequence diagram will typically look something like Figure 5.21.

FIGURE 5.21

Sequence diagram with control object

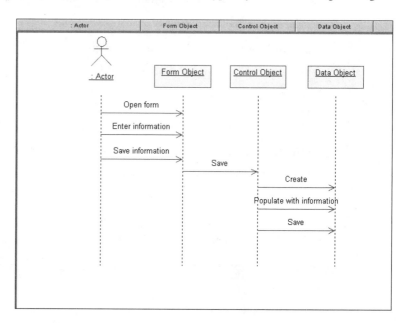

Notice that the control object doesn't carry out any business processing; it just sends off messages to the other objects. The control object is responsible for coordinating the efforts of the other objects and delegating responsibility. For this reason, control objects are sometimes called *manager* objects.

The benefit of using a control object is separating the business logic from the sequencing logic. If the sequencing needs to change, only the control object will be affected.

You may also want to add some objects to handle things like security, error handling, or database connectivity. Many of these objects are generic enough to be built once and reused in many applications. Let's take a look at the database issues, for example.

There are two commonly used options when trying to save information to a database or retrieve information from a database. Say we're trying to save a new employee, John Doe, to the database. The John Doe object can either know about the database, in which case it saves itself to the database, or it can be completely separated from the database logic, in which case another object has to handle saving John to the database. Let's start with John knowing about the database, as shown in Figure 5.22.

In this situation, there is no separation of application logic and database logic. The John Doe object takes care of application logic, such as hiring and firing John Doe, as well as database logic, including saving John to the database and retrieving him later. Should the database need to change, the change will ripple through more of the application this way, because many objects will contain some database logic. On the other hand, this approach can be easy to model and implement.

FIGURE 5.22

Application logic integrated with database logic

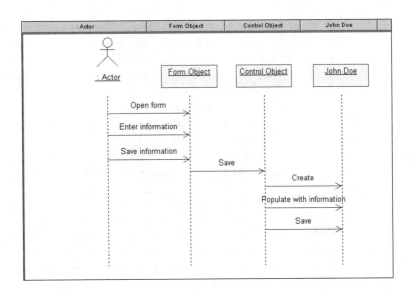

Another option is to separate the application logic from the database logic. In this situation, you will need to create another object to deal with the database logic. We'll call this new object *Transaction Manager*. The John Doe object will still hold the business logic; it will know how to hire or fire John, or how to give him a raise. The Transaction Manager object will know how to retrieve John from the database or save him to the database. The Sequence diagram might look something like Figure 5.23.

FIGURE 5.23

Application logic separated from database logic

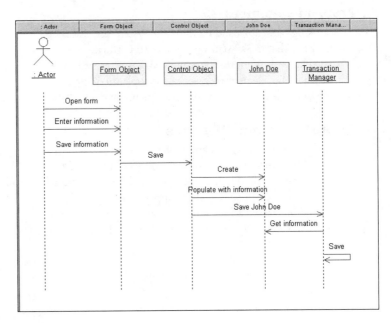

The advantage of this approach is that now it's easier to reuse the John Doe object in another application with a different database, or with no database at all. It also helps minimize the impact of a requirement change. Database changes won't affect the application logic, and application changes won't affect the database logic. The disadvantage here can be that you'll need a little more time to model and implement this solution.

These are two of the more common approaches, although there are some other approaches you can take when dealing with database issues. Whichever decision you make, be sure to keep the approach consistent across Interaction diagrams.

Aside from database issues, you may add objects now for things like error handling, security, or interprocess communication. These details won't interest the customer, but will be critical for the developers.

Once you've added all of the objects, the next step is to map each of the objects to classes. You can map the objects to existing classes or create new classes for the objects (see the earlier section titled "Mapping an Object to a Class"). Then, you map each of the messages in the diagram to an operation (see the earlier section titled "Mapping a Message to an Operation"). Finally, you go into the object and message specifications if you need to set things like object persistence, message synchronization, and message frequency.

Exercise

In this exercise, we'll build a Sequence and a Collaboration diagram to add an item to the shopping cart in our web-based e-commerce system.

Problem Statement

After talking with April and building the system use case model, Andy began looking at the particular functionality that the system would have to perform. Andy started a detailed analysis of the features needed. The "Add Item to Shopping Cart" use case was one with a higher priority to the users and one with a higher element of risk. To allow plenty of time to deal with the risks of this use case, Andy decided to tackle it first by creating a Sequence and a Collaboration diagram.

Create Interaction Diagrams

Create the Sequence diagram and Collaboration diagram to add an item to the shopping cart. Your completed Sequence diagram should look like Figure 5.24.

This is just one of the diagrams you would need to model the full "Add Item to Shopping Cart" use case. This diagram shows what happens when everything goes right. You would need some additional diagrams to model what happens when things go wrong, or when the user selects different options. Each alternate flow in the use case may be modeled in its own Interaction diagram.

FIGURE 5.24

Sequence diagram to add an item to the shopping cart

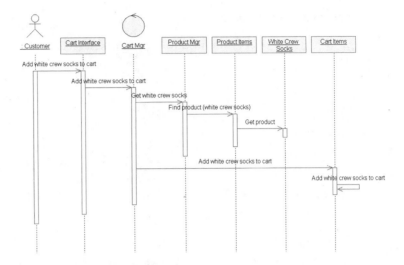

EXERCISE STEPS:

SETUP

1. Select Tools ➤ Options.

2. Select the Diagram tab.

3. Be sure that Sequence Numbering, Collaboration Numbering, and Focus of Control are all checked.

4. Click OK to exit the Options window.

CREATE THE SEQUENCE DIAGRAM

1. Right-click Add Item to Shopping Cart in the system use case model in the browser.

2. Select New ➤ Sequence Diagram.

3. Name the new diagram **Main Flow**.

4. Double-click the new diagram to open it.

ADD ACTOR AND OBJECTS TO THE DIAGRAM

1. Drag the Customer actor from the browser onto the diagram.

2. Select the Object button from the toolbar.

3. Click near the top of the diagram to add the object.

4. Name the new object **Cart Interface**.

Continued on next page

EXERCISE STEPS *(continued)*:

5. Repeat steps 3 and 4 to add the other objects to the diagram.

    ◆ Cart Mgr

    ◆ Product Mgr

    ◆ Product Items

    ◆ White Crew Socks

    ◆ Cart Items

ADD MESSAGES TO THE DIAGRAM

1. Select the Object Message toolbar button.

2. Drag from the lifeline of the Customer actor to the lifeline of the Cart Interface object.

3. With the message selected, type **Add white crew socks to cart**.

4. Repeat steps 2 and 3 to add additional messages to the diagram, as shown below.

    ◆ Add white crew socks to cart (between Cart Interface and Cart Mgr)

    ◆ Get white crew socks (between Cart Mgr and Product Mgr)

    ◆ Find product (white crew socks) (between Product Mgr and Product Items)

    ◆ Get product (between Product Items and White Crew Socks)

    ◆ Add white crew socks to cart (between Cart Mgr and Cart Items)

5. Select the Message to Self button from the toolbar.

6. Below the last message, click on the lifeline of the Cart Items object to add a reflexive message.

7. Name this new message **Add white crew socks to cart**.

CREATE A COLLABORATION DIAGRAM

To create a Collaboration diagram from the Sequence diagram, you can press F5, or if you would rather create a Collaboration diagram from scratch, follow the steps outlined here.

CREATE THE COLLABORATION DIAGRAM

1. Right-click Add Item to Shopping Cart in the system use case model in the browser.

2. Select New ➤ Collaboration diagram.

3. Name the new diagram **Main Flow**.

4. Double-click the new diagram to open it.

Continued on next page

ADD ACTOR AND OBJECTS TO THE DIAGRAM

1. Drag the Customer actor from the browser onto the diagram.

2. Select the Object button from the toolbar.

3. Click anywhere inside the diagram to add the object.

4. Name the new object **Cart Interface**.

5. Repeat steps 2 through 4 to add the other objects to the diagram, as shown below.

   - Cart Mgr
   - Product Mgr
   - Product Items
   - White Crew Socks
   - Cart Items

ADD MESSAGES TO THE DIAGRAM

1. Select the Object Link toolbar button.

2. Drag from the Customer actor to the Cart Interface object.

3. Repeat steps 1 and 2 to add links between the following:

   - Cart Interface and Cart Mgr
   - Cart Mgr and Product Mgr
   - Product Mgr and Product Items
   - Product Items and White Crew Socks
   - Cart Mgr and Cart Items

4. Select the Link Message toolbar button.

5. Click on the link between Customer and Cart Interface.

6. With the message selected, type **Add white crew socks to cart**.

7. Repeat steps 4 through 6 to add additional messages to the diagram, as shown in Figure 5.25.

   - Add white crew socks to cart (between Cart Interface and Cart Mgr)
   - Get white crew socks (between Cart Mgr and Product Mgr)
   - Find product (white crew socks) (between Product Mgr and Product Items)
   - Get product (between Product Items and White Crew Socks)
   - Add white crew socks to cart (between Cart Mgr and Cart Items)

FIGURE 5.25

Collaboration
diagram

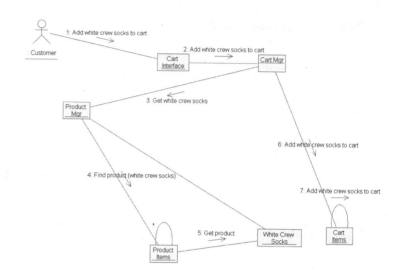

Summary

In this chapter, we have discussed one of the most versatile concepts in UML: Interaction diagrams. Object Interaction diagrams show how objects work together in order to implement the functionality of a use case. There are two types of Interaction diagrams: Sequence diagrams and Collaboration diagrams. Both of these show the same information, just from different perspectives.

Sequence diagrams show the flow of control through time. A Sequence diagram is created for each alternative path through a use case. They are useful for viewing the functionality as a use case progresses.

Collaboration diagrams show the flow of control, but not across time. Collaboration diagrams illustrate the relationships between objects and show messages between objects. From a Collaboration diagram, a system designer can see which objects may be bottlenecks or discover which objects need to directly communicate with each other. Collaboration diagrams can also show data flows between objects; Sequence diagrams do not have this capability. Through Rose, Sequence diagrams and Collaboration diagrams are interchangeable. When a change is made on one, the corresponding diagram changes as well.

Typically, each Interaction diagram goes through a two-pass approach. In the first pass, most of the technical details are left off of the diagrams. These diagrams can be shown to the users who can verify that the process is captured correctly. Once the first-pass diagrams have been validated, the second-pass diagrams can be created. The audience of the second-pass diagrams is not the users, but the project team, including the designer, developers, and analysts. The second pass incorporates many details into the Interaction diagrams. Each object of the diagrams is mapped to a class. Each message on the diagrams is mapped to an operation of a class. Model-quality reports can be generated to show any unmapped objects or messages.

After completing the second-pass Interaction diagrams, some classes that the system requires have been created in Rose. In the next chapter, we will discuss how to create the class diagrams that developers use to actually develop classes.

Chapter 6

Classes and Packages

IN THE PREVIOUS CHAPTER, we discussed how objects interact in order to give a system its functionality. Now we will look at the classes themselves and how to organize them into packages. Objects that are modeled in Rose correspond to classes in the Logical view. In this chapter, we will discuss how to create classes, packages, and Class diagrams in the Logical view.

- ◆ Creating Class diagrams

- ◆ Adding classes to the model

- ◆ Working with classes and packages

Logical View of a Rose Model

In this chapter, we'll discuss some of the items that are stored in the Logical view of a Rose model. As we mentioned in the previous chapter, you can create Sequence and Collaboration diagrams in the Logical view. Other items that you can add to the Logical view include:

- ◆ Classes, including attributes and operations

- ◆ Packages

- ◆ Class diagrams

- ◆ Use Case diagrams

- ◆ Associations

- ◆ State/activity models with Statechart diagrams

We'll begin by creating classes and Class diagrams. In the next few chapters, we'll add details, such as attributes and operations, to the Class diagrams and add relationships between the classes and packages.

Class Diagrams

A *Class diagram* is used to display some of the classes and packages in your system. It gives you a static picture of the pieces in the system and of the relationships between them. In Rose, a Class diagram has the following symbol next to it:

You will usually create several Class diagrams for a single system. Some will display a subset of the classes and their relationships. Others might display a subset of classes, including their attributes and operations. Still others may display only the packages of classes and the relationships between the packages. You can create as many Class diagrams as you need to get a full picture of your system.

By default, there is one Class diagram, called Main, directly under the Logical View entry. This Class diagram displays the packages of classes in your model. Inside each package is another diagram called Main, which includes all of the classes inside that package. In Rose, double-clicking a package in a Class diagram will automatically open its Main Class diagram. If a Main Class diagram does not exist, double-clicking the package will create it.

NOTE   In the `Rose.ini` configuration file, set *AutoConstructMainDiagrams=Yes to automatically create a Package Overview diagram for each package.*

Class diagrams are good design tools for the team. They help the developers see and plan the structure of the system before the code is written, helping to ensure that the system is well designed from the beginning. An example of a Class diagram is shown in Figure 6.1.

FIGURE 6.1

Class diagram

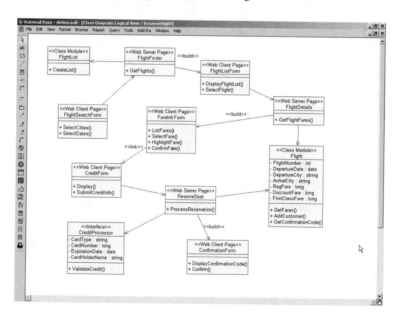

What Is a Class?

A *class* is something that encapsulates information and behavior. Traditionally, we've approached systems with the idea that we have the information over here on the database side and the behavior over there on the application side. One of the differences with the object-oriented approach is the joining of a little bit of information with the behavior that affects the information. We take a little bit of information and a little bit of behavior, and encapsulate them into something called a class.

For example, in a personnel system, we may have a class called Employee. This class will contain some information, such as an employee ID, name, address, and phone number. The Employee class will also have some behavior, such as knowing how to hire or fire an employee or giving an employee a raise.

In UML, a class is shown using the following notation:

The top section of the class holds the class name and, optionally, its stereotype. The middle section holds the attributes, or the information that a class holds. The lower section holds the operations, or the behavior of a class. If you would like, you can hide the attributes and/or the operations of the class in order to make your diagrams easier to read.

You can also show the visibility of each attribute and operation, the data type of each attribute, and the signature of each operation on these diagrams. We will discuss these options in the next chapter.

This Employee class will become a template for employee objects. An object is an instance of a class. For example, objects of the Employee class might be John Doe, Fred Smith, and the other employees of the company.

The Employee class dictates what information and behavior the employee objects will have. Continuing the above example, a John Doe object can hold the following information: John Doe's name, his address, his phone number, and his salary. The John Doe object will also know how to hire John Doe, fire John Doe, and give John Doe a raise. The object has the information and the behavior specified in its class.

Finding Classes

A good place to start when finding classes is the flow of events for your use cases. Looking at the nouns in the flow of events will let you know what some of the classes are. When looking at the nouns, they will be one of four things:

- ◆ An actor
- ◆ A class
- ◆ An attribute of a class
- ◆ An expression that is not an actor, a class, or an attribute

By filtering out all of the nouns except for the classes, you will have many of the classes identified for your system.

Alternatively, you can examine the objects in your Sequence and Collaboration diagrams. Look for commonality between the objects to find classes. For example, you may have created a Sequence diagram that shows the payroll process. In this diagram, you may have illustrated how John Doe and Fred Smith were paid. Now, you examine the John Doe and Fred Smith objects. Both have similar attributes: Each holds the appropriate employee's name, address, and telephone number. Both have similar operations: Each knows how to hire and fire the appropriate employee. So at this point, an *Employee* class is created, and it will become the template for the John Doe and Fred Smith objects.

In our airline example, we use two instances of the flight #1020 object. Now that we are defining classes, we can create a single class, called Flight, which will serve as the template for these two objects.

Each object in your Sequence and Collaboration diagrams should be mapped to the appropriate class. Please refer to the previous chapter for details about mapping objects to classes in Interaction diagrams.

Along with the flow of events, Interaction diagrams are a great place to start when looking for classes. However, there are some classes you may not find in these places. There are three different stereotypes to consider when looking for classes: entity, boundary, and control. Not all of these will be found in the flow of events or the Interaction diagrams. We'll talk about entity, boundary, and control classes in the stereotypes section later in this chapter.

Before we do, however, there's an important process note to make here. In some organizations, people prefer to create the Sequence and Collaboration diagrams first, and then create the Class diagrams, as we have done here. However, others prefer to create the Class diagrams first, and then use the classes as a "dictionary" of objects and relationships that are available on the Sequence and Collaboration diagrams.

If you prefer to create Class diagrams first, you would begin, as we described earlier, by examining the flow of events and looking at the nouns. You would use this as a basis, and decide what other classes you would need in order to implement the system. You would review any foundation class libraries you might have, and include these classes on the diagram. You would group your classes into packages and architectural layers, and then build the Sequence and Collaboration diagrams.

There are pros and cons to both approaches. In either case, a majority of the design work and design decisions is performed in the two steps of creating Sequence/Collaboration diagrams and creating Class diagrams.

One of the benefits of creating Sequence diagrams first is that you can carefully examine, step-by-step, what objects are needed to carry out the functionality in the flow of events, and be sure each class is used. You don't have to worry too much, however, that you may include a class in your model that isn't really used. Also, Sequence diagrams are wonderful group exercises. Creating them first gives you the flexibility to get a bunch of designers together and brainstorm the most efficient design, creating and deleting objects as needed until you have the best design. You are not limited to the list of classes you've already defined.

On the other hand, this opens up the team to design problems. Different subgroups may design the diagrams very differently, leading to overlaps in class responsibilities, inconsistencies in design, and, ultimately, architectural problems. For example, without laying out the classes and their relationships first, a team is free to allow the user interface to communicate directly with the database.

If you create the Class diagrams first, then you have the opportunity to decide the architectural layers and communication patterns before you build the Sequence diagrams. When you are building the Sequence diagrams later, you know you won't violate the architecture as long as you follow the relationships laid out on the Class diagram. This approach can be a little restrictive, however, and teams may need to revisit the Class diagrams to make modifications as they lay out the design of the Sequence diagrams.

Either way, you should be able to trace requirements through the process. The flow of events should reflect the rules laid out in the requirements. The steps in the Sequence and Collaboration diagrams should map to the steps in the flow of events (not a one-for-one mapping, but the sequence should be the same). The objects in the Sequence and Collaboration diagrams should map to the classes in the Class diagrams. A single class may appear on many Sequence and Collaboration diagrams and may even appear several times on the same Sequence or Collaboration diagram as different objects of the same class.

Creating Class Diagrams

In Rose, Class diagrams are created in the Logical view. Again, you can create as many Class diagrams as you need to provide a complete picture of your system.

When you create a new model, Rose automatically creates a Main Class diagram under the Logical view. Typically, you use this diagram to display the packages of classes in your model. You can create additional Class diagrams directly underneath the Logical view or within any existing package.

In Rose 2002, you can set a default Main diagram for each package, even if the diagram is not titled "Main." In the browser, right-click the diagram you wish to make the default, and select the Set as Default Diagram option.

To access the Main Class diagram:

1. Click the + (plus sign) next to the Logical View entry in the browser to open it.

2. The Main Class diagram will be visible. Note that Class diagrams in Rose have the following icon on their right:

3. Double-click the Main Class diagram to open it.

NOTE   *When you first start Rose and load a model, the Main Class diagram will automatically open.*

To create a new Class diagram:

1. Right-click the Logical View entry in the browser.

2. Select New ➤ Class diagram from the shortcut menu.

3. Enter the name of the new diagram.

4. Double-click the diagram in the browser to open it.

To open an existing Class diagram:

1. Locate the Class diagram in the Logical view of the browser.

2. Double-click the diagram to open it.

OR

1. Select Browse ➤ Class Diagram. The window displayed in Figure 6.2 will appear.

2. In the Package list box, select the package that contains the diagram you want to open.

3. In the Class Diagrams list box, select the diagram you want to open.

4. Press OK.

FIGURE 6.2

Opening an existing
Class diagram

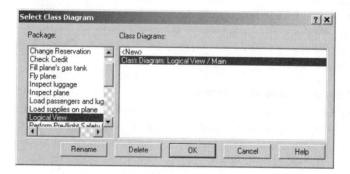

To add an item to a Class diagram, use the Class Diagram toolbar buttons to add items to the diagram. Or, you can go to Tools ➤ Create and select the item you wish to create. In the following sections, we'll describe how to add the various items to a Class diagram.

There are two ways to remove an item from the diagram. To remove an item from the current diagram only:

1. Select the item on the diagram.

2. Press Delete.

To remove an item from the model:

1. Select the item on the diagram.

2. Select Edit ➤ Delete from Model, or press Ctrl+D.

OR

1. Right-click the item in the browser.

2. Select Delete from the shortcut menu.

Deleting Class Diagrams

As you add and remove classes from your model, you may need to delete some of the Class diagrams you have created. In Rose, you can delete Class diagrams using the browser. When you delete a diagram, the classes contained on the diagram will not be deleted. They will still exist in the browser and on other diagrams.

To delete a Class diagram:

1. Right-click the Class diagram in the browser.

2. Select Delete from the shortcut menu.

Organizing Items on a Class Diagram

As more and more classes and relationships are added to a diagram, it can become very cluttered and difficult to read. Rose provides the option of automatically arranging all of the classes on the diagram.

As you add attributes and operations to a class or resize the classes on the diagram, you may end up with a class that is too large or too small. Rose can automatically resize all of the classes to fit the text within them. Using these two options, you can turn a diagram that looks like Figure 6.3 into a diagram that looks like Figure 6.4.

FIGURE 6.3

Class diagram without resizing and automatic layout

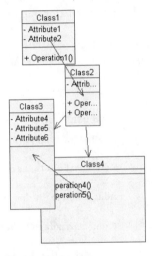

FIGURE 6.4

Class diagram with resizing and automatic layout

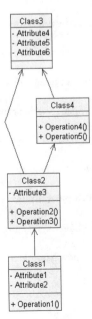

To lay out the items on a Class diagram, select Format ➤ Layout Diagram. Rose will automatically align the classes in the diagram.

To resize the items on a Class diagram, select Format ➤ Autosize All. Rose will automatically resize each class on the diagram to fit the class name, attributes, and operations within the class.

Using the Class Diagram Toolbar

In this chapter, we'll discuss how to add classes to the model and to a diagram. In the following sections, we'll talk about the options provided by each of these toolbar buttons, with the exception of those dealing with relationships. We will discuss the relationship toolbar buttons in Chapter 8, "Relationships."

If you don't see all of these buttons on the toolbar, right-click the toolbar and select Customize. From this dialog box, you can add each of the buttons listed in Table 6.1.

TABLE 6.1: ICONS USED IN THE CLASS DIAGRAM TOOLBAR

ICON	BUTTON	PURPOSE
	Selects or Deselects an Item	Returns the cursor to an arrow to select an item.
ABC	Text Box	Adds a text box to the diagram.
	Note	Adds a note to the diagram.
	Anchor Note to Item	Connects a note to an item on the diagram.
	Class	Adds a new class to the diagram.
	Interface	Adds a new interface class to the diagram.
	Association	Draws an association relationship.
	Aggregation	Draws an aggregation relationship.
	Association Class	Links an association class to an association relationship.
	Package	Adds a new package to the diagram.
	Dependency or Instantiates	Draws a dependency relationship.
	Generalization	Draws a generalization relationship.
	Realize	Draws a realizes relationship.
	Parameterized Class	Adds a new parameterized class to the diagram.

Continued on next page

TABLE 6.1: ICONS USED IN THE CLASS DIAGRAM TOOLBAR *(continued)*

ICON	BUTTON	PURPOSE
	Class Utility	Adds a new class utility to the diagram.
	Parameterized Class Utility	Adds a new parameterized class utility to the diagram.
	Instantiated Class	Adds a new instantiated class to the diagram.
	Instantiated Class Utility	Adds a new instantiated class utility to the diagram.
	Domain	Adds a new domain to the diagram.
	Domain Package	Adds a new domain package to the diagram.
	Server Page	Adds a new server page to the diagram.
	Client Page	Adds a new client page to the diagram.
	Form	Adds a new HTML form to the diagram.
	COM Object	Adds a new COM object to the diagram.
	Applet	Adds a new applet to the diagram.

Working with Classes

Once you've created your Class diagrams, the next step is to add classes to the model. There are several types of classes you can add: regular classes, parameterized classes, instantiated classes, class utilities, and so on. We'll talk about each of these types of classes in the sections that follow.

We'll also discuss the options Rose provides to add detail to your classes. You can name each class, assign it a stereotype, set its visibility, and set a number of other options. We'll discuss each of these options below.

In this chapter, we'll cover how to view the attributes, operations, and relationships for your classes. In the next few chapters, we'll discuss the details of adding and maintaining attributes, operations, and relationships.

Adding Classes

To begin, let's add a standard class. You can add a class by using the toolbar, the browser, or the menu.

First, you can add a new class to the browser only. In this case, it will be available to add to any diagram, but won't exist on a diagram to start with. Alternatively, you can add a new class to a diagram. If you add a new class to a diagram, it will be automatically added to the browser as well.

To add a new class to a Class diagram:

1. Select the Class button from the toolbar. The cursor changes to a plus sign (+) when moved to the diagram.

2. Click anywhere inside the Class diagram. The new class will be named NewClass by default.

3. Rose will display a list of all existing classes. To place an existing class on the diagram, double-click the existing class in the list, as shown in Figure 6.5. To create a new class, replace the word NewClass with the new class name. Note that the new class has also been automatically added to the browser in the Logical view.

NOTE   If you want to create a new class with the same name as a class in a different package, open the class specification window and enter the class name. You will see a warning telling you that classes with the same name now exist in multiple packages.

FIGURE 6.5

Adding a new class

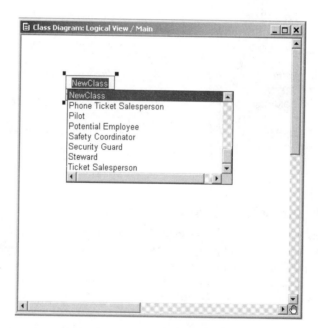

OR

1. Select Tools ➢ Create ➢ Class.

2. Click anywhere inside the Class diagram to place the new class. The new class will be named NewClass by default.

3. Rose will display a list of all existing classes. To place an existing class on the diagram, double-click the existing class in the list. To create a new class, replace the word NewClass with the new class name. Note that the new class has automatically been added to the browser in the Logical view.

NOTE *You may also create new parameterized classes, class utilities, parameterized class utilities, instantiated classes, and instantiated class utilities using the Tools ➤ Create menu. A detailed discussion of these types of classes appears later in this chapter.*

To add a new class using an Interaction diagram:

1. Open a Sequence or Collaboration diagram.

2. Right-click an object in the diagram.

3. Select Open Specification from the shortcut menu.

4. Select <New> in the Class drop-down list box. Rose will take you to the specification window for the new class.

5. In the class specification window, enter the class name in the Name field.

NOTE *Because Interaction diagrams are in the Use Case view of the browser, new classes created with this method are created in the Use Case view. To move them to the Logical view, drag and drop the classes in the browser.*

To add an existing class to a Class diagram:

Drag the class from the browser to the open Class diagram.

OR

1. Select Query ➤ Add Classes. The Add Classes dialog box will appear, as shown in Figure 6.6.

2. In the Package drop-down list box, select the package that contains the class(es) you want to add to the diagram.

3. Move the class(es) you want to add from the Classes list box to the Selected Classes list box. To add all the classes, press the All button.

4. Press OK.

5. Rose will add the selected class(es) to the open diagram.

FIGURE 6.6

Adding existing classes to a Class diagram

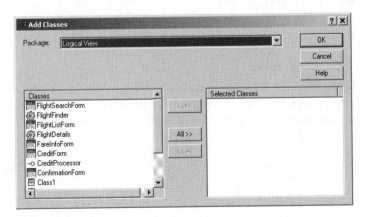

To add a class to the browser:

1. Right-click Logical View in the browser. To add a class to a package, right-click the package name.

2. From the shortcut menu, select New ➢ Class. To add a class utility or an interface, select New ➢ Class Utility or New ➢ Interface. The new class, called NewClass by default, will appear in the browser.

3. Select the new class and type its name.

4. To then add the new class to a Class diagram, drag it from the browser to the open diagram.

Class Stereotypes

A stereotype is a mechanism you can use to categorize your classes. Say, for example, you want to quickly find all of the forms in the model. You could create a Form stereotype, and to find your forms later, you would just need to look for the classes with the Form stereotype.

This feature helps you more thoroughly understand the responsibilities of each class in your model. Classes with a Form stereotype are responsible for displaying information to the user and receiving information from the user. Classes with the Visual Basic Collection stereotype are responsible for grouping entities together into a dataset or other type of collection. Each stereotype has its own types of responsibilities.

Stereotypes also help in the code-generation process. When Rose generates code, it looks at the class stereotypes to determine what type of class to create in the target programming language.

Rose comes with a number of built-in stereotypes. Some are used during the analysis process, when you haven't yet determined what language you will be using. Others are specific to a particular language, and are used in the detailed design process. These different types of stereotypes are important; they allow you to start assigning responsibilities to classes in the analysis process without tying the model to a specific language.

In this section, we will discuss the stereotypes for analysis and language-dependent design that come with Rose.

Analysis Stereotypes

During analysis, you may want to categorize your classes according to the functions they perform. There are three primary class stereotypes in UML that are used for analysis: boundary, entity, and control.

BOUNDARY CLASSES

Boundary classes are those classes that lie on the boundary between your system and the rest of the world. These would include all of your forms, reports, interfaces to hardware such as printers or scanners, and interfaces to other systems. The UML representation of a boundary class looks like this:

BoundaryClass

To find and identify boundary classes, you can examine your Use Case diagram. At a minimum, there must be one boundary class for every actor–use case interaction. The boundary class is what allows the actor to interact with the system.

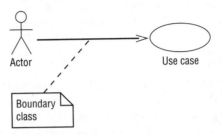

You don't necessarily have to create a unique boundary class for every actor–use case pair. For example, say you have two actors that both initiate the same use case. They might both use the same boundary class to communicate with the system.

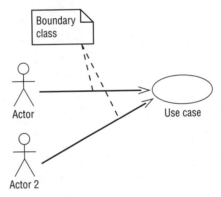

ENTITY CLASSES

Entity classes hold information that you may save to persistent storage. In our airline reservation system, the Flight class is a good example of an entity class. Entity classes are usually found in the flow of events and in Interaction diagrams. They are the classes that have the most meaning to the user and are typically named using business-domain terminology.

Look at the nouns in your flow of events. Many of these nouns will be the entity classes in the system. Another good place to look is in the database structure. If some database design has already been done, look at the table names. An entity class may need to be created for a table. While the table holds a record's information permanently, the entity class will hold the information in memory while the system is running.

In UML, entity classes are represented by the following symbol:

EntityClass

By tying our database design to the object model, we can trace many of the fields in the database back to a requirement. The requirements determine the flow of events. The flow of events determines the objects, the classes, and the attributes of the classes. Each attribute in an entity class may become a field in the database. Using this approach, we can trace each database field back to a requirement and reduce the risk of collecting information no one uses.

CONTROL CLASSES

Finally, let's take a look at control classes. *Control classes* are responsible for coordinating the efforts of other classes. They are optional, but if a control class is used, there is typically one control class per use case, which controls the sequencing of events through the use case. On an Interaction diagram, a control class has coordinating responsibilities, as you can see in Figure 6.7.

FIGURE 6.7

Control class on a
Sequence diagram

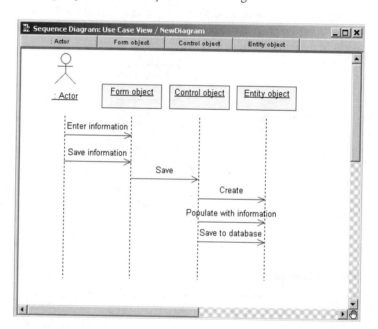

Notice that the control class doesn't carry out any functionality itself, and other classes don't send many messages to it. Instead, it sends out a lot of messages. The control class simply delegates responsibility to the other classes. Control classes are responsible for knowing and carrying out the business rules of an organization. They execute alternative flows and know what to do in case of an error. For this reason, control classes are sometimes called manager classes. In UML, control classes are drawn using the following symbol:

ControlClass

There may be other control classes that are shared among several use cases. For example, we may have a SecurityManager class that is responsible for controlling events related to security. We may have a TransactionManager class that is responsible for coordinating messages related to database transactions. We may have other managers to deal with other common functionality, such as resource contention, distributed processing, or error handling.

These types of control classes can be a good way to isolate functionality that is used across the system. Encapsulating security coordination, for example, into a SecurityManager can help minimize the impact of change. If the sequencing of the security logic needs to change, only the SecurityManager will be affected.

ADDITIONAL CLASS STEREOTYPES

In addition to the stereotypes mentioned above, you can add your own stereotypes to the model. In the Stereotype field, you can enter the new stereotype, and from that point on, it will be available in your current Rose model.

To assign a class stereotype:

1. Open the class specification window by right-clicking the class and selecting Open Specification.

2. Select a stereotype from the drop-down list box or type in the stereotype name.

To display the stereotype name on the diagram:

1. Right-click a class on a Class diagram.

2. From the shortcut menu, select Options ➤ Stereotype Display ➤ Label. The stereotype name will appear, enclosed in double angle brackets (<< >>), just above the class name.

To display the Stereotype icon on the diagram:

1. Right-click a class on a Class diagram.

2. From the shortcut menu, select Options ➤ Stereotype Display ➤ Icon.

3. The representation of the class will change to the appropriate icon. This example shows the icon for an Interface class:

BoundaryClass

NOTE *Not all of the stereotypes have icons. If there is no icon for a stereotype, only the stereotype name will appear on the diagram.*

To turn off the stereotype display on the diagram:

1. Right-click a class on a Class diagram.

2. From the shortcut menu, select Options ➤ Stereotype Display ➤ None. The class will still have a stereotype, visible in the class specification window, but the stereotype will not display on the diagram.

To change the default stereotype display option:

1. Select Tools ➤ Options.

2. Select the Diagram tab.

3. In the Compartments area, as shown in Figure 6.8, select or deselect the Show Stereotypes check box to control whether or not the stereotype will display.

4. In the Stereotype Display area, select the default display type (None, Label, Decoration, or Icon).

FIGURE 6.8

Changing the default stereotype display

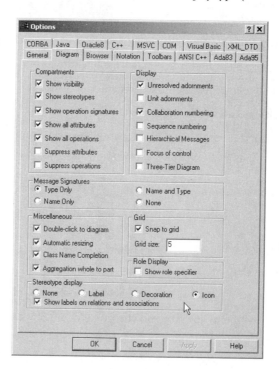

To add a new stereotype to the current Rose model:

1. Open the class specification window.

2. Type a new stereotype in the Stereotype field. The new stereotype will now be available in the drop-down list box as you add more classes, but only in the current Rose model.

3. To add a new Stereotype icon for the new stereotype, see the online help ("Stereotype Configuration File").

Class Types

In design, we want to categorize our classes using the terminology of the particular programming language we are going to use. For example, if we are using Visual Basic, we may have stereotypes such as Class Module, Collection, or Form. If we are using Java, we would need stereotypes for session objects, servlets, interfaces, and so on.

Rose supports a number of different stereotypes for its different language options. This section describes the types of classes that are available. In the following sections, we'll discuss stereotypes for several of the languages supported by Rational Rose.

PARAMETERIZED CLASS

A *parameterized class*, the first of the special types of classes we'll discuss, is a class that is used to create a family of other classes. Typically, a parameterized class is some sort of container; it is also known as a template. Not all languages directly support templates; you can use them in C++, Visual C++, or Ada.

For example, you may have a parameterized class called List. Using instances of the parameterized class, you can create some classes called EmployeeList, OrderList, or AccountList, as described below.

In UML, a parameterized class is displayed using this notation:

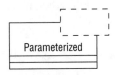

To add a parameterized class:

1. Select the Parameterized Class button from the toolbar.

2. Click anywhere inside the diagram to place the new class.

3. Type the name of the class.

OR

1. Add a class to a Class diagram or to the browser using one of the methods listed above.

2. Open the class specification window.

3. In the Type field, select ParameterizedClass.

4. Press OK.

OR

1. Select Tools ➢ Create ➢ Parameterized Class.

2. Click anywhere inside the diagram to place the new class.

3. Type the name of the class.

Setting Arguments for a Parameterized Class

The arguments for the class are displayed in the dashed-line box. The arguments are placeholders for the items that the parameterized class will contain. Using our example from the last section, we can replace the parameter item with a specific thing, such as Employee, to instantiate an EmployeeList class.

The argument can be another class, a data type, or a constant expression. You can add as many arguments as you need.

To add an argument:

1. Open the class specification window by right-clicking the class and selecting Open Specification.

2. Select the Detail tab.

3. Right-click anywhere inside the white space in the Formal Arguments area.

4. Select Insert from the shortcut menu.

5. Type the argument name.

6. Click below the Type column header to display a drop-down list of argument types, as shown in Figure 6.9. Select one of the types in the list or enter your own.

7. Click below the Default Value column header to enter a default value for the argument. A default value is not required.

FIGURE 6.9

Adding an argument to a parameterized class

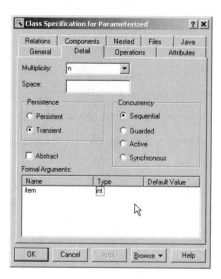

To delete an argument:

1. Open the class specification window.

2. Select the Detail tab.

3. Right-click on the argument you wish to delete.

4. Select Delete from the shortcut menu.

INSTANTIATED CLASS

An *instantiated class* is a parameterized class that has actual values for the arguments. From our last example, we know that we have a list of items. Now, we can supply a value for the Items argument, to see that we have a list of employees. UML notation for an instantiated class is a class with the argument name enclosed in angle brackets (< >):

The number of actual values in an instantiated class must match the number of formal arguments in the parameterized class that it instantiates. If an argument is another class, then there should be a dependency on that class.

To add an instantiated class:

1. Select the Instantiated Class button from the toolbar.

2. Click anywhere inside the diagram to place the new class.

3. Type the name of the class with the arguments in angle brackets (< >).

OR

1. Add a class to a Class diagram or to the browser using one of the methods listed above.

2. Open the class specification window.

3. In the Type field, select InstantiatedClass.

4. Click OK.

OR

1. Select Tools ➢ Create ➢ Instantiated Class.

2. Click anywhere inside the diagram to place the new class.

3. Type the name of the class.

CLASS UTILITY

A *class utility* is a collection of operations. For example, you may have some mathematical functions—squareroot(), cuberoot(), and so on—that are used throughout your system but don't fit well into any particular class. These functions can be gathered together and encapsulated into a class utility for use by the other classes in the system.

Utility classes are frequently used to extend the functionality provided by the programming language or to hold collections of generic, reusable pieces of functionality that are used in many systems.

A class utility will appear as a shadowed class on the diagram with this symbol:

To add a class utility:

1. Select the Class Utility button from the toolbar.

2. Click anywhere inside the diagram to place the new class.

3. Type the name of the class.

OR

1. Add a class to a Class diagram or to the browser using one of the methods listed above.

2. Open the class specification window.

3. In the Type field, select ClassUtility.

4. Press OK.

OR

1. Select Tools ➤ Create ➤ Class Utility.

2. Click anywhere inside the diagram to place the new class.

3. Type the name of the class.

PARAMETERIZED CLASS UTILITY

A *parameterized class utility* is a parameterized class that contains a set of operations. It is the template that is used to create class utilities. It appears on a Class diagram with the following symbol:

To add a parameterized class utility:

1. Select the Parameterized Class Utility button from the toolbar.

2. Click anywhere inside the diagram to place the new class.

3. Type the name of the class.

OR

1. Add a class to a Class diagram or to the browser using one of the methods listed above.

2. Open the class specification window.

3. In the Type field, select ParameterizedClassUtility.

4. Press OK.

OR

1. Select Tools ➤ Create ➤ Parameterized Class Utility.

2. Click anywhere inside the diagram to place the new class.

3. Type the name of the class.

INSTANTIATED CLASS UTILITY

An *instantiated class utility* is a parameterized class utility that has values set for the parameters. It appears on a Class diagram as follows:

To add an instantiated class utility:

1. Select the Instantiated Class Utility button from the toolbar.

2. Click anywhere inside the diagram to place the new class.

3. Type the name of the class.

OR

1. Add a class to a Class diagram or to the browser using one of the methods listed above.

2. Open the class specification window.

3. In the Type field, select InstantiatedClassUtility.

4. Click OK.

OR

1. Select Tools ➤ Create ➤ Instantiated Class Utility.

2. Click anywhere inside the diagram to place the new class.

3. Type the name of the class.

Interfaces

One guideline in object-oriented programming is to separate the implementation of a class from its interface. Most object-oriented languages now support the concept of an interface, which contains only the method signatures (without the implementation) for a class.

For example, we may have a class that deals with security. It has methods called CheckID, Check-Password, and LogSecurityViolation. The CheckID operation takes the user ID as a parameter and returns a Boolean signifying whether or not the ID is valid. CheckPassword takes the password entered by the user and also returns a Boolean. LogSecurityViolation takes no parameters.

Various pieces of the system will need to call the CheckID operation, for example. The typical approach is to create a class, which we'll call SecurityImplementer, that contains all three of the security methods as well as code to implement the functions.

One option is to allow the rest of the system to directly call methods of the SecurityImplementer class whenever they need security functionality. A problem could occur, however, if the Security-Implementer class changes. What happens if we change the way that the methods work or if we want to replace our C++-based security class with a Java-based security class? There could be ripple effects throughout the system.

So rather than take this approach, we create the SecurityImplementer class with its methods and their implementations, but we also create a SecurityInterface class, which holds only the operation signatures. Other classes will reference the interface rather than the implementer class so that if the implementer needs to change, the rest of the system won't be affected.

This concept has been used as the basis for interface definition language (IDL), which allows you to define language-independent interfaces. In Rose, an interface is modeled as a class with a circle icon, which is often called a "lollipop," as follows:

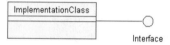

Interface

Web Modeling Stereotypes

One of the new features in Rose is the support of web modeling stereotypes. Using this feature, you can more thoroughly describe the structure of your web applications, labeling which classes in the model correspond to client pages, server pages, applets, session objects, or other web constructs.

NOTE *You can read more about this topic in Chapter 19, "Web Modeling."*

In this section, we'll briefly discuss each of the stereotypes available in Rose Web Modeler. If you are using these stereotypes, you may first want to customize the Class Diagram toolbar to be able to see buttons for these. To do so, open a Class diagram and right-click the Class Diagram toolbar. Select Customize, find the web stereotype buttons, and then add them to the toolbar.

Many of these stereotypes have their own symbols on a Class diagram. In Rose, you can view the classes with their symbols by right-clicking the class and selecting Options ➤ Stereotype Display ➤ Icon. To switch back to stereotypes with text labels instead, select the Label option.

NOTE *If you have changed the stereotype display to Icon but you're still not seeing the symbols, be sure the default language on the Notation tab of Tools ➤ Options is set to Web Modeler before you create the classes. If the classes are already created, be sure they are mapped to a component whose language is set to Web Modeler (see Chapter 10, "Component View," for component mapping).*

CLIENT PAGE

A client page is an HTML-formatted page that is displayed on the client machine by a web browser. A client page may have some embedded logic with JavaScript or VBScript, but typically will carry out only user interface logic. In most situations, business logic should, whenever possible, be carried out on the server.

In Rose, a client page is modeled with the following symbol:

SERVER PAGE

A server page is a page that is executed on the server and typically carries out business, rather than user interface, functionality. The server page can communicate with the resources available on the server, such as the database, other server pages, and business objects. The separation between client and server pages helps the team to separate the business logic from the user interface.

In Rose, a server page is modeled with the following symbol:

FORM

A form is a simple HTML page that doesn't do business processing. It exists only to display information to the end user and to allow the end user to enter some information in simple fields. Once the user enters the information, the form passes control to a server page, which carries out any business logic in response to the information on the form.

On a Class diagram, a form looks like this:

APPLICATION

One of the challenges in web programming is the inability to keep track of the client's state. In other words, once a client has made a request to the server and the server has processed the request, the server does not keep track of where the client is or what it is doing. If the client needs something else, it needs to establish a new connection to the server and send a new request.

When using Active Server Pages (ASP), an application object helps with this problem. It allows the server to keep track of some information across all of the clients that are currently using the system. All clients share the same application object.

In Rose, an application object is modeled as a class with a Web Application stereotype:

APPLET

An applet is a Java construct. It is a (typically small) compiled program that is downloaded to the client and runs on the client machine. Applets are frequently used to add some functionality to the user interface that is not generally available. Although ActiveX controls serve the same purpose, they are not currently supported by all browsers.

Applets are shown on a Class diagram with the following symbol:

SESSION

Session objects exist for largely the same reason as application objects. The difference is that while all clients share the same application object, a session object is unique to a particular client. It allows the server to keep track of what the client is doing and what it has requested in the past—in other words, the state of the client.

A session object is modeled as a class with a Web Session stereotype:

COM OBJECT

The COM object stereotype is used to model ActiveX components. Although not all browsers currently support ActiveX, there are a number of ActiveX controls in use today (and more are being created all the time!). As long as you know that your clients are running Microsoft's Internet Explorer or another browser that supports ActiveX, you can use these controls to enhance the user interface. Like applets, ActiveX controls run on the client machine.

COM objects appear on the Class diagram with the following symbol:

Other Language Stereotypes

In addition to the stereotypes discussed above, Rose supports different stereotypes for Visual Basic, Java, XML, CORBA, COM, and other types of classes. Table 6.2 lists the stereotypes for the different languages available in Rose.

TABLE 6.2: LANGUAGE-SPECIFIC STEREOTYPES IN ROSE

LANGUAGE	STEREOTYPES	LANGUAGE	STEREOTYPES
Visual Basic	Add-InDesigner	CORBA	Constant
	ADO Class		Enumeration
	Class Module		Exception
	Collection		Struct
	Custom Webitem		Typedef
	Data Environment		Union
	Data Report		Value
	DHTML Page		Custom Value
	Enum	COM	Alias
	Form		Coclass
	MDI Form		Enum
	Module		Module
	MTS Class		Struct
	Property Page		Union
	Template Webitem	Oracle 8	Nested Table
	Type		Object Table
	User Control		Object Type
	User Document		Object View
	User Connection		Relational Table
	Web Class		Relational View
Java	EJB Entity		VARRAY
	EJB Home Interface	XML	DTD Element
	EJBPrimaryKey		DTD Entity
	EJBRemoteInterface		DTD Sequence Group
	EJBSession		DTD Notation
	Generic Servlet		
	HTTP Servlet		

Class Specifications

Most of the options that you can set for a class are available on the class specification window, as shown in Figure 6.10. For example, this window allows you to set the class stereotype, visibility, and persistence. In the following sections, we'll talk about each of the options available on the tabs of this window.

FIGURE 6.10

Class specification window

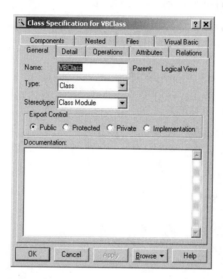

If you are examining the specifications for a Java, XML, or CORBA class, the specification window that appears is slightly different, as shown below in Figure 6.11. All of the options on this window are also available through the standard specification window.

FIGURE 6.11

Java specification window

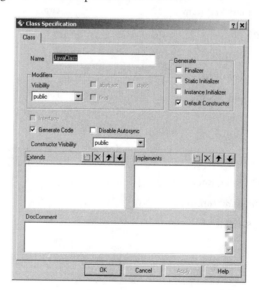

To open the class specifications:

1. Right-click the class on a Class diagram.

2. Select Open Specification from the shortcut menu.

OR

1. Right-click the class in the browser.

2. Select Open Specification from the shortcut menu.

OR

1. Select the class on a Class diagram.

2. Select Browse ➤ Specification, or press Ctrl+B.

Naming a Class

Each class in your Rose model should be given a unique name. Most organizations have a naming convention to follow when naming a class. In general, however, classes are named using a singular noun. In our airline reservation system, for example, we may have a class called Flight and another called Airplane. (We would not call them flights and airplanes.)

Class names typically do not include spaces. This is for practical reasons as well as readability—many programming languages do not support spaces in class names. Try to keep your class names relatively short. While ListOfEmployeesThatAreOnProbation is a very good description of what that class does, it can make the code rather unreadable. EmployeeList might be a better class name in this case.

Whether to use uppercase or lowercase letters really depends on your organization. If we have a class that is a list of employees, it could be called employeelist, Employeelist, EmployeeList, or EMPLOYEELIST. Again, each company typically has a naming convention. Just be sure that whichever approach is decided upon is used for all classes.

To name a class:

1. Select the class in the browser or on the Class diagram.

2. Type the class name.

OR

1. Open the class specification window.

2. In the Name field, enter the class name.

To add documentation to a class:

1. Select the class in the browser.

2. In the documentation window, type the class documentation.

OR

1. Open the class specification window.

2. In the specification window, type the information in the Documentation area.

Setting Class Visibility

The Visibility option determines whether or not a class can be seen outside of its package. It is controlled through the Export Control field in the specification window. There are three visibility options for a class:

Public   Suggests that the class can be seen by all of the other classes in the system.

Protected or Private   Suggests that the class can be seen in nested classes, friends, or within the same class.

Package or Implementation   Suggests that the class can be seen only by other classes in the same package.

To set class visibility:

1. Right-click the class in the browser or on a Class diagram.

2. Select Open Specification from the shortcut menu.

3. Set the export control to Public, Protected, Private, or Implementation.

If a class has protected, private, or package visibility, it cannot be seen by classes in other packages. An access violation occurs in one of two situations:

◆ When there is a relationship between two classes in different packages, but there is no dependency relationship between the packages themselves

◆ When there is a relationship between classes in different packages, and the supplier class has implementation visibility

In Rose, open a Class diagram and select Report ➤ Show Access Violations to check for one of these two problems.

Setting Class Multiplicity

The Multiplicity field gives you a place to set the number of instances that you expect to have of a class. In the employee tracking system, we can probably expect to have many instances of the Employee class—one for John Doe, one for Fred Smith, and so on. The multiplicity for the Employee class, then, would be n. Control classes, however, frequently have a multiplicity of 1. As you're running the application, you probably need only one instance of a security manager.

In Rose, the following multiplicity options are available in the drop-down list box:

Multiplicity	Meaning
n (default)	Many
0..0	Zero
0..1	Zero or one
0..n	Zero or more
1..1	Exactly one
1..n	One or more

Or you can enter your own multiplicity, using one of the following formats:

Format	Meaning
<number>	Exactly <number>
<number 1>..<number 2>	Between <number 1> and <number 2>
<number>..n	<number> or more
<number 1>,<number 2>	<number 1> or <number 2>
<number 1>, <number 2>.. <number 3>	Exactly <number 1> or between <number 2> and <number 3>
<number 1>..<number 2>, <number 3>..<number 4>	Between <number 1> and <number 2> or between <number 3> and <number 4>

To set class multiplicity:

1. Open the class specification window.
2. Select the Detail tab.
3. From the Multiplicity drop-down list box, select the multiplicity. Or type in a multiplicity option that is not available in the drop-down list box.

Setting Storage Requirements for a Class

As you are building your model, you may want to note the amount of relative or absolute memory you expect each object of the class to require. The Space field in the class specification window is used for this purpose.

You cannot use the Space field for class utilities, instantiated class utilities, or parameterized class utilities.

To set class space:

1. Open the class specification window.
2. Select the Detail tab.
3. Enter the storage requirements for the class in the Space field.

Setting Class Persistence

In Rose, you can generate DDL (data definition language) from your model. The DDL defines the structure of your database.

When you generate DDL, Rose will look for classes that have been set to Persistent. The Persistence field in the class specification window is used to specify whether a class is Persistent or Transient:

Persistent   Suggests that the class will live beyond the execution of the application. In other words, the information in objects of the class will be saved to a database or some other form of persistent storage.

Transient   Suggests that information in objects of the class will not be saved to persistent storage.

You cannot use the Persistence field for class utilities, instantiated class utilities, or parameterized class utilities.

To set the persistence of a class:

1. Open the class specification window.

2. Select the Detail tab.

3. Select Persistent or Transient in the Persistence area.

Setting Class Concurrency

Concurrency is used to describe how the class behaves in the presence of multiple threads of control. There are four concurrency options:

Sequential   This is the default setting, and suggests that the class will behave normally (i.e., the operations will perform as expected) when there is only one thread of control, but the behavior of the class is not guaranteed in the presence of multiple threads of control.

Guarded   Suggests that the class will behave as expected when there are multiple threads of control, but the classes in the different threads will need to collaborate with each other to ensure that they don't interfere with each other.

Active   Suggests that the class will have its own thread of control.

Synchronous   Suggests that the class will behave as expected, with multiple threads of control. There won't be any collaboration required with other classes, because the class will deal with the mutual exclusion on its own.

To set the concurrency of a class:

1. Open the class specification window.

2. Select the Detail tab.

3. Select a concurrency radio button in the Concurrency area.

Creating an Abstract Class

An *abstract class* is a class that will not be instantiated. In other words, if Class A is abstract, there will never be any objects of Type A in memory. A class is defined as being abstract if at least one operation of the class is abstract. Rose does not enforce this rule.

Abstract classes are typically used in inheritance structures. They hold some information and behavior that is common to some other classes. For example, we may have an Animal class, which has some attributes called height, color, and species. From this class, we inherit three other classes—Cat, Dog, and Bird. Each of these will inherit height, color, and species from the Animal class, and will have its own unique attributes and operations as well.

When the application is run, there are no animal objects created—all of the objects are cats, dogs, or birds. The Animal class is an abstract class that just holds the commonality between cats, dogs, and birds.

In UML, an abstract class is shown on a Class diagram with its name in italics:

```
┌─────────────────┐
│  AbstractClass  │
├─────────────────┤
├─────────────────┤
└─────────────────┘
```

To create an abstract class:

1. Create a class using one of the methods described above.

2. Open the class specification window.

3. Select the Detail tab.

4. Check the Abstract check box.

Viewing Class Attributes

In the next chapter, we'll talk in detail about adding, deleting, and working with attributes for a class. Part of the class specification window allows you to see the attributes that have already been created for a class. For additional information about attributes and operations, please refer to Chapter 7, "Attributes and Operations."

To view the class attributes:

1. Open the class specification window.

2. Select the Attributes tab. The attributes for the class, including the attribute visibility, stereotype, name, data type, and default value, will be listed on this tab.

Viewing Class Operations

In the next chapter, we'll discuss the details of adding, deleting, and maintaining the operations for a class. Here, in the class specification window, you can view the operations for a class. For additional information about operations, please refer to the next chapter.

To view the class operations:

1. Open the class specification window.

2. Select the Operations tab. The operations for the class, including the operation visibility, stereotype, signature, and return type, will be listed on this tab.

Viewing Class Relationships

In Chapter 8, we will discuss in detail the different types of relationships you can add to classes. We'll talk about adding and deleting relationships and setting the detailed information about each relationship. In the class specification window, you can view all of the relationships that have been added to a class. For additional information about relationships between classes, please refer to Chapter 8.

To view the class relationships:

1. Open the class specification window.

2. Select the Relations tab. All of the relationships in which the class participates will be listed on this tab.

Using Nested Classes

In Rose, you can nest one class inside another. You can also nest additional classes inside the nested class, to as many levels of depth as necessary.

To create a nested class:

1. Open the class specification window for the parent class.

2. Select the Nested tab.

3. Right-click anywhere inside the white space on the Nested tab.

4. Select Insert from the shortcut menu.

5. Type the name of the nested class.

OR

1. Create and name the parent class.

2. Create and name a class for the nested class.

3. In the browser, drag and drop the nested class onto the parent class.

To display a nested class on a Class diagram:

1. Open a Class diagram.

2. Select Query ➤ Add Classes.

3. Move the nested class from the Classes list box to the Selected Classes list box. The nested class will display with the format ParentClass::NestedClass.

4. Click OK. The nested class will appear on the diagram, with the parent class name in parentheses.

To delete a nested class from the model:

1. Open the class specification window for the parent class.

2. Select the Nested tab.

3. Right-click on the name of the nested class you wish to delete.

4. Select Delete from the shortcut menu. The nested class will be removed from all Class diagrams.

OR

1. Right-click the nested class in the browser.

2. Select Delete.

Viewing the Interaction Diagrams That Contain a Class

When you need to change a class, it can be helpful to know exactly where in the system the class is being used. The two types of Interaction diagrams—Sequence diagrams and Collaboration diagrams—will let you know exactly where and how each class is being used. You can use the Report menu to see which Sequence and Collaboration diagrams contain objects of a particular class.

To view all Sequence and Collaboration diagrams that contain a certain class:

1. Select the class on a Class diagram.

2. Select Report ➤ Show Instances.

3. Rose will display a list of all Sequence and Collaboration diagrams that contain objects of that class, as shown in Figure 6.12. To open a diagram, double-click it in the list, or click the Browse button.

FIGURE 6.12

Viewing class instances

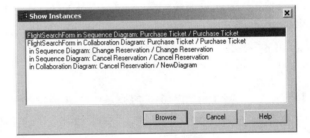

Setting Java Class Specifications

In Rose, Java classes have two specification windows: the standard specification, as described above, and a Java specification window. The Java specification window is used to set Java-specific fields, such as whether to generate a default constructor. Figure 6.13 shows the Java Class Specification window. Using this window, you can set the following:

Name is equivalent to setting the name on the standard specification window.

Visibility controls whether the class is public and can be seen by all classes, or is visible only to classes in the same package. Possible values are Public or Package. Setting the value to Package is equivalent to setting the Export Control to Implementation in the standard specification window.

Abstract sets the class to be abstract, which implies that the class will never be directly instantiated. Setting this flag on the Java specification window is equivalent to checking the Abstract check box on the Detail tab of the standard specification window.

Final determines whether subclasses of the class may be created. If the Final flag is set to True, subclasses may not be created.

Generate is a set of four flags that determine whether to generate a finalize method, static initializer, instance initializer, and/or default constructor when generating code.

Interface sets whether this class is an interface. Checking this box is equivalent to setting the class stereotype to Interface in the standard specification window.

Generate Code controls whether Rose will generate code for this class. By default, this option is selected.

Disable Autosync will disable autosync for this class. Autosync is a feature that will automatically initiate the code-generation process when a Java element is modified. To enable or disable autosync for the entire model, select Tools ➤ Java ➤ Project Specification and then the Detail tab. At the bottom of the screen is an option for autosynchronization.

Constructor Visibility sets the visibility of the class's constructor to Public, Package, Private, or Protected.

Extends indicates whether the class is a subclass of another. If so, the parent class is listed.

Implements indicates whether the class implements the functionality listed in an interface. If so, the interface is listed.

DocComment provides comments for the class. This is equivalent to typing comments in the Documentation field of the standard specification window.

FIGURE 6.13

Java Class
Specification
window

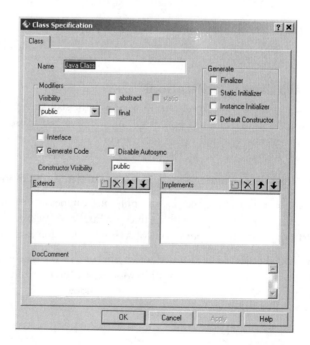

Setting CORBA Class Specifications

As with Java, CORBA classes have their own specification window. You can use this window to set CORBA-specific information, such as enumeration attribute ordering or constant types and values. The specification window will vary slightly, depending upon the stereotype of the CORBA class you are working with. An example of the CORBA specification window is shown in Figure 6.14.

FIGURE 6.14

CORBA Class
Specifications

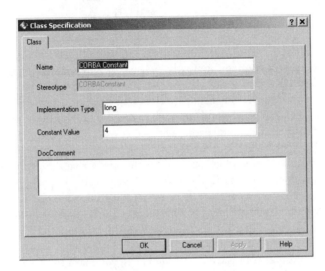

Using the CORBA specification window, you can set the following information. Note that some of these options are available only for certain CORBA stereotypes.

Name sets the name of the class. This is equivalent to setting the name on the standard specification window.

Stereotype displays the stereotype of the class. To change the stereotype, open the standard specification window.

Implementation Type (Constant, Typedef) sets the data type of the constant or typedef.

Constant Value (Constant) sets the value of the constant.

Array Dimensions (Typedef) sets the dimensions of the typedef's declarator.

Attribute/Role Ordering (Enumeration, Union, Exception, Struct, Value, Custom Value) is used to set the order of the attributes in the class. When code is generated, the attributes will be generated in this order.

Inherits From (Value, Custom Value) sets the parent class, if the class is inherited.

Switch Type (Union) is the variable used for the case statements generated for the class.

Working with Packages

A package is used to group together classes that have some commonality. In UML, a package is displayed with this symbol:

There are a few common approaches when packaging classes, but you can group the classes together however you'd like. One approach is to group the classes together by stereotype. With this approach, you have one package with your client page classes, one with your server page classes, one with your applets, and so on. This can be a helpful approach to take for deployment's sake—all the forms that will go on the client machine are already packaged together.

Another approach is to group the classes together by functionality. For example, you might have a package called Security, which holds all of the classes that deal with application security. You might have some other packages called Employee Maintenance, Reporting, or Error Handling. The advantage of this approach is in reuse. If you carefully group your classes together, you end up with packages that are fairly independent of one another. In this example, you can just pick up the Security package and reuse it in other applications.

Finally, you can use a combination of these approaches. Packages can be nested inside each other to further organize your classes. At a high level, you may group your classes by functionality to create your Security package. Within this package, you can have some other packages, grouping the security classes by functionality or stereotype.

Adding Packages

The next step in creating your model is adding some packages. Class packages are created in the Logical view of the browser.

To add an existing package to a Class diagram:

Drag the package from the browser onto the Class diagram.

To add a new package to a Class diagram:

1. Select the Package toolbar button.

2. Click anywhere inside the Class diagram to place the package.

3. Type the package name.

To add a package to the browser:

1. Right-click Logical View in the browser. To create a package inside an existing package, right-click the existing package in the browser.

2. Select New ➤ Package.

3. Type the name of the new package.

To move an item into a package:

In the browser, drag the item from its existing location to the new package.

Deleting Packages

You can delete a package from a Class diagram or from the entire model. If you delete a package from the model, the package and all of its contents will be removed.

To remove a package from a Class diagram:

1. Select the package on the Class diagram.

2. Press the Delete key.

Note that the package has been removed from the Class diagram, but still exists in the browser and on other Class diagrams.

To remove a package from the model:

1. Right-click the package in the browser.

2. Select Delete from the shortcut menu.

OR

1. Select the package on a Class diagram.

2. Select Edit ➤ Delete from Model, or press Ctrl+D.

WARNING   *When you delete a package from the model, all classes and diagrams within the package will also be deleted.*

Exercise

In this exercise, we'll take the classes we created last time and group them into packages. Then we'll create some Class diagrams to show the classes in the system and the packages.

Problem Statement

From the Interaction diagrams, Andy could see that the system met the business needs of the company. So he spoke with Karen, the lead developer.

"Here are the Interaction diagrams for adding a new order."

"Great! I'll get going on development."

Karen took a look at the classes in the Rose model. She decided to group them together by stereotype. So, she created packages called Entities, Boundaries, and Control, and moved each class into the appropriate package. Then, she created a Class diagram in each package: a Main Class diagram to display the packages and an Enter New Order Class diagram to show all of the classes for that use case.

Creating a Class Diagram

Group the classes that we've identified so far into packages. Create a Class diagram to display the packages, Class diagrams to display the classes in each package, and a Class diagram to display all of the classes in the "Enter New Order" use case.

EXERCISE STEPS:

SETUP

1. Select Tools ➢ Options.

2. Select the Diagram tab.

3. Be sure the Show Stereotypes check box is selected.

4. Be sure the Show All Attributes and Show All Operations check boxes are selected.

5. Be sure the Suppress Attributes and Suppress Operations check boxes are *not* checked.

CREATE PACKAGES

1. Right-click Logical View in the browser.

2. Select New ➢ Package.

3. Name the new package **Entities**.

4. Repeat steps 1–3 to create a **Boundaries** package and a **Control** package.

At this point, the browser should look like Figure 6.15.

FIGURE 6.15

Packages for the shopping cart system

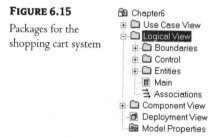

CREATE MAIN CLASS DIAGRAM

1. Double-click the Main Class diagram, directly underneath the Logical View in the browser, to open the diagram.

2. Drag the Entities package from the browser to the diagram.

3. Drag the Boundaries and Control packages from the browser to the diagram.

The Main Class diagram should look like Figure 6.16.

Continued on next page

EXERCISE STEPS *(continued)*:

FIGURE 6.16

Main Class diagram
for the shopping
cart system

CREATE CLASS DIAGRAM WITH ALL CLASSES IN THE "ADD ITEM TO SHOPPING CART" USE CASE

1. Right-click Logical View in the browser.

2. Select New ➤ Class Diagram.

3. Name the new Class diagram **Add Item to Shopping Cart**.

4. Double-click the Add Item to Shopping Cart Class diagram in the browser to open it.

5. Select the Class toolbar button and add the following classes to the diagram: CartMgr, CartInterface, ProductMgr, Product, ProductCollection, CartCollection, and CartItem.

The Class diagram should look like Figure 6.17.

FIGURE 6.17

Add Item to
Shopping Cart
Class Diagram

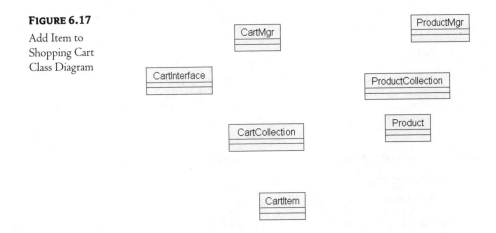

Continued on next page

EXERCISE STEPS *(continued)*:

ADD STEREOTYPES TO THE CLASSES

1. Right-click the CartInterface class in the diagram.

2. Select Open Specification from the shortcut menu.

3. In the stereotype field, type **Boundary**.

4. Click OK.

5. Right-click the CartMgr class in the diagram.

6. Select Open Specification from the shortcut menu.

7. In the stereotype field, type **Control**.

8. Click OK.

9. Repeat steps 1–4 to assign the CartCollection, Product, ProductCollection, and CartItem classes the entity stereotype.

The Class diagram should look like Figure 6.18.

FIGURE 6.18

Stereotypes for classes in Add Item to Shopping Cart use case

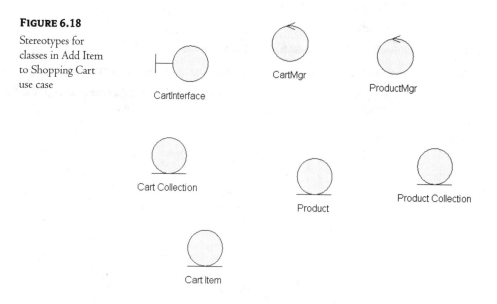

CartInterface

CartMgr

ProductMgr

Cart Collection

Product

Product Collection

Cart Item

GROUP CLASSES INTO PACKAGES

1. In the browser, drag the CartInterface class to the Boundaries package.

2. Drag the CartMgr and ProductMgr classes to the Control package.

3. Drag the CartCollection, Product, ProductCollection, and CartItem classes to the Entities package.

Continued on next page

EXERCISE STEPS *(continued)*:

The classes and packages in the browser are shown in Figure 6.19.

FIGURE 6.19

Classes and packages in the Add Item to Shopping Cart use case

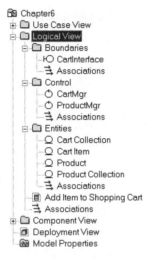

ADD CLASS DIAGRAMS TO EACH PACKAGE

1. In the browser, right-click the Boundaries package.

2. Select New ➤ Class Diagram.

3. Name the new diagram **Main**.

4. Double-click the new diagram to open it.

5. Drag the CartInterface class from the browser to the diagram.

   The Main Class diagram for the Boundaries package should look like Figure 6.20.

6. Close the diagram.

7. Right-click the Entities package in the browser.

8. Select New ➤ Class Diagram.

9. Name the new diagram Main.

FIGURE 6.20

Main Class diagram for Boundaries package

CartInterface

10. Double-click the new diagram to open it.

Continued on next page

EXERCISE STEPS *(continued)*:

11. Drag the CartCollection, Product, ProductCollection, and CartItem classes from the browser to the diagram.

    The Main Class diagram for the Entities package should look like Figure 6.21.

12. Close the diagram.

13. Right-click the Control package in the browser.

14. Select New ➢ Class Diagram.

15. Name the new diagram **Main**.

16. Double-click the new diagram to open it.

17. Drag the CartMgr and ProductMgr classes from the browser to the diagram.

18. Close the diagram.

FIGURE 6.21

Main Class diagram for Entities package

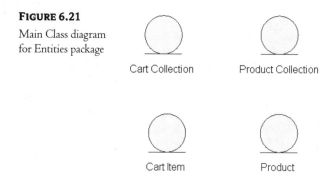

Cart Collection   Product Collection

Cart Item   Product

The Main Class diagram for the Control package should look like Figure 6.22.

FIGURE 6.22

Main Class diagram for Control package

CartMgr   ProductMgr

Summary

In this chapter, we discussed classes, Class diagrams, and packages. By now, we have greatly improved our view of the system that is being built. By the end of the last chapter, we had created Object Interaction diagrams such as Collaboration diagrams and Sequence diagrams. These illustrate the interactions required for the system to perform its functions. In this chapter, we created Class diagrams to show the static behavior in the system. We also organized the classes into packages in order to better understand the system. Next, we will look in detail at the attributes and operations of the classes.

Chapter 7

Attributes and Operations

IN THE PREVIOUS CHAPTER, we looked at classes and packages. Remember that classes are encapsulated attributes (data) and the operations (behaviors) that act on those attributes. Now we will discuss working with attributes and operations. We will begin by talking about how to find attributes, add them to the Rose model, and add details about the attributes. We will then look at finding operations, adding them to the model, and adding details to the operations. Next, we will look at displaying attributes and operations on Class diagrams. Lastly, we will discuss how to map operations to messages on Interaction diagrams.

- ◆ Working with attributes

- ◆ Working with operations

- ◆ Displaying attributes and operations on Class diagrams

- ◆ Mapping operations to messages

Working with Attributes

An *attribute* is a piece of information associated with a class. For example, a Company class might have attributes called Name, Address, and NumberOfEmployees. A Ticket class might have attributes called FlightNumber, Cost, and PassengerName.

In Rose, you may add one or more attributes to each of the classes in the model. The following sections describe how to find attributes, add them to the model, delete them from the model, and set the detailed specifications for each attribute.

Finding Attributes

There are many sources of attributes. To begin, you can take your use case documentation and look for nouns in your flow of events. Some of the nouns will be objects or classes, some will be actors, and others will be attributes. For example, your flow of events may read "The user enters the employee's name, address, social security number, and phone number," letting you know that the Employee class has attributes called Name, Address, SSN, and Phone. In our airline example, the user is looking for a flight and enters a departure and destination city as well as a departure date.

From this, we know that a Flight class would have attributes called DepartureCity, DestinationCity, and DepartureDate.

Another good place to look is the requirements document. There may be requirements that outline what information should be collected by the system. Any piece of information that is collected should be an attribute in a class.

Finally, you can check the database structure. If your database structure has already been defined, the fields in the tables will give you a good idea of what your attributes are. Frequently, there's a one-to-one mapping between database tables and entity classes. Going back to our previous example, a Flight table may have fields called DepartureCity, DestinationCity, and DepartureDate. The corresponding class, called Flight, will have attributes called DepartureCity, DestinationCity, and DepartureDate. It's important to note that there isn't always a one-to-one mapping between the database tables and the classes. There are different considerations when designing your database and designing your classes. Relational databases, for example, don't directly support inheritance.

However, when you identify attributes, be sure that each one can be traced back to a requirement. This can help solve the classic problem of an application capturing a great deal of information that nobody uses. Each requirement should be traced back to the flow of events of a use case, to a particular requirement, or to an existing database table. If you cannot trace the requirement, you cannot be sure that it is needed by the customer. This can be a bit of a deviation from some older methodologies—rather than create the database structure first and then wrap the system around it, you're building the system and the database at the same time to conform to the same requirements.

As you identify attributes, carefully assign them to the appropriate classes. An attribute should be a piece of information related to the class. For example, an Employee class might have name and address information, but shouldn't include information about the products the employee's company manufactures. A Product class would be a better place to store information about products.

Be cautious of classes with too many attributes. If you find that a particular class has a large number of attributes, it might be an indication that the class should be split into two smaller classes. If you have a class with more than about 10 or 15 attributes, be sure to take a close look at it. The class may be perfectly legitimate; just be sure that all of the attributes are needed and truly belong to that class. Similarly, be cautious of classes with too few attributes. Again, it may be perfectly legitimate. Control classes, for example, tend to have very few attributes. However, it may also be a sign that two or more classes should be combined. If you have a class with only one or two attributes, it may be worth a closer look.

Sometimes you may run into a piece of information and wonder whether it's an attribute or a class. For example, let's look at an attribute like Company Name. The question you face might be: Is the company name an attribute of a Person class, or should Company be its own class? The answer really depends on the application you are writing. If you need to keep information about the company and there is some behavior associated with a company, it may be its own class. For example, you may be building a system to keep track of your customers. In this case, you'll want to keep some information about the companies you sell products or services to. You may want to know how many employees the company has, the company's name and address, the name of your contact with the company, and so on.

On the other hand, you may not need to know specific information about the company. You may be writing an application that will generate letters to your contacts in other organizations. When generating the letters, you will need to know a company name. However, you don't need to know any more information about the company. In this case, you could consider the company name to be an attribute of a Contact class.

Another thing to consider is whether the piece of information in question has behavior. If the Company has some behavior in your application, it is better modeled as a class. If the company has no behavior, it may be better modeled as an attribute.

Once you've identified the attributes, the next step is to add them to your Rose model. In the following sections, we'll discuss how to add attributes and add details to the attributes, such as the data type and default value.

Adding Attributes

As you identify attributes, you can add them to the appropriate class in your Rose model. There are three main pieces of information you can supply for each attribute: the attribute name, the data type, and the initial value. Before you can generate code for your model, you must supply a name and data type for each attribute. Initial values are optional.

There are three ways to add an attribute. You may type the attribute directly onto a Class diagram, add the attribute using the browser, or add the attribute using the class specification window.

Once you've added an attribute, you can add documentation for it. Typically, attribute documentation would include a short description or definition of the attribute. Any attribute documentation will be included as a comment in the code generated from the model. By documenting the attributes as you go along, you are beginning to document the code as well.

To add an attribute to a class:

1. Right-click the class on a Class diagram.

2. Select New ➤ Attribute.

3. Type the attribute name, using the format Name : Data Type = Initial Value. For example:

    Address : String

    IDNumber : Integer = 0

    The data type is required in order to generate code, but the initial value is optional.

4. To add more attributes, press Enter and type the new attributes directly on the Class diagram.

OR

1. Right-click the class in the browser.

2. Select New ➤ Attribute.

3. A new attribute, called "name" by default, will appear under the class in the browser. Type the name of the new attribute. Attribute data types and default values cannot be assigned in the browser; you can enter them on the Class diagram, as we'll discuss shortly.

OR

1. Open the class specification window for the attribute's class.

2. Select the Attributes tab. If the class already has some attributes, they will be listed here.

3. Right-click anywhere inside the Attributes area, as in Figure 7.1.

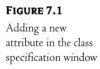

FIGURE 7.1

Adding a new attribute in the class specification window

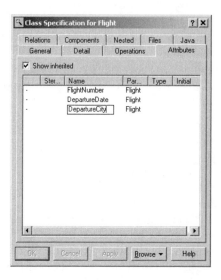

4. Select Insert from the shortcut menu.

5. Type the name of the new attribute.

6. Enter the visibility, stereotype, data type, and initial value in the appropriate columns. We'll discuss each of these in detail in the following sections.

To add documentation to an attribute:

1. Select the attribute in the browser.

2. Type the attribute documentation in the documentation window.

OR

1. Select the attribute on a Class diagram.

2. Type the attribute documentation in the documentation window.

OR

1. Right-click the attribute in the browser.

2. Select Open Specification from the shortcut menu.

3. Enter the attribute documentation in the Documentation area of the class attribute specification window.

OR

1. Open the class specification window for the attribute's class.

2. Select the Attributes tab.

3. Select the attribute.

4. Type the attribute documentation in the documentation window.

Deleting Attributes

At times, you may find that you need to delete an attribute you have created. This is most common when the system requirements change, removing the need for a particular attribute. In Rose, the quickest way to delete an attribute is typically through the browser. However, you can also use a Class diagram to delete an attribute. When an attribute is deleted from one Class diagram, Rose will automatically remove it from the model, including any other Class diagrams on which it appeared.

To delete an attribute from a class:

1. Right-click the attribute in the browser.

2. Select Delete from the shortcut menu.

OR

1. Select the attribute on a Class diagram.

2. Use the Backspace key to erase the attribute name, data type, and initial value from the diagram.

3. Single-click anywhere on the diagram.

4. Rose will confirm the deletion before the attribute is removed.

OR

1. Open the class specification window for the attribute's class.

2. Select the Attributes tab.

3. Right-click the attribute you want to delete.

4. Select Delete from the shortcut menu.

5. Rose will confirm the deletion before the attribute is removed.

Setting Attribute Specifications

As with other Rose model elements, there are a number of detailed specifications you can add to an attribute. These include, among other things, the attribute data type, initial value, stereotype, and visibility. In the next several sections, we'll take a look at each specification.

All of the specifications are viewed or changed on the attribute specification window, as shown in Figure 7.2.

FIGURE 7.2

Attribute
specification
window

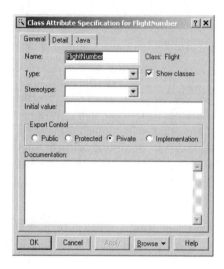

To open the attribute specifications:

1. Right-click the attribute in the browser.

2. Select Open Specification from the shortcut menu.

OR

1. Open the class specification window for the attribute's class.

2. Select the Attributes tab.

3. Double-click the appropriate attribute.

NOTE   *In the following sections, if you are working with a Java, COM, or CORBA class, the specification window will be different. To open the standard specifications, right-click and select Open Standard Specification from the shortcut menu.*

SETTING THE ATTRIBUTE DATA TYPE

One of the main pieces of information you specify about an attribute is its data type. The data type is the language-specific type, such as string, integer, long, or Boolean. Before you can generate code, you must enter a data type for each attribute.

When you are entering the data type, you can either use built-in data types (string, integer, long, etc.) for your programming language or the names of classes that you have defined in your Rose model. To see the classes you have defined in the drop-down list box, select the Show Classes check box.

To set the attribute data type:

1. Right-click the attribute in the browser.

2. Select Open Specification from the shortcut menu. Rose will open the class attribute specification window.

3. Select a data type from the Type drop-down list box or enter a new data type.

OR

1. Select the attribute on a Class diagram.

2. Type a colon and the data type after the attribute name. For example, if you have an attribute called Address that you want to set as a string, type **Address : String.**

SETTING THE ATTRIBUTE STEREOTYPE

Like actors, use cases, and classes, attributes can be stereotyped. An attribute stereotype is a way to classify the attribute. For example, you may have some attributes that map to fields in your database, and other attributes that do not. You can define two stereotypes, one for each of these types of attributes.

In Rose, you are not required to assign stereotypes to attributes. You can generate code without using attribute stereotypes. Stereotypes can, however, improve the readability and comprehensibility of your model.

To set the attribute stereotype:

1. Right-click the attribute in the browser.

2. Select Open Specification from the shortcut menu. Rose will open the Class Attribute Specification window.

3. Select a stereotype from the drop-down list box or enter a new stereotype.

OR

1. Select the attribute in the browser.

2. Single-click the attribute again to edit the name. Before the name, the double angle bracket characters (<< >>) will appear:

3. Type the stereotype between the double angle brackets:

Flight
<<Stereotype>> - FlightNumber
- DepartureDate
- DepartureCity

SETTING THE ATTRIBUTE INITIAL VALUE

Many attributes will have some sort of a default value associated with them. For example, you may have a class called Order, which holds information and behavior about purchase orders for your company. The Order class may have an attribute called TaxRate for the sales tax rate of the purchase. In your city, for example the tax rate may be 7.5%, so most of your orders would be at the 7.5% rate. You can assign an initial value of .075 to the TaxRate attribute.

Like attribute stereotypes, initial values aren't required in order to generate code. However, if an initial value is present, Rose will generate the code necessary to initialize the attribute.

To set the attribute initial value:

1. Right-click the attribute in the browser.

2. Select Open Specification from the shortcut menu. The class attribute specification window will appear.

3. In the Initial Value field, enter the attribute's default value.

OR

1. Select the attribute on a Class diagram.

2. After the attribute data type, enter an equals sign (=), followed by the default value. For example, if you have an integer attribute called EmployeeID and you wish to set its default value to 0, your Class diagram would look like this:

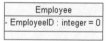

SETTING THE ATTRIBUTE VISIBILITY

One of the central concepts of object-oriented programming is that of encapsulation. Each class, by having attributes and operations, encapsulates a little bit of information and a little bit of behavior. One of the benefits of this approach is the ability to have small, self-contained pieces of code. The Employee class, for example, has all of the information and behavior related to an employee.

You can view a class like this:

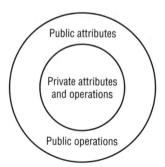

The private attributes are contained inside the class, hidden away from other classes. Because the attributes are encapsulated within a class, you will need to define which classes have access to view and change the attribute. This is known as the *attribute visibility*.

There are four visibility options for an attribute. Let's look at each in the context of an example: We have an Employee class with an attribute called Address, and a Company class.

Public   Suggests that the attribute is visible to all other classes. Any other class can view or modify the value of the attribute. In this case, the Company class could view or modify the value of the Address attribute of the Employee class. The UML notation for a public attribute is a plus sign (+).

Private   Means that the attribute is not visible to any other class. The Employee class would know what the value of the Address attribute is, and would be able to change the value, but the Company class wouldn't be able to view or edit the Address attribute. If the Company class needed to view or edit Address, it would have to ask the Employee class to view or edit the attribute. This is typically done through public operations. We'll talk more about this in the operations part of this chapter. The UML notation for a private attribute is a minus sign (-).

Protected   Suggests that the class and any of its descendants have access to the attribute. In our example, assume we have two different types of employees, hourly employees and salaried employees. The classes HourlyEmp and SalariedEmp are inherited from the Employee class. If the Address attribute has protected visibility, it can be viewed or changed by the Employee class, the HourlyEmp class, or the SalariedEmp class, but not by the Company class. The UML notation for a protected attribute is a pound sign (#).

Package or implementation   Indicates that the attribute is public, but only to classes in the same package. In our example, assume the Address attribute of the Employee class has package visibility. Address could be modified by Company only if Company and Employee are in the same package. With implementation visibility, no icon appears next to the attribute.

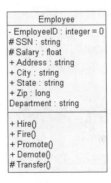

In general, private or protected visibility is recommended for attributes. Using these options helps you maintain better control of your code and the attribute. By using private or protected attributes, you won't have a situation where an attribute is being modified by all sorts of classes throughout the system. Instead, the logic for modifying an attribute is encapsulated in a single class, along with the attribute.

The visibility options you select will affect the generated code. For example, Figure 7.3 is the Java code generated for the class in the previous example.

FIGURE 7.3

Attribute visibility in generated code

```
//Source file: C:\\Employee.java

public class Employee
{
    private integer EmployeeID = 0;
    protected string SSN;
    protected float Salary;
    public string Address;
    public string City;
    public string State;
    public long Zip;
    string Department;

    public Employee()
    {
    }

    /**
    @roseuid 3AA2D20D0109
    */
    public void Hire()
    {
    }

    /**
    @roseuid 3AA2D20F00EE
    */
    public void Fire()
    {
    }

    /**
    @roseuid 3AA2D210010E
    */
    public void Promote()
    {
    }

    /**
    @roseuid 3AA2D2120020
    */
    public void Demote()
    {
    }

    /**
    @roseuid 3AA2D21501AB
    */
    protected void Transfer()
    {
    }
}
```

Rose supports two sets of visibility notations. The first is UML notation (+, -, #) for public, private, and protected attributes, respectively. The second notation includes four Rose icons, as shown in Table 7.1.

TABLE 7.1: ROSE VISIBILITY ICONS

ICON	DESCRIPTION
	Public
	Private
	Protected
	Package or implementation

On a Class diagram, you can use either of these notations. See the upcoming numbered steps for a description of how to switch between these two notations. Figure 7.4 shows an example of a class using UML visibility notation. Figure 7.5 shows the same class using Rose visibility notation. Rose and UML visibility notations are summarized in Table 7.2.

FIGURE 7.4

UML visibility notation

SampleClass
+ Public attribute - Private attribute # Protected attribute Implementation attribute
+ Public operation() - Private operation() # Protected operation() Implementation operation()

FIGURE 7.5

Rose visibility notation

SampleClass
◇Public attribute 🔒Private attribute 🔑Protected attribute 📋Implementation attribute
◆Public operation() 🔒Private operation() 🔑Protected operation() 📋Implementation operation()

TABLE 7.2: ROSE AND UML VISIBILITY NOTATIONS

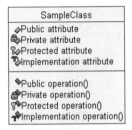

ROSE NOTATION	IF YOU WANT TO...	USE...	UML NOTATION
◇	Make an attribute visible to all classes	Public visibility	+
🔒	Make an attribute visible to only one class	Private visibility	-
🔑	Make an attribute visible to a class and its descendants	Protected visibility	#
📋	Make an attribute visible to all classes in the same package	Package or implementation visibility	<no icon>

To set the attribute visibility:

1. Right-click the attribute in the browser.

2. Select Open Specification from the shortcut menu. The class attribute specification window will appear.

3. In the Export Control field, select the attribute's visibility: Public, Protected, Private, or Implementation. By default, all attributes have private visibility.

OR

1. Select the attribute on a Class diagram.

2. If you are using UML notation for visibility, single-click the icon (+, -, or #) next to the attribute. Select a visibility option from the list of Rose visibility icons that appears.

3. If you are using Rose notation for visibility, single-click the Rose visibility icon to the left of the attribute name. Select a visibility option from the list of icons that appears.

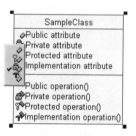

To change the visibility notation:

1. Select Tools ➤ Options.

2. Select the Notation tab.

3. Check the Visibility as Icons check box to use Rose notation, or uncheck it to use UML notation.

NOTE   Changing this option changes only the diagrams. The browser will always use the icon notation.

Setting the Attribute Containment

The attribute's containment describes how the attribute is *stored* within the class. There are three containment options:

By value   Suggests that the attribute is contained within the class. For example, if you have an attribute of type "string," the string is contained within the class definition.

By reference   Suggests that the attribute is located outside the class, but the class has a pointer to it. For example, you may have an attribute of type "employee" within a Timecard class. The employee object itself is located outside of the timecard. The attribute inside the timecard is simply a pointer to this external object.

Unspecified   Suggests that the containment has not yet been specified. You should specify either By Value or By Reference prior to generating code. When generating code, Rose will assume By Value if the containment is unspecified.

To set the attribute containment:

1. Right-click the attribute in the browser.

2. Select Open Specification from the shortcut menu. The class attribute specification window will appear.

3. Select the Detail tab.

4. Select the attribute's containment: By Value, By Reference, or Unspecified. By default, all attributes are set to an unspecified containment.

Making an Attribute Static

When an attribute is added to a class, each instance of the class will receive its own copy of the attribute. For example, let's look at our Employee class. At runtime, we may instantiate three employees: John Doe, Bill Jones, and Jane Smith. Each of these three objects has its own copy of the attribute Salary.

A *static* attribute is one that is shared by all instances of a class. Returning to the previous example, if Salary was a static attribute, it would be shared by John, Bill, and Jane. When an attribute is marked as static, it will be underlined on the Class diagram. In this example, the Salary attribute is static:

To make an attribute static:

1. Right-click the attribute in the browser.

2. Select Open Specification from the shortcut menu. The class attribute specification window will appear.

3. Select the Detail tab.

4. Select the Static check box to mark the attribute as static. Rose will underline the attribute name on the Class diagram.

Specifying a Derived Attribute

A *derived attribute* is one that is created from one or more other attributes. For example, a Rectangle class might have attributes called Width and Height. It might also have an attribute called Area, which is calculated from the width and height. Because Area is derived from the Width and Height, two other attributes, it is considered a derived attribute.

In UML, derived attributes are marked with a slash (/) before the attribute name. In the above example, the Area attribute would be written as /Area.

To specify a derived attribute:

1. Right-click the attribute in the browser.

2. Select Open Specification from the shortcut menu. The class attribute specification window will appear.

3. Select the Detail tab.

4. Select the Derived check box to mark the attribute as derived. Rose will place a slash (/) before the attribute name on the Class diagram.

Working with Operations

An *operation* is a behavior associated with a class. An operation has three parts: the operation name, the operation parameters, and the operation return type. The parameters are arguments the operation receives as input. The return type is the output of the operation.

On a Class diagram, you can view either the operation name or the operation name followed by the parameters and return type. To reduce clutter on Class diagrams, it can be helpful to have some Class diagrams with operation names only and others with the full operation signature, including parameters and the return type.

In UML, operations are displayed using the following notation:

Operation Name(argument1 : argument1 data type, argument2 : argument2 data type, …) : return type

Operations define the responsibilities of your classes. As you identify operations and examine your classes, keep a few things in mind:

♦ Be suspicious of any classes with only one or two operations. It may be perfectly legitimate, but it may also indicate that the class should be combined with another.

♦ Be very suspicious of classes with no operations. A class typically encapsulates both behavior and information. A class with no behavior might be better modeled as an attribute or two.

♦ Be wary of classes with too many operations. A class should have a manageable set of responsibilities. If you have a class with too many operations, it may be difficult to maintain. Dividing it instead into two smaller classes may ease maintenance.

In this section, we'll talk about finding operations, adding them to your Rose model, and adding the operation details. We'll also take a look at how operations can be displayed on the Class diagrams.

Finding Operations

Finding operations is fairly straightforward. As you created your Sequence and Collaboration diagrams, you did most of the work necessary to find operations.

There are four different types of operations to consider: implementer, manager, access, and helper.

IMPLEMENTOR OPERATIONS

Implementor operations implement some business functionality. They are found by examining Interaction diagrams. The Interaction diagrams focus on business functionality, and each message on the diagram will most likely be mapped to an implementor operation.

Each implementor operation should be able to be traced back to a requirement. This is achieved through the various pieces of the model. Each operation comes from a message on an Interaction diagram, which comes from the details in the flow of events, which comes from the use case, which comes from the requirements. This ability to trace can help you ensure that each requirement is implemented in the code and that each piece of code can be traced back to a requirement.

MANAGER OPERATIONS

Manager operations manage the creation and destruction of objects. For example, the constructor and destructor operations of a class fall into this category.

In Rose, you don't need to manually create constructor and destructor operations for each of your classes. When you generate code, Rose gives you the option of automatically generating constructors and destructors.

ACCESS OPERATIONS

Attributes are typically private or protected. However, other classes may need to view or change the attributes of a particular class. This can be accomplished through *access operations*.

For example, if we have an attribute called Salary in an Employee class, we wouldn't want all of the other classes to be able to go in and change the Salary. Instead, we add two access operations to the Employee class: GetSalary and SetSalary. The GetSalary operation, which is public, can be called by other classes. It will go in and get the value of the Salary attribute, and return this value to the calling class. The SetSalary operation, which is also public, will help another class set the value of the Salary attribute. SetSalary can contain any validation rules for the salary that must be checked before the value in Salary is changed.

This approach keeps the attributes safely encapsulated inside a class and protected from other classes, but still allows controlled access to the attributes. The industry standard has been to create a Get and Set operation for each attribute in a class.

As with manager operations, you don't have to manually enter each access operation. When you generate code, Rose can automatically create Get and Set operations for each of the attributes in the class.

HELPER OPERATIONS

Helper operations are those operations that one class needs to carry out its responsibilities but that other classes don't need to know about. These are the private and protected operations of a class.

Like implementor operations, helper operations are found by examining the Sequence and Collaboration diagrams. Frequently, helper operations appear as reflexive messages on a Sequence or Collaboration diagram.

To identify operations, you can perform the following series of steps:

1. Examine Sequence and Collaboration diagrams. Most messages will become implementor operations. Reflexive messages may become helper operations.

2. Consider manager operations. You may want to add constructors and destructors. Again, this isn't required; Rose can generate these for you when code is generated.

3. Consider access operations. Create a Get and Set operation for any attribute that will need to be viewed or changed by another class. As with manager operations, these don't need to be manually added; Rose can generate them for you when code is generated.

Adding Operations

Like attributes, operations can be added to your Rose model through a Class diagram or through the browser. You can also add operations to a class through the class specification window.

Once you've added an operation, you can add documentation to it. Any documentation you add to an operation will be included as a comment in the generated code. Documentation for operations typically includes information like the purpose of the operation, a short description of the operation's parameters, and the operation return type.

To add an operation to a class:

1. Right-click the class on a Class diagram.

2. Select New Operation.

3. Type the operation name, using the following format:

   Name(Argument1 : Argument1 data type): Operation Return Type

   For example:

   ```
   Add(X : Integer, Y: Integer) : Integer
   Print(EmployeeID : Long) : Boolean
   Delete() : Long
   ```

4. To add more operations, press Enter and type the new operations directly on the Class diagram.

OR

1. Right-click the class in the browser.

2. Select New ➤ Operation.

3. A new operation, called "opname" by default, will appear under the class in the browser. Type the name of the new operation. Rose does not allow you to enter the operation arguments or return type value in the browser; as with attributes, you can enter these details on the Class diagram.

OR

1. Open the class specification window for the operation's class.

2. Select the Operations tab. If the class already has some operations, they will be listed here.

3. Right-click anywhere inside the operations area, as shown in Figure 7.6.

FIGURE 7.6

Adding a new operation in the class specification window

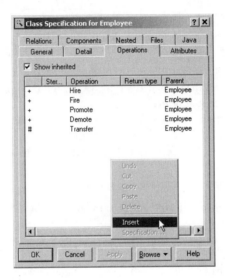

4. Select Insert from the shortcut menu.

5. Type the name of the new operation in the Operation column.

6. Enter the visibility, stereotype, and return type in the appropriate columns.

To add documentation to an operation:

1. Select the operation in the browser.

2. Type the operation documentation in the documentation window.

OR

1. Select the operation on a Class diagram.

2. Type the operation documentation in the documentation window.

OR

1. Right-click the operation in the browser.

2. Select Open Specification from the shortcut menu.

3. Enter the operation documentation in the DocComment area of the operation specification window.

OR

1. Open the class specification window for the operation's class.

2. Select the Operations tab.

3. Select the operation.

4. Type the operation documentation in the documentation window.

Deleting Operations

If you need to delete an operation, you can do so through a Class diagram or the browser. When an operation is deleted from one diagram, it is automatically removed from the entire model, including any other diagrams on which it appeared.

When deleting an operation, be sure to keep the model consistent. You may have used the operation in a Sequence or Collaboration diagram. If you delete the operation, it will be automatically converted into a message on all Sequence and Collaboration diagrams. Be sure to update the Sequence or Collaboration diagram appropriately.

To determine which diagrams reference an operation:

1. Open the class specification window (or standard specification window in 98i) for the operation's class.

2. Select Browse ➤ Show Usage at the bottom of the dialog box.

To delete an operation from a class:

1. Right-click the operation in the browser.

2. Select Delete from the shortcut menu.

OR

1. Select the operation on a Class diagram.

2. Use the Backspace key to erase the operation name and signature from the diagram.

3. Single-click anywhere on the diagram.

4. Rose will confirm the deletion before the operation is removed.

OR

1. Open the class specification window for the operation's class.

2. Select the Operations tab.

3. Right-click the operation you want to delete.

4. Select Delete from the shortcut menu.

5. Rose will confirm the deletion before the operation is removed.

Setting Operation Specifications

In the operation specifications, you can set details such as the operation parameters, return type, and visibility. In the next several sections, we'll take a look at each specification.

All of the specifications are viewed or changed on the operation specification window, as shown in Figure 7.7.

FIGURE 7.7

Operation
specification
window

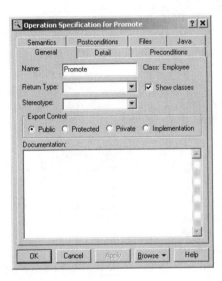

To open the operation specifications:

1. Right-click the operation in the browser.

2. Select Open Specification from the shortcut menu.

OR

1. Open the class specification window for the operation's class.

2. Select the Operations tab.

3. Double-click the appropriate operation.

NOTE *In the following sections, if you are working with a Java, COM, or CORBA class, the specification window will be different. To open the standard specifications, right-click and then select Open Standard Specification from the shortcut menu.*

SETTING THE OPERATION RETURN CLASS

The return class of an operation is the data type of the operation's result. For example, say we have an operation called Add, which takes as parameters two strings, X and Y. The operation will convert X and Y to integers, add them, and return the result as an integer. The return class of Add will be "integer."

When specifying the return class, you can either use built-in data types of your programming language—such as string, char, or integer—or use classes that you have defined in your Rose model.

To set the operation return class:

1. Right-click the operation in the browser.

2. Select Open Specification from the shortcut menu.

3. Select a return class from the drop-down list box, or enter a new return type.

OR

1. Select the operation on a Class diagram.

2. After the operation name, enter a colon, followed by the return type. For example, if you have an operation called Print that should return an integer, your Class diagram will look like this:

SETTING THE OPERATION STEREOTYPE

As with other model elements, operations can be stereotyped to classify them. As discussed above, there are four commonly used operation stereotypes:

Implementor   Operations that implement some business logic.

Manager   Constructors, destructors, and memory management operations.

Access   Operations that allow other classes to view or edit attributes. Typically, these are named Get<attribute name> and Set<attribute name>.

Helper   Private or protected operations used by the class but not seen by other classes.

Setting stereotypes for operations isn't required to generate code. However, stereotypes can help improve the understandability of the model. Also, they can help you to be sure that you haven't missed any operations.

To set the operation stereotype:

1. Right-click the operation in the browser.

2. Select Open Specification from the shortcut menu. Rose will open the operation specification window.

3. Select a stereotype from the drop-down list box or enter a new stereotype.

OR

1. Select the operation in the browser.

2. Single-click the operation again to edit the name. Before the name, the double angle bracket characters (<<>>) will appear:

3. Type the stereotype between the brackets.

SETTING THE OPERATION VISIBILITY

As we discussed before, visibility has to do with how information and behavior is encapsulated in a class. There are four visibility options for operations. (To familiarize yourself with the way these are represented visually, see Table 7.2.)

Public   Suggests that the operation is visible to all other classes. Any other class can request that the operation be executed.

Private   Means that the operation is not visible to any other class.

Protected   Suggests that the class and any of its descendants have access to the operation.

Package or implementation   Indicates that the operation is public, but only to classes in the same package.

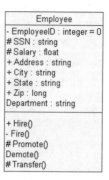

While attributes are typically private or protected, operations may be public, private, protected, or package. When making this decision, think about what other classes, if any, will need to know that the operation exists. When you generate code, Rose will generate the appropriate visibility. For example, the code generated for the class above is shown in Figure 7.8.

FIGURE 7.8

Operation visibility
in generated code

```
//Source file: C:\\Employee.java
public class Employee
{
    private integer EmployeeID = 0;
    protected string SSN;
    protected float Salary;
    public string Address;
    public string City;
    public string State;
    public long Zip;
    string Department;

    public Employee()
    {
    }

    /**
    @roseuid 3AA2D20D0109
    */
    public void Hire()
    {
    }

    /**
    @roseuid 3AA2D20F00EE
    */
    private void Fire()
    {
    }

    /**
    @roseuid 3AA2D210010E
    */
    protected void Promote()
    {
    }

    /**
    @roseuid 3AA2D2120020
    */
    void Demote()
    {
    }

    /**
    @roseuid 3AA2D21501AB
    */
    protected void Transfer()
    {
    }
}
```

As mentioned earlier in this chapter, you can use either UML or Rose notation on a Class diagram. See the upcoming numbered steps for a description of how to switch between these two notations. Refer to Figure 7.4 to see a class using UML visibility notation and to Figure 7.5 to see the same class using Rose visibility notation. To revisit a summary of the possible visibility options, including their Rose and UML notations, see Table 7.2.

To set the operation visibility:

1. Right-click the operation in the browser.

2. Select Open Specification from the shortcut menu. The Operation Specification window will appear.

3. In the Export Control field, select the operation's visibility: Public, Protected, Private, or Implementation. By default, all operations have public visibility.

OR

1. Select the operation on a Class diagram.

2. If you are using UML notation for visibility, single-click the icon (+, -, or #) next to the operation. Select a visibility option from the list of Rose visibility icons that appears.

3. If you are using Rose notation for visibility, single-click the Rose visibility icon to the left of the operation name. Select a visibility option from the list of icons that appears.

Adding Arguments to an Operation

Operation arguments, or parameters, are the input data the operation receives. An Add operation, for example, may take two arguments, X and Y, and add them together.

There are two pieces of information to supply for each argument. The first is the argument name. The second is its data type. On a Class diagram, the arguments and data types appear in parentheses after the operation name:

Employee
- EmployeeID : integer = 0 ＃ SSN : string ＃ Salary : float + Address : string + City : string + State : string + Zip : long Department : string
+ Hire() - Fire() ＃ Promote(EmpID : integer, PromoDate : date, NewSalary : float) Demote() ＃ Transfer()

If you'd like, you can also specify a default value for each argument. If you include a default value, the UML notation is:

Operation name(argument1 : argument1 data type = argument1 default value) : operation return type

Employee
- EmployeeID : integer = 0 # SSN : string # Salary : float + Address : string + City : string + State : string + Zip : long Department : string

+ Hire()
- Fire()
# Promote(EmpID : integer, PromoDate : date, NewSalary : float = 50000) 	
Demote()
# Transfer() 	

When you generate code, Rose will generate the operation name, arguments, argument data types, argument default values, and return type. Rose will also create comments if any documentation was added to the operation.

To add an argument to an operation:

1. Open the operation specification window.

2. Select the Detail tab.

3. Right-click in the Arguments box, then select Insert from the menu.

4. Enter the name of the argument, as shown in Figure 7.9.

5. Click on the Type column and enter the data type of the argument.

6. Click on the Default column and enter the default for the argument, if desired.

FIGURE 7.9

Operation arguments

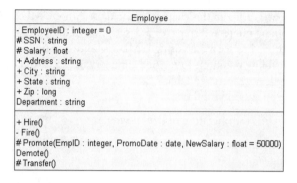

To delete an argument from an operation:

1. Open the operation specification window.

2. Select the Detail tab.

3. Right-click the argument to be deleted in the Arguments box, and then select Delete from the menu.

4. Confirm the deletion.

Specifying the Operation Protocol

The operation protocol describes what operations a client may perform on the object, and in which order the operations must be executed. For example, if operation A should not be executed until operation B has been executed, you can note this in the Protocol field of operation A. The information you enter here will not have an impact on what code is generated for the operation. The operation protocol screen is shown in Figure 7.10.

To specify the operation protocol:

1. Open the operation specification window.

2. Select the Detail tab.

3. Enter the protocol in the Protocol field.

FIGURE 7.10

Operation protocol

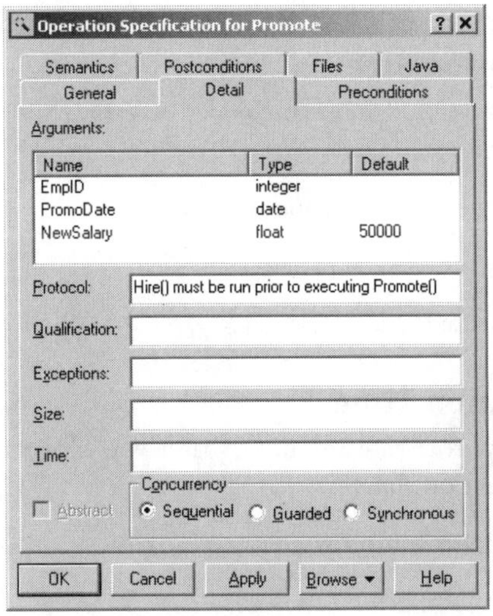

Specifying the Operation Qualifications

This field lets you identify any language-specific qualifications for the operation. It will not affect the code generated for the operation.

To specify the operation qualifications:

1. Open the operation specification window.

2. Select the Detail tab.

3. Enter the qualifications in the Qualification field.

Specifying the Operation Exceptions

The operation Exceptions field gives you a place to list the exceptions that the operation may throw. In some languages, the exception information will affect the code generated for the operation. For example, Figure 7.11 is some Java code generated with exception information.

FIGURE 7.11

Operation exceptions
in generated code

```
/**
@roseuid 3AA2D210010E
*/
protected void Promote(integer EmpID, date PromoDate, float NewSalary) throws throw Problem("an error has occurred")
{
}
```

To specify the operation exceptions:

1. Open the operation specification window.

2. Select the Detail tab.

3. Enter the exceptions in the Exceptions field.

Specifying the Operation Size

The Size field is a place to note how much memory you expect the operation to require at runtime. To specify the operation size:

1. Open the operation specification window.

2. Select the Detail tab.

3. Enter the size in the Size field.

Specifying the Operation Time

The operation time is the approximate amount of time you expect this operation to require as it executes. To specify the operation time:

1. Open the operation specification window.

2. Select the Detail tab.

3. Enter the time in the Time field.

Specifying the Operation Concurrency

The Concurrency field specifies how the operation will behave in the presence of multiple threads of control. There are three concurrency options:

Sequential   Suggests that the operation will run properly only if there is a single thread of control. The operation must run to completion before another operation may be run.

Guarded   Suggests that the operation will run properly with multiple threads of control, but only if the classes collaborate to ensure that mutual exclusion of running operations is achieved.

Synchronous   Suggests that the operation will run properly with multiple threads of control. When called, the operation will run to completion in one thread. However, other operations can run in other threads at the same time. The class will take care of mutual exclusion issues, so collaboration with other classes is not required.

To specify the operation concurrency:

1. Open the operation specification window.

2. Select the Detail tab.

3. Select the desired concurrency from the Concurrency box.

Specifying the Operation Preconditions

A precondition is some condition that must be true before the operation can run. You can enter any preconditions for the operation on the Preconditions tab of the operation specification window, as shown in Figure 7.12.

FIGURE 7.12

Operation
preconditions

Preconditions will not affect the code that is generated for the operation. If you have an Interaction diagram that illustrates the operation preconditions, you can enter the Interaction diagram name at the bottom of the Preconditions tab.

To specify the operation preconditions:

1. Open the operation specification window.

2. Select the Preconditions tab.

3. Enter the preconditions in the Preconditions field.

Specifying the Operation Postconditions

Postconditions are conditions that must always be true after the operation has finished executing. Postconditions are entered on the Postconditions tab of the operation specification window, as shown in Figure 7.13.

FIGURE 7.13

Operation postconditions

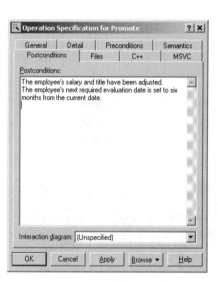

Like preconditions, the postconditions will not affect the code generated for an operation, but will appear as a comment in the generated code. If you have an Interaction diagram that includes information about the postconditions, you can enter its name at the bottom of the Postconditions tab.

To specify the operation postconditions:

1. Open the operation specification window.

2. Select the Postconditions tab.

3. Enter the postconditions in the Postconditions field.

Specifying the Operation Semantics

The Semantics field of the operation specification window gives you a place to describe what the operation will do, as shown in Figure 7.14. You can use pseudocode here, or just a description, to spell out the operation logic. If you have an Interaction diagram related to the operation's semantics, you can enter it at the bottom of this tab page.

FIGURE 7.14

Operation semantics

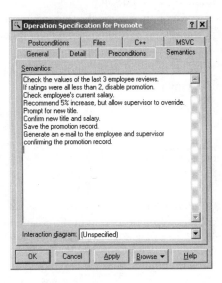

To specify the operation semantics:

1. Open the operation specification window.

2. Select the Semantics tab.

3. Enter the semantics in the Semantics field.

Displaying Attributes and Operations on Class Diagrams

UML is very flexible; it allows for either all details to be shown on a Class diagram or only those details you'd like to see. In Rose, you can customize your Class diagrams to do the following:

◆ Show all attributes and operations

◆ Hide the attributes

◆ Hide the operations

◆ Show selected attributes and operations

◆ Show operation signatures or operation names only

◆ Show or hide attribute and operation visibility

◆ Show or hide operation and attribute stereotypes

In the following sections, we'll take a look at each of these options. In a typical project, you'll have many Class diagrams. Some will focus on the relationships, and will show little attribute and operation detail. Others may focus on the classes, and may not show attributes and operations at all. Still others may focus on the attributes and operations, showing all of the detailed information. In Rose, you can place a class on as many Class diagrams as you'd like. You can then use the following options to show or hide the attribute and operation details.

You can set the defaults for each of these options using the Tools ➤ Options window. The specific instructions for setting the defaults are listed in the following sections.

Showing Attributes

For a given class on a Class diagram, you can:

- ◆ Show all attributes
- ◆ Hide all attributes
- ◆ Show selected attributes
- ◆ Suppress attributes

Suppressing the attributes will not only hide the attributes on the diagram, but will remove the line indicating where the attributes would be located in the class. To illustrate the difference between hiding and suppressing attributes, let's look at an example. Here we have Employee class with hidden attributes:

Here, we have the same class, but the attributes have been suppressed:

There are two ways to change the attribute display options. You can visit each class individually and set the appropriate options. Or, you can change the default attribute display options before you create the Class diagram. When you change the defaults, only new diagrams will be affected.

To show all attributes for a class:

1. Select the desired class on a diagram.

2. Right-click on the class to display the shortcut menu.

3. Select Options ➤ Show All Attributes.

To show selected attributes for a class:

1. Select the desired class on a diagram.

2. Right-click on the class to display the shortcut menu.

3. Select Options ➤ Select Compartment Item.

4. Select the desired attributes in the Edit Compartment window.

OR

1. Select the desired class on a diagram.

2. Select Edit ➤ Compartment.

3. Select the desired attributes in the Edit Compartment window, as shown in Figure 7.15.

FIGURE 7.15

Selecting attributes
in the Edit
Compartment
window

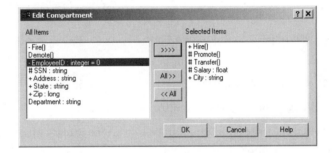

To suppress all attributes for a class on a diagram:

1. Select the desired class.

2. Right-click on the class to display the shortcut menu.

3. Select Options ➤ Suppress Attributes.

To change the default option for showing attributes:

1. Select Tools ➤ Options.

2. Select the Diagram tab.

3. Use the Suppress Attributes and Show All Attributes check boxes to set the default options.

NOTE   When the default is changed, only new diagrams will be affected. Existing Class diagrams will not be changed.

Showing Operations

As with attributes, you have several choices for displaying operations:

◆ Show all operations

◆ Show selected operations

◆ Hide all operations

◆ Suppress operations

In addition, you have the following options:

◆ Display operation name only, which will display the operation name on the Class diagram, but hide the operation's arguments and return type.

◆ Display full operation signature, which will show not only the operation's name, but all of the parameters, parameter data types, and the operation return type.

To show all operations for a class:

1. Select the desired class on a diagram.

2. Right-click on the class to display the shortcut menu.

3. Select Options ➢ Show All Operations.

To show selected operations for a class:

1. Select the desired class on a diagram.

2. Right-click on the class to display the shortcut menu.

3. Select Options ➢ Select Compartment Items.

4. Select the desired operations in the Edit Compartment window.

OR

1. Select the desired class on a diagram.

2. Select Edit ➢ Compartment.

3. Select the desired operations in the Edit Compartment window.

To suppress all operations for a class:

1. Select the desired class on a diagram.

2. Right-click on the class to display the shortcut.

3. Select Options ➢ Suppress Operations.

OR

1. Select the desired class on a diagram.

2. Select Edit ➢ Diagram Object Properties ➢ Suppress Operations.

To show operation signatures on a Class diagram:

1. Select the desired class on a diagram.

2. Right-click on the class to display the shortcut menu.

3. Select Options ➢ Show Operation Signature.

To change the default option for showing operations:

1. Select Tools ➤ Options.

2. Select the Diagram tab.

3. Use the Suppress Operations, Show All Operations, and Show Operation Signatures check boxes to set the default options.

NOTE When the default is changed, only new diagrams will be affected. Existing Class diagrams will not be changed.

Showing Visibility

There are four visibility options for attributes and operations: public, private, protected, and package. In UML, these are represented by icons (+, -, and #) for public, private, and protected, and no icon for implementation.

Rather than using UML notation, you can use Rose notation for attribute and operation visibility. The Rose and UML notations for attribute and operation visibility are listed in Table 7.3.

TABLE 7.3: ROSE AND UML VISIBILITY NOTATIONS

ROSE NOTATION	VISIBILITY	UML NOTATION
	Public	+
	Private	-
	Protected	#
	Package or implementation	<no icon>

You can use either UML or Rose notation for visibility, or you can hide the visibility icons altogether.

To show attribute and operation visibility for a class:

1. Select the desired class on a diagram.

2. Right-click on the class to display the shortcut menu.

3. Select Options ➤ Show Visibility.

To change the default visibility display option:

1. Select the Tools ➤ Options.

2. Select Diagram tab.

3. Use the Show Visibility check box to set the default option.

To switch between Rose and UML visibility notations:

1. Select Tools ➤ Options.

2. Select the Notation tab.

3. Use the Visibility as Icons check box to switch between notations. If the check box is selected, Rose notation will be used. If the check box is not selected, UML notation will be used.

Showing Stereotypes

In Rose, you can show or hide the stereotypes of your operations and attributes. If you show the stereotypes, they will be displayed before the attribute and operation names, enclosed in double angle brackets (<<>>):

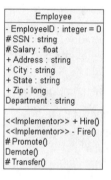

To show attribute and operation stereotypes for a class:

1. Select the desired class on a diagram.

2. Right-click on the class to display the shortcut menu.

3. Select Options ➤ Show Compartment Stereotypes.

To change the default stereotype display option:

1. Select Tools ➤ Options.

2. Select the Diagram tab.

3. Use the Show Stereotypes check box to set the default option.

NOTE   *When you change the default, only new diagrams will be affected. Existing diagrams will not be changed.*

Mapping Operations to Messages

As we discussed above, each message on a Sequence or Collaboration diagram will be mapped to an operation. If your Sequence diagram looks like this:

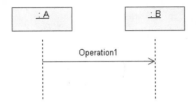

the operation Operation1 will be placed inside Class B. When you first create your Sequence and Collaboration diagrams, you may use message names that are English phrases rather than operation names, as shown in Figure 7.16.

However, as you are identifying operations, you'll want to map each message to the appropriate operation. The Sequence diagram above will be changed to look like Figure 7.17.

Mapping an Operation to a Message on an Interaction Diagram

As you identify operations, go through each message on your Sequence and Collaboration diagrams. Before you generate code, be sure that each message has been mapped to the appropriate operation. Figures 7.16 and 7.17 show a Sequence diagram without and with operation mapping, respectively.

NOTE *Operations can be mapped to messages only if the Interaction Diagram object has been mapped to a class.*

FIGURE 7.16

Sequence diagram without operation mapping

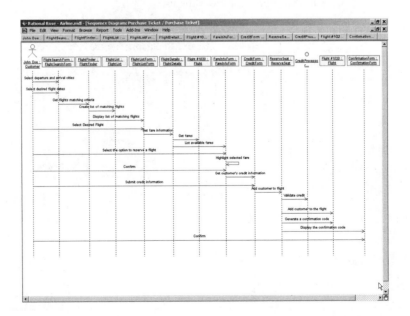

FIGURE 7.17

Sequence diagram
with operation
mapping

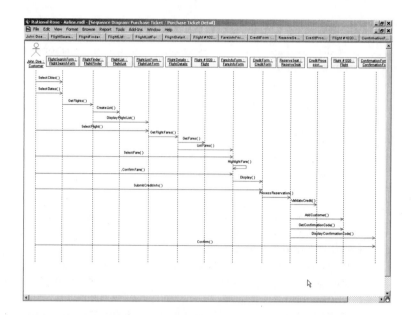

To map a message to an existing operation:

1. Be sure the receiving object (the supplier) has been mapped to a class.

2. Right-click the message in the Sequence or Collaboration diagram.

3. A list of the supplier's operations will appear, as shown in Figure 7.18.

4. Select the operation from the list.

FIGURE 7.18

Mapping a message
to an existing
operation

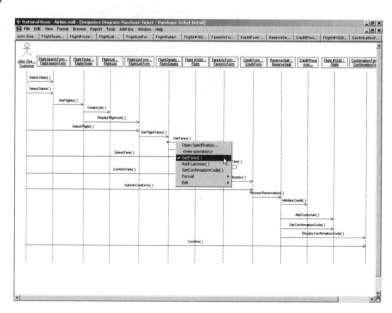

To remove a message's operation mapping:

1. Double-click the message in the Sequence or Collaboration diagram.

2. In the Name field, delete the operation name and enter the new message name.

To create a new operation for the message:

1. Be sure the receiving object (the supplier) has been mapped to a class.

2. Right-click the message in the Sequence or Collaboration diagram.

3. Select <new operation>.

4. Enter the new operation's name and details. (The options available on the operation specification window are discussed in earlier in this chapter.)

5. Click OK to close the operation specification window and add the new operation.

To ensure each message has been mapped to an operation:

1. Select Report ➤ Show Unresolved Messages.

2. Rose will display a list of all messages that have not yet been mapped to operations, as shown in Figure 7.19.

FIGURE 7.19

Show Unresolved
Messages window

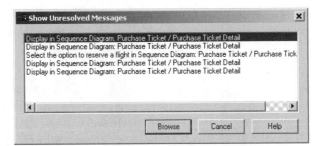

Exercise

In the exercise for Chapter 5, "Object Interaction," we created Sequence and Collaboration diagrams for the "Add Item to Shopping Cart" use case. These diagrams include messages that translate to some of the operations for the classes in our problem. In the Chapter 6 ("Classes and Packages") exercise, we diagrammed the classes on a Class diagram and packaged the classes. In this exercise, we'll add details to the classes, such as the operations for the class, including parameters and return types. We'll also add attributes to the classes.

Problem Statement

Once Karen had a Class diagram with the classes for the "Add Item to Shopping Cart" use case, she began to fill in the details. She chose C++ as a programming language, then proceeded to add operations. She went back and looked at the Sequence and Collaboration diagrams to help define operations. She copied the Sequence and Collaboration diagrams and added more details to them. First, she mapped each object to a class. Then, she mapped each message to an operation. This is the method she used to define her operations.

She also went back to the flow of events to identify attributes. She added the attributes Order Number and Customer Name to the Order class on the Class diagram. She also took a look at the order items. Because there are many order items on a particular order and each has some information and behavior, she decided to model them as a class rather than an attribute of Order. To keep the model consistent, she updated the Sequence diagram, as shown in Figure 7.20.

FIGURE 7.20

Updated Sequence diagram

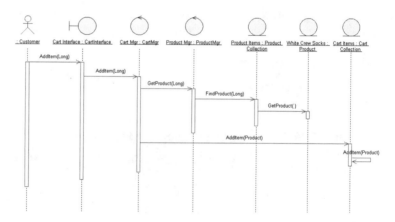

Just then, Bob came in with a requirement change.

"We need to start keeping track of the order date and order fill date. Also, we've got some new suppliers, and the procedure for restocking the inventory has changed quite a bit."

Karen first documented the new date requirements, and took a high-level look at the changes to the restocking procedures. Because she was currently working on the "Enter New Order" use case, she was primarily concerned with how the procedural changes would affect this use case. She was planning to work on the "Restock Inventory" use case next month, and would worry about the details of the restocking procedures then. It turned out that the new procedures, while they drastically affected the "Restock Inventory" use case, didn't affect the "Enter New Order" use case.

The new date requirements necessitated the addition of a couple of new attributes to the Order class. With these added, the model again reflected the most current requirements.

Add Attributes and Operations

Add attributes and operations to the classes using the Add Item to Shopping Cart Class diagram. Add language-specific details to the attributes and operations. Set the options to display all attributes, all operations, and the operation signatures. Set the options to display the visibility using UML notation.

EXERCISE STEPS:

SETUP

1. Select Tools ➤ Options.

2. Select the Diagram tab.

3. Be sure the Show Visibility check box is checked.

4. Be sure the Show Stereotypes check box is checked.

5. Be sure the Show Operation Signatures check box is checked.

6. Be sure the Show All Attributes and Show All Operations check boxes are checked.

7. Be sure the Suppress Attributes and Suppress Operations check boxes are *not* checked.

8. Select the Notation tab.

9. Be sure the Visibility as Icons check box is *not* checked.

CREATE A DETAILED SEQUENCE DIAGRAM

1. Locate the Main Flow Sequence diagram for the "Add Item to Shopping Cart" use case in the browser.

2. Double-click to open the diagram.

3. Press Ctrl+A to select all elements of the diagram

4. Press Ctrl+C to copy all elements of the diagram.

5. Right-click the "Add Item to Shopping Cart" use case in the browser.

6. Select New ➤ Sequence Diagram from the shortcut menu.

7. Name the new sequence diagram **Main Flow: Detailed**.

8. Double-click to open the diagram.

9. Press Ctrl+V to paste all items of the previous diagram into the new diagram.

10. Double-click the CartInterface object to open its specification.

11. Select CartInterface as the class for the object.

12. Click OK to close the specification.

13. Repeat steps 10–12 to set the classes for the following objects:

>   CartMgr : CartMgr
>
>   ProductMgr : ProductMgr
>
>   ProductItems : ProductCollection
>
>   White Crew Socks : Product
>
>   CartItems : CartCollection

Continued on next page

EXERCISE STEPS *(continued)*:

ADD OPERATIONS

1. Locate the Add Item to Shopping Cart Class diagram in the browser.

2. Double-click to open the diagram.

3. Right-click the CartInterface class.

4. Select New Operation from the shortcut menu.

5. Enter the new operation as follows:

   AddItem(ItemNo: Long): Boolean

6. Click outside of the class to stop adding operations.

7. Repeat steps 3–6 to add the following operations to the following classes:

   ◆ To CartMgr, add AddItem(ItemNo: Long): Boolean

   ◆ To ProductMgr, add GetProduct(ItemNo: Long) : Product

   ◆ To CartCollection, add AddItem(NewItem: Product) : Boolean

   ◆ To ProductCollection(FindProduct), add FindProduct(ItemNo: Long) : Product

ADD ATTRIBUTES

1. Right-click the Product class.

2. Select New Attribute from the shortcut menu.

3. Enter the new attribute as follows:

   ProductID: Long

4. Press Enter.

5. Enter the other new attributes as follows:

   ProductDescription: String

   ProductUnitPrice: Double

6. Click outside of the class.

The Class diagram for the Add Item to Shopping Cart Class diagram, after the operations and attributes have been added, should appear as in Figure 7.21.

FIGURE 7.21

Add Item to
Shopping Cart
Class diagram with
attributes and
operations

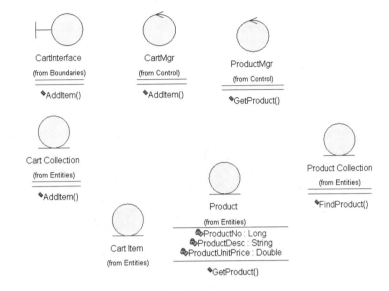

CartInterface
(from Boundaries)

◆AddItem()

CartMgr
(from Control)

◆AddItem()

ProductMgr
(from Control)

◆GetProduct()

Cart Collection
(from Entities)

◆AddItem()

Cart Item
(from Entities)

Product
(from Entities)
🔷ProductNo : Long
🔷ProductDesc : String
🔷ProductUnitPrice : Double

◆GetProduct()

Product Collection
(from Entities)

◆FindProduct()

Summary

In this chapter, we looked at the details of classes, including their attributes and operations. We discussed adding attributes, their names, data types, and default values. We also examined operations, including adding them to the model. We looked at operation details such as the arguments, data types, and return types.

So far, we have looked at classes individually. In the next chapter, we will focus on the relationships between the classes. It is this coordination between classes that lets the application do what it needs to do.

Chapter 8

Relationships

AT THIS POINT, WE'VE looked at classes, their attributes, and their operations. In the Interaction diagrams, we began to look at how classes communicate with one another. Now, we'll focus on the relationships between the classes.

A relationship is a semantic connection between classes. It allows one class to know about the attributes, operations, and relationships of another class. In order for one class to send a message to another on a Sequence or Collaboration diagram, there must be a relationship between the two classes.

In this chapter, we'll take a look at the different types of relationships that can be established between classes and between packages. We'll discuss the implications of each type of relationship and explore how to add the relationship to your Rose model.

- ◆ Adding association, dependency, aggregation, and generalization relationships to a Rose model through a Class diagram

- ◆ Adding relationship names, stereotypes, role names, static relationships, friend relationships, qualifiers, link elements, and constraints

- ◆ Setting multiplicity, export control, and containment

Relationships

This section includes a description of the five types of relationships you can use in a Rose model. We'll also take a look at how to find relationships. Much of the work in finding relationships has already been done by this point in the process. Here, we formally look at relationships and add them to the model. Relationships are shown on Class diagrams.

Types of Relationships

There are five types of relationships you can set up between classes: associations, dependencies, aggregations, realizes relationships, and generalizations. We'll take a close look at each of these types of relationships later in this chapter, but let's talk about them briefly here.

Associations are semantic connections between classes. They are drawn on a Class diagram with a single line, as shown in Figure 8.1.

FIGURE 8.1

Association
relationship

When an association connects two classes, as in the above example, each class can send messages to the other in a Sequence or a Collaboration diagram. Associations can be bidirectional, as shown above, or unidirectional. In UML, bidirectional associations are drawn either with arrowheads on both ends or without arrowheads altogether. Unidirectional associations contain one arrowhead showing the direction of the navigation.

With an association, Rose will place attributes in the classes. For example, if there is an association relationship between a Flight class and a Customer class, Rose would place a Customer attribute inside Flight to let the flight know who the passengers are, and a Flight attribute inside Customer to let the customer know which flight they are on.

Associations can also be labeled to further clarify them. For example, the relationship between a server page and client page is labeled with the stereotype <<build>>, indicating that the server page builds the client page. There are other stereotypes available for associations that we will discuss later in this chapter.

Dependencies also connect two classes, but in a slightly different way than associations. Dependencies are always unidirectional and show that, although one class does not instantiate the other, it does need to send messages to the other class. In other words, although object A does not instantiate and "own" object B, it does need to send messages to object B. Rose will not generate attributes for the classes in a dependency relationship.

Dependency relationships are also needed when a class is needed as a parameter or return type in an operation of a class. Going back to the airline example, if there is a dependency from Flight class to Customer class, a Customer attribute will *not* be created in the Flight class. Dependencies are shown with dashed arrows, as shown in Figure 8.2.

FIGURE 8.2

Dependency
relationship

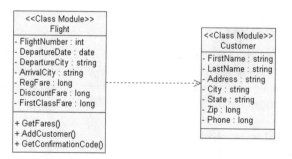

Aggregations are a stronger form of association. An aggregation is a relationship between a whole and its parts. For example, you may have a Car class, as well as an Engine class, a Tire class, and classes for the other parts of a car. In this case, a Car object will be made up of an Engine object, four

Tire objects, and so on. Aggregations are shown as a line with a diamond next to the class representing the whole, as shown in Figure 8.3.

FIGURE 8.3

Aggregation
relationship

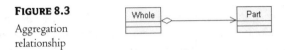

Realizes relationships are used to show the relationship between a class and its interface, between a package and its interface, between a component and its interface, or between a use case and a use case realization. The relationship connects a publicly visible interface (interface class or use case) to the detailed implementation of the interface (class, package, or use case realization). In other words, this relationship helps separate an interface from its implementation.

A realization relationship looks slightly different when using the icon stereotype display for the interface rather than the label stereotype display. Figure 8.4 includes both options.

FIGURE 8.4

Realizes relationship

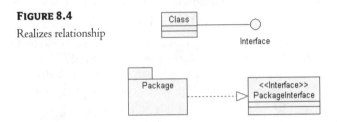

Generalizations are used to show an inheritance relationship between two modeling elements (actors, use cases, classes, or packages). Most object-oriented languages directly support the concept of inheritance. Inheritance allows one class to inherit all of the attributes, operations, relationships, and semantics of another modeling element. In UML, an inheritance relationship is known as a generalization, and is shown as an arrow from the child class to the parent class, as shown in Figure 8.5.

FIGURE 8.5

Generalization
relationship

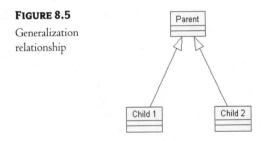

Finding Relationships

To find relationships, you can examine the model elements you've created so far. Much of the relationship information has already been outlined in the Sequence and Collaboration diagrams. Now, you can revisit those diagrams to get association and dependency information. You can then examine your classes to look for aggregations and generalizations.

To find relationships, you can do the following:

1. Begin by examining your Sequence and Collaboration diagrams. If Class A sends a message to Class B on a Sequence or Collaboration diagram, there must be a relationship between them. Typically, the relationships you find with this method are associations or dependencies.

2. Examine your classes and look for any whole-part relationships. Any class that is made up of other classes may participate in an aggregation.

3. Examine your classes to look for generalization relationships. Try to find any class that may have different types. For example, you may have an Employee class. In your company, there are two different types of employees, hourly and salaried. This may indicate that you should have an HourlyEmp class and a SalariedEmp class, each of which inherit from an Employee class. Attributes, operations, and relationships that are common to all employees are placed in the Employee class. Attributes, operations, or relationships that are unique to hourly or salaried employees are placed in the HourlyEmp or SalariedEmp classes.

4. Examine your classes to look for additional generalization relationships. Try to find classes that have a great deal in common. For example, you may have two classes called CheckingAccount and SavingsAccount. Both have similar information and behavior. You can create a third class, called Account, to hold the information and behavior common to a checking and a savings account.

Be cautious of classes with too many relationships. One goal of a well-designed application is to reduce unnecessary relationships in the system. A class with many relationships may need to know about a great many other classes. It can therefore be harder to reuse, and your maintenance effort may also be greater. If any of the other classes change, the original class may be affected.

Associations

An association is a semantic connection between classes. An association allows one class to know about the public attributes and operations of another class. For example, in Figure 8.6, we have a bidirectional association between Flight and Customer.

FIGURE 8.6

Association relationship between the Flight class and the Customer class

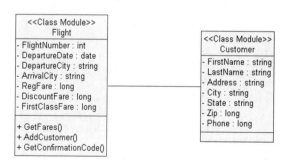

The Flight class knows about the public attributes and operations of Customer, and the Customer class knows about the public attributes and operations of Flight. On a Sequence diagram, therefore, Flight can send messages to Customer, and Customer can send messages to Flight.

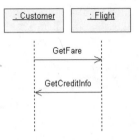

In the example above, the relationship is bidirectional. However, you will want to refine most of your associations to be unidirectional. Unidirectional relationships are easier to build and to maintain, and can help you find classes that can be reused. Let's look at the above example again, but this time the association is unidirectional. Figure 8.7 shows the unidirectional relationship.

FIGURE 8.7

Unidirectional
association
relationship

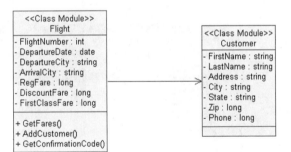

In this case, the Flight class knows about the public attributes and operations of Customer, but Customer does not know about the public attributes and operations of Flight. Messages on a Sequence or Collaboration diagram can be sent by Flight and received by Customer, but cannot be sent by Customer.

You can determine the direction of an association by looking at the Sequence and Collaboration diagrams. If every message on the Interaction diagrams is sent by Flight and received by Customer, there is a unidirectional relationship from Flight to Customer. If there is even one message from Customer to Flight, you will need a bidirectional relationship.

Unidirectional relationships can help you identify classes that are good candidates for reuse. If the association between Flight and Customer is bidirectional, each class needs to know about the other; neither class can, therefore, be reused without the other. But assume instead that there is a unidirectional relationship from Flight to Customer. Flight needs to know about Customer, so it can't be reused without Customer. However, Customer doesn't need to know about Flight, so Customer can be easily reused. Any class that has many unidirectional relationships coming out of it is hard to reuse; any class that has only unidirectional relationships coming into it is easy to reuse, as shown in Figure 8.8.

FIGURE 8.8

Reuse with
unidirectional
associations

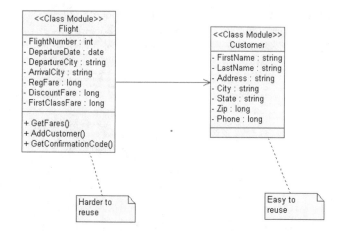

When you generate code for a bidirectional association, Rose will generate attributes in each class. In our Flight and Customer example, Rose will place a Flight attribute inside Customer, and a Customer attribute inside Flight. Figure 8.9 is an example of the code generated for these two classes.

FIGURE 8.9

Code generated for
a bidirectional
association

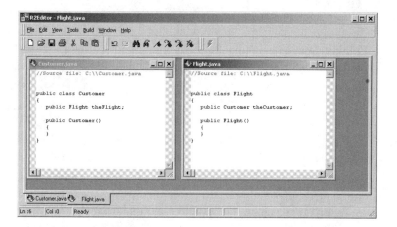

If, instead, we have a unidirectional association, Rose will place a Customer attribute inside Flight, but not a Flight attribute inside Customer. Figure 8.10 is an example of the code generated for a unidirectional association.

Associations can also be reflexive. A reflexive association suggests that one instance of a class is related to other instances of the same class. For example, we may have a Person class. One person can be the parent of one or more other people. Because there are separate instances of Person with a relationship to each other, we have a reflexive association, as shown in Figure 8.11.

FIGURE 8.10

Code generated for a unidirectional association

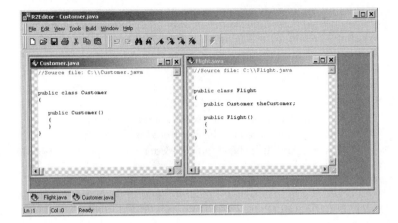

FIGURE 8.11

Reflexive association

Using Web Association Stereotypes

With the inclusion of web modeling, Rose now supports four stereotypes for associations. These are the link, submit, build, and redirect stereotypes.

The link stereotype is used to show a hypertext link between two client pages or from a client page to a server page. It is represented on a Class diagram as a unidirectional association with a stereotype of <<link>>:

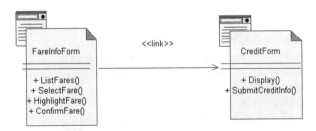

The submit stereotype is used when a form sends the information in its fields to a server page for processing. This submittal of information is shown on a Class diagram as a unidirectional association relationship with a stereotype of <<submit>>.

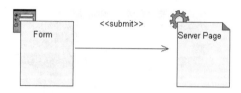

The build stereotype is used when a server page builds a client page. Once the client page has been built, it can be displayed on the client browser. The relationship shows which server page builds which client page. It is shown on a class diagram as a unidirectional relationship with a stereotype of <<build>>:

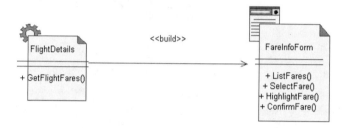

Finally, the redirect stereotype is used to show one page passing processing control to another page. A redirect relationship is shown as a unidirectional association with a stereotype of <<redirect>>:

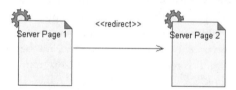

Creating Associations

In Rose, you create associations directly on a Class diagram. The Diagram toolbar includes buttons for creating both unidirectional and bidirectional associations.

If you create a bidirectional association, you can later change it to a unidirectional association by changing its navigability. Later in this chapter, in the "Working with Relationships" section, we will discuss the detailed specifications of an association, including navigability.

To create a bidirectional association on a Class diagram:

1. Select the Association icon from the toolbox.

2. Drag the association line from one class to the other class.

OR

1. Select Tools ➤ Create ➤ Association.

2. Drag the association line from one class to the other class.

To create a unidirectional association on a Class diagram:

1. Select the Unidirectional Association icon from the toolbox.

2. Drag the association line from one class to the other class.

OR

1. Select Tools ➤ Create ➤ Unidirectional Association.

2. Drag the association line from one class to the other class.

To set the navigability of a relationship:

1. Right-click the desired relationship at the end to be navigated.

2. Select Navigable from the menu.

OR

1. Open the desired relationship's specification window.

2. Select the Role Detail tab for the end to be navigated.

3. Change the navigability using the Navigable check box.

To create a reflexive association on a Class diagram:

1. Select the Association icon from the toolbox.

2. Drag the association line from the class to somewhere outside of the class.

3. Release the association line.

4. Drag the association line back into the class.

OR

1. Select Tools ➤ Create ➤ Association.

2. Drag the association line from the class to somewhere outside of the class.

3. Release the association line.

4. Drag the association line back into the class.

To add documentation to an association:

1. Double-click the desired association.

2. Select the General tab.

3. Enter documentation in the Documentation field.

OR

1. Select the desired association.

2. Select Browse ➢ Specification.

3. Select the General tab.

4. Enter documentation in the Documentation field.

To change a relationship to an association:

1. Select the desired relationship.

2. Select Edit ➢ Change Into ➢ Association.

Deleting Associations

There are two ways to delete an association. The first is to delete it from a single diagram. In this case, Rose still knows the association exists, and keeps track of it behind the scenes. Although the association may be deleted from one diagram, it may still exist on other Class diagrams.

The second way to delete an association is to remove it from the entire Rose model. In this case, the relationship is removed from all Class diagrams, and Rose no longer keeps track of it.

To delete an association from the diagram only:

1. Select the desired association.

2. Press the Delete key.

OR

1. Select the desired association.

2. Select Edit ➢ Delete.

NOTE   *Deleting an association from the diagram does not delete it from the model.*

To delete an association from the model:

1. Select the desired association.

2. Press Ctrl+D.

OR

1. Select the desired association.

2. Select Edit ➤ Delete from Model.

OR

1. Open the specification window for either class participating in the relationship.

2. Select the Relations tab.

3. Right-click the relationship.

4. Select Delete from the shortcut menu.

Dependencies

A dependency relationship shows that a class references another class. Therefore, a change in the referenced class specification may impact the using class. When there is a dependency between two classes, Rose does not add any attributes to the classes for the relationship, which is one of the differences between an association and a dependency.

Returning to our example above, assume there is a dependency relationship between Flight and Customer. A dependency relationship is shown as a dashed arrow, as shown in Figure 8.12.

FIGURE 8.12

Dependency relationship

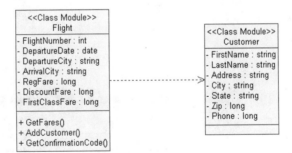

When we generate code for these two classes, attributes will not be added to either class for the relationship, as shown in Figure 8.13. However, any language-specific statements needed to support the relationship will be generated. For example, in C++, the necessary #include statements will be included in the generated code.

The implication here is that Flight will need some other way to know that Customer exists. The direction of the arrow indicates that Flight depends on Customer. In other words, there is a Sequence or Collaboration diagram in which Flight sends a message to Customer. Had there been a regular association between these two, Flight would have a Customer attribute. To send a message to Customer, Flight would just look at its own Customer attribute.

With a dependency, however, Flight won't have a Customer attribute. It therefore has to find out about Customer some other way. There are three ways it can know about Customer. Customer could be global, in which case Flight would know it exists. Or, Customer could be instantiated as a local variable inside an operation of Flight. Finally, Customer could be passed in as a parameter to some operation inside Flight. When there is a dependency, one of these three approaches must be taken.

FIGURE 8.13

Code generated for a dependency relationship

Although we are now at the detailed coding level, this decision may affect the model. We may need to add an argument to an operation of Flight.

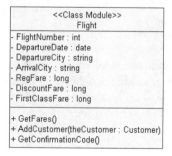

The second difference between an association and a dependency lies in the direction. Associations can be bidirectional, but dependencies are unidirectional. Dependencies are also used for relationships between packages and between components. This will be discussed later in this chapter.

Creating Dependencies

After you've added associations, you may want to revisit them to see if any should be dependencies instead. If so, you can change the relationship from an association to a dependency using the method outlined below. (This is preferred if you have an association displayed in several diagrams, because Rose will change the association globally.)

To create a new dependency, you can use the Dependency icon on the Class Diagram toolbar.

To create a dependency on a Class diagram:

1. Select the Dependency icon from the toolbox.

2. Click the class to be dependent.

3. Drag the dependency line to the other class.

OR

1. Select Tools ➤ Create ➤ Dependency.

2. Click the class to be dependent.

3. Drag the dependency line to the other class.

To add documentation to a dependency:

1. Double-click the desired dependency.

2. Select the General tab.

3. Enter documentation in the Documentation field.

OR

1. Select the desired dependency.

2. Select Browse ➤ Specification.

3. Select the General tab.

4. Enter documentation in the Documentation field.

To change a relationship to a dependency on a Class diagram:

1. Select the desired relationship.

2. Select Edit ➤ Change Into ➤ Uses Dependency.

Deleting Dependencies

As with associations, there are two ways to delete a dependency. You can remove it from a single Class diagram or from the entire model. The following are the procedures for deleting a dependency.

To delete a dependency from the diagram:

1. Select the desired dependency.

2. Press the Delete key.

OR

1. Select the desired dependency.

2. Select Edit ➤ Delete.

NOTE *Deleting a dependency from the diagram does not delete it from the model.*

To delete a dependency from the model:

1. Select the desired dependency.

2. Press Ctrl+D.

OR

1. Select the desired dependency.

2. Select Edit ➤ Delete from Model.

OR

1. Open the specification window for either class participating in the relationship.

2. Select the Relations tab.

3. Right-click the relationship.

4. Select Delete from the shortcut menu.

Package Dependencies

Dependencies can be drawn between packages as well as classes. A package dependency, like a class dependency, is drawn as a dashed arrow. Figure 8.14 is an example of a package dependency.

A package dependency from package A to package B suggests that some class in package A has a unidirectional relationship to some class in package B. In other words, some class in A needs to know about some class in B.

FIGURE 8.14

Package dependency

This has reuse implications. If our dependencies look like this, package A depends on package B. Therefore, we can't just pick up package A and reuse it in another application. We would also have to pick up B and reuse it. Package B, on the other hand, is easy to reuse because it doesn't depend on anything else.

You can find package dependencies by examining the relationships on your Class diagram. If two classes from different packages have a relationship, their packages must have a relationship as well.

As you are creating package dependencies, try to avoid circular dependencies whenever possible. A circular dependency looks like Figure 8.15.

FIGURE 8.15

Circular dependency

This suggests that some class in A needs to know about some class in B, while some class in B needs to know about some class in A. In this case, neither package can be easily reused, and a change to one package may affect the other. We've lost some of the benefits of packaging classes with this approach—the packages are too interdependent. To break circular dependencies, you can split apart one package into two. In our example, we can take the classes in B that A depends on, and move them to another package we'll call C. Now our package dependencies look like this:

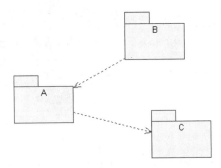

Creating Package Dependencies

As you identify package dependencies, you can add them to your Rose model through a Class diagram. Typically, you will have one Class diagram which displays all of the packages and the relationships between them. As with class dependencies, you use the Dependency toolbar button to draw the relationships.

To create a package dependency on a Class diagram:

1. Select the Dependency icon from the toolbox.

2. Drag the dependency line from the dependent package to the other package.

OR

1. Select Tools ➤ Create ➤ Dependency.

2. Drag the dependency line from the dependent package to the other package.

Deleting Package Dependencies

As with a class dependency, there are two ways to delete a package dependency—from a single Class diagram or from the entire model.

If you delete a package dependency, but classes from the two packages still have relationships to each other, you will have difficulty generating code. You can use the Report ➤ Show Access Violations option to see if this has happened.

To delete a package dependency from a Class diagram:

1. Select the desired package dependency.

2. Press the Delete key.

OR

1. Select the desired package dependency.

2. Select Edit ➤ Delete.

Aggregations

An aggregation is a stronger form of association. An aggregation is a relationship between a whole and its parts. For example, a FlightList might be made up of Flights. In UML, an aggregation is shown as a line connecting the two classes, with a diamond next to the class representing the whole, as shown in Figure 8.16.

FIGURE 8.16

Aggregation
relationship

One class may have several aggregation relationships with other classes. For example, a Car class might have relationships to its many parts.

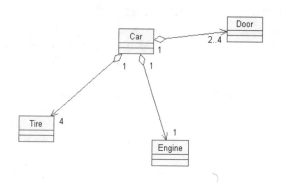

Like associations, aggregations can be reflexive, as shown in Figure 8.17. A reflexive aggregation suggests that one instance of a class is made up of one or more other instances of the same class. For example, when cooking, you may combine some ingredients, which form ingredients for other things. In other words, each ingredient can be made up of other ingredients.

FIGURE 8.17

Reflexive aggregation relationship

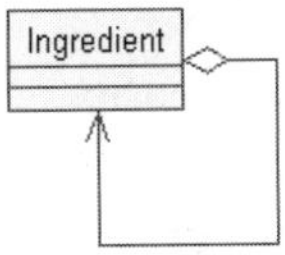

When you generate code for an aggregation, Rose will generate attributes to support the aggregation. In the Car example, the Car class will have attributes for the door, engine, tire, and all of the other parts in the aggregation relationship.

Creating Aggregations

Aggregations are created on the Class diagrams. To create an aggregation, you can use the Aggregation button on the Class Diagram toolbar.

To create an aggregation on a Class diagram:

1. Select the Unidirectional Aggregation icon from the toolbox.

2. Drag the aggregation line from the whole class to the part class.

OR

1. Select Tools ➢ Create ➢ Aggregation.

2. Drag the aggregation line from the whole class to the part class.

To create a reflexive aggregation on a Class diagram:

1. Select the Unidirectional Aggregation icon from the toolbox.

2. Drag the aggregation line from the class to somewhere outside of the class.

3. Release the aggregation line.

4. Drag the aggregation line back into the class.

OR

1. Select Tools ➢ Create ➢ Aggregation.

2. Drag the aggregation line from the class to somewhere outside of the class.

3. Release the aggregation line.

4. Drag the aggregation line back into the class.

To add documentation to the aggregation:

1. Double-click the desired aggregation.

2. Select the General tab.

3. Enter documentation in the Documentation field.

OR

1. Select the desired aggregation.

2. Select Browse ➢ Specification.

3. Select the General tab.

4. Enter documentation in the Documentation field.

To change a relationship to an aggregation on a Class diagram:

1. Select the desired relationship.

2. Select Edit ➢ Change Into ➢ Aggregation.

OR

1. Open the relationship specification window for the desired relationship.

2. Select the Role Detail tab.

3. Select the Aggregate check box.

Deleting Aggregations

You can delete an aggregation either from a single Class diagram or from the entire model. Here we list the procedures for both.

To delete an aggregation from the diagram:

1. Select the desired aggregation.

2. Press the Delete key.

OR

1. Select the desired aggregation.

2. Select Edit ➢ Delete.

NOTE *Deleting an aggregation from the diagram does not delete it from the model.*

To delete an aggregation from the model:

1. Select the desired aggregation.

2. Press Ctrl+D.

OR

1. Select the desired aggregation.

2. Select Edit ➢ Delete from Model.

OR

1. Open the specification window for either class participating in the relationship.

2. Select the Relations tab.

3. Right-click the relationship.

4. Select Delete from the shortcut menu.

Generalizations

A generalization is an inheritance relationship between two model elements such as classes, actors, use cases, and packages. It allows one class to inherit the public and protected attributes and operations of another class. For example, we may have the relationship shown in Figure 8.18.

FIGURE 8.18

Generalization
relationship

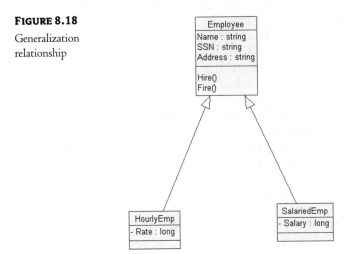

In this example, we have two types of employees: hourly and salaried, both of which inherit from the Employee class. The Employee class is known as the *superclass*, and the HourlyEmp and SalariedEmp classes are known as the *subclasses*. The arrow points from the subclass to the superclass.

The elements that are common to both types are placed in the Employee class. Both HourlyEmp and SalariedEmp inherit the Name, Address, and SSN attributes of the Employee class and the Hire() and Fire() operations of the Employee class.

Each subclass can have its own unique attributes, operations, and relationships in addition to those it inherits. For example, only hourly employees have an hourly rate, and only salaried employees have a salary.

Generalization relationships can save a great deal of time and effort in both development and maintenance. In the above example, you don't need to program and maintain two separate copies of the Hire() operation (one in HourlyEmp and one in SalariedEmp). Instead, you can create and maintain one copy of the operation. Any changes you make to the operation will be automatically inherited by HourlyEmp and SalariedEmp, and any other subclasses of Employee.

When you are defining your generalizations, you can build your inheritance structure either from the top down or the bottom up. To build the structure from the top down, look for classes that might have different types. For example, you would start with the Employee class and soon realize that there are different types of employees. To build the structure from the bottom up, look for classes with commonality. Here, you would start with the HourlyEmp and SalariedEmp classes and then realize that they are similar. You would then create an Employee class to hold the common elements.

Be careful not to create an inheritance structure that isn't maintainable. A hierarchy with too many layers can become very difficult to maintain. Every change toward the top of the structure will ripple down through the hierarchy to the classes below. While this can be an advantage, it can also make change analysis and control even more essential. In some languages, too many layers can also slow down the application.

Creating Generalizations

As you discover generalization relationships, you can add them to your Rose model using a Class diagram. Frequently, an organization will create a single Class diagram or two that are dedicated to the inheritance structure. These Class diagrams will typically show only limited attribute or operation information.

As you add generalizations, you may need to move some of the attributes and operations. For example, you may start with the HourlyEmp and SalariedEmp classes, each of which has an attribute called Address, and now, you want to move the Address attribute up the structure to the Employee class. In the browser, you can drag the Address attribute from either the HourlyEmp or the Salaried-Emp class to the Employee class. Be sure to remember to remove the other copy of Address from HourlyEmp or SalariedEmp.

To create a generalization on a Class diagram:

1. Select the Generalization icon from the toolbox.

2. Drag the generalization line from the subclass to the superclass.

OR

1. Select Tools ➤ Create ➤ Generalization.

2. Drag the generalization line from the subclass to the superclass.

To add documentation to a generalization:

1. Double-click the desired generalization.

2. Select the General tab.

3. Enter documentation in the Documentation field.

OR

1. Select the desired generalization.

2. Select Browse ➢ Specification.

3. Select the General tab.

4. Enter documentation in the Documentation field.

To change a relationship to a generalization:

1. Select the desired relationship.

2. Select Edit ➢ Change Into ➢ Generalization.

Deleting Generalizations

As with the other relationships, you can delete a generalization from a single diagram or from the model. If you delete a generalization from the entire model, keep in mind that the attributes, operations, and relationships of the superclass will no longer be inherited by the subclass. Therefore, if the subclass needs those attributes, operations, or relationships, they will have to be added to the subclass.

To delete a generalization from the diagram:

1. Select the desired generalization.

2. Press the Delete key.

OR

1. Select the desired generalization.

2. Select Edit ➢ Delete.

NOTE   *Deleting a generalization from the diagram does not delete it from the model.*

To delete a generalization from the model:

1. Select the desired generalization.

2. Press Ctrl+D.

OR

1. Select the desired generalization.

2. Select Edit ➢ Delete from Model.

OR

1. Open the specification window for either class participating in the relationship.

2. Select the Relations tab.

3. Right-click the relationship.

4. Select Delete from the shortcut menu.

Working with Relationships

In this section, we'll take a look at the detailed specifications of the relationships in Rose. In your model, you can add things like association names, role names, and qualifiers to specify why the relationship exists.

Before you generate code, you should specify the relationship multiplicity; otherwise Rose will provide a default. Most of the other specifications we present in this section, however, are optional. Rose will notify you if a required specification has not been set when you attempt to generate code.

Setting Multiplicity

Multiplicity indicates how many instances of one class are related to a single instance of another class at a given point in time. For example, if we're looking at a course registration system for a university, we may have classes called Course and Student. There is a relationship between them; courses have students and students have courses. The questions answered by the multiplicity are "How many courses can a student take at one time?" and "How many students can be enrolled in a single course at one time?"

Because the multiplicity answers both questions, the multiplicity indicators are included at both ends of the relationship. In the course registration example, we decide that each student can be enrolled in 0 to 4 classes, and each course can have 10 to 20 students. On a Class diagram, this would be shown as in Figure 8.19.

FIGURE 8.19

Relationship multiplicity

In this figure, the 0..4 means that each student can be enrolled in 0 through 4 classes, and the 10..20 means that each class can have 10 to 20 students.

Keep in mind that the multiplicity settings will let you know whether the relationship is optional. In our example above, a student can take from 0 to 4 courses at any one time. Therefore, someone is still considered a student if they have taken a semester off. Had the multiplicity been 1..4 instead, every student would be required to take at least 1 course per semester. The multiplicity, therefore, implements business rules such as "every student must take at least one course per semester."

Typically, multiplicity between forms, screens, or windows will be 0..1 on each side of the relationship. Although this doesn't always hold true, this multiplicity would indicate that each form can exist independently of the other.

UML notations for multiplicity are as follows:

Multiplicity	Meaning
*	Many
0	Zero
1	One
0..*	Zero or more
1..*	One or more
0..1	Zero or one
1..1	Exactly one

Or, you can enter your own multiplicity, using one of the following formats:

Format	Meaning
<number>	Exactly <number>
<number 1>..<number 2>	Between <number 1> and <number 2>
<number>..n	<number> or more
<number 1>,<number 2>	<number 1> or <number 2>
<number 1>, <number 2>..<number 3>	Exactly <number 1> or between <number 2> and <number 3>
<number 1>..<number 2>, <number 3>..<number 4>	Between <number 1> and <number 2> or between <number 3> and <number 4>

To set relationship multiplicity:

1. Right-click the desired relationship on one end.
2. Select Multiplicity from the shortcut menu.
3. Select the desired multiplicity.
4. Repeat steps 1–3 for the other end of the relationship.

OR

1. Open the desired relationship's specification window.
2. Select the Role Detail tab for one end.
3. Change the multiplicity using the cardinality field.
4. Repeat steps 1–3 for the other end of the relationship.

Using Relationship Names

Relationships can be refined using relationship names or role names. A relationship name is usually a verb or verb phrase that describes why the relationship exists. For example, we may have an association between a Person class and a Company class. From this, though, we might ask these questions: Why does this relationship exist? Is the person a customer of the company, an employee, or an owner? We can name the relationship *employs* to specify why the relationship exists. Figure 8.20 is an example of a relationship name.

FIGURE 8.20

Relationship name

Relationship names are optional, and are typically used only when the reason for the relationship is not obvious. Relationship names are shown along the relationship line.

In Rose, you can also set the relationship direction. In the example above, we can say that the company employs the person, but can't say that the person employs the company. You can set the name direction in the relationship specification window.

To set the relationship name:

1. Select the desired relationship.

2. Type in the desired name.

OR

1. Open the desired relationship's specification window.

2. Select the General tab.

3. Enter the name in the Name field.

To set the name direction:

1. Open the desired relationship's specification window.

2. Select the Detail tab.

3. Set the name direction using the Name Direction field.

Using Stereotypes

Like other model elements, you can assign a stereotype to a relationship. Stereotypes are used to classify relationships. In particular, when modeling web applications, you may want to set the stereotypes of the association relationships. As we discussed earlier in this chapter, there are four stereotypes in the Rose Web Modeler add-in: a link relationship, a submit relationship, a build relationship, and a redirect relationship. A link relationship is used to show one page that contains a hyperlink to another. A submit relationship shows a form submitting information to a server page. A build relationship is used to show a server page building a client page. Finally, a redirect relationship shows how processing control is passed from one page to another.

Stereotypes are shown along the association line and are enclosed in double angle brackets (<<>>). To set the relationship stereotype, you can use the General tab of the relationship specification window, as shown in Figure 8.21.

FIGURE 8.21

Relationship specification window

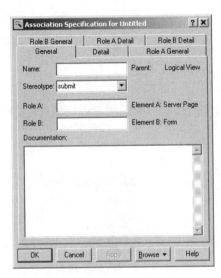

To set a relationship stereotype:

1. Open the desired relationship's specification window.

2. Select the General tab.

3. Enter the stereotype in the Stereotype field.

Using Roles

Role names can be used instead of relationship names in associations or aggregations to describe the reason the relationship exists. Returning to our Person and Company example, we can say that a Person playing the role of an employee is related to a Company. Role names are typically nouns or noun phrases, and are shown next to the class playing the role. Typically, you would use either a relationship name or a role name, but not both. Like relationship names, role names are optional, and are only used when the purpose of the relationship is not obvious. Figure 8.22 shows an example of roles.

FIGURE 8.22

Roles in a relationship

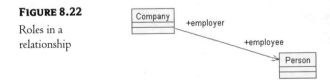

You can add documentation to a role using the relationship specification window. Any documentation you add to a role will be generated as a comment when you generate code. To view the role on the diagram, right-click the relationship and select the Role Name option, as shown in Figure 8.23.

To set a role name:

1. Right-click the desired association on the end to be named.

2. Select Role Name from the shortcut menu.

3. Type in the role name.

FIGURE 8.23

Setting role
documentation

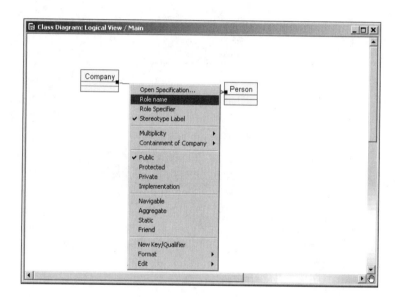

OR

1. Open the desired association's specification window.

2. Select the Role General tab for the role to be named.

3. Enter the role name in the Role field.

To add role documentation:

1. Open the desired association's specification window.

2. Select the Role General tab for the desired role.

3. Enter the documentation in the Documentation field.

Setting Export Control

In an association relationship, Rose will create attributes when you generate code. The visibility of the generated attributes is set through the Export Control field. As with other attributes, there are four visibility options:

Public   Indicates that the attribute will be visible to all other classes

Private   Indicates that the attribute is not visible to any other class

Protected   Suggests that the attribute is visible only to the class and its subclasses

Package or implementation   Means that the attribute is visible to all other classes in the same package

In a bidirectional relationship, you can set the export control of two attributes, one created at each end of the relationship. In a unidirectional relationship, only one will need to be set. The export control can be set using the Role A General and Role B General tabs of the relationship specification window.

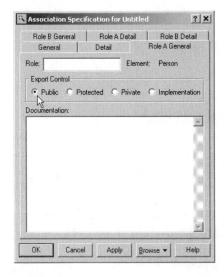

To set export control for a role:

1. Right-click the desired role's name.

2. Select Export Control from the shortcut menu.

OR

1. Open the desired relationship's specification window.

2. Select the Role General tab for the desired role.

3. Set the export control to Public, Protected, Private, or Implementation.

Using Static Relationships

As we mentioned earlier, Rose will generate attributes for association and aggregation relationships. A static attribute is one that is shared by all instances of a class. You use the Static field to determine whether or not the generated attributes will be static.

If you set one of the roles to be static, the associated attribute that is generated will be static. On the Class diagram, the static role will appear with a dollar sign ($) in front of it, as shown in Figure 8.24.

To classify an association as static:

1. Right-click the desired end of the association to be static.

2. Select Static from the pop-up menu.

OR

1. Open the desired association's specification window.

2. Select the Detail tab for the role to be static.

3. Select the Static check box.

FIGURE 8.24

Static role

Using Friend Relationships

A friend relationship indicates that the Client class has access to the non-public attributes and operations of the Supplier class. You can set the friend property for an association, aggregation, dependency, or generalization. The source code for the Supplier class will include logic to allow the Client class to have friend visibility.

For example, say we have a unidirectional association from a Person class to a Company class, and we've set the Friend check box for the relationship. When we generate C++ code, the Company .h file will include the line "friend class Person." This suggests that the Person class has access to the non-public parts of the Company class.

To classify a relationship as a friend:

1. Right-click the appropriate end of the desired relationship.

2. Select Friend from the pop-up menu.

OR

1. Open the desired relationship's specification window.

2. Select the Role Detail tab for the appropriate end.

3. Select the Friend check box.

Setting Containment

The Containment field determines whether the generated attributes of an aggregation will be contained by value or by reference. In an aggregation, the whole class will have attributes added for each of the part classes. Whether these attributes are by value or by reference is set here.

A by-value attribute suggests that the whole and the part are created and destroyed at the same time. For example, if there is a by-value aggregation between a Window class and a Button class, the Window and the Button are created and destroyed at the same time. In UML, a by-value aggregation is shown with a filled diamond, as shown in Figure 8.25.

FIGURE 8.25

By-value aggregation

A by-reference aggregation suggests that the whole and the part are created and destroyed at different times. If we have an EmployeeList class that is made up of Employees, a by-reference aggregation would suggest that the Employee may or may not be around in memory, and the EmployeeList may or may not be around in memory. If they are both there, they are related via an aggregation. The Employee and EmployeeList are created and destroyed at different times. A by-reference aggregation is shown with a clear diamond, as in Figure 8.26.

To set containment:

1. Right-click the desired end of the association to set containment.

2. Select Containment from the pop-up menu.

3. Select the containment as By Reference, By Value, or Unspecified.

FIGURE 8.26

By-reference aggregation

OR

1. Open the desired relationship's specification window.

2. Select the Role Detail tab for the desired role.

3. Select the containment as By Reference, By Value, or Unspecified, as shown in Figure 8.27.

FIGURE 8.27

Setting containment

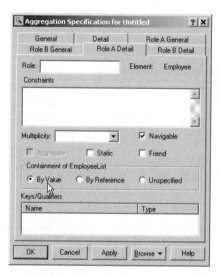

Using Qualifiers

A qualifier is used to reduce the scope of an association. For example, we may have an association between a Person class and a Company class. Suppose we want to say that for a given value of Person ID, there are exactly two related companies. We can add a qualifier called Person ID to the Person class. The diagram would look like Figure 8.28.

FIGURE 8.28

Using a qualifier

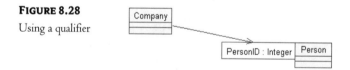

To add a qualifier:

1. Right-click the desired association at the end to add a qualifier.

2. Select New Key/Qualifier from the pop-up menu.

3. Enter the new qualifier's name and type.

OR

1. Open the desired association's specification window.

2. Select the Role Detail tab for the desired role.

3. Right-click the Keys/Qualifiers box.

4. Select Insert from the pop-up menu.

5. Enter the new qualifier's name and type.

To delete a qualifier:

1. Open the desired association's specification window.

2. Select the Role Detail tab for the desired role.

3. Right-click the qualifier to be deleted.

4. Select Delete from the pop-up menu.

Using Link Elements

A *link element*, also known as an association class, is a place to store attributes related to an association. For example, we may have two classes, Student and Course. Where should the attribute Grade be placed? If it is inside the Student class, we will need to add an attribute to Student for every course the student is enrolled in. This can clutter the Student class. If we put the attribute in Course, we will need an additional attribute for every student enrolled in the course.

To get around this problem, we can create an association class. The attribute Grade, because it's more related to the link between a student and a course than to each individually, can be placed in this new class. UML notation for an association class is shown in Figure 8.29.

FIGURE 8.29

Link element
(association class)

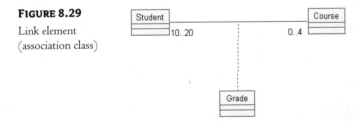

To set a link element for the relationship:

1. Open the desired relationship's specification window.

2. Select the Detail tab.

3. Set the link element using the Link Element field.

Using Constraints

A constraint is some condition that must be true. In Rose, you can set constraints for the relationship or for a single role. Any constraints you enter will be generated as comments in the generated code.

To set a relationship constraint:

1. Open the desired relationship's specification window, as shown in Figure 8.30.

2. Select the Detail tab.

3. Enter constraints in the Constraints field.

To add constraints to a role:

1. Open the desired relationship's specification window.

2. Select the Role Detail tab for the desired role.

3. Enter the constraints in the Constraints field, as shown in Figure 8.31.

Exercise

In this exercise, we will add the relationships between the classes that participate in the "Add Item to Shopping Cart" use case.

Problem Statement

Once Karen had added the attributes and operations to the classes, she was nearly ready to generate code. First, though, she had to take a look at the relationships between the classes.

She examined the Sequence diagrams for any existing messages between two objects, which indicated the need for a relationship between the classes. Any classes that communicated in the Sequence diagram needed a relationship on the Class diagram. Once she identified the relationships, she added them to the model.

Adding Relationships

Add relationships to the classes that participate in the "Add Item to Shopping Cart" use case.

EXERCISE STEPS:

SETUP

1. Locate the Add Item to Shopping Cart Class diagram in the browser.

2. Double-click to open the diagram.

3. Look for a Unidirectional Association button on the Diagram toolbar. If one does not exist, continue through step 5. Otherwise, skip to the next section of the exercise.

4. Right-click the Diagram toolbar and select Customize from the shortcut menu.

5. Add the button labeled Creates a Unidirectional Association to the toolbar.

ADD ASSOCIATIONS

1. Select the Unidirectional Association toolbar button.

2. Draw an association from the CartInterface class to the CartMgr class.

3. Repeat steps 1 and 2 to draw the following associations:

   ◆ From CartMgr to ProductMgr

   ◆ From ProductMgr to ProductCollection

   ◆ From ProductCollection to Product

   ◆ From CartMgr to CartCollection

   ◆ From CartCollection to CartItem

Continued on next page

EXERCISE STEPS *(continued)*:

4. Right-click the unidirectional association between the CartInterface class and the CartMgr class, near the CartInterface class.

5. Select Multiplicity ➤ Zero or One from the shortcut menu.

6. Right-click the other end of the unidirectional association.

7. Select Multiplicity ➤ Zero or One from the shortcut menu.

8. Repeat steps 4–7 to add the remaining multiplicity to the diagram, as shown in Figure 8.32.

9. Right-click the unidirectional association between the CartCollection class and CartItem class, near the CartCollection class.

10. Select Aggregate from the shortcut menu.

11. Repeat steps 9 and 10 to add an aggregation between the ProductCollection class and Product class.

FIGURE 8.32

Associations for the "Add Item to Shopping Cart" use case

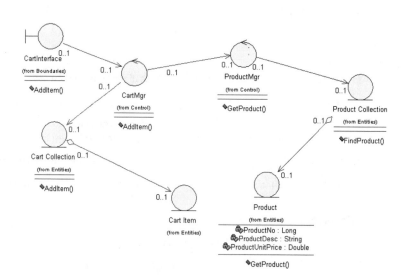

Summary

In this chapter, we discussed the different types of relationships in UML: associations, dependencies, aggregations, and generalizations. Each of these types of relationships can be added to a Rose model through a Class diagram.

Once the relationships have been added, you can add various details, such as relationship names, role names, qualifiers, and multiplicity. In the next chapter, we'll take a look at object behavior. We'll focus on a single class and examine the various states in which the class can exist and the ways the class transitions from one state to another.

Chapter 9

Object Behavior

WE'VE LOOKED AT CLASSES and their relationships; we'll now examine the life of a single object. A given object can exist in one or more states. For example, an employee can be employed, fired, on probation, on leave, or retired. An Employee object may behave differently in each of these states.

In this chapter, we discuss Statechart diagrams, which include information about the various states in which an object can exist, how the object transitions from one state to another, and how the object behaves differently in each of the states.

- ◆ Creating a Statechart diagram

- ◆ Adding activities, entry actions, exit actions, events, and state histories to states

- ◆ Adding events, arguments, guard conditions, actions, and send events to transitions

- ◆ Adding start, stop, and nested states

Statechart Diagrams

A Statechart diagram shows the life cycle of a single object, from the time that it is created until it is destroyed. These diagrams are a good way to model the dynamic behavior of a class. In a typical project, you do not create a Statechart diagram for every class. In fact, many projects do not use them at all. Figure 9.1 is an example of a Statechart diagram for our Flight class.

In this chapter, we discuss the different pieces of notation in this diagram. Briefly, however, we can read the diagram as follows:

A flight begins in a Tentative state. Someone reviews the schedule to determine whether or not to include the flight. If the schedule is rejected, the flight is deleted and no further action can be taken. If the schedule is approved, the flight moves into a Scheduled status. The flight schedule is posted to the Internet, and as soon as it is 60 days or less before the flight, the flight becomes open. We can add and remove passengers from the flight, but as soon as the last seat is sold, the flight is full. If someone then cancels their reservation, the flight can become open again. Ten minutes before takeoff, the flight is closed for reservations. If the plane has not yet arrived, the flight is delayed until either the plane arrives or it has been four hours. After four hours, the flight is canceled. If the plane has arrived, but there are fewer than 50 people, the flight is canceled. If the flight is canceled, the airline will find an alternate flight for the passengers. If the plane does arrive, it takes off and lands, which is the conclusion of this particular flight.

FIGURE 9.1

Statechart diagram for a Flight class

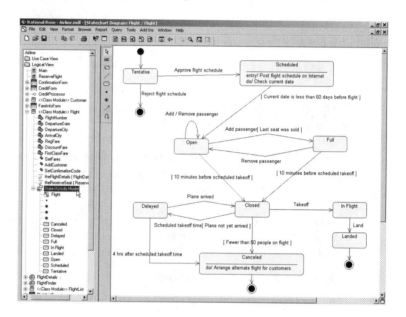

If you have a class that has some significant dynamic behavior, it can be helpful to create a Statechart diagram for it. A class with significant dynamic behavior is one that can exist in many states. In our airline example, a flight may be scheduled, open, full, or canceled.

To decide whether a class has significant dynamic behavior, begin by looking at its attributes. Consider how an instance of the class might behave differently with different values in an attribute. If you have an attribute called Status, this can be a good indicator of various states. How does the object behave differently as different values are placed in this attribute?

You can also examine the relationships of a class. Look for any relationships with a zero in the multiplicity. Zeroes indicate that the relationship is optional. Does an instance of the class behave differently when the relationship does or does not exist? If it does, you may have multiple states. For example, let's look at a relationship between a person and a company. If there is a relationship, the person is in an employed state. If there is no relationship, the person may be fired or retired.

In Rose, no source code is generated from a Statechart diagram. These diagrams serve to document the dynamic behavior of a class so that developers and analysts will have a clear understanding of the behavior. The developers are ultimately responsible for implementing the logic outlined in the diagram. As with the other UML diagrams, Statechart diagrams give the team a chance to discuss and document the logic before it is coded.

Creating a Statechart Diagram

In Rose, you can create one or more Statechart diagrams per class. In the browser, the Statechart diagrams appear underneath the class. The Rose icon for a Statechart diagram in the browser is shown below:

To create a Statechart diagram:

1. Right-click the desired class in the browser.

2. Select New ➤ Statechart Diagram from the pop-up menu.

Rose will create an entry under the class in the browser called State/Activity Model. Underneath this entry will be a new Statechart diagram called NewDiagram. You can create additional Statechart or activity diagrams for the class by right-clicking State/Activity Model in the browser and selecting New ➤ Statechart Diagram or New ➤ Activity Diagram.

Adding States

A *state* is one of the possible conditions in which an object may exist. You can examine two areas to determine the state of an object: the values of the attributes and the relationships to other objects. Consider the different values that can be placed in the attributes and the state of the object if a relationship does or does not exist. Our Flight class, for example, might have an attribute called NumPassengers. Consider how the flight behaves depending upon the value of NumPassengers. If there are 0 passengers, should the flight be able to leave at all? What if there are 500 scheduled passengers on a flight that holds 150? What if there are only 50? 10? 5? At what point does the flight go ahead, and at what point is it canceled?

We can also look at the attribute DepartureDate. If the departure date is three years in the future, do we let passengers reserve the flight? We might want to put the flight in a Scheduled status until it's a little closer to the departure date. On the other hand, we may want to open the flight immediately, even if it doesn't depart for three years. The business requirements will dictate the system behavior.

Examining attributes like these can help us determine what some of the states of the object might be. So far, we have states called Full, Open, and Scheduled. We may even want to include an Overbooked state if we can put 500 reservations on a 150-person flight.

We can also look at the relationships between the flight and other objects to look for states. If there is a relationship to a Schedule object, the flight has been scheduled. If there is no relationship to a Pilot object, we will put the flight into the Canceled state.

As with other Rose elements, you can add documentation to a state. However, because code is not generated from these diagrams, comments will not be inserted into generated code for state documentation.

In UML, a state is shown as a rounded rectangle:

```
Full
```

To add a state:

1. Select State from the toolbox toolbar.

2. Click on the Statechart diagram where the state should appear.

OR

1. Select Tools ➤ Create ➤ State.

2. Click on the Statechart diagram where the state should appear.

To add documentation to a state:

1. Double-click the desired state to open the state specification window.

2. Select the General tab.

3. Enter documentation in the Documentation field.

OR

1. Select the desired state.

2. Select Browse ➤ Specification.

3. Select the General tab.

4. Enter documentation in the Documentation field.

Adding State Details

While an object is in a particular state, there may be some activity that it performs. A report may be generated, some calculation may occur, or an event may be sent to another object. For example, while a flight is in the Scheduled state, it may check the current date periodically to see when it is 60 days before the flight date. As soon as it is 60 days before, the flight will be moved to the Open state. In Rose, you can include this type of information in the model through the state specification window.

There are five types of information you can include for a state: an activity, an entry action, an exit action, an event, or a state history. Let's look at each of these in the context of our example. Figure 9.2 is the Statechart diagram for the Flight class.

ACTIVITY

An *activity* is some behavior that an object carries out while it is in a particular state. For example, when an account is in the Closed state, the account holder's signature card is pulled. When a flight is in a Canceled state, the airline tries to find alternate flights for its customers. An activity is an interruptible behavior. It may run to completion while the object is in that state, or it may be interrupted by the object moving to another state.

An activity is shown inside the state itself, preceded by the word "do" and a slash.

```
┌─────────────────────────────────────────┐
│                 Canceled                 │
├─────────────────────────────────────────┤
│  do/ Arrange alternate flight for customers │
└─────────────────────────────────────────┘
```

FIGURE 9.2

Statechart diagram
for Flight class

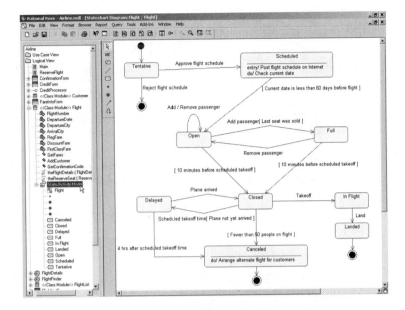

ENTRY ACTION

An *entry action* is a behavior that occurs while the object is transitioning into the state. Using our flight example, as soon as a flight becomes scheduled, the system posts the schedule to the Internet. This happens while the flight is transitioning into the Scheduled state. Unlike an activity, an entry action is considered to be noninterruptible. While the posting of a schedule record for use on the Internet is technically interruptible, it happens very fast and the user does not have the ability to easily cancel the transaction while it is occurring. Therefore, it can be modeled as an action. There is a fine line between an action and an activity, but the distinguishing characteristic is whether or not it is interruptible.

An entry action is shown inside the state, preceded by the word "entry" and a slash.

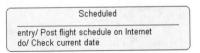

EXIT ACTION

An *exit action* is similar to an entry action. However, an exit action occurs as part of the transition out of a state. For example, when the plane lands and transitions out of the In Flight state, the system records the landing time. Like an entry action, an exit action is considered to be noninterruptible.

An exit action is shown inside the state, preceded by the word "exit" and a slash.

The behavior in an activity, entry action, or exit action can include sending an event to some other object. For example, if the flight is delayed for more than four hours, the flight object may need to send an event to a flight scheduler object, which will automatically reschedule the flight for another day. In this case, the activity, entry action, or exit action is preceded by a caret (^). The diagram would then read:

Do/ ^Target.Event(Arguments)

where Target is the object receiving the event, Event is the message being sent, and Arguments are parameters of the message being sent. In Rose, you can add all of these details to a send event.

An activity may also happen as a result of some event being received. For example, an account may be in the Open state. When some event occurs, the activity will be run.

All of these items can be added to your Rose model through the action specification window, as shown in Figure 9.3.

To add an activity:

1. Open the specification window for the desired state.

2. Select the Action tab.

3. Right-click the Actions box.

4. Select Insert from the pop-up menu.

5. Double-click the new action.

6. Enter the action in the Actions field.

7. In the When box, select Do to make the new action an activity.

FIGURE 9.3

Action specification
window

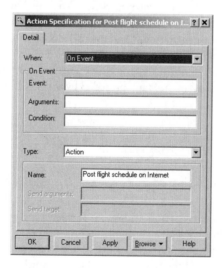

To add an entry action:

1. Open the specification window for the desired state.

2. Select the Action tab.

3. Right-click the Actions box.

4. Select Insert from the pop-up menu.

5. Double-click the new action.

6. Enter the action in the Actions field.

7. In the When box, select On Entry.

To add an exit action:

1. Open the specification window for the desired state.

2. Select the Action tab.

3. Right-click on the Actions box.

4. Select Insert from the pop-up menu.

5. Double-click the new action.

6. Enter the action in the Actions field.

7. In the When box, select On Exit.

To add an action that occurs on a specific event:

1. Open the specification window for the desired state.

2. Select the Action tab.

3. Right-click the Actions box.

4. Select Insert from the pop-up menu.

5. Double-click the new action.

6. Enter the action in the Actions field.

7. In the When box, select On Event.

8. Enter the event that triggers the action, along with any arguments of the event and any guard conditions that control whether or not the action should occur. If the guard condition is true, the action will occur on the event. If not, the action will not occur, even if the event happens.

To send an event:

1. Open the specification window for the desired state.

2. Select the Detail tab.

3. Right-click the Actions box.

4. Select Insert from the pop-up menu.

5. Double-click the new action.

6. Select Send Event as the type.

7. Enter the event, arguments, and target in their respective fields.

Adding Transitions

A *transition* is a movement from one state to another. The set of transitions on a diagram shows how the object moves from one state to another. On the diagram, each transition is drawn as an arrow from the originating state to the succeeding state.

Transitions can also be reflexive. Something may happen that causes an object to transition back to the state it is currently in. For example, when we add a passenger to an open flight or remove a passenger, the flight is still open. Reflexive transitions are shown as an arrow starting and ending on the same state.

To add a transition:

1. Select Transition from the toolbox toolbar.

2. Click on the state where the transition begins.

3. Drag the transition line to the state where the transition ends.

To add a reflexive transition:

1. Select Transition to Self from the toolbox toolbar.

2. Click on the state where the reflexive transition occurs.

OR

1. Select Tools ➢ Create ➢ Transition to Self.

2. Click on the state where the reflexive transition occurs.

To add documentation to a transition:

1. Double-click the desired transition to open the specification window.

2. Select the General tab.

3. Enter documentation in the Documentation field.

Adding Transition Details

There are various specifications you can include for each transition. These include events, arguments, guard conditions, actions, and send events. Let's look at each of these, again in the context of our airline example. Figure 9.2 from earlier in this chapter shows the Statechart diagram for a Flight class.

EVENT

An *event* is something that causes a transition from one state to another to occur. In the airline example, the event Land transitions the flight from an In Flight status to a Landed status. If the flight was Delayed, it becomes Closed once the Plane Arrived event happens. An event is shown on the diagram along the transition arrow.

On the diagram, an event can be drawn using an operation name or simply using an English phrase. In the airline example, all events are given English names. If you use operations instead, the Add Passenger event might be written as AddPassenger().

Events can have arguments. For example, when removing a passenger, we will need the name of the passenger to be removed. The Remove Passenger event may therefore have an argument called PassengerName. In your Rose model, you can add arguments to your events.

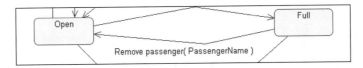

Most transitions will have events—the events are what cause the transition to occur in the first place. However, you can also have an automatic transition, which has no event. With an automatic transition, an object automatically moves from one state to another as soon as all the entry actions, activities, and exit actions have occurred.

GUARD CONDITION

A *guard condition* controls when a transition can or cannot occur. In the airline example, adding a passenger will move the flight from the Open to the Full state, but *only if* the last seat was sold. The guard condition in this example is "Last seat was sold."

A guard condition is drawn along the transition line, after the event name, and enclosed in square brackets.

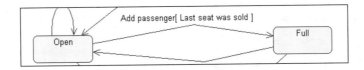

Guard conditions are optional. If there is more than one automatic transition out of a state, however, there must be mutually exclusive guard conditions on each automatic transition. This will help the reader of the diagram understand which path is automatically taken.

ACTION

An *action*, as we mentioned above, is a noninterruptible behavior that occurs as part of a transition. Entry and exit actions are shown inside states, because they define what happens every time an object enters or leaves a state. Most actions, however, will be drawn along the transition line, because they won't apply every time an object enters or leaves a state.

For example, when transitioning from the Scheduled state to the Open state, we may want to initialize the number of passengers at 0. This initialization can happen while the transition is occurring, and can therefore be modeled as an action.

An action is shown along the transition line, after the event name, and preceded by a slash.

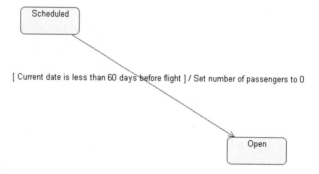

An event or action may be a behavior that occurs inside the object or a message that is sent to another object. If an event or action is sent to another object, it is preceded by a caret (^) on the diagram.

To add an event:

1. Double-click the desired transition to open the specification window.

2. Select the General tab.

3. Enter the event in the Event field.

To add arguments to an event:

1. Double-click the desired transition to open the specification window.

2. Select the General tab.

3. Enter the arguments in the Arguments field.

To add a guard condition:

1. Double-click the desired transition to open the specification window.

2. Select the Detail tab.

3. Enter the guard condition in the Condition field.

To add an action:

1. Double-click the desired transition to open the specification window.

2. Select the Detail tab.

3. Enter the action in the Action field.

To send an event:

1. Double-click the desired transition to open the specification window.

2. Select the Detail tab.

3. Enter the event in the Send Event field.

4. Enter any arguments in the Send Arguments field.

5. Enter the target in the Send Target field.

Adding Special States

There are two special states that can be added to the diagram: the start state and the stop state.

START STATE

The *start state* is the state the object is in when it is first created. In the airline example, a flight begins in the Tentative state. A start state is shown on the diagram as a filled circle.

A transition is drawn from the circle to the initial state.

A *start state* is mandatory: the reader of the diagram will need to know what state a new object is in. There can be only one start state on the diagram.

To add a start state:

1. Select Start State from the toolbox toolbar.

2. Click on the Statechart diagram where the start state should appear.

STOP STATE

The *stop state* is the state an object is in when it is destroyed. A stop state is shown on the diagram as a bull's-eye.

Stop states are optional, and you can add as many stop states as you need.
To add a stop state:

1. Select End State from the toolbox toolbar.

2. Click on the Statechart diagram where the stop state should appear.

Using Nested States and State History

To reduce clutter on your diagram, or as a design decision, you can nest one or more states inside another. The nested states are referred to as *substates*, while the larger state is referred to as a *superstate*.

If two or more states have an identical transition, they can be grouped together into a superstate. Then, rather than maintaining two identical transitions (one for each state), the transition can be moved to the superstate. Figure 9.4 is a portion of our Statechart diagram for the Flight class. As you can see, the flight moves into the Closed state 10 minutes before takeoff, regardless of whether it was in the Open or Full state before.

FIGURE 9.4

Statechart diagram
without nested states

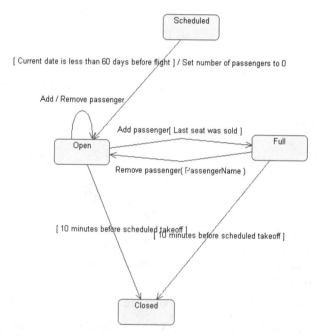

To reduce the number of arrows on the diagram, we can create a superstate around Open and Full, and then just model a single transition to the Closed state. Figure 9.5 is the same portion of the diagram with nested states. (As you can see, superstates can help to reduce the clutter on a Statechart diagram.)

FIGURE 9.5

Statechart diagram
with nested states

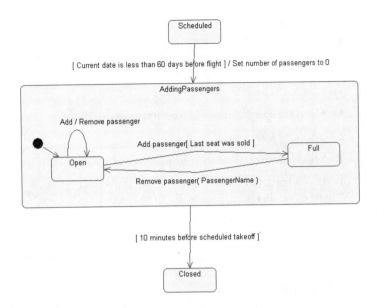

At times, you may need the system to remember which state it was last in. If you have three states in a superstate and then leave the superstate, you may want the system to remember where you left off inside the superstate. In our example, if we want to temporarily suspend reservations while the system is undergoing routine maintenance, we may transition to a SuspendReservations state while the maintenance is occurring. Once the maintenance is done, we want to return to whatever state the flight was in before the maintenance started.

There are two things you can do to resolve this issue. The first is to add a start state inside the superstate. The start state will indicate where the default starting point is in the superstate. The first time the object enters that superstate, this is where the object will be.

The second is to use state history to remember where the object was. If the History option is set, an object can leave a superstate and then return and pick up right where it left off. The History option is shown with a small "H" in a circle at the corner of the diagram, as shown in Figure 9.6.

FIGURE 9.6

Superstate history

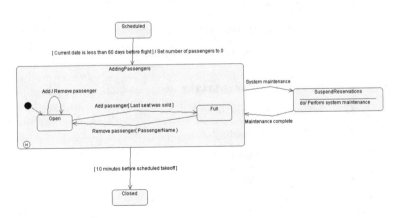

To nest a state:

1. Select State from the toolbox.

2. Click on the state in which to nest the new state.

To use state history:

1. Open the specification window for the desired state.

2. Select the General tab.

3. Select the State/Activity History check box.

4. If you have states within states within states, you can apply the history feature to all nested states within the superstate. To do so, select the Substate/Activity History check box.

Exercise

In this exercise, we will create a Statechart diagram for the Product class.

Problem Statement

In designing the Product class, Karen realized that it was a class that may require special attention. Many of the requirements varied significantly as the state of a product changed. For example, products that were backordered could not be purchased.

To be sure the design was sound, she sat down with the other developers in the group and worked out a Statechart diagram for the class. With this information, the developers had a very good sense of what it was going to take to code the class.

Create a Statechart Diagram

Create the Statechart diagram shown in Figure 9.7 for the Order class.

EXERCISE STEPS:

CREATE THE DIAGRAM

1. Locate the Product class in the browser.

2. Right-click the class and select New Statechart Diagram.

ADD THE START AND STOP STATES

1. Select Start State from the toolbox.

2. Place the state on the diagram.

3. Select End State from the toolbox.

4. Place the state on the diagram.

Continued on next page

ADD THE STATES

1. Select State from the toolbox.

2. Place the state on the diagram.

3. Name the state **Ordered**.

4. Select State from the toolbox.

5. Place the state on the diagram.

6. Name the state **Inventoried**.

7. Select State from the toolbox.

8. Name the state **Out of Stock**.

9. Select State from the toolbox.

10. Name the state **Selected for Purchase**.

11. Select State from the toolbox.

12. Place the state on the diagram.

13. Name the state **Purchased**.

ADD TRANSITIONS

1. Select Transition from the toolbox.

2. Click the Start State.

3. Drag the transition line to the Ordered state.

4. Repeat steps 1–3 to add the following transitions:

   - Ordered to Out of Stock

   - Ordered to Inventoried

   - Inventoried to Selected for Purchase

   - Selected for Purchase to Inventoried

   - Selected for Purchase to Purchased

   - Purchased to End State

   - Out of Stock to End State

   - Inventoried to End State

Continued on next page

EXERCISE STEPS *(continued)*:

ADD TRANSITION DETAILS

1. Double-click the Ordered to Out of Stock transition to open the specification.

2. Select the Detail tab.

3. In the Guard Condition field, enter **backordered.**

4. Click OK to close the specification.

5. Repeat steps 1–4 to add the guard conditions to the following transitions:

   ◆ [received] between Ordered and Inventoried

   ◆ [in shopping cart] between Inventoried and Selected for Purchase

   ◆ [paid] between Selected for Purchase and Purchased

FIGURE 9.7

Statechart diagram
for the Product class

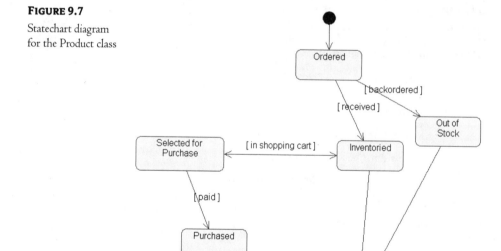

Summary

In this chapter, we took a look at the Statechart diagram, another of the UML diagrams supported by Rose. Although source code is not generated from these diagrams, they can prove invaluable when examining, designing, and documenting the dynamic behavior of a class.

A Statechart diagram shows the various states in which an object can exist, how the object moves from one state to another, what happens in each state, and what happens during the transitions from one state to another. All of this information is part of the detailed design of the class. The developers can use this information when programming the class.

In Rose, you can create a Statechart diagram for a class, an operation, a package, or a use case. You can create as many Statechart diagrams per class as you'd like to show the states and transitions for the class. Not every class will need a Statechart diagram, only those with significant dynamic behavior. To determine whether a class has significant dynamic behavior, you can examine the values its attributes can have and the relationships the class can have.

In the next chapter, we'll prepare for source code generation by examining the Component view of Rose. In the Component view, we'll move from the logical design to the physical design and look at the code libraries, executable files, and other components of a system.

Chapter 10

Component View

WE MOVE NOW TO the Component view of Rose. In the Component view, we'll focus on the physical organization of the system. First, we'll decide how the classes will be organized into code libraries. Then, we'll take a look at the different executable files, dynamic link library (DLL) files, and other runtime files in the system. We won't concern ourselves yet with where the different files will be placed on the network. We'll consider these issues in the Deployment view.

- ◆ Exploring types of components
- ◆ Creating components and mapping classes to components
- ◆ Using Component diagrams

What Is a Component?

A *component* is a physical module of code. Components can include both source code libraries and runtime files. For example, if you are using C++, each of your .cpp and .h files is a separate component. The .exe file that you create after the code is compiled is also a component.

Before you generate code, you map each of your files to the appropriate component(s). In C++, for example, each class is mapped to two components—one representing the .cpp file for that class and one representing the .h file. In Java, you map each class to a single component, representing the .java file for that class. When you generate code, Rose will use the component information to create the appropriate code library files.

Once the components are created, they are added to a Component diagram and relationships are drawn between them. The only type of relationship between components is a dependency. A dependency suggests that one component must be compiled before another. We'll look at this in more detail in the "Adding Component Dependencies" section later in this chapter.

Types of Components

In Rose, you can use several different icons to represent the different types of components. As we mentioned earlier, there are two primary types of components: source code libraries and runtime components. Within each of these two groups are a number of different component icons you can use. Let's start by looking at the source code library icons:

Component   The Component icon represents a software module with a well-defined interface. In the component specification, you specify the type of component in the Stereotype field (e.g., ActiveX, Applet, Application, DLL, and Executables). See Table 10.1 in the stereotypes section for a discussion of the different stereotypes you can use with this icon.

Subprogram Specification and Body   These icons represent a subprogram's visible specification and the implementation body. A subprogram is typically a collection of subroutines. Subprograms do not contain class definitions.

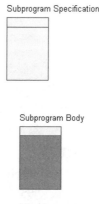

Main Program   The Main Program icon represents the main program. A main program is the file that contains the root of a program. In PowerBuilder, for example, this is the file that contains the application object.

Package Specification and Body   A package is the implementation of a class. A package specification is a header file, which contains function prototype information for the class. In C++, package specifications are the .h files. In Java, you use the Package Specification icon to represent the .java files.

A package body contains the code for the operations of the class. In C++, package bodies are the .cpp files.

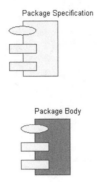

Package Specification

Package Body

There are additional Component icons that are used for runtime components. Runtime components include executable files, DLL files, and tasks.

Task Specification and Body   These icons represent packages that have independent threads of control. An executable file is commonly represented as a task specification with a .exe extension.

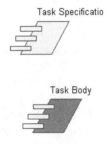

Task Specificatio

Task Body

Database   This icon represents a database, which may contain one or more schemas. On a Component diagram, a database is shown with the following icon:

Database

In addition to modeling the component itself, you can model the relationship between a component and its interface. On a Component diagram, a component with its interface would look like this:

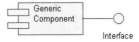

Interface

Component Diagrams

A *Component diagram* is a UML diagram that displays the components in the system and the dependencies between them. Figure 10.1 is an example of a Component diagram.

FIGURE 10.1

Component diagram

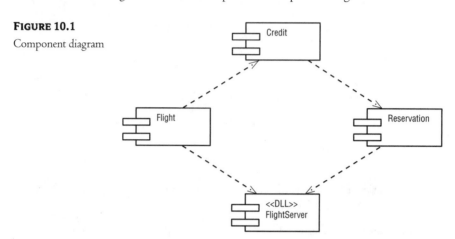

With this diagram, the staff responsible for compiling and deploying the system will know which code libraries exist and which executable files will be created when the code is compiled. Developers will know which code libraries exist and what the relationships are between them. The component dependencies will let those who are responsible for compiling know in which order the components need to be compiled.

In the example in Figure 10.1, there are four components. The FlightServer component realizes the classes Customer, Flight, and FlightList, all of which are on the server. The Flight component realizes the server pages and client pages that are responsible for searching for flights and displaying flight information. The Credit component realizes the CreditForm class, and the Reservation component realizes the ReserveSeat and ConfirmationForm server and client pages.

Creating Component Diagrams

In Rose, you can create Component diagrams in the Component view. Once the diagrams are created, you can either create components directly on the diagram or drag existing components from the browser to the diagram.

In the browser, Component diagrams are displayed with the following icon:

To create a Component diagram in the Component view:

1. In the browser, right-click the package that will contain the Component diagram.

2. Select New ➤ Component Diagram from the pop-up menu.

3. Enter the name of the new Component diagram.

OR

1. Select Browse ➤ Component Diagram. This displays the Select Component Diagram window.

2. Select the desired package.

3. Select <New> from the Component Diagram box and click OK.

4. Enter the name of the new Component Diagram and click OK.

To delete a Component diagram:

1. In the browser, right-click the Component diagram.

2. Select Delete from the pop-up menu.

OR

1. Select Browse ➤ Component Diagram. This displays the Select Component Diagram window.

2. Select the desired package.

3. Select the component to delete.

4. Click the Delete button.

Adding Components

Once you've created the Component diagram, the next step is to add components. You begin by creating a generic component and then assigning the appropriate stereotype to it. In the Component Diagram toolbar, buttons are available for all the different types of icons listed in the earlier section titled "Types of Components."

You can add documentation to the components as well. Documentation may include a description of the purpose of the component or a description of the class(es) in the component.

Like classes, components can be packaged together to organize them. Typically, you create one Component view package for each Logical view package. For example, if a Logical view package called Orders contains classes called Order, OrderItem, and OrderForm, the corresponding Component view package would contain the components that hold the Order, OrderItem, and OrderForm classes.

To add a component:

1. Select Component from the toolbox toolbar.

2. Click on the diagram where the new component will be placed.

3. Enter a name for the new component.

OR

1. Select Tools ➤ Create ➤ Component.

2. Click on the diagram where the new component will be placed.

3. Enter a name for the new component.

OR

1. In the browser, right-click the package to contain the component.

2. Select New ➤ Component from the pop-up menu.

3. Enter a name for the new component.

To add documentation to a component:

1. Right-click the desired component.

2. Select Open Specification from the pop-up menu. This opens the component's specification window.

3. Select the General tab.

4. Enter documentation in the Documentation field.

OR

1. Double-click the desired component. This opens the component's specification window.

2. Select the General tab.

3. Enter documentation in the Documentation field.

OR

1. Select the desired component.

2. Select Browse ➤ Specification. This opens the component's specification window.

3. Select the General tab.

4. Enter documentation in the Documentation field.

OR

1. Select the desired component.

2. Enter documentation in the documentation window.

To delete a component from the diagram only:

1. Select the component in the diagram.

2. Press Delete.

NOTE *The component has been removed from the diagram, but still exists in the browser and on other Component diagrams.*

To delete a component from the model:

1. Select the component on a Component diagram.

2. Select Edit ➢ Delete from Model, or press Ctrl+D.

OR

1. Right-click the component in the browser.

2. Select Delete from the shortcut menu.

NOTE *Rose will remove the component from all Component diagrams, as well as from the browser.*

Adding Component Details

As with other Rose model elements, there are a number of detailed specifications you can add to each component. These include stereotypes, languages, declarations, and classes.

STEREOTYPES

The first detail is a component stereotype. The stereotype controls which icon will be used to represent the component.

As listed earlier, the stereotypes are <none> (which uses the Component icon), subprogram specification, subprogram body, main program, package specification, package body, executable, DLL, task specification, and task body.

In addition, Rose includes a number of other stereotypes for the different languages it supports. The language-specific stereotypes available in Rose are included in Table 10.1.

TABLE 10.1: LANGUAGE-SPECIFIC COMPONENT STEREOTYPES

LANGUAGE	STEREOTYPES
Java	EJBDeploymentDescriptor, EJB JAR, ServletDeploymentDescriptor, and WAR
Oracle8	Database, Schema
Visual Basic	ActiveX Control

You can create additional stereotypes if you'd like to represent new types of components in your particular programming language and application.

To assign a stereotype:

1. Open the desired component's standard specification window.

2. Select the General tab, as shown in Figure 10.2.

3. Enter the stereotype in the Stereotype field.

FIGURE 10.2

Assigning a stereotype to a component

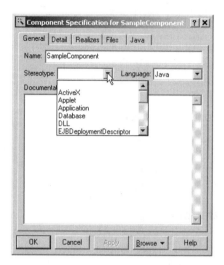

OR

1. Select the desired component.

2. Type the stereotype within the double angle brackets: **<< Name >>**.

If the component is a Java, XML, or CORBA component, an additional component specification window is provided, as shown below:

LANGUAGES

In Rose, you can assign languages on a component-by-component basis. Therefore, you can generate part of your model in C++, part in Java, part in Visual Basic, and so on, provided you have the Enterprise version of Rose installed.

Rose Enterprise contains add-ins for ANSI C++, Ada 83, Ada 95, CORBA, C++, Java, Visual Basic, Visual C++, Web Modeler, XML/DTD, and Oracle 8. Many more add-ins are available from various vendors to extend the capabilities of Rose. Add-ins for other languages (PowerBuilder, Forte, Visual Age for Java, etc.) may be purchased as well. For a complete list of Rose Link Partners, visit the Rational Rose website at `www.rational.com`.

To assign a language:

1. Open the desired component's standard specification window.

2. Select the General tab.

3. Enter the language in the Language field.

DECLARATIONS

In Rose, there is a place to include supplementary declarations that will be added during code generation for each component. Declarations include language-specific statements that are used to declare variables, classes, and so on. A C++ #include statement is also considered a declaration.

To add declarations:

1. Open the desired component's standard specification window.

2. Select the Detail tab, as shown in Figure 10.3.

3. Enter the declarations in the Declarations field.

FIGURE 10.3

Adding declarations to a component

CLASSES

Before code can be generated for a class, it must be mapped to a component. This mapping helps Rose know in which physical file the code for the class should be stored.

You can map one or more classes to each component. After you have mapped a class to a component, the component name will appear in parentheses after the class name in the Logical view.

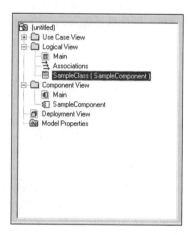

To map classes to a component:

1. Open the desired component's standard specification window.

2. Select the Realizes tab, as shown in Figure 10.4.

FIGURE 10.4

Mapping classes to a component

3. Right-click the class to map.

4. Select Assign from the pop-up menu.

OR

1. In the browser, select the class to map.

2. Drag the class to the desired component, either in the browser or on a diagram.

Adding Component Dependencies

The only type of relationship that exists between components is a *component dependency*. A component dependency suggests that one component depends on another. A component dependency is drawn as a dashed arrow between the components:

In this example, Component A depends upon Component B. In other words, there is some class in A that depends on some class in B.

These dependencies have compilation implications. In this example, because A depends on B, A cannot be compiled until B has been compiled. Someone reading this diagram will know that B should be compiled first, followed by A.

As with package dependencies, you want to avoid circular dependencies with components. If A depends on B, and B depends on A, you cannot compile either until the other has been compiled. Thus, you have to treat the two as one large component. All circular dependencies should be removed before you attempt to generate code.

The dependencies also have maintenance implications. If A depends on B, any change to B may have an impact on A. Maintenance staff can use this diagram to assess the impact of a change. The more components that a single component depends on, the more likely it is to be affected by a change.

Finally, the dependencies will let you know what may or may not be easily reused. In this example, A is difficult to reuse. Because A depends on B, you cannot reuse A without also reusing B. B, on the other hand, is easy to reuse, since it does not depend on any other components. The fewer components that a single component depends on, the easier it is to reuse.

To add a component dependency:

1. Select the Dependency icon from the toolbox.

2. Drag the dependency line from the Client component to the Supplier component.

OR

1. Select Tools ➤ Create ➤ Dependency.

2. Drag the dependency line from the Client component to the Supplier component.

To delete a component dependency:

1. Select the desired component dependency.

2. Press the Delete key.

OR

1. Select the desired component dependency.

2. Select Edit ➤ Delete.

Exercise

In this exercise, we will create the Component diagram for the shopping cart application. At this point, we've identified the classes that are needed for the "Add Item to Shopping Cart" use case. As other use cases are built, new components will be added to the diagram.

Problem Statement

With the analysis and design completed, Dan, one of the members of the deployment team, created the Component diagrams. By now, the team had decided to use Java, so he set about creating the appropriate components for each class.

Figure 10.5 shows the main Component diagram for the entire system. This main diagram focuses on the packages of components you will create.

FIGURE 10.5

Main Component diagram

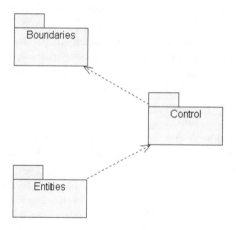

Figure 10.6 includes all of the components in the Entities package. These are the components that will contain the classes in the Entities package in the Logical view.

Figure 10.7 includes the components in the Control package. These components will contain the classes in the Control package in the Logical view.

Figure 10.8 includes the components in the Boundaries package. These components will contain the classes in the Boundaries package in the Logical view.

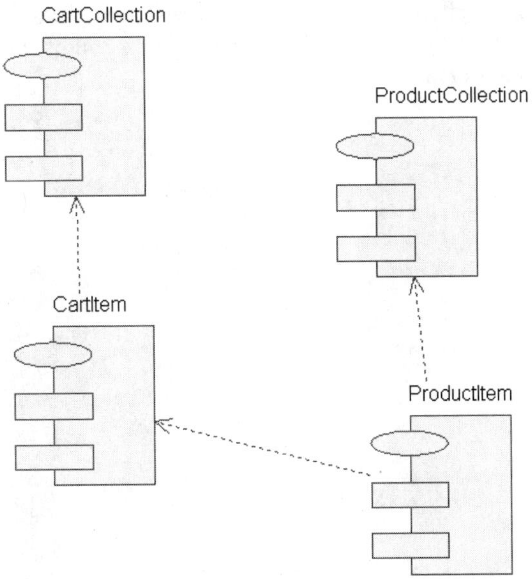

FIGURE 10.6

Entities package
Component diagram

CartCollection

ProductCollection

CartItem

ProductItem

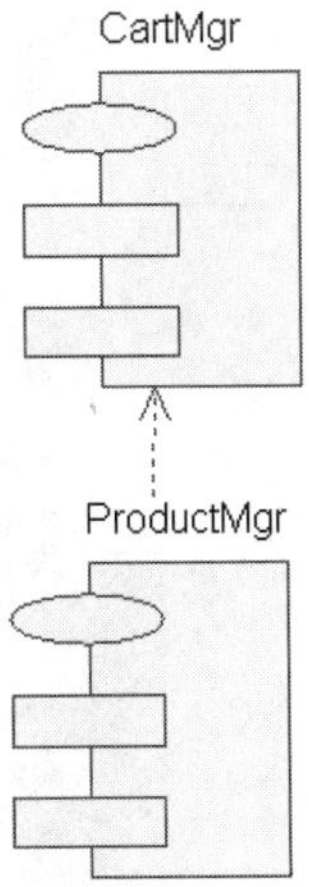

FIGURE 10.7

Control package
Component diagram

CartMgr

ProductMgr

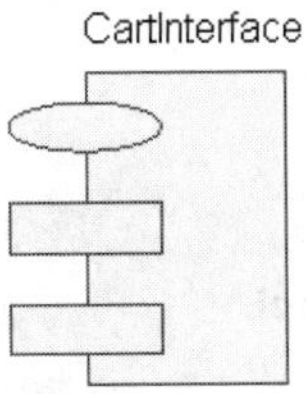

FIGURE 10.8

Boundaries package
Component diagram

CartInterface

Figure 10.9 shows all of the components in the system. We've named this diagram the System Component diagram. With this one diagram, you can see all of the dependencies between all of the components in the system.

FIGURE 10.9

System Component diagram

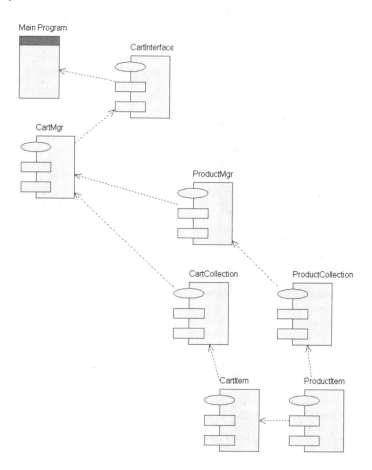

EXERCISE STEPS:

CREATE THE COMPONENT PACKAGES

1. Right-click the Component view in the browser.
2. Select New ➢ Package.
3. Name the new package **Entities**.
4. Repeat steps 1–3 for packages **Boundaries** and **Control**.

Continued on next page

ADD THE PACKAGES TO THE MAIN COMPONENT DIAGRAM

1. Open the main Component diagram by double-clicking it.
2. Drag the Entities, Boundary, and Control packages from the browser to the main Component diagram.

DRAW PACKAGE DEPENDENCIES

1. Select Dependency from the toolbox.
2. On the main Component diagram, click the Entities package.
3. Drag the dependency to the Control package.
4. Repeat steps 1–3 to add a dependency from the Control package to the Boundaries package.

ADD THE COMPONENTS FOR THE PACKAGES AND DRAW DEPENDENCIES

1. Double-click the Entities package in the main Component diagram to open the main Component diagram for the Entities package.
2. Select Package Specification from the toolbox.
3. Place the package specification on the diagram.
4. Enter the name of the package specification as **CartCollection**.
5. Repeat steps 2–4 to add the **CartItem**, **ProductCollection**, and **ProductItem** package specifications.
6. Select Dependency from the toolbox.
7. Click on the CartItem package specification.
8. Drag the dependency line to the CartCollection package specification.
9. Repeat steps 6-8 to add dependencies from the ProductItem package specification to the Product-Collection package specification and from the ProductItem package specification to the CartItem package specification.
10. Use this method to create the following components and dependencies:
    - CartInterface package specification for the Boundaries package
    - CartMgr package specification for the Control package
    - ProductMgr package specification for the Control package
    - ProductMgr package specification to CartMgr package specification for a dependency in the Control package

CREATE THE SYSTEM COMPONENT DIAGRAM

1. Right-click the Component view in the browser.
2. Select New ➢ Component Diagram from the pop-up menu.

Continued on next page

EXERCISE STEPS *(continued)*:

3. Name the new diagram **System**.

4. Double-click the System Component diagram.

PLACE COMPONENTS ON THE SYSTEM COMPONENT DIAGRAM

1. If needed, expand the Entities component package in the browser to open the package.

2. Click the CartItem package specification within the Entities component package.

3. Drag the CartItem package specification onto the diagram.

4. Repeat steps 2 and 3 to place the CartCollection, ProductItem, and ProductCollection package specifications on the diagram.

5. Use this method to place the following components on the diagram:

- ◆ CartInterface package specification in the Boundaries component package
- ◆ CartMgr package specification in the Control component package
- ◆ ProductMgr package specification in the Control component package

6. Select Main Program from the toolbox.

7. Place a main program on the diagram and name it **MainProgram**.

ADD REMAINING DEPENDENCIES TO THE SYSTEM COMPONENT DIAGRAM

The dependencies that already exist are automatically displayed on the System Component diagram after you add the components. Next, we add the remaining dependencies.

1. Select Dependency from the toolbox.

2. Click the ProductCollection package specification.

3. Drag the dependency line to the ProductMgr package specification.

4. Repeat steps 1–3 to add the following dependencies:

- ◆ CartCollection package specification to CartMgr package specification
- ◆ CartMgr package specification to CartInterface package specification
- ◆ CartInterface package specification to MainProgram task specification

MAP CLASSES TO COMPONENTS

1. In the Logical view of the browser, locate the ProductItem class in the Entities package.

2. Drag the ProductItem class to the ProductItem component package specification in the Component view. This maps the ProductItem class to the ProductItem component package specification.

Continued on next page

3. Repeat steps 1–2 to map the following classes to components:

    ◆ CartItem class to CartItem package specification

    ◆ CartCollection class to CartCollection package specification

    ◆ ProductCollection class to ProductCollection package specification

    ◆ CartMgr class to CartMgr package specification

    ◆ ProductMgr class to ProductMgr package specification

    ◆ CartInterface class to CartInterface package specification

Summary

In this chapter, we examined the Component view of Rose. The Component view is concerned with the physical structure of the system. A component is simply a file associated with the system. It may be a source code file, an executable file, or a DLL file. In Rose, there are various icons you can use to distinguish the different types of components.

Classes are mapped to specific languages by first mapping them to components. Each component is assigned a specific language. In the Enterprise version of Rose, you can generate part of your code in one language and part in another.

Component dependencies give you information about the compilation dependencies. These relationships will let you know in what order the various components must be compiled.

In the next chapter, we'll discuss how the components are deployed on the network.

Chapter 11

Deployment View

IN THIS CHAPTER, WE'LL examine the final view of Rose, the Deployment view. The Deployment view is concerned with the physical deployment of the application. This includes issues such as the network layout and the location of the components on the network. We'll also consider deployment issues such as how much network bandwidth we have, how many concurrent users we can expect, what we do if a server goes down, and so on.

The Deployment view contains processors, devices, processes, and connections between processors and devices. All of this information is diagrammed on a Deployment diagram. There is only one Deployment diagram per system, and therefore one Deployment diagram per Rose model.

- ◆ Creating and using a Deployment diagram

- ◆ Adding processors

- ◆ Adding devices

- ◆ Adding connections

- ◆ Adding processes

Deployment Diagrams

A Deployment diagram shows all of the nodes on the network, the connections between them, and the processes that will run on each one. Figure 11.1 is an example of a Deployment diagram.

Opening the Deployment Diagram

In Rose, the Deployment diagram is created in the Deployment view. Because there is only one diagram, it isn't shown in the browser as a package. To access the Deployment diagram, you need to use the browser.

To open the Deployment diagram:

1. Double-click Deployment View entry in the browser.

2. Rose will open the Deployment diagram for the model.

FIGURE 11.1

Deployment diagram
for the airline system

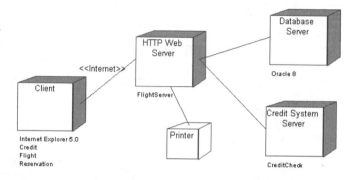

In the following sections, we'll examine each piece of this diagram.

Adding Processors

A processor is any machine that has processing power. The servers, workstations, and other machines with processors are included in this category.

In UML, processors are displayed with this symbol:

To add a processor:

1. Select Processor from the toolbox.

2. Click the Deployment diagram to place the processor.

3. Enter the name of the processor.

OR

1. Select Tools ➤ Create ➤ Processor.

2. Click the Deployment diagram to place the processor.

3. Enter the name of the processor.

OR

1. Right-click the Deployment view in the browser.

2. Select New ➤ Processor from the pop-up menu.

3. Enter the name of the processor.

To add documentation to a processor:

1. Right-click the desired processor.

2. Select Open Specification from the pop-up menu. This opens the processor's specification window.

3. Select the General tab.

4. Enter documentation in the Documentation field.

OR

1. Double-click the desired processor. This opens the processor's specification window.

2. Select the General tab.

3. Enter documentation in the Documentation field.

OR

1. Select the desired processor.

2. Select Browse ➤ Specification. This opens the processor's specification window.

3. Select the General tab.

4. Enter documentation in the Documentation field.

OR

1. Select the desired processor.

2. Enter documentation in the documentation window.

To delete a processor from the diagram only:

1. Select the processor in the diagram.

2. Press Delete.

OR

1. Select the processor in the diagram.

2. Select Edit ➤ Delete.

NOTE *Note that the processor has been removed from the diagram, but still exists in the browser.*

To delete a processor from the model:

1. Select the processor on the Deployment diagram.

2. Select Edit ➤ Delete from Model, or press Ctrl-D.

OR

1. Right-click the processor in the browser.

2. Select Delete from the shortcut menu.

NOTE *Rose will remove the processor from the Deployment diagram, as well as from the browser.*

Adding Processor Details

In the processor specification window, you can add information about the processor's stereotype, characteristics, and scheduling.

The stereotype, as with other model elements, is used to classify the processor. For example, you may have some Unix machines and some PC machines. You may want to define stereotypes to differentiate between the two.

A processor's characteristics are physical descriptions of the processor. For example, these could include the processor's speed or amount of memory.

The Scheduling field documents the type of process scheduling used by the processor. The options are as follows:

Preemptive Indicates that high-priority processes can preempt lower-priority processes.

Non-preemptive Indicates that the processes have no priority. The current process executes until it is finished, at which time the next process begins.

Cyclic Indicates the control cycles between the processes; each process is given a set amount of time to execute, and then control passes to the next process.

Executive Indicates that there is some sort of computational algorithm that controls the scheduling.

Manual Indicates that the processes are scheduled by the user.
To assign a stereotype:

1. Open the desired processor's specification window.

2. Select the General tab, as shown in Figure 11.2.

3. Enter the stereotype in the Stereotype field.

OR

1. Select the desired processor.

2. Type the stereotype within double-angle brackets: << **Name** >>.

To add characteristics to a processor:

1. Open the desired processor's specification window.

2. Select the Detail tab, as shown in Figure 11.3.

3. Enter the characteristics in the Characteristics field.

FIGURE 11.2

Entering a processor
stereotype

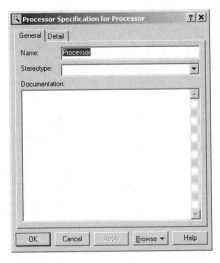

FIGURE 11.3

Entering processor
characteristics

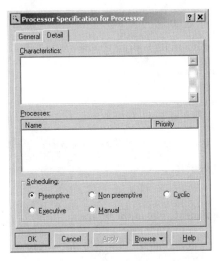

To set scheduling for a processor:

1. Open the desired processor's specification window.

2. Select the Detail tab.

3. Select one of the following for scheduling: Preemptive, Non-preemptive, Cyclic, Executive, or Manual.

To show scheduling on the diagram:

1. Right-click the desired processor.

2. Select Show Scheduling from the pop-up menu.

To show processes on the diagram:

1. Right-click the desired processor.

2. Select Show Processes from the pop-up menu.

Adding Devices

A device is hardware with a single purpose or a limited purpose. Devices include items such as dumb terminals, printers, and scanners. Both processors and devices can also be referred to as *nodes* on a network.
In UML, devices are displayed with this symbol:

To add a device:

1. Select Device from the toolbox.

2. Click the Deployment diagram to place the device.

3. Enter the name of the device.

OR

1. Select Tools ➤ Create ➤ Device.

2. Click on the Deployment diagram to place the device.

3. Enter the name of the device.

OR

1. Right-click the Deployment view in the browser.

2. Select New ➤ Device from the pop-up menu.

3. Enter the name of the device.

To add documentation to a device:

1. Right-click the desired device.

2. Select Open Specification from the pop-up menu. This opens the device's specification window.

3. Select the General tab.

4. Enter documentation in the Documentation field.

OR

1. Double-click the desired device. This opens the device's specification window.

2. Select the General tab.

3. Enter documentation in the Documentation field.

OR

1. Select the desired device.

2. Select Browse ➤ Specification. This opens the device's specification window.

3. Select the General tab.

4. Enter documentation in the Documentation field.

OR

1. Select the desired device.

2. Enter documentation in the documentation window.

To delete a device from the diagram only:

1. Select the device in the diagram.

2. Press Delete.

OR

1. Select the device in the diagram.

2. Select Edit ➤ Delete.

NOTE   *Note that the device has been removed from the diagram, but still exists in the browser.*

To delete a device from the model:

1. Select the device on the Deployment diagram.

2. Select Edit ➤ Delete from Model, or press Ctrl+D.

OR

1. Right-click the device in the browser.

2. Select Delete from the shortcut menu.

NOTE   *Rose will remove the device from the Deployment diagram, as well as from the browser.*

Adding Device Details

Like processors, there are various details that can be added to a device. The first is the stereotype, which is used to classify the device. The second are the characteristics, which, as with processors, are the physical descriptions of the device.

To assign a stereotype:

1. Open the desired device's specification window.

2. Select the General tab, as shown in Figure 11.4.

3. Enter the stereotype in the Stereotype field.

FIGURE 11.4

Entering a device stereotype

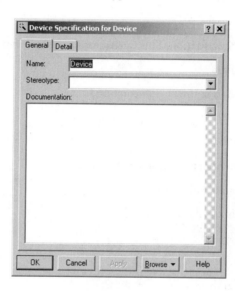

OR

1. Select the desired device.

2. Type the stereotype within double-angle brackets: **<< Name >>**.

To add characteristics to a device:

1. Open the desired device's specification window.

2. Select the Detail tab, as shown in Figure 11.5.

3. Enter the characteristics in the Characteristics field.

Adding Connections

A connection is a physical link between two processors, two devices, or a processor and a device. Most commonly, connections represent the physical network connections between the nodes on your network. A connection can also be an Internet link between two nodes.

To add a connection:

1. Select Connection from the toolbox.

2. Click on the node to connect.

3. Drag the connection line to another node.

OR

1. Select Tools ➤ Create ➤ Connection.

2. Click on the node to connect.

3. Drag the connection line to another node.

To delete a connection:

1. Select the connection in the diagram.

2. Press Delete.

OR

1. Select the connection in the diagram.

2. Select Edit ➤ Delete.

FIGURE 11.5

Entering device
characteristics

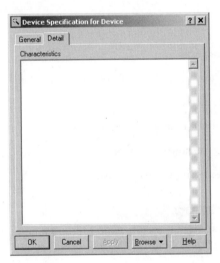

Adding Connection Details

Connections may be assigned stereotypes. Connections can also be given characteristics, which are used to provide details about the physical connection. For example, a connection might be a T1 line. This type of note would be added in the Characteristics field.

To assign a stereotype:

1. Open the desired connection's specification window.

2. Select the General tab, as shown in Figure 11.6.

3. Enter the stereotype in the Stereotype field.

FIGURE 11.6

Entering a connection
stereotype

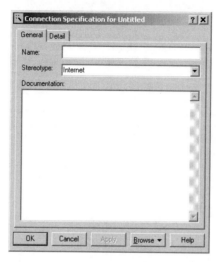

OR

1. Select the desired connection.

2. Type the stereotype within double-angle brackets: << **Name** >>.

To add characteristics to a connection:

1. Open the desired connection's specification window.

2. Select the Detail tab, as shown in Figure 11.7.

3. Enter the characteristics in the Characteristics field.

FIGURE 11.7

Entering connection
characteristics

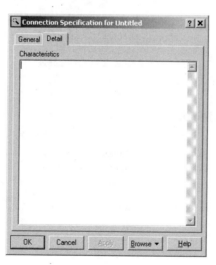

Adding Processes

A process is a single thread of execution that runs on a processor. An executable file, for example, is considered a process. When adding processes to the diagram, focus on only the processes related to the system being built.

Processes can be displayed on a Deployment diagram or hidden from view. If they are displayed, they are listed directly below the processor(s) on which they are run.

Processes may be assigned a priority. If the processor on which they are run uses preemptive scheduling, the priority of the process will determine when it can run.

To add a process:

1. Right-click the desired processor in the browser.

2. Select New ➤ Process from the pop-up menu.

3. Enter the name of the new process.

OR

1. Open the desired processor's specification window.

2. Click the Detail tab.

3. Right-click in the Processes box.

4. Select Insert from the pop-up menu.

5. Enter the name of the new process.

To add documentation to a process:

1. Open the desired processor's specification window.

2. Select the Detail tab.

3. Enter documentation in the Documentation field.

OR

1. Double-click the desired process in the browser.

2. Select the Detail tab.

3. Enter documentation in the Documentation field.

OR

1. Right-click the desired process in the browser.

2. Select Open Specification from the pop-up menu.

3. Select the Detail tab.

4. Enter documentation in the Documentation field.

To add a priority to a process:

1. Open the desired processor's specification window.

2. Select the General tab, as shown in Figure 11.8.

3. Enter the priority in the Priority field.

FIGURE 11.8

Entering process
information

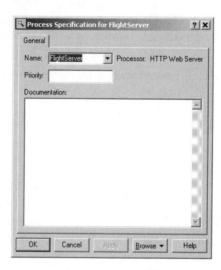

To delete a process:

1. Right-click the desired process in the browser.

2. Select Delete from the pop-up menu.

OR

1. Open the desired processor's specification.

2. Click the Detail tab.

3. Right-click the desired process.

4. Select Delete from the pop-up menu.

Exercise

In this exercise, we'll create a Deployment Diagram.

Problem Statement

The project team had done quite a bit of analysis and design up to this point. The use cases, object interaction, and components were all nicely defined. However, the network management unit needed to know which components would reside on which machines. So, the team put together a Deployment diagram for the system.

Create Deployment Diagram

Create the Deployment diagram for the Order Processing system. Your completed diagram should look like Figure 11.9.

FIGURE 11.9

Deployment diagram for the Order Processing system

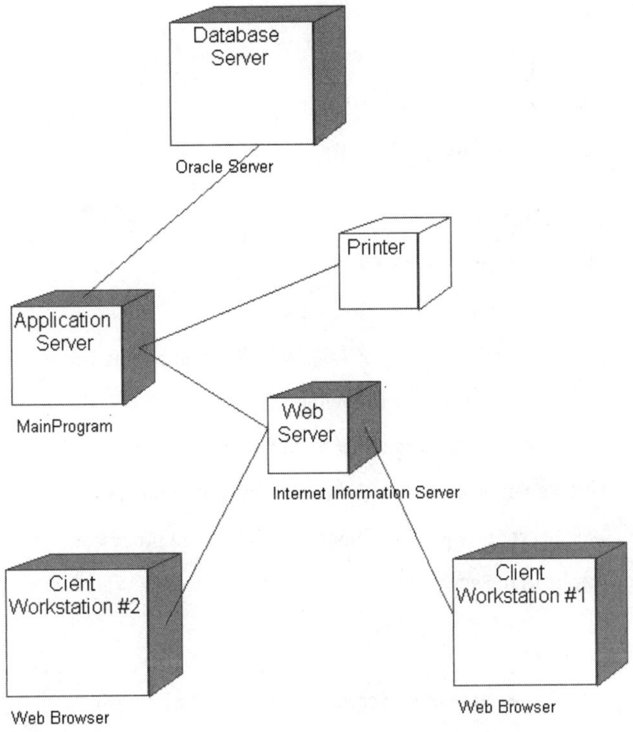

EXERCISE STEPS:

ADD THE NODES TO THE DEPLOYMENT DIAGRAM

1. Double-click the Deployment view in the browser to open the Deployment diagram.

2. Select Processor from the toolbox.

3. Click the diagram to place the processor.

4. Enter the processor name as **Database Server**.

Continued on next page

EXERCISE STEPS *(continued)*:

5. Repeat steps 2–4 to add the following processors:

    ◆ Application Server

    ◆ Client Workstation #1

    ◆ Client Workstation #2

    ◆ Web Server

6. Select Device from the toolbox.

7. Click the diagram to place the device.

8. Enter the device name as **Printer**.

ADD CONNECTIONS

1. Select Connection from the toolbox.

2. Click on the Database Server processor.

3. Drag the connection line to the Application Server processor.

4. Repeat steps 1–3 to add the following connections:

    ◆ Application Server processor to Web Server processor

    ◆ Web Server processor to Client Workstation #1 processor

    ◆ Web Server processor to Client Workstation #2 processor

    ◆ Application Server processor to Printer device

ADD PROCESSES

1. Right-click the Application Server processor in the browser.

2. Select New ➢ Process from the menu.

3. Enter the process name as **MainProgram**.

4. Repeat steps 1–3 to add the following processes:

    ◆ For the Client Workstation #1 processor: **Web Browser**

    ◆ For the Client Workstation #2 processor: **Web Browser**

    ◆ For the Database Server processor: **Oracle Server**

    ◆ For the Web Server: **Internet Information Server**

Continued on next page

EXERCISE STEPS *(continued)*:

SHOW THE PROCESSES

1. Right-click the Application Server process.

2. Select Show Processes from the menu.

3. Repeat steps 1 and 2 to show the processes for the following processors:

- ◆ Client Workstation #1 processor

- ◆ Client Workstation #2 processor

- ◆ Web Server

- ◆ Database Server

Summary

In this chapter, we covered the Deployment view of Rose. In the Deployment diagram, the team describes the network structure and where the various processes are run.

You now have the information you need to do the following:

- ◆ Define the system scope with use cases and actors, and diagram the use cases and actors on a Use Case diagram.

- ◆ Analyze a problem with use cases and Use Case documentation.

- ◆ Describe the objects in the system and the system flow in a Sequence or Collaboration diagram.

- ◆ Create the classes needed to implement the functionality in the flow of events, and diagram the classes.

- ◆ Define and diagram the attributes, operations, and relationships of the classes.

- ◆ Examine the dynamic behavior of a class by creating a Statechart diagram.

- ◆ Perform an architectural assessment by grouping the classes into packages and examining the relationships between the classes and the packages.

- ◆ Define and view the physical structure of the system in a Component diagram.

- ◆ View the network structure and deployment information on a Deployment diagram.

In the next chapter, we'll take a close look at the code-generation features of Rose. The next few chapters will discuss how to generate C++, Java, Visual Basic, and CORBA/IDL code from a Rose model. We'll also look at how to design a database using Rose, how to work with XML and Rose, and how to model a web application in Rose.

Chapter 12

Introduction to Code Generation and Reverse Engineering Using Rational Rose

ONE OF THE MOST powerful features of Rational Rose is its ability to generate code that represents a model. In this chapter, we'll take a look at the fundamental steps you must take before you can generate code from your Rose model. Then, we'll examine the reverse-engineering process, and see what is reverse engineered into a Rose model.

The code-generation options you have available will vary by the version of Rose you have installed. There are three different versions of Rose currently available:

- Rose Modeler allows you to create a model for your system, but will not support code generation or reverse engineering.

- Rose Professional allows you to generate code in one language.

- Rose Enterprise allows you to generate code in Ada 83, Ada 95, ANSI C++, CORBA, Java, COM, Visual Basic, Visual C++, C++, and XML. It also supports the generation and reverse engineering of databases.

A number of Rose partner companies have developed add-ins to support code generation and reverse engineering in other languages. Check Rational's website, www.rational.com, for information about add-in products available for Rose.

- Checking your Rose model

- Setting code-generation properties

- Generating code using Rational Rose

- Preparing for reverse engineering

- Reverse engineering code into a Rose model

Preparing for Code Generation

There are six basic steps to generating code:

1. Check the model.

2. Create the components.

3. Map the classes to the components.

4. Set the code-generation properties.

5. Select a class, component, or package.

6. Generate the code.

Not all of these steps are necessary in each language. For example, you can generate C++ code without first creating components. You can create code in any language without running the Check Model step, although you may have some errors during the code generation. In the following chapters, we'll discuss the details of generating and reverse engineering code in the various languages.

Although not all of these steps are required, we recommend completing the first five steps before generating code. The model check will help to find inconsistencies and problems in your model that you certainly wouldn't want to affect the code. The component steps serve as a way to map your logical system design to its physical implementation, and they provide you with a great deal of useful information. If you skip these steps, Rose will use the package structure in the Logical view to create components.

Step One: Check the Model

Rose includes a language-independent model check feature that you can run to ensure that your model is consistent before you generate code. It's always a good idea to run this check before you attempt to generate code, because it can find inconsistencies and errors in your model that might prevent code from being generated correctly.

To check your Rose model:

1. Select Tools ➢ Check Model from the menu.

2. Any errors that are found will be written to the log window.

Common errors include things like messages on a Sequence or Collaboration diagram that are not mapped to an operation, or objects on a Sequence or Collaboration diagram that are not mapped to a class. The rest of this section explores some of the common errors and their solutions.

The message below indicates that you have an object in a Sequence or a Collaboration diagram that has not been mapped to a class.

```
Unresolved reference from use case "<Use case name>" to ClassItem with name
(Unspecified) by object <Object name>>
```

First, look at the objects on your Sequence or Collaboration diagram. Each box should contain the object name, followed by a colon, followed by the class name:

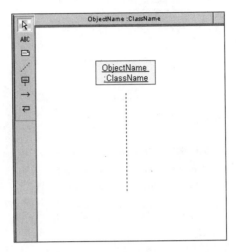

Next, find the object without the class name. Right-click the object and select Open Specification from the shortcut menu. In the object specification window, select the object's class using the Class drop-down list box.

The following message lets you know that you have a message on a Sequence or a Collaboration diagram that has not been mapped to an operation.

```
Unresolved reference to Operation with name <Message name> in message <Message
name> between <Class name> and <Class name> in Sequence diagram <Use case
name>/<Sequence diagram name>
```

Right-click the appropriate message on the diagram (the error in the log window will let you know the name of the offending message and its Sequence or Collaboration diagram), and map the message to an operation. If necessary, create a new operation for the message.

FINDING ACCESS VIOLATIONS

The Check Model menu item will find most of the inconsistencies and problems in a model. The Access Violations menu item will find violations that occur when there is a relationship between two classes in different packages but no relationship between the packages themselves. For example, if we have an Order class in an Entities package that has a relationship to an OrderManager class in a Control package, there must be a relationship between the Entities package and the Control package. If there is not, Rose will find an access violation.

To find access violations:

1. Select Report ➤ Show Access Violations from the menu.

2. Rose will display any access violations in the Access Violations window, as shown in Figure 12.1.

FIGURE 12.1

Access Violations
window

RUNNING A LANGUAGE-INDEPENDENT CHECK

To run a language-independent check, choose Tools ➤ Check Model. If you are using Java, you can run a Java-specific syntax check by selecting Tools ➤ Java ➤ Syntax Check. This check will find errors such as multiple public classes in a single compilation unit. If you are using CORBA, run Tools ➤ CORBA ➤ Syntax Check to perform a similar analysis. Select Tools ➤ XML_DTD ➤ Syntax Check for XML.

If any of these checks find errors, they will appear in the Rose log. Once all errors have been corrected, move on to step two.

Step Two: Create Components

The second step in the code-generation process is to create components to hold the classes. There are many types of components: source code files, executable files, runtime libraries, ActiveX components, and applets, to name a few. Before you generate code, you can map each of your classes to the appropriate source code component.

Once the components are created, you can add dependencies between them on a Component diagram. Dependencies between the components are the compilation dependencies in the system. (See Chapter 10, "Component View," for more information about components and component dependencies.)

If you are generating C++, Java, or Visual Basic, you aren't required to complete this step in order to generate code. In Java or Visual Basic, Rose will automatically create the appropriate component for each of your classes.

To create a component:

1. Open a Component diagram.

2. Use the Component icon on the Diagram toolbar to add a new component to the diagram. See Chapter 10 for more information about adding components.

Step Three: Map Classes to Components

Each source code component represents the source code file for one or more classes. In C++, for example, each class is mapped to two source code components, one representing the header file and one representing the body file. In PowerBuilder, many classes are mapped to a single component. A

PowerBuilder source code component is a PowerBuilder library (`.pb1`) file. In Java, each source code component represents a single `.java` file. Components are also created for ActiveX controls, applets, DLL files, executable files, and other source and compiled files.

The third step in the code-generation process is to map each of your classes to the appropriate components. For PowerBuilder, you must map each class to a component before you can generate code. However, this is an optional step with C++, Java, or Visual Basic. If you are generating Java or Visual Basic code, Rose will also generate the appropriate components and map the classes for you. However, components will not be automatically created for C++. It's a good idea to go ahead and complete this step regardless of the language you are using.

To map a class to a component:

1. Right-click the component on a Component diagram or in the browser.

2. Select Open Specification from the shortcut menu.

3. Select the Realizes tab.

4. On the Realizes tab, right-click the appropriate class or classes and select Assign from the shortcut menu.

5. The browser will show the component name in parentheses after the class name in the Logical view.

OR

1. Locate the class in the Logical view of the browser.

2. Drag the class to the appropriate component in the Component view.

3. The component name will appear in parentheses after the class name in the Logical view.

Step Four: Set the Code-Generation Properties

There are a number of code-generation options you can set for classes, attributes, components, and other model elements. These properties control how the code will be generated. Common default settings are provided in Rose.

For example, one of the code-generation properties for a C++ attribute is GenerateGetOperation, which controls whether or not a Get() operation will be created for the attribute. One of the properties for a Java class is GenerateDefaultConstructor, which controls whether or not a constructor should automatically be created for the class. One of the properties for a relationship in Visual Basic is GenerateDataMember, which controls whether or not an attribute will automatically be created to support the relationship.

Each language in Rose has a number of code-generation properties. In the following chapters, we'll discuss the code-generation properties for specific languages. Before you generate code, it's a good idea to examine the code-generation properties and make any needed changes.

To view the code-generation properties, select Tools ➤ Options, then select the appropriate language tab. For example, here is the tab for the Visual Basic properties:

From the drop-down list box, you can select Class, Attribute, Operation, or the other types of model elements. Each language will have different model elements available in the drop-down list box. As you select different values, different property sets will appear. We just saw the Class properties in Visual Basic. Here are the Attribute properties.

Any changes you make to a property set in the Tools ➤ Options window will affect all model elements using that set. For example, if you change the GenerateDefaultConstructor Class property on the Java tab, this change will affect all classes in your model that will be implemented in Java.

At times, you may want to change the code-generation properties for a single class, attribute, operation, or other model element. To do so, open the standard specification window for the model element, and then select the appropriate language tab. Any changes you make in the specification window for a model element will affect only that model element.

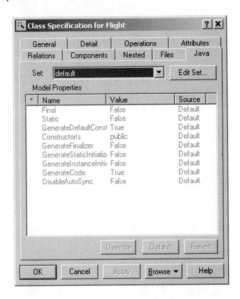

CLONING PROPERTY SETS

Rather than making changes directly to the default property sets, you can clone them and then make changes to the copy. To clone a property set, press the Clone button on the Clone the Property Set window. Rose will prompt you to enter a name for the new property set.

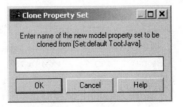

Once you've cloned a property set, it will be available by opening the Set drop-down list box on the Clone Property Set window.

You can make as many changes as you'd like to this cloned set, without affecting the original default set. We recommend leaving the default set alone and only changing cloned sets.

DELETING PROPERTY SETS

If you no longer need a cloned property set, you can remove it from the model through the Tools ➤ Options window. Select the tab for the appropriate language and then select the cloned property set in the Set drop-down list box.

Once you've selected the appropriate set, select the Remove button. Rose will remove that property set from the model. Note that you cannot remove the default property set. Once you remove a property set, you can no longer generate code for an item using that property set. When viewing the item's specification, you will see the cloned property set in parentheses, which indicates that the property set has been deleted or is not loaded. To generate code for the item, assign a different property set to it.

Step Five: Select a Class, Component, or Package

When generating code, you can generate a class at a time, a component at a time, or an entire package at a time. Code can be generated from a diagram or from the browser. If you generate code from a package, you can select either a Logical View package on a Class diagram or a Component View package on a Component diagram. If you select a Logical View package, all of the classes in that package will be generated. If you select a Component View package, all of the components in that package will be generated.

You can also generate code for a number of classes, components, or packages at once. On a diagram, use the Ctrl key to select the classes, components, or packages you want to generate code for, then select the appropriate code-generation command from the menu.

Step Six: Generate Code

If you have Rose Professional or Enterprise installed, you will have some language-specific menu options available on the Tools menu, as shown in Figure 12.2.

FIGURE 12.2

Code-generation
menu items

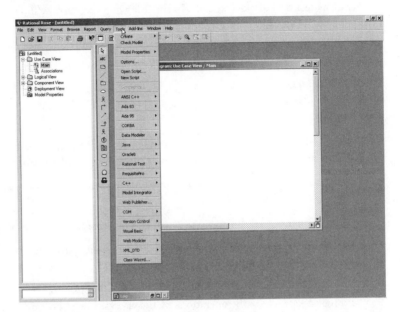

To show or hide these menu options, select the Add-Ins ➤ Add-In Manager menu option. In the Add-In Manager dialog box, as shown in Figure 12.3, use the check boxes to show or hide the options for various languages.

FIGURE 12.3

Add-In Manager

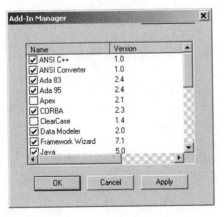

Once you have a class or component selected on a diagram, select the appropriate code-generation option from the menu. If any errors are encountered as the code generation progresses, these errors will be noted in the log window.

What Gets Generated?

When you generate code, Rose collects information from the Logical view and the Component view of your model. Although no modeling tool can create a completed application for you, Rose will generate a great deal of skeletal code. In the following chapters, we'll discuss specifically what is generated for a given language.

Elements generated by the code include the following:

Classes   All classes in the model will be generated in the code.

Attributes   The code will include the attributes of each class, including the visibility, data type, and default value. In some languages, Get and Set operations can also be automatically generated for the attributes.

Operation signatures   The operations will be declared in the code, along with any parameters, the data types of the parameters, and the return type of the operation.

Relationships   Some of the relationships in your model will cause attributes to be created when you generate code.

Components   Each component will be implemented by the appropriate source code file.

Documentation   When documentation has been added, the code generator will insert the documentation at the appropriate place.

Once the files have been generated, there are two steps remaining. First, the developers take the files, and they code each of the operations of the classes. Then, the graphical user interface is designed.

Rose is not intended to be a GUI design tool—you can use your programming language's environment to design the screens and forms. Instead, this approach helps you ensure that the system you're building has a solid design. The team can review the Rose model to reach an agreement on the best architecture and the best design, and then generate code from the model. Rather than having 20 different programmers designing in 20 different directions, everyone is working off of the same blueprint.

When generating code, Rose will use the package structure you've set up in the Component view to create the appropriate directories. By default, the root directory it uses for code generation is the directory with the Rose application file in it. You can change the directory through the code-generation properties for your language.

If you don't have components set up, Rose will use the package structure in the Logical view to set up the directory structure. Again, the default directory is the Rose directory, but you can change it through the code-generation properties.

Introduction to Reverse Engineering Using Rational Rose

Reverse engineering is the ability to take information from source code and create or update a Rose model. Through its integration with C++, Java, Visual Basic, and many other languages, Rose supports the reverse engineering of code into a UML model. One of the challenges with information technology projects is keeping the object model consistent with the code. As requirements change, it can be tempting to change the code directly, rather than changing the model and then generating the changed code from the model. If this happens in Rose, the team can reverse engineer the changes from the code back into the model. Reverse engineering helps us keep the model synchronized with the code.

In the reverse-engineering process, Rose will read components, packages, classes, relationships, attributes, and operations from the code. Once this information is in a Rose model, you can make any needed changes to the model and then regenerate the code through the forward-engineering features of Rose.

The options you will have available will depend on the version of Rose you are using:

◆ Rose Modeler will not include any reverse-engineering functionality.

◆ Rose Professional includes reverse-engineering capabilities for one language.

◆ Rose Enterprise includes ANSI C++, Visual C++, C++, CORBA, XML, Visual Basic, Ada, and Java reverse engineering, as well as database generation and reverse engineering.

◆ A new feature of Rose is the ability to reverse engineer a web application.

◆ Rose add-ins will give you reverse-engineering capabilities in other languages, such as Power-Builder or Forte.

Model Elements Created During Reverse Engineering

During the reverse-engineering process, Rose will collect information about:

◆ Classes

◆ Attributes

◆ Operations

◆ Relationships

◆ Packages

◆ Components

Using this information, Rose will create or update an object model. Depending upon the language you are reverse engineering, you can create a new Rose model or update the current Rose model.

Let's begin by examining classes, attributes, and operations. If you have a source code file that contains a class, the reverse-engineering process will create a corresponding class in your Rose model. Each of the attributes and operations of the class will appear as attributes and operations of the new class in the Rose model. Along with the attribute and operation names, Rose pulls in information about their visibility, data types, and default values.

For example, when reverse engineering the following Java class, Rose will produce the model shown in Figure 12.4.

```
//Source file: C:\\Flight.java


public class Flight
{
    private int FlightNumber;
    private long DepartureDate;
    private int GateNumber;
```

```java
    public Flight()
    {
    }

    /**
    @roseuid 3942C4F50253
    */
    public boolean AddPassenger(int PassengerID)
    {
    }

    /**
    @roseuid 3942C4FE02B0
    */
    public boolean RemovePassenger(int PassengerID)
    {
    }

    /**
    @roseuid 3942C5060211
    */
    public boolean SwitchGate(int NewGate)
    {
    }
}
```

FIGURE 12.4

Reverse engineering
a Java class

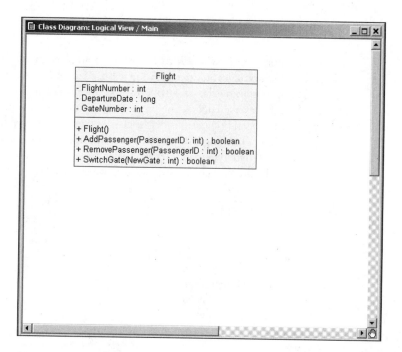

If you originally created the classes using Rose, and then made some changes to the classes in the code, these changes will be reflected in the model during the reverse-engineering process. For example, if you deleted an operation in the code, the operation will be deleted from the model during reverse engineering. If you added an attribute or operation directly into the code, this new attribute or operation will be added to the model during reverse engineering.

In addition to classes, Rose will collect information about the relationships in the code. If one class contains an attribute whose data type is another class, Rose will create a relationship between the two classes. For example, given the following two Java classes, Rose will create an association relationship between them, as shown in Figure 12.5.

```java
//Source file: C:\\Class_A.java


public class Class_A
{
    public Class_B theClass_B;

    public Class_A()
    {
    }
}



//Source file: C:\\Class_B.java


public class Class_B
{

    public Class_B()
    {
    }
}
```

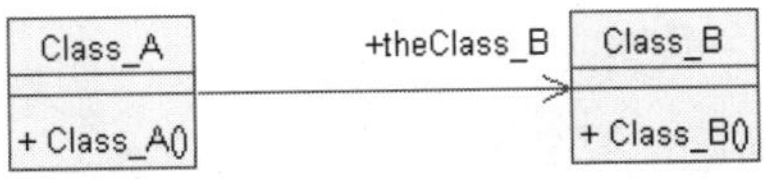

FIGURE 12.5

Reverse engineering an association relationship

Inheritance relationships are also generated in the Rose model. Rose will create generalization relationships to support any inheritance in the code. If you have packages of foundation classes in your model, such as the JDK or PowerBuilder system types, Rose will add generalization relationships between the reverse-engineered classes and the base classes.

The components in the code will also be represented in Rose after the reverse-engineering process. Each language deals with components differently. We'll discuss the reverse engineering of components in the following chapters.

Round-Trip Engineering

When you generate code using Rose, there are identification numbers placed in the generated code. For example, you may see a line like this in the code:

```
@roseuid 36730C530302
```

These strings of numbers and letters are used to help identify the classes, operations, and other model elements in the code and to synchronize the code with your Rose model.

In addition to the ID numbers, Rose generates protected regions in the code during the code-generation process. Any code you write in these protected regions will be safe during round-trip engineering.

For example, let's look at a portion of C++ code that was generated by Rose:

```
void SampleClass::DoSomething ()
{
   //## begin SampleClass::DoSomething%36EAB3DB03AC.body preserve=yes
   // – Code for the operation goes here –
   //## end SampleClass::DoSomething%36EAB3DB03AC.body
}
```

When the developers write code for this class, they code the DoSomething operation in the space between the //begin and //end statements, in a protected region. If this class is reverse engineered, changes are made, and it is then regenerated, the code of the DoSomething operation will remain safe.

NOTE   *When reverse engineering, Rose only examines files. It does not keep any of the source code, such as operation code, stored within Rose.*

Summary

In this chapter, we presented an overview of the code-generation and reverse-engineering capabilities of Rose.

To review, the steps for generating code are as follows:

1. Check the model.

2. Create the components.

3. Map the classes to the components.

4. Set the code-generation properties.

5. Select a class, component, or package.

6. Generate the code.

When reverse engineering code, Rose gathers information about the classes, attributes, operations, and relationships between the classes to generate the appropriate model elements. Using round-trip engineering, you can modify the model and then change the corresponding code, or change the code directly and then update the model. Either way, round-trip engineering helps keep your code and object model synchronized. In the next chapters, we'll take a look at code generation and reverse engineering in more detail for specific languages.

Chapter 13

ANSI C++ and Visual C++ Code Generation and Reverse Engineering

C++ IS ONE OF the most widely used object-oriented languages in the industry. Rational Rose supports integration with C++ through its code-generation and reverse-engineering capabilities. In this chapter, we'll discuss how to generate C++ code from your Rational Rose model and how to reverse engineer C++ code into a Rose model.

There are three versions of C++ integration with Rational Rose. First is the C++ add-in that has been available in Rose since October 1994. It contains a great deal of functionality, but can prove difficult to use. The second is an add-in for Microsoft's Visual C++. This add-in is simpler to use, but will integrate only with Microsoft's Visual C++. Rational, therefore, has introduced the third add-in, ANSI C++, which is an easy-to-use C++ code-generation and reverse-engineering tool that will work with C++ tools other than Microsoft's Visual C++.

In this chapter, we will discuss the ANSI C++ and Visual C++ add-ins. The original C++ add-in is still supported, but will not be covered here. We'll discuss the code-generation properties that can be set, and take a close look at how each Rose model element is implemented in the code.

- ◆ Setting C++ code-generation properties

- ◆ Mapping Rose elements to C++ constructs

- ◆ Generating C++ code from your Rose model

- ◆ Reverse engineering C++ code into your Rose model

Generating Code in ANSI C++ and Visual C++

You will need to follow these steps to generate code in ANSI C++:

1. Create components (see Chapter 10, "Component View").

2. Assign classes to components (see Chapter 10).

3. Set the code-generation properties.

4. Select a class or component to generate on a Class or Component diagram.

5. Select Tools ➢ ANSI C++ ➢ Generate Code.

6. Select Tools ➢ ANSI C++ ➢ Browse Header or Browse Body to view the generated code.

The first step in code generation is to create components for the classes. In ANSI C++, the file is located in the class file. The component has only the Root directory. Once components have been created and the classes mapped, the next step is to set the code-generation properties for your classes, components, operations, and other model elements. The code-generation properties control certain aspects of the code that is generated.

If you are generating code in Visual C++, you will use a wizard. To start the wizard, select Tools ➢ Visual C++ ➢ Update Code. The Visual C++ Code Update tool will start, and a welcome screen will be displayed. Click Next to continue. Rose will display the Select Components and Classes window. Before you can generate a class in Visual C++, the class must be assigned to a component. If you have not assigned the class to a component, select the Create a VC++ Component and Assign New Classes to It (Ctrl+R) option in the wizard window. Using this option, you can create as many components as you need before you generate the code. Then select the components and/or classes in your model for which you wish to generate code.

To change the code-generation properties for your Visual C++ components and classes, right-click the VC++ folder on this screen. You can then edit any of the code-generation properties, such as the container class, to support relationship multiplicity, to automatically generate a constructor and destructor, and to automatically generate Get and Set operations or other member functions. The code-generation properties are discussed in greater detail in the upcoming section, "Visual C++ Code-Generation Properties."

Once all classes have been assigned to components, you have selected the classes and/or components you wish to generate, and all code-generation properties have been set, click Next to continue. A summary page will be displayed to let you know which classes or components were generated and which errors were encountered during the code-generation process.

Rose will use a lot of information from the model to generate code. For example, it will look at the multiplicity, role names, containment, and other details of each relationship. It will look at the attributes, operations, visibility, and other details of each class. From all of the information you entered using the specification windows for the various model elements, Rose will gather what it needs to generate code.

Converting a C++ Model to an ANSI C++ Model

Previous versions of Rose contained a C++ add-in, but not an ANSI C++ add-in. As we discussed earlier, the ANSI C++ add-in is a more user-friendly version of the C++ code-generation and reverse-engineering tool. Although you can continue to use the C++ add-in, Rose provides a means of converting an older C++ model to an ANSI C++ model.

First, select Add Ins ➢ Add In Manager, and be sure the ANSI Converter add-in is selected. Select Tools ➢ ANSI C++ ➢ Convert from Classic C++.

You can choose the following options:

- Convert selected classes, which will convert any classes that you selected on a Class diagram before starting the conversion wizard

- Convert all classes in selected packages, which will convert all classes within any package(s) that you selected on a Class diagram before starting the conversion wizard

- Convert all classes in selected package and its subpackages, which will convert all classes within the package that you selected on a Class diagram, as well as all classes in subpackages of the selected package

- Convert Entire Model, which will convert all classes in all packages

WARNING   *This operation will make significant changes to your model, so it's a good idea to make a backup of the model before performing the conversion.*

ANSI C++ Code-Generation Properties

C++ code generation using Rational Rose is extremely flexible. You have full control over what gets generated and many of the details of how the generated code will look. For example, for each class, you can decide if a constructor, copy constructor, and destructor will automatically be created. For each attribute, you control the visibility, name, and whether Get and Set operations should automatically be created. For each operation, you control the name, parameters, visibility, and return type.

In ANSI C++, you can manage these types of settings using the code-generation properties and the C++ class and component specification windows. The ANSI C++ add-in includes code-generation properties for classes, attributes, operations, operation parameters, packages, components, associations, and generalizations. You can see all of these properties by selecting Tools ➤ Options, and then selecting the ANSI C++ tab.

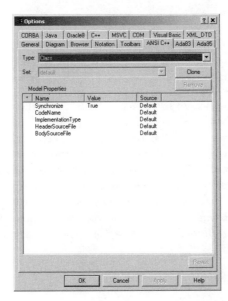

Code-generation properties can be set for the entire model or for a specific model element. You can change the default code-generation properties for the entire model by selecting Tools ➢ Options, then selecting the ANSI C++ tab. Code-generation properties can be set for a single class, attribute, operation, or other model element, which will override the default setting. To do so, open the specification window for the model element, select the ANSI C++ tab, modify the property value, and press the Override button. In the following sections, we'll examine the code-generation properties for classes, attributes, operations, operation parameters, packages, components, associations, and generalizations.

Class Properties

Class properties are the ANSI C++ code-generation properties that apply specifically to classes. These properties will let you change the class name, decide whether or not the class should be generated or reverse engineered, set the header filename, and set other class-specific properties.

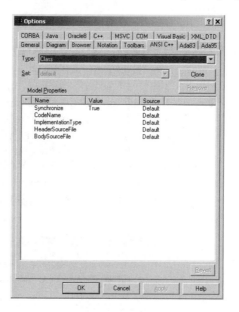

There are two places to set these properties. To set them for all classes, select Tools ➢ Options, then click the ANSI C++ tab and select Class from the drop-down list box. To set them for only one class, select the ANSI C++ tab on the class specification window and edit the properties there.

Using stereotypes, you can control the generation of keywords such as "static" or "virtual." Rose generates the text of the class stereotype in front of the "class" keyword.

Table 13.1 lists the ANSI C++ class properties, their purposes, and their default values.

In addition to these properties, you can control the code generation through the ANSI C++ class specification window. To open this window, select one or more classes on a Class diagram, then right-click it, and select ANSI C++ ➢ Class Customization. The customization window is shown in Figure 13.1.

TABLE 13.1: CLASS CODE-GENERATION PROPERTIES

PROPERTY	PURPOSE	DEFAULT
Synchronize	Controls whether the class will participate in code generation and reverse engineering.	True
CodeName	The name of the class in the generated code.	By default, Rose will use the class name in the model.
ImplementationType	Controls whether a class is generated using a class definition or elemental data type.	<blank> (generates class definition)
HeaderSourceFile	Filename for the . h file for this class.	<blank>
BodySourceFile	Filename for the . cpp file for this class.	<blank>

FIGURE 13.1

ANSI C++ Class Customization window

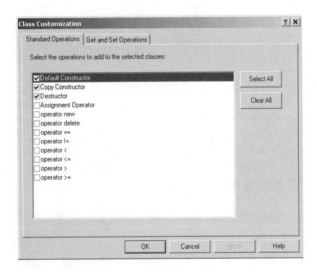

On the Standard Operations tab, select the method(s) you would like Rose to generate for the selected classes. When you close this window, Rose will add the selected methods to the classes, and they will be included in the code-generation process.

On the Get and Set Operations tab, select the attribute(s) for which you would like to generate Get and Set operations. For each selected operation, check the Generate Get Operation and/or Generate Set Operation to control which operations are generated.

Attribute Properties

Attribute properties are the ANSI C++ properties that relate specifically to attributes. Using these properties, you can control whether the attribute will be included in code generation and reverse engineering and you can set the name of the attribute in the generated code.

There are two places to set these properties. To set them for all attributes, select Tools ➤ Options, then click the ANSI C++ tab and select Attribute from the drop-down list box. To set them for only one attribute, select the ANSI C++ tab on the attribute specification window and edit the properties there.

In addition, stereotypes can be set on attributes to control whether a keyword, such as "static," is included for each attribute. Export control determines if an attribute is created as public or private. The default is to make all attributes private, which is good programming practice.

Table 13.2 lists the attribute properties, their purposes, and their default values.

TABLE 13.2: ATTRIBUTE CODE-GENERATION PROPERTIES

PROPERTY	PURPOSE	DEFAULT
Synchronize	Controls whether the attribute will be included in code generation and reverse engineering.	True
CodeName	Sets the attribute's name in the generated code.	\<blank\> (uses attribute name from the model)

Operation Properties

The operation properties are the ANSI C++ code-generation properties that are specific to operations. These properties will let you set the name of the operation, control whether the operation is inline, and set other code-generation specifications for each operation.

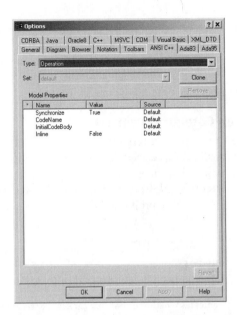

There are two places to set these properties. To set them for all operations, select Tools ➤ Options, then click the ANSI C++ tab and select Operation from the drop-down list box. To set them for only one operation, select the ANSI C++ tab on the operation specification window and edit the properties there.

Table 13.3 lists the operation code-generation properties, their purposes, and their default values.

TABLE 13.3: OPERATION CODE-GENERATION PROPERTIES

PROPERTY	PURPOSE	DEFAULT
Synchronize	Controls whether the operation will be included in code generation and reverse engineering.	True
CodeName	Sets the name of the generated operation.	<blank> (uses the operation name from the model)
Generate FunctionBody (Rose 2002)	Determine if function body is to be generated. If true, function body will be generated. If false, function body will not be generated. If default, then a body will be generated unless it is a non-inline friend or a non-inline abstract operation other than a destructor.	Default
InitialCodeBody	Code to include within the operation itself. This code will be generated within the operation the first time the code-generation process is run. Subsequent code-generation processes will not replace the operation code with the value of the InitialCodeBody property. You must include opening and closing braces in this property.	<blank>
Inline	Controls whether or not to inline the operation.	False

In addition to these, each parameter in the operation also has a property called CodeName. (The CodeName property in Table 13.3 applies to the overall operation, but there is also a CodeName property for each parameter in the operation.) If you supply a value to this property, Rose will use that value as the parameter's name when generating code. If you do not supply a value, Rose will use the parameter name as it appears in the model.

Package (Class Category) Properties

The class category properties are those ANSI C++ properties that apply to packages of classes. To set these properties for all packages, select Tools ➤ Options, then click the ANSI C++ tab and select Class Category from the drop-down list box. To set them for a single package, open the package specification window, select the ANSI C++ tab, and set the properties there.

Table 13.4 lists the package properties, their descriptions, and their default values.

TABLE 13.4: PACKAGE CODE-GENERATION PROPERTIES

PROPERTY	PURPOSE	DEFAULT
CodeName	Namespace	\<blank\>
IsNameSpace	Indicates whether or not this package represents a namespace	False

Component (Module Specification) Properties

The component properties are related to the `.cpp` and `.h` files generated and reverse engineered by Rose. These properties allow you to control items such as copyright statements and #include statements in the code.

To set these properties for all components, select Tools ➤ Options, then click the ANSI C++ tab and select Module Specification from the drop-down list box. To set them for a single component, open the component specification window and select the ANSI C++ tab. Table 13.5 lists the component properties.

TABLE 13.5: COMPONENT CODE-GENERATION PROPERTIES

PROPERTY	PURPOSE	DEFAULT
Synchronize	Controls whether this component will be included in code generation and reverse engineering.	True
Copyright	Copyright statement to include in the generated code.	\<blank\>
RootPackage	Logical view package under which reverse-engineered classes and packages will be placed.	C++ Reverse Engineered
InitialHeaderIncludes	#Include statements to include in the generated `.h` file.	\<blank\>
InitialBodyIncludes	#Include statements to include in the generated `.cpp` file.	\<blank\>
RevEngRootDirectory (Rose 2002)	Sets the default directory to search for files when reverse engineering	\<blank\>

Continued on next page

TABLE 13.5: COMPONENT CODE-GENERATION PROPERTIES *(continued)*

PROPERTY	PURPOSE	DEFAULT
RevEngDirectoriesAs-Packages (Rose 2002)	Creates a Logical view package to correspond to each directory used in reverse engineering	False
HeaderFileExtension (Rose 2002)	Sets the file extension to use when generating header files	.h
ImplementationFile-Extension (Rose 2002)	Sets the file extension to use when generating implementation files	.cpp
NewHeaderFileDirectory (Rose 2002)	Subdirectory of root directory for generated header files	<blank>
NewImplementation-FileDirectory (Rose 2002)	Subdirectory of root directory for generated implementation files	<blank>
FileCapitalization (Rose 2002)	Sets case to use in generated file names (upper case, lower case, lower case with underscores, same as model)	Same as model
CodeGenExtraDirectories (Rose 2002)	Controls what directories will be created on code generation	<blank>
StripClassPrefix (Rose 2002)	Character(s) to strip from the class name when a file is generated	<blank>
UseTabs (Rose 2002)	Indents the generated code with tabs rather than spaces	False
TabWidth (Rose 2002)	Number of characters to indent for each tab	8
IndentWidth (Rose 2002)	Column width in spaces between indent locations	4
AccessIndentation (Rose 2002)	Number of spaces that the public, private, and protected keywords will be indented	-2
ModelIdCommentRules (Rose 2002)	Controls when model IDs are generated (on code generation, on code generation and reverse engineering, or never)	Code generation only
PageWidth (Rose 2002)	Number of characters in a line in the generated file	80
ClassMemberOrder (Rose 2002)	Sets the order of the generated attributes (public first, private first, order by kind, unordered)	Public First
OneParameterPerLine (Rose 2002)	Controls whether or not each parameter in an operation is written on a separate line	False
NamespaceBraceStyle (Rose 2002)	Sets the style for namespace braces. Use the ANSI C++ component specification window for examples of the five available styles.	B2
ClassBraceStyle (Rose 2002)	Sets the style for class braces. Use the ANSI C++ component specification window for examples of the five available styles.	B2
FunctionBraceStyle (Rose 2002)	Sets the style for function braces. Use the ANSI C++ component specification window for examples of the five available styles.	B2

These properties and others can also be controlled through the C++ component specification window, shown in Figure 13.2. To open this window, right-click the component and select ANSI C++ ➢ Open ANSI C++ Specification.

FIGURE 13.2

ANSI C++
component
customization
window's Files tab

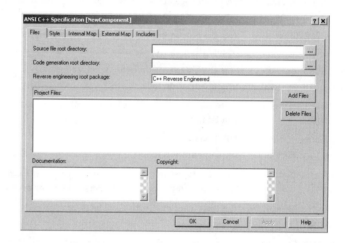

In the first field on the Files tab, you enter the root directory of all the source files. In the Code Generation Root Directory field, enter the directory into which Rose should generate code. The Reverse Engineering Root Package field corresponds to the RootPackage property discussed above, and sets the package into which files will be reverse engineered. The Project Files section includes the .cpp, .h, and other source code files relevant to this component. Finally, the Documentation and Copyright fields are the places to enter comments and copyright information for the component.

In Rose 2002, there are additional fields available on the Files tab. The Reverse Engineer Directories As Packages check box controls whether or not directories are reverse engineered as Logical view packages. The Header and Implementation File Extension fields allow you to set the file extension that will be used for these types of files when generating code. In Rose 2002, you can generate source and body files into different directories. Use the Subdirectory of Root for Header Files field to set the directory for header files, and use the Subdirectory of Root for Implementation Files field to set the directory for implementation files. Filename Capitalization controls whether filenames are generated in upper or lower case. The Additional Directories field controls whether subdirectories will be created for namespaces or packages. Finally, the Prefix to Strip from Class Name When Constructing Filename field will strip specific characters from the class name to generate the header and implementation files.

The Style tab is shown in Figure 13.3. This tab controls formatting options for the component.

Under the Indentation area, you choose whether to use spaces or tabs for indentation and the number of spaces or tabs to use. Under Round-Trip Engineering Options, select Code Generation Only for Model IDs if you would like model IDs generated in the source code. Select Code Generation and Reverse Engineering if you would also like to insert model IDs into code that has been reverse engineered. Select Never Generate Model IDs if you don't want to use the IDs at all. Although the IDs are optional, they are recommended if you plan to do round-trip engineering. The ID will help Rose map the appropriate source code to the appropriate class or other model element, even if the class name has been changed.

Under the Brace Styles area, select one of the five indentation styles for namespaces, classes, and functions.

Use the Internal Map tab to set the #include statements that will be created for references to classes within the component. Use the External Map tab to set the #include statements that will be created for references to classes within the component by classes outside of the component. Finally, enter any #include statements for the header or body in the Includes tab.

FIGURE 13.3

ANSI C++ component customization window's Style tab

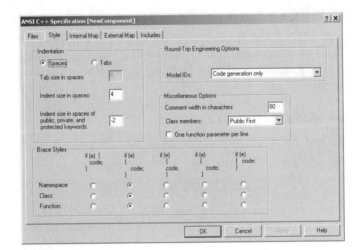

Role Properties

Role properties are the C++ code-generation properties that affect the code generated for relationships. As with most of the other property sets, there are two places to set these properties. To set them for all relationships, select Tools ➤ Options, then click the ANSI C++ tab and select Role from the drop-down list box. To set them for a single relationship, open the relationship specification window. On the ANSI C++ tab of the relationship specification window, you can change the properties for that relationship.

Table 13.6 lists the role properties, their meanings, and their default values.

TABLE 13.6: ROLE CODE-GENERATION PROPERTIES

PROPERTY	PURPOSE	DEFAULT
Synchronize	Controls whether the relationship will be included in code generation and reverse engineering.	True
CodeName	Sets the name of the relationship in the generated code.	\<blank\>
Const (Rose 2000A)	Controls whether the attribute created to support the relationship is a constant.	False
InitialValue	Sets the initial value of the attribute created to support the relationship.	\<blank\>

Generalization Properties

As with other relationships, you can set code-generation properties for generalization (inheritance) relationships in C++. There is, however, only one property you can set for a generalization relationship. The Synchronize property controls whether the relationship will be included in code generation and reverse engineering. The default value is True.

Visual C++ Code-Generation Properties

The Visual C++ add-in includes a Model Assistant, which you use to set the code-generation properties for your classes, attributes, operations, and other model elements. Once the properties have been set, the Visual C++ add-in includes a wizard that will walk you through all the steps needed to generate your code.

Class Model Assistant

To start the Model Assistant, right-click a class or component and select Model Assistant. The Model Assistant for a class is shown here:

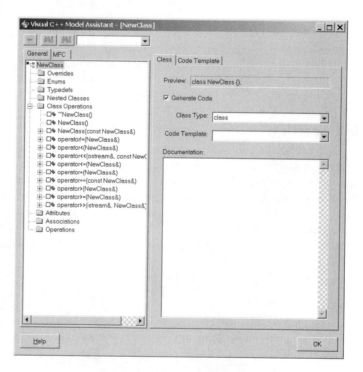

As you can see, the Model Assistant lets you set code-generation properties for the class, as well as its attributes, operations, and associations. In Rose, you can automatically generate certain operations, such as a constructor and a destructor, by selecting them in the Class Operations section of the treeview.

To begin, select the class name (in this example "NewClass" at the top level of the treeview). Select the Generate Code check box if you would like Rose to generate Visual C++ code for this class. In the Class Type list box, select the class stereotype: class, structure, union, typedef, or enum. In the Code Template list box, you can optionally select a template to use. A template contains attributes, operations, and code that can be used to create a class. In the Documentation field, you can enter text that will be generated as comments in the code.

In the Attributes section of the treeview, you can select an attribute to modify. Once you select an attribute, you can then set its data type using the Type field. Standard Visual C++ data types will appear in the list. If the attribute should have a default value, fill in the Initial Value field. Set the attribute's visibility (public, private, or protected). By default, Rose sets all attributes to Private. The Static check box will add the "static" keyword to the generated code. As with classes, text entered in the Documentation field will appear as a comment in the generated code.

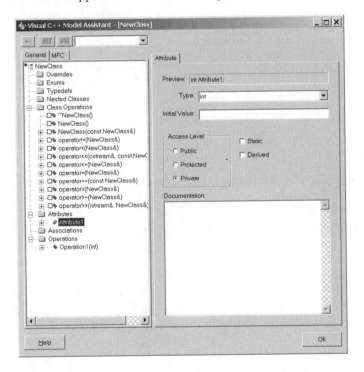

Select an operation in the Operations section of the treeview. In the Return Type field, set the data type of the operation's return value. Standard Visual C++ data types are listed in this field. Set the visibility (public, protected, or private) using the Access Level field. By default, an operation has public visibility. You can create a virtual or abstract operation by setting the Operation Kind field. Select the Inline check box to include the "inline" keyword with the operation. An inline operation's definition is generated in the header file for the class. Select the Const check box to add the "const" keyword to the operation and to signify that the operation will return a constant. To make an operation static or to give it friend visibility, select Static or Friend from the list in the Linkage field.

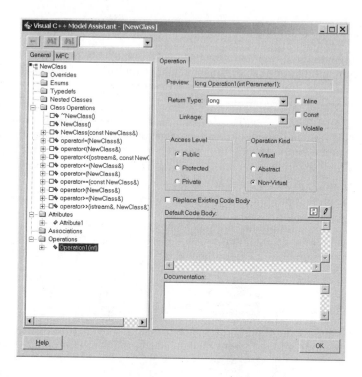

By default, Rose will not add code to the body of a generated method. To add some default code, select the Replace Existing Code Body check box and add the text in the Default Code Body field. Add comments to the Documentation field.

An operation's parameters are listed in the treeview under the operation name. To edit a parameter, select it in the treeview. You can then change its data type, default value, and documentation.

As with ANSI C++, associations in Visual C++ are generated as attributes. In the Model Assistant, the attributes generated for associations are listed in the Associations portion of the treeview. In the Implementation field, you can set the type of reference to generate. By default, Rose will generate a pointer to the referenced class. You can also use an array, reference, or user-defined type. Select the appropriate value from the Implementation list box.

As with attributes, you set the default value in the Initial Value field, set the visibility to Public, Private, or Protected, and check the Const or Static boxes if these keywords are needed. In the Multiplicity field, enter the multiplicity of the relationship.

Component Properties

The Model Assistant is also used to set the code-generation properties for components. Specifically, each component must be assigned to a Visual C++ project before code generation can be completed. You can also assign each component to a project during the code-generation process—the wizard will give you the option to assign components to projects. The Component Model Assistant window is shown here:

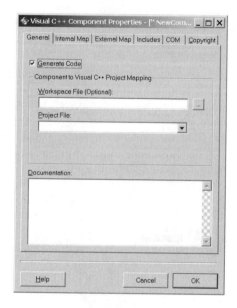

To open the Model Assistant for a component, right-click the component and select Properties. On the General tab, map the component to an existing Visual C++ project file. Optionally, you can set a Visual C++ workspace file as well. If the file is an IDL file, set the IDL filename and path.

The Internal Map tab is used to set up the mapping of classes within the component to include statements. For each mapping, set the class (an asterisk [*] refers to all classes), include the filename, and include the file location. You can add as many mappings as needed.

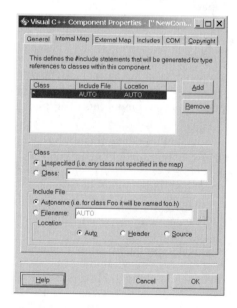

The External Map tab is very similar, but is used to set up the include statements needed by classes in other components to reference classes in this component.

On the Includes tab, you can set up includes statements to be generated in the header and body files for each class in the component. Add as many includes statements as you need, adding each on a separate line.

Use the COM tab to control how ATL objects will be generated for this component. The Update ATL Artifacts check box controls whether code is generated for ATL objects at all. If you do update the code, complete the rest of the settings on this screen to control how the code is updated:

- The Use Smart Pointers for Interface Associations check box will use the Visual C++ smart pointer functionality during code generation and reverse engineering.

- The Generate #Import Statements check box controls whether #import statements are created and where they are created.

- If there is a value in the Put #Import Statements In field, Rose will put all #import statements in that file.

- If Include Full Path on Imports is checked, Rose will use the full path in the #import statement.

- If Use Default Attributes is checked and there is a value in that field, Rose will use the field value when attributes are unspecified in the model.

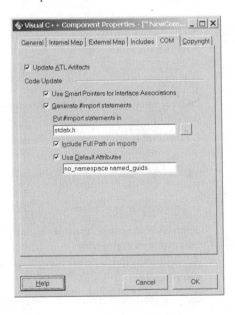

Finally, you can use the Copyright tab to set copyright information for the component. Text you enter here will be entered into the header and implementation files for the classes in that component.

Project Properties

Using the menu command Tools ➤ Visual C++ ➤ Properties, you can set properties that apply to the whole Rose model.

Table 13.7 lists each Visual C++ project property, its purpose, and the tab on the Visual C++ Properties window you use to set the property.

TABLE 13.7: VISUAL C++ PROJECT PROPERTIES

PROPERTY	PURPOSE	TAB
Generate Model IDs	Controls whether Rose model IDs are inserted into the source code.	Code Update
Generate Documentation	Controls whether comments you entered into the Documentation field of a class or other model element are generated as comments in the source code.	Code Update
Generate #Include Statements	Controls whether #include statements are added to the header file.	Code Update
Apply Pattern on Code Generation	Controls whether to apply the selections you made on the Operations and Accessors tabs to the generated code.	Code Update
Generate Debug Operations for MFC Classes	Controls whether AssertValid and Dump operations are created for MFC classes.	Code Update
Create Backup Files	Controls whether backup files are created for source code before Rose modifies them.	Code Update
Support CodeName	Gives the user the option of naming an element differently in the model and the source code.	Code Update
Reverse Engineer Documentation	Pulls comments from the source code into the Documentation field of the model element.	Model Update
Create Overview Diagrams	Creates an overview diagram for reverse-engineered code.	Model Update
Update Model IDs in Code	Adds model IDs to the code during the reverse-engineering process.	Model Update
Default Package	Sets the package in which reverse-engineered elements are placed.	Model Update
Attribute Types	Controls which types will be modeled as attributes rather than roles in reverse engineering.	Model Update
Containers	Sets the container classes that can be used in the Implementation field for a role.	Containers
Class Operations	Controls which operations will be generated for a class.	Class Operations
Accessors	Controls whether Get and Set operations are generated for an attribute or role.	Accessors

Visual C++ and ATL Objects

The Rose Visual C++ add-in includes support for ATL objects. If you are using ATL in your model, you should first import the standard ATL classes. This step will help ensure that the round-trip engineering process works properly. You can import ATL 3.0 classes into your model by selecting Tools ➤ Visual C++ ➤ Quick Import ATL 3.0. The ATL 3.0 classes will be imported into a package called ATL 3.0 in the Logical view. Once the import is complete, you can create relationships between your classes and the ATL classes.

CONVERTING AN EXISTING CLASS TO AN ATL OBJECT

You can create new ATL objects in Rose or simply convert existing classes in your Rose model to ATL. To convert an existing class:

1. Right-click the class and select COM ➤ New ATL Object.

2. You will see the ATL Object Properties window.

3. In the C++ section, enter the short name of the C++ class. The Class field will already be completed for you.

4. If the appropriate component already exists in the Rose model, select the C++ component and project for the C++ class. Otherwise, leave these fields blank.

5. In the COM section, enter the name of the CoClass and interface. When you press OK, Rose will create the CoClass and interface class and set their relationships.

6. If the appropriate component already exists in the Rose model, select the COM component and project for the COM classes. Otherwise, leave these fields blank.

NOTE *In Rose 2002, reverse-engineered MIDL components will be added to the model as components with the <<MIDL>> stereotype. Any classes with a stereotype of <<coclass>> or <<interface>> will be automatically mapped to the MIDL components.*

Generated Code

In the following sections, we'll take a look at the C++ code generated for a class, an attribute, an operation, and for the different types of relationships between classes. In each of these sections, we'll include some sample code to give you an idea of what will be generated from your Rose model.

Rose uses the information in the specifications of the model elements when generating code. For example, it will look at the different specifications for a class (visibility, attributes, operations, and so on) when generating code for the class.

Code Generated for Classes

Let's begin by looking at the code generated for a typical class. A class in your object model will become a C++ class when you generate code. Each class will generate code similar to the following:

```
Class TheClass
{
public:
TheClass();
~TheClass();
};
```

However, a great deal of additional information will also be generated in the code. (We'll look at a complete header and implementation file shortly.) All of the attributes, operations, and relationships of the class will be reflected in the generated code. The major elements generated for each class include:

- The class name
- The class visibility
- A constructor for the class (optional)
- A destructor for the class (optional)
- Get() and Set() operations for each attribute (optional)
- Class documentation
- Attributes
- Operations
- Relationships

Each class in the model will generate two C++ files, a header file, and an implementation file. Each file will be named using the class name. For example, an Employee class will generate an `Employee.h` file and an `Employee.cpp` file.

When generating code with ANSI C++, Rose will use the package structure you established in the Component view of your model to generate the appropriate directories. A directory will be created for each package in the model. Within each of the directories Rose creates, there will be the `.cpp` and `.h` files for the classes in that package. If you have not created components and packages in the Component view, Rose will use the package structure in the Logical view to create the directory structure.

Much of the information in your Rose model will be used directly when generating code. For example, the attributes, operations, relationships, and class name of each class will directly affect the code generated. Other model fields, such as the documentation entered for the class, will not directly affect the code. These field values are created as comments in the generated code.

Table 13.8 lists the fields available in the class specification window and notes which of these fields will directly affect the code generated.

TABLE 13.8: EFFECT OF CLASS SPECIFICATIONS ON GENERATED CODE

FIELDS	EFFECT ON CODE
Name	Name in model will become class name
Type	Directly affects the type of class created
Stereotype	No effect
Export Control	Directly affects the class visibility
Documentation	Becomes a comment
Cardinality	No effect
Space	No effect

Continued on next page

TABLE 13.8: Effect of Class Specifications on Generated Code *(continued)*

FIELDS	EFFECT ON CODE
Persistence	No effect
Concurrency	No effect
Abstract	Creates an abstract class
Formal Arguments	Formal arguments are included in the code for a parameterized class
Operations	Generated in code
Attributes	Generated in code
Relationships	Generated in code

Let's look at the code generated for the following class:

Flight
- FlightNumber : int - DepartureDate : date - DepartureCity : string - ArrivalCity : string
+ AddPassenger(PassengerID : int) : boolean + RemovePassenger(PassengerID : int) : boolean + CancelFlight() : int

GENERATED HEADER FILE

The following code is the header file that was generated for this class.

```
#ifndef FLIGHT_H_INCLUDED_C6AD4E5A
#define FLIGHT_H_INCLUDED_C6AD4E5A


//##ModelId=39528510031C
//##Documentation
//## This class holds information about airline flights.
class Flight
{
  public:
    //##ModelId=3952853300EC
    boolean AddPassenger(int PassengerID);

    //##ModelId=3952853B013D
    boolean RemovePassenger(int PassengerID);

    //##ModelId=3952854302B1
    int CancelFlight();

  private:
    //##ModelId=395285160108
    int FlightNumber;
```

```
//##ModelId=395285190365
date DepartureDate;

//##ModelId=3952851E0037
string DepartureCity;

//##ModelId=3952852B009A
string ArrivalCity;

};



#endif /* FLIGHT_H_INCLUDED_C6AD4E5A */
```

Let's begin by discussing the annotations that Rose inserts into the source code. Rose adds these model IDs so that code can be modified and regenerated (round-trip engineering) without overwriting any changes. Use of the model IDs is optional. To turn model IDs on or off, open the ANSI C++ component specification for the component. On the Style tab, set model IDs to the Never Generate Model IDs option.

The generated file will include header information for the attributes and operations of the class. It can also include headers for a constructor, a destructor, a copy constructor, and other standard methods. To include any of these, open the ANSI C++ Class Customization window and select the method(s) to generate. Or, if you are using Visual C++, use the Model Assistant.

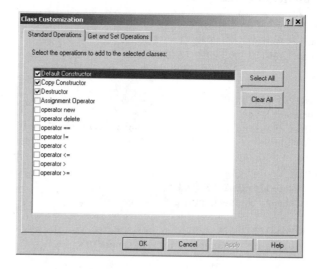

As you can see, Rose includes the visibility, parameters, parameter data types, and return type for each operation. Although Rose cannot code the operation itself, it does provide a "skeleton" framework for the programmers to use. You can generate code for the operation by adding default code in the operation's InitialCodeBody property.

GENERATED IMPLEMENTATION FILE

The other file generated by Rose is an implementation file, with the default extension .cpp. The following is the implementation file generated along with the header file we just examined.

```
#include "c:/Flight.h"

//##ModelId=3954129803B3
boolean Flight::AddPassenger(int PassengerID)
{
}

//##ModelId=395412A00093
boolean Flight::RemovePassenger(int PassengerID)
{
}

//##ModelId=395412A80121
int Flight::CancelFlight()
{
}
```

Again, notice that Rose includes the operation visibility, parameters, parameter data types, and operation return type in the generated code. Had we selected the option to generate the constructor, destructor, or other standard methods (by right-clicking the class and selecting ANSI C++ Code Customization), these would be included in the code as well. With Visual C++, use the Model Assistant to determine whether or not to generate these methods.

Code Generated for Attributes

Aside from the class itself, Rose will generate the attributes for the class. For each attribute, Rose will include:

- Visibility
- Data type
- Default value
- Get operation (optional)
- Set operation (optional)

For a given attribute, Rose will generate code similar to the following:

```
Class TheClass
{
public:
int PublicAttribute;
int GetPublicAttribute();
int GetProtectedAttribute();
int GetPrivateAttribute();
```

```
void set_PublicAttribute (int value);
void set_ProtectedAttribute (int value);
void set_PrivateAttribute (int value);

protected:
    int ProtectedAttribute;

private:
    int PrivateAttribute;
};
```

A great deal more, including comments and Rose identifiers, will be generated in a full header and implementation file. Let's look in detail at the code generated for the following class:

In this example, we opened the ANSI C++ Class Customization window and selected the option to generate Get and Set methods for the FlightNumber attribute. Using Visual C++, you can use the Model Assistant to control whether Get and Set methods are created. The header file now reads as follows:

```
#ifndef FLIGHT_H_INCLUDED_C6ABFE6A
#define FLIGHT_H_INCLUDED_C6ABFE6A

//##ModelId=39541274036B
class Flight
{
  public:
    //##ModelId=3954129803B3
    boolean AddPassenger(int PassengerID);

    //##ModelId=395412A00093
    boolean RemovePassenger(int PassengerID);

    //##ModelId=395412A80121
    int CancelFlight();

    //##ModelId=395413D80055
    int get_FlightNumber() const;

    //##ModelId=395413D800BA
    void set_FlightNumber(int left);
```

```
private:
    //##ModelId=3954127801F4
    int FlightNumber;

    //##ModelId=3954128202DF
    date DepartureDate;

    //##ModelId=395412860122
    string DepartureCity;

    //##ModelId=3954128E0097
    string ArrivalCity;

};

#endif /* FLIGHT_H_INCLUDED_C6ABFE6A */
```

The implementation file also includes the Get and Set methods. Note that Rose will include more than just the method signature; it will actually code these methods for you. The implementation file for the Flight class is shown here:

```
#include "c:/Flight.h"

//##ModelId=3954129803B3
boolean Flight::AddPassenger(int PassengerID)
{
}

//##ModelId=395412A00093
boolean Flight::RemovePassenger(int PassengerID)
{
}

//##ModelId=395412A80121
int Flight::CancelFlight()
{
}

//##ModelId=395413D80055
int Flight::get_FlightNumber() const
{
    return FlightNumber;
}

//##ModelId=395413D800BA
void Flight::set_FlightNumber(int left)
{
    FlightNumber = left;
}
```

Code Generated for Operations

Rose generates code for each of the operations in the class. For each operation, the generated code includes the operation name, the parameters, the parameter data types, and the return type. Each operation will generate code similar to the following:

```
Class TheClass
{
public:
void PublicOperation();

protected:
void ProtectedOperation();

private:
void PrivateOperation();
};
```

We'll examine the code generated for the following class:

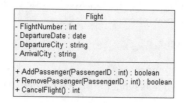

In the header file, Rose will generate the signatures for the operations:

```
#ifndef FLIGHT_H_INCLUDED_C6ABEA96
#define FLIGHT_H_INCLUDED_C6ABEA96

//##ModelId=39541274036B
class Flight
{
  public:
    //##ModelId=3954129803B3
    boolean AddPassenger(int PassengerID);

    //##ModelId=395412A00093
    boolean RemovePassenger(int PassengerID);

    //##ModelId=395412A80121
    //##Documentation
    //## The CancelFlight operation will cancel all reservations for the
    //## flight, notify all passengers with reservations, and disable future
    //## reservations for the flight.
    int CancelFlight();
```

```
    private:
       //##ModelId=3954127801F4
       int FlightNumber;

       //##ModelId=3954128202DF
       date DepartureDate;

       //##ModelId=395412860122
       string DepartureCity;

       //##ModelId=3954128E0097
       string ArrivalCity;

    };



#endif /* FLIGHT_H_INCLUDED_C6ABEA96 */
```

As you can see, the full operation signature is generated in the code. Any documentation you entered for the operation is also generated, as a comment in the code. If you enter information for the operation protocol, qualifications, exceptions, time, space, preconditions, semantics, or post-conditions, this information will not appear in the generated code.

Rose will also generate code for the operation in the implementation file. We just examined the header file for the Flight class, so now let's take a look at the implementation file for this class.

```
#include "c:/Flight.h"

//##ModelId=3954129803B3
boolean Flight::AddPassenger(int PassengerID)
{
}


//##ModelId=395412A00093
boolean Flight::RemovePassenger(int PassengerID)
{
}


//##ModelId=395412A80121
int Flight::CancelFlight()
{
}
```

As you can see, Rose includes each operation in the implementation file. Developers now need to go into the implementation file and code each operation between the opening and closing braces.

Visual C++ Code Generation

For the most part, the code generated in Visual C++ is the same as that generated in ANSI C++, and follows the rules described in the "Generated Code" section earlier in this chapter. Each class in the model becomes a class in the Visual C++ project. Attributes become data members in Visual C++, and the data type, default value, access type, and other code-generation settings from Rose are directly translated into Visual C++. Operations create member functions in Visual C++. The code-generation add-in examines the operation visibility, parameters, parameter data types, return type, and other code-generation properties to create the member function. Attributes are created for relationships, as described in the "Generated Code" section.

The differences between ANSI C++ and Visual C++ code generation lie in the components. Each component in the Rose model will become either a Visual C++ project or an IDL file within a project. Classes are assigned to components during the code-generation process. Interfaces are generated in the IDL files, and are created using the process described earlier in the "Visual C++ and ATL Objects" section.

Reverse Engineering ANSI C++

To reverse engineer in ANSI C++, you must first select a component. All or some of the classes assigned to that component can then be reverse engineered.

To reverse engineer one or more classes that are not in the Rose model at all:

1. Create a new component in the Component view.

2. Open the ANSI C++ specification window for the new component.

3. In the Project Files area, click Add Files to browse the source file(s) you want to reverse engineer.

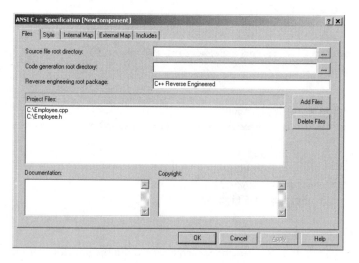

4. Click OK to close the ANSI C++ specification window.

5. Right-click the component and select ANSI C++ ➤ Reverse Engineer.

6. Select the class(es) to reverse engineer and press OK.

7. The classes will be brought into the Rose model and added to the Logical view, under a package named C++ Reverse Engineered.

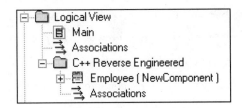

NOTE *To reverse engineer classes into a package other than C++ Reverse Engineered, open the C++ specification window for the component and change the package name in the Reverse Engineering Root Package field.*

To reverse engineer a class that already exists in your model, right-click its component and select ANSI C++ ➤ Reverse Engineer. Select the class(es) to reverse engineer and press OK. Alternately, you can right-click the class you want to reverse engineer and select ANSI C++ ➤ Reverse Engineer.

When you reverse engineer a class, all of its attributes, operations, and relationships are reverse engineered as well. The C++-to-Rose mapping we've discussed in the past several sections controls how the C++ code is represented in the Rose model.

Reverse Engineering Visual C++

You can reverse engineer a Visual C++ project into an existing component or into a new component in Rose. To begin either process, select Tools ➤ Visual C++ ➤ Update Model from Code. Rose will display a list of existing components in your Rose model.

To reverse engineer the project into a new component, right-click Visual C++ and select Add Component. Select the Visual C++ project to reverse engineer into the new component.

To reverse engineer the project into an existing component, right-click the appropriate component, select Properties, and select the element(s) in the project that you wish to reverse engineer.

Click Next to show a summary, and then Finish to complete the reverse-engineering process. The elements in the project will be mapped to Rose elements as we've discussed in this chapter.

Summary

In this chapter, we took a look at how various Rose model elements are implemented in C++. Using the code-generation properties for classes, packages, attributes, operations, roles, and other model elements, you have a great deal of control over what gets generated.

Again, the steps needed to generate ANSI C++ code are:

1. Create components.

2. Assign classes to components.

3. Set the code-generation properties.

4. Select a class or component to generate on a Class or Component diagram.

5. Select Tools ➤ ANSI C++ ➤ Class Customization.

6. Select Tools ➤ ANSI C++ ➤ Code Generation.

7. Select Tools ➤ ANSI C++ ➤ Browse Header or Browse Body to view the generated code.

The steps to generate Visual C++ code are:

1. Create component(s) corresponding to the project(s).

2. Select Tools ➤ Visual C++ ➤ Model Assistant.

3. Select Tools ➤ Visual C++ ➤ Update Code.

4. Select the component(s) to update.

5. Set code-generation properties.

6. Select Finish to complete the process.

The steps needed to reverse engineer ANSI C++ code are:

1. Create a new component.

2. Use the ANSI C++ specification window to select the file(s) to reverse engineer.

3. Right-click the component and select ANSI C++ ➤ Reverse Engineer.

4. Select the class(es) to reverse engineer and press OK.

The steps needed to reverse engineer Visual C++ code are:

1. Select Tools ➤ Visual C++ ➤ Update Model from Code.

2. Select an existing component to reverse engineer, or create a new component.

3. Select the project element(s) to reverse engineer.

In the next chapter, we'll examine the Java add-in for Rose. Using this powerful feature, you can model Java classes, interfaces, attributes, operations, relationships, JAR files, and WAR files. Through the new support for J2EE, you can now also model EJBs, servlets, and other constructs. The enhanced functionality in Rose 2001, 2001A, and 2002 provide the ability to create a complete model of your Java application. The forward- and reverse-engineering features provide you with the ability to keep the code and the object model consistent.

Chapter 14

Java Code Generation and Reverse Engineering

IN THIS CHAPTER, WE'LL discuss how to generate Java code from your Rational Rose model and reverse engineer a Rose model from your Java code. We'll discuss the code-generation properties that can be set for Java and take a close look at how each Rose model element is implemented in the code. Then, we'll look at how to reverse engineer Java code and how to keep your model and code synchronized.

To generate code, you'll need to follow these steps:

1. Create the components (see Chapter 10, "Component View").

2. Assign classes to the components (see Chapter 10).

3. Set the code-generation properties.

4. Select a class or component to generate on a Class or Component diagram.

5. Select Tools ➢ Java ➢ Code Generation.

6. Select Tools ➢ Java ➢ Browse Java Source to view the generated code.

Rose will take a lot of information from the model to generate code. For example, it will look at the multiplicity, role names, containment, and other details of each relationship. It will look at the attributes, operations, visibility, and other details of each class. From all of the information you entered using the specification windows for the various model elements, Rose will gather what it needs to generate code.

- ◆ Setting Java code-generation properties

- ◆ Generating Java code from your Rose model

- ◆ Mapping Rose elements to Java constructs

- ◆ Importing the Java Development Kit

- ◆ Reverse engineering Java into your Rose model

Introduction to Rose J

Rose J is the add-in to Rational Rose that supports the generation and reverse engineering of Java constructs. This feature includes:

◆ Integration with VisualAge Java and Visual J++

◆ Support for Java 2 Platform Enterprise Edition (J2EE) constructs

◆ Generation of Java code

◆ Reverse engineering Java constructs into a Rose model

◆ Support for Java frameworks, such as the Java™ Development Kit (JDK™) and Java™ Foundation Classes (JFC).

Let's begin with code generation. Rose J will examine the classes and components that you have created in your Rose model and generate the appropriate source code for these components. There are a number of code-generation properties that will affect the generated source code. Using Rose J, Rose ID numbers will also be created in the source code. These numbers help to keep the code from being overwritten during round-trip engineering.

There is an auto-synchronization feature in Rose J, which automatically starts the code-generation process anytime a Java class has changed in the model. This feature will help ensure that the model and the source code remain consistent.

Once you create your classes, components, attributes, operations, and other model elements, you can begin the code-generation process. Before generating code, check the syntax of the model using the Tools ➢ Java ➢ Syntax Check menu option. If there are any problems, they will appear in the log window.

After you resolve any problems, you can set the code-generation properties and generate code. In this chapter, we will discuss in detail how to set the properties and how each Rose modeling element maps to a Java construct. Table 14.1 lists the Java constructs and their corresponding model elements.

TABLE 14.1: JAVA-TO-ROSE MAPPING

JAVA CONSTRUCT	ROSE ELEMENT
Class	Class
Variable	Attribute
Method	Operation
Interface	Interface (class with stereotype of Interface)
.java file	Component
Java package	Component package
Java Bean	Attribute
EJB (Enterprise Java Bean)	Class

Continued on next page

TABLE 14.1: JAVA-TO-ROSE MAPPING *(continued)*

JAVA CONSTRUCT	ROSE ELEMENT
Servlet	Class
Inner class	Nested class
Implements relationship	Realization relationship
Extends relationship	Generalization relationship
Import statement	Association, dependency, or generalization

Beginning a Java Project

When first creating a Java model, there are four steps you may want to follow. First, when working on a project that will be primarily implemented in Java, you always want to set the default language to Java. This is done through the Tools ➤ Options menu. Click the Notation tab and set the default language to Java.

Next, select the framework you would like to use for your project. This is an optional step, but can provide you with the foundation you need to model your application. We will discuss specific frameworks shortly.

Third, if you are using either Microsoft Visual J++ or IBM VisualAge for Java, you should enable the links between Rose and these tools. Once you enable the links, you can generate code and reverse engineer VisualAge or Visual J++ projects directly from Rose.

Finally, be sure that the ClassPath environment variable is set. The ClassPath is used by Rose J to determine the location of class libraries and other files while generating code and reverse engineering. To view the ClassPath settings, select Tools ➤ Java ➤ Project Specification. The ClassPath entries will be displayed, and you can add or remove entries using this dialog box.

Selecting a Java Framework

When you first create a Rational Rose model, you are given the option to base your model on an existing framework. Create a new Rose model, and you will see the window shown in Figure 14.1.

NOTE   If you do not see the frameworks window, select Add-Ins ➤ Add-In Manager, and be sure Framework Wizard is checked.

There are several Java frameworks available: J2EE, J2SE 1.2, J2SE 1.3, jdk-116, jdk-12, and jfc-11. (The last three are, respectively, Java Development Kit version 1.1.6, Java Development Kit version 1.2, and the Java Foundation Classes version 1.1.)

Simply select whichever framework you will be using for your project. Rose will automatically load classes, relationships, attributes, operations, and components from the selected framework into your new model. You can then use these elements as a foundation to create your own project.

FIGURE 14.1

Rose frameworks

FIGURE 14.1

Rose frameworks

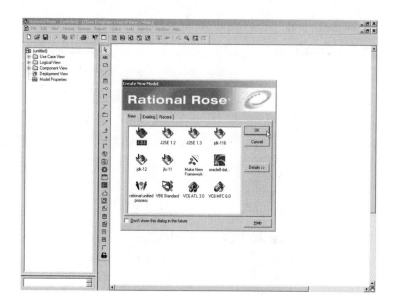

Figure 14.2 is an example of a new Rose model using the J2EE framework. No new information has yet been added to the model. The figure shows only what is imported with the J2EE framework. Note that, for readability, many of the packages in Figure 14.2 are not expanded; however, classes and other model elements are inside each one.

FIGURE 14.2

Rose model with J2EE framework

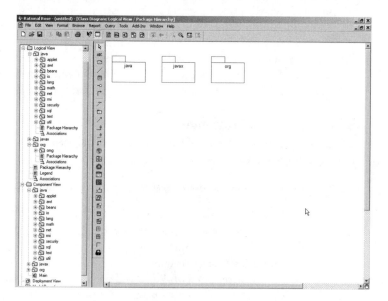

You can also use a framework on an existing Rose model. To do so, you need to load the appropriate controlled units. Each package in the frameworks is stored as controlled units. Select File ➤ Units ➤ Load, and then navigate to the `Rose 2000\framework\frameworks\shared components` directory. The `.cat` files in this directory are the controlled units for the frameworks. Each `.cat` file begins with the name of the framework, such as `j2ee` or `j2se_1_2`, so you know which files to import for which framework. Select the `.cat` files appropriate for your framework, and Rose will import them into your model.

Linking to IBM VisualAge for Java

Establishing a link between Rational Rose and IBM's VisualAge will allow you to update a VisualAge project directly from within Rose or to reverse engineer a VisualAge project into Rose.

To set up the link between the two tools, first start VisualAge. Select File and then Quick Start. On the dialog box, select Basic and then RoseLink Plug-In Toggle. This will establish the link from the VisualAge side.

To complete the process, start Rose. Select Tools ➤ Java ➤ Project Specification. On the Detail tab, set the Virtual Machine setting to IBM, as shown in Figure 14.3.

FIGURE 14.3

Java Virtual Machine setting

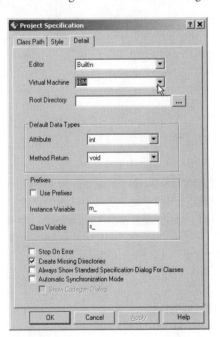

Select Tools ➤ Java ➤ IBM VisualAge for Java Project. Select the appropriate VisualAge project. The link between the two tools is now set.

Linking to Microsoft Visual J++

Similar to the link with IBM's VisualAge, the link to Microsoft Visual J++ will allow you to generate code and to reverse engineer using Rose and Visual J++. Once the link has been established, Rose can launch Visual J++ or Visual J++ can launch Rose in order to generate code or reverse engineer.

To set up the link to Visual J++, select Tools ➤ Java ➤ Project Specification. On the Detail tab, set the Virtual Machine setting to Microsoft.

You are now ready to work with Rose and Visual J++. From Rose, select Tools ➤ Java ➤ Generate Java to launch Visual J++ and generate code. From Visual J++, select the elements you wish to reverse engineer and select Tools ➤ Update Rose Model. Rose will be launched, and the elements will be reverse engineered into the Rose model.

Java Code-Generation Properties

The Java code-generation properties can be set in two places. The defaults are set by using the Tools ➤ Options menu item and then selecting the Java tab, as shown in Figure 14.4. You can set properties for the following items:

- ◆ Attributes
- ◆ Classes
- ◆ Module bodies
- ◆ Module specifications
- ◆ Operations
- ◆ Projects
- ◆ Roles

We'll discuss using these various properties throughout this chapter. We'll begin with a brief description of the available code-generation properties, then cover projects, modules, classes, attributes, operations, and roles.

FIGURE 14.4

Java code-generation
properties window

Project Properties

The project properties affect all aspects of Java code generation in Rose. This section provides a listing of the properties and their common settings.

The project properties are code-generation properties that apply more to the whole project than to any specific model element, such as a class or relationship. The options in this section include things like the default directory to use when generating code, the file extensions to use, and whether or not to stop generation if an error occurs. The project properties are listed in Table 14.2, along with their purposes and default value. (In this and subsequent code-generation property tables, we list the most commonly used properties.)

TABLE 14.2: Java Project Properties

PROPERTY	PURPOSE	DEFAULT
RootDir	Directory to hold the Java project.	\<blank\>
CreateMissingDirectories	If True, creates any directories that are required if they do not exist.	True
StopOnError	If True, Rose will stop code generation at the first error.	False
UsePrefixes	If True, Rose will add user-defined prefixes to the variable names.	False
AutoSync	Automatically begins the code-generation process when a Java element changes in the Rose model.	False
ShowCodeGenDlg	Shows a progress dialog box while generating code.	False
JavadocDefaultAuthor	Sets the value of the Javadoc @author tag.	\<blank\>
JavadocDefaultVersion	Sets the value of the Javadoc @version tag.	\<blank\>
JavadocDefaultSince	Sets the value of the Javadoc @since tag.	\<blank\>
JavadocNumAsterisks	Number of asterisks to use with the Javadoc comments.	0
MaxNumChars	Maximum number of characters in a line of generated Java code.	80
Editor	Select the editor to use while browsing code.	Rose's built-in editor
VM	Select the version of the Java Virtual Machine (Sun, IBM, or Microsoft).	Sun
ClassPath	Specifies the directory where code will be generated.	\<blank\> (use current directory)
InstanceVariablePrefix	If UsePrefixes is True, then this prefix will be added to all instance variables.	m_
ClassVariablePrefix	If UsePrefixes is True, then this prefix will be added to all class variables.	s_
DefaultAttributeDataType	If no type is selected for an attribute, this type will be used.	Integer

Continued on next page

TABLE 14.2: JAVA PROJECT PROPERTIES *(continued)*

PROPERTY	PURPOSE	DEFAULT
DefaultOperationReturnType	If no return type is selected for an operation, this type will be used.	Void
NoClassCustomDlg	Determines whether the custom specification window will be suppressed for Java classes and other elements.	False
GlobalImports	Sets import statements to be generated. Each class or package listed will generate an import statement.	\<blank\>
OpenBraceClassStyle	Sets whether an opening brace will start on a new line.	True
OpenBraceMethodStyle	Sets whether an opening brace for a method will start on a new line.	True
UseTabs	Determines whether to use tabs (as opposed to spaces) to indent the generated Java code.	False
UseSpaces	Determines whether to use spaces (as opposed to tabs) to indent the generated Java code.	True
SpacingItems	Number of tabs or spaces (depending on the values of UseTabs and UseSpaces) to use to indent the generated Java code.	3
RoseDefaultCommentStyle	Use the default Rose comment style in generated code.	True
AsteriskCommentStyle	Use asterisk comment style in generated code.	False
JavaCommentStyle	Use Javadoc tags for comments in generated code.	False
JavadocAuthor	Controls whether the Javadoc @author tag is enabled.	True
JavadocSince	Controls whether the Javadoc @since tag is enabled.	False
JavadocVersion	Controls whether the Javadoc @version tag is enabled.	False

Most of these project properties can also be set in the Project Specification window. To open the Project Specification window, select Tools ➢ Java ➢ Project Specification. On the Class Path tab, you can set the ClassPath project property.

Figure 14.5 shows the Style tab of the Java Project Specification window. On this tab, you can set the values of the following properties:

◆ UseTabs

◆ UseSpaces

◆ SpacingItems (Number to Use)

◆ OpenBraceClassStyle (On New Line for Classes)

◆ OpenBraceMethodStyle (On New Line for Methods)

◆ RoseDefaultCommentStyle (Rose Default)

- AsteriskCommentStyle (Asterisk Style)

- JavaCommentStyle (Javadoc Style)

- MaxNumChars (Maximum Number of Characters in a Line)

- JavadocAuthor, JavadocDefaultAuthor (@Author)

- JavadocVersion, JavadocDefaultVersion (@Version)

- JavadocSince, JavadocDefaultSince (@Since)

- JavadocNumAsterisks (Number of Asterisks)

Refer to Table 14.2 for a description of each of these properties.

FIGURE 14.5

Style tab of the Java Project Specification window

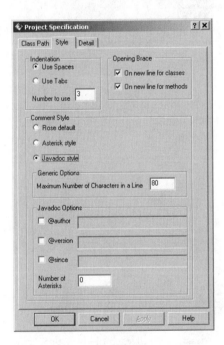

On the Detail tab of the Project Specification window, you can set additional project properties. Figure 14.6 shows the Detail tab. It includes the following properties:

- Editor

- VM (Virtual Machine)

- RootDir (Root Directory)

- DefaultAttributeDataType (Attribute)

- DefaultOperationReturnType (Method Return)

- UsePrefixes

- ◆ InstanceVariablePrefix
- ◆ ClassVariablePrefix
- ◆ StopOnError
- ◆ CreateMissingDirectories
- ◆ NoClassCustomDlg (Always Show Standard Specification Dialog for Classes)
- ◆ AutoSync (Automatic Synchronization Mode)
- ◆ ShowCodeGenDlg (Show Codegen Dialog)

FIGURE 14.6

Detail tab of the Java Project Specification window

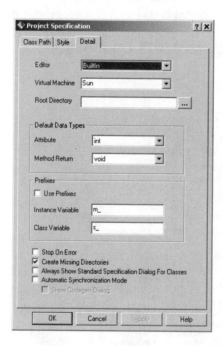

Refer to Table 14.2 for a description of each of these properties.

Class Properties

In this section, we discuss the Java code-generation properties that apply to classes. These properties will let you change the class name, decide whether or not constructors should be created for the class, and set other class-specific properties.

There are three places to set these properties. To set them for all classes, select Tools ➢ Options, then click the Java tab and select Class from the drop-down list box. To set them for only one class, either select the Java tab on the standard class specification window and edit the properties there or open the custom Java class specification window for the class.

Table 14.3 lists the Java class properties, their purposes, and their default values.

TABLE 14.3: JAVA CLASS PROPERTIES

PROPERTY	PURPOSE	DEFAULT
Final	Includes the final modifier in the generated code.	False
Static	Declares that a nested Java class is static and that only one instance of the class can exist.	False
GenerateDefaultConstructor	Controls whether or not a constructor will automatically be generated for the class.	True
ConstructorIs	Sets the visibility (public, private, protected) of the constructor.	Public
GenerateFinalizer	Includes a finalizer in the class.	False
GenerateStaticInitializer	Includes a static initializer in the class.	False
GenerateInstanceInitializer	Includes an instance initializer in the class.	False
GenerateCode	Generate code for the class.	True
DisableAutoSync	Disables the automatic generation of code when the class changes. (Automatic generation is always disabled if the AutoSync project property is set to False.)	False

These properties can also be set using the custom Java specification window for the class, as shown in Figure 14.7. As you can see on this window, you can set each of the class properties using the fields with corresponding names. The ConstructorIs property is set through the Constructor Visibility field.

In addition, you can mark the class as abstract using this window. An abstract class will never directly be instantiated. You can mark the class as an interface, in which case the final modifier, finalizer, static initializer, and instance initializer will no longer be available. Using the Extends area, you can list any classes of which this is a subclass. Using the Implements area, you can list any interfaces that this class implements.

FIGURE 14.7

Setting class properties through the Java Class Specification window

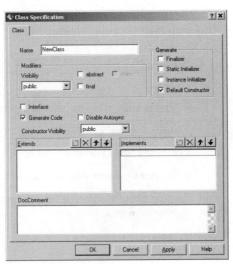

Attribute Properties

In this section, we cover the Java code-generation properties that relate to attributes. Using these properties, you can, for example, decide whether or not the attribute will be generated in the code.

There are three places to set these properties. To set them for all attributes, select Tools ➤ Options, then click the Java tab and select Attribute from the drop-down list box. To set them for only one attribute, select the Java tab on the standard attribute specification window (right-click the attribute in the browser and select Open Standard Specification) or open the Java attribute specification window (right-click the attribute in the browser and select Open Specification) and edit the properties there. Figure 14.8 shows the Java tab under Tools ➤ Options, with which you can set properties for all attributes.

FIGURE 14.8

Setting Java attribute properties

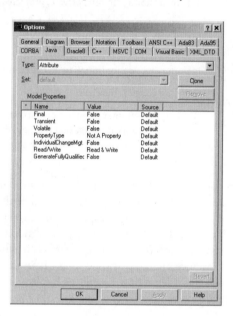

Table 14.4 lists the attribute properties, their purposes, and their default values.

TABLE 14.4: JAVA ATTRIBUTE PROPERTIES

PROPERTY	PURPOSE	DEFAULT
Final	If True, includes a final modifier in the attribute.	False
Transient	Includes a transient modifier in the attribute.	False
Volatile	Includes a volatile modifier in the attribute.	False
PropertyType	Specifies the property type for a Java Bean.	Not a Property
IndividualChangeMgt	Specifies whether or not the Java Bean gets its own registration mechanism.	False

Continued on next page

TABLE 14.4: JAVA ATTRIBUTE PROPERTIES *(continued)*

PROPERTY	PURPOSE	DEFAULT
Read/Write	Sets whether or not Rose will generate a Get and/or a Set method for the attribute.	Read & Write
GenerateFullyQualifiedTypes	Include the complete file path in the generated code for reference attributes.	False

You can set the values of these properties using the Java attribute specification window, as shown in Figure 14.9.

FIGURE 14.9

Setting attribute properties through the Java Field Specification window

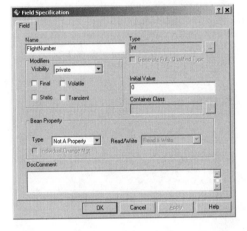

Using this window, you can also set the static flag, the attribute visibility, the initial value, and the data type for the attribute. The static flag marks the attribute as a class variable as opposed to an instance variable. The attribute visibility (public, private, protected, or package) controls what other classes will be able to access the attribute. The attribute's initial value is set using this window, and will be generated in the code. The data type can be set by pressing the "…" button next to the Type field and selecting from the list of Java types presented. The Container Class field is also displayed on this window, but is used only for relationships.

Operation Properties

Next, we discuss the Java code-generation properties that are specific to operations. These properties will let you, for example, control whether the operation is abstract or not.

There are three places to set these properties. To set them for all operations, select Tools ➢ Options, then click the Java tab and select Operation from the drop-down list box. To set them for only one operation, select the Java tab on the standard operation specification window, or open the Java operation specification window and edit the properties there.

Table 14.5 lists the operation code-generation properties, their purposes, and their default values.

TABLE 14.5: JAVA OPERATION PROPERTIES

PROPERTY	PURPOSE	DEFAULT
Abstract	Includes an abstract modifier in the operation.	False
Static	Includes a static modifier in the operation.	False
Final	Includes a final modifier in the operation.	False
Native	Includes a native modifier in the operation.	False
Synchronized	Includes a synchronized modifier in the operation.	False

As with attributes, you can set the values of these properties using the Java specification window. Figure 14.10 shows the Java specification window for an operation.

Using this window, you can also set the operation visibility (public, private, protected, or package), set the operation return type, set the operation arguments, or list the exceptions that the operation will throw.

FIGURE 14.10

Setting operation properties through the Java Method Specification window

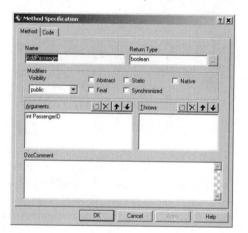

Module Properties

The module specification and body properties are those properties that are related to the files you will generate from Rose. These properties give you the ability to decide whether or not to include a copyright notice in the file and whether or not to list any configuration management strings to be generated in the code.

There are three places to set these properties. To set them for all files, select Tools ➢ Options, then click the Java tab and select Module Specification or Module Body from the drop-down list box. To set them for only one file, select the Java tab on the standard component specification window or open the Java component specification window and edit the properties there.

Table 14.6 lists the code-generation properties for module specifications, their purposes, and their default values.

TABLE 14.6: JAVA MODULE SPECIFICATION PROPERTIES

PROPERTY	PURPOSE	DEFAULT
CMIdentification	Specifies a user-defined configuration management identification string.	<blank>
CopyrightNotice	Specifies a user-defined copyright string to include in the code as a comment.	<blank>

Using the Java Component Specification window, as shown in Figure 14.11, you can set these properties. You can also list any Java import statements you would like to include in the generated code.

FIGURE 14.11

Setting component properties through the Java Component Specification window

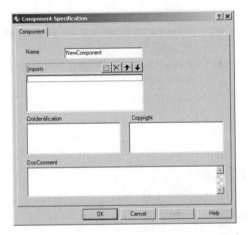

You can also set code-generation properties for a module body in Java. The available properties are CMIdentification and CopyrightNotice, as described in Table 14.6.

Role Properties

Role properties are the Java code-generation properties that affect the code generated for relationships. Using these properties, you can set the container class to be used for the attribute and change other specifics of the generated code for a role.

As with most of the other property sets, there are three places to set these properties. To set them for all relationships, select Tools ➢ Options, then click the Java tab and select Role from the drop-down list box. To set them for a single relationship, open the relationship specification. On the Java tab of the relationship specification window, you can change the properties for that relationship.

Table 14.7 lists the role properties, their purposes, and their default values.

TABLE 14.7: JAVA ROLE PROPERTIES

PROPERTY	PURPOSE	DEFAULT
ContainerClass	Specifies the container class to use if the relationship's multiplicity is greater than one.	\<blank\>
InitialValue	Specifies the default value for the attribute.	\<blank\>
Final	Includes a final modifier in the attribute.	False
Transient	Includes a transient modifier in the attribute.	False
Volatile	Includes a volatile modifier in the attribute.	False
PropertyType	Specifies the property type for a Java Bean.	Not a Property
IndividualChangeMgt	Specifies whether or not the Java Bean gets its own registration mechanism.	False
Read/Write (98i)	Sets whether or not Rose will generate a Get and/or a Set method.	Read & Write
GenerateFullyQualifiedTypes	Include the complete file path in the generated code for reference attributes.	False
IsNavigable	Indicates navigability	True

Generating Code

Once you have created the classes, relationships, attributes, operations, EJBs, servlets, and other Java elements in your Rose model, you can generate code. To generate code, follow these steps:

1. Create the needed components.

2. Assign the Java classes to the appropriate components.

3. Set the code-generation properties.

4. Select Tools ➢ Check Model to check for language-independent model errors. Check the log window for any errors found, and resolve the errors.

5. Select Tools ➢ Java ➢ Syntax Check to check for Java-specific problems. Again, check the log window for a list of errors found, and resolve the errors.

6. Select the class(es) or component(s) to generate.

7. Select Tools ➢ Java ➢ Code Generation.

8. To view the generated code for a class, right-click the class on a diagram and select Java ➢ Browse Java Source.

Generated Code

In the following sections, we'll take a look at the Java code generated for a class, attribute, and operation, and for the different types of relationships between classes. In each of these sections, we'll include some sample code to give you an idea of what will be generated from your Rose model.

Rose uses the information in the specifications of the model elements when generating code. For example, it will look at the different specifications for a class (visibility, attributes, operations, and so on) when generating code for the class.

Let's begin by looking at the code generated for a typical class.

Classes

A class in your object model will become a Java class when you generate code. All of the attributes, operations, and relationships of the class will be reflected in the generated code. The major elements generated for each class include:

- The class name
- The class visibility
- A constructor for the class
- Class documentation
- Attributes
- Operations
- Relationships

Without a component mapping, each class in the model will generate one file with the .java extension. Each file will be named using the class name. For example, an Employee class will generate an Employee.java file. With a component mapping, the class (or classes) mapped to each component will be generated in a .java file for the component.

Much of the information in your Rose model will be used directly when generating code. For example, the attributes, operations, relationships, and class name of each class will directly affect the code generated. Other model properties, such as the documentation entered for the class, will not directly affect the code. These properties are created as comments in the generated code.

Table 14.8 lists the properties available in the class specification window and notes which properties will directly affect the code that is generated.

TABLE 14.8: EFFECT OF CLASS SPECIFICATIONS ON GENERATED CODE

PROPERTY	EFFECT ON CODE
Name	Name in model will become class name.
Type	Directly affects the type of class created.
Stereotype	Directly affects the type of class created.

Continued on next page

TABLE 14.8: EFFECT OF CLASS SPECIFICATIONS ON GENERATED CODE *(continued)*

PROPERTY	EFFECT ON CODE
Export Control	Directly affects the class visibility.
Documentation	Appears as a comment.
Persistence	Affects whether DDL can be generated for the class.
Abstract	Creates an abstract class.
Formal Arguments	Formal arguments are included in the code for a parameterized class.
Operations	Generated in code.
Attributes	Generated in code.
Relationships	Generated in code.

Let's look at the code generated for the following class:

Flight
- FlightNumber : int
+ AddPassenger(PassengerID : int) : boolean

The following code is the Java file that was generated for this class.

```
//Source file: C:\\Flight.java

/* Copyright Notice */


/**
Comments for Flight Class
*/
public class Flight
{
   private int FlightNumber;

   public Flight()
   {
   }

   /**
   @roseuid 394461CB01F3
   */
   public boolean AddPassenger(int PassengerID)
   {
   }
}
```

COPYRIGHT NOTICE SECTION

The copyright notice section includes the following line of code:

```
/* Copyright Notice */
```

By default, there is no copyright notice generated for your code. If, however, you'd like to add a copyright notice to all files, you can change the code-generation properties. Select Tools ➤ Options from the menu, then select the Java tab. Select Module Specification from the drop-down list box to display the module specification code-generation properties. Change the CopyrightNotice field to include any copyright information. If information is entered, it will be generated.

You can override the default for a specific component by changing the value in the Copyright field in the component specification window or in the CopyrightNotice property on the Java tab of the component's standard specification window.

Attributes

Aside from the class itself, Rose will generate the attributes for the class. For each attribute, Rose will include information about the attribute visibility, data type, and default value in the code. Let's look again at the code generated for the Flight class.

```
//Source file: C:\\Flight.java

/* Copyright Notice */


/**
Comments for Flight Class
*/
public class Flight
{
    private int FlightNumber;

    public Flight()
    {
    }

    /**
    @roseuid 394461CB01F3
    */
    public boolean AddPassenger(int PassengerID)
    {
    }
}
```

As you can see, the code includes the attribute visibility and data type. If the default value is set, it will also be included in the generated code.

To apply one of the modifiers, such as the transient modifier, to an attribute, set the appropriate property to True. In this case, you set the transient property to True, and the attribute generates with the modifier, as in the following code:

```
//Source file: C:\\Flight.java

/* Copyright Notice */


/**
Comments for Flight Class
*/
public class Flight
{
    private transient int FlightNumber;

    public Flight()
    {
    }

    /**
    @roseuid 394461CB01F3
    */
    public boolean AddPassenger(int PassengerID)
    {
    }
}
```

The visibility options affect the generated attribute. In the above example, and as the default, attributes are given private visibility. If you set an attribute to Protected or Public, the following code is an example of what you will generate:

```
//Source file: C:\\Flight.java

/* Copyright Notice */


/**
Comments for Flight Class
*/
public class Flight
{
    private transient int FlightNumber;
    public long DepartureDate;
    protected int GateNumber;

    public Flight()
    {
    }
```

```
    /**
    @roseuid 394461CB01F3
    */
    public boolean AddPassenger(int PassengerID)
    {
    }
}
```

Operations

Rose generates each of the operations in the class. For each operation, the generated code includes the operation name, the parameters, the parameter data types, and the return type. Again, we'll examine the code generated for the Flight class:

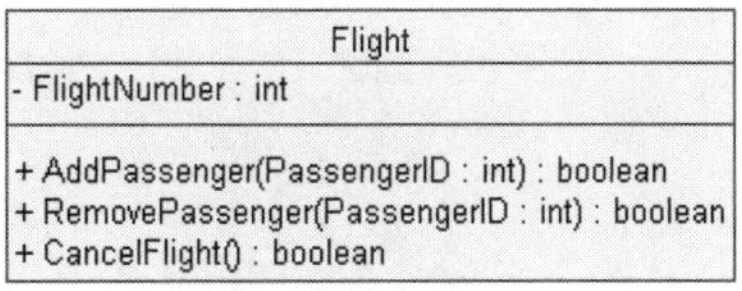

Flight
- FlightNumber : int
+ AddPassenger(PassengerID : int) : boolean + RemovePassenger(PassengerID : int) : boolean + CancelFlight() : boolean

```
//Source file: C:\\Flight.java


public class Flight
{
    private int FlightNumber;

    public Flight()
    {
    }

    /**
    @roseuid 39446D1B0084
    */
    public boolean AddPassenger(int PassengerID)
    {
    }

    /**
    @roseuid 39446D230253
    */
    public boolean RemovePassenger(int PassengerID)
    {
    }

    /**
    @roseuid 39446D2B02AE
```

```
        */
        public boolean CancelFlight()
        {
        }
    }
```

As you can see, the full operation signature is generated in the code. Any documentation you enter for the operation is also generated as a comment in the code.

Rose generates skeletal code for operations. That is, the operation signature is generated. Once you have generated the code, you insert the implementation code for each operation between the { and } delimiters of the operation. This protects the code during round-trip engineering.

You can enter exception information using the Java operation specification window, as shown here:

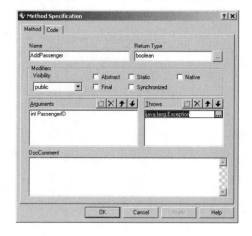

In the Throws field, select the appropriate Java exception class. When you generate code, the exception information will be generated as well:

```
//Source file: C:\\Flight.java


public class Flight
{
    private int FlightNumber;

    public Flight()
    {
    }

    /**
    @roseuid 39446ECD011F
    */
    public boolean AddPassenger(int PassengerID) throws java.lang.Exception
    {
```

```
    }

    /**
    @roseuid 39446ED40101
    */
    public boolean RemovePassenger(int PassengerID)
    {
    }

    /**
    @roseuid 39446EDB03BE
    */
    public boolean CancelFlight()
    {
    }
}
```

As with other model elements, you can control the code generated for an operation by modifying its code-generation properties.

Bidirectional Associations

To support bidirectional associations, Rose will generate attributes in the code. Each of the classes in the relationship will contain an attribute to support the association. By default, Rose names the roles by appending "the" to the class name. Let's look at the code generated for the following relationship:

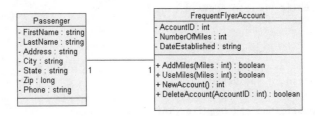

The following is the code for Passenger:

```
//Source file: C:\\Passenger.java


public class Passenger
{
    private string FirstName;
    private string LastName;
    private string Address;
    private string City;
    private string State;
    private long Zip;
```

```java
    private string Phone;
    public FrequentFlyerAccount theFrequentFlyerAccount;

    public Passenger()
    {
    }
}
```

The following is the code for FrequentFlyerAccount:

```java
//Source file: C:\\FrequentFlyerAccount.java


public class FrequentFlyerAccount
{
    private int AccountID;
    private int NumberOfMiles;
    private string DateEstablished;
    public Passenger thePassenger;

    public FrequentFlyerAccount()
    {
    }

    /**
    @roseuid 394590F100A2
    */
    public boolean AddMiles(int Miles)
    {
    }

    /**
    @roseuid 394590FE0209
    */
    public boolean UseMiles(int Miles)
    {
    }

    /**
    @roseuid 394591060124
    */
    public int NewAccount()
    {
    }

    /**
    @roseuid 39459113021D
    */
    public boolean DeleteAccount(int AccountID)
```

```
      {
      }
}
```

As you can see, Rose will automatically generate attributes on both sides of the bidirectional association relationship. With the FrequentFlyerAccount attribute, Passenger can access the public attributes and operations of FrequentFlyerAccount. With the Passenger attribute, FrequentFlyerAccount can access the public attributes and operations of Passenger. If you want to use different names for the attributes instead of thePassenger and theFrequentFlyerAccount, you can set role names for the association. These names will be used instead, as in the following code for Passenger. In this example, we set the role names to MyAccount and AccountHolder.

```
//Source file: C:\\Passenger.java


public class Passenger
{
    private string FirstName;
    private string LastName;
    private string Address;
    private string City;
    private string State;
    private long Zip;
    private string Phone;
    public FrequentFlyerAccount myAccount;

    public Passenger()
    {
    }
}
```

The following is the code for FrequentFlyerAccount:

```
//Source file: C:\\FrequentFlyerAccount.java


public class FrequentFlyerAccount
{
    private int AccountID;
    private int NumberOfMiles;
    private string DateEstablished;
    public Passenger AccountHolder;

    public FrequentFlyerAccount()
    {
    }

    /**
    @roseuid 394590F100A2
```

```
  */
  public boolean AddMiles(int Miles)
  {
  }

  /**
  @roseuid 394590FE0209
  */
  public boolean UseMiles(int Miles)
  {
  }

  /**
  @roseuid 394591060124
  */
  public int NewAccount()
  {
  }

  /**
  @roseuid 39459113021D
  */
  public boolean DeleteAccount(int AccountID)
  {
  }
}
```

Rose will use the role name to generate the attribute name. By default, each generated attribute will have public visibility. To change the visibility, open the association specification window. Select either the Role A General or Role B General tab, and change the Export Control property.

Note that this association has a multiplicity of one to one. See the upcoming sections titled "Associations with a Multiplicity of One to Many" or "Associations with a Multiplicity of Many to Many" for a discussion of how other multiplicity settings will affect code generation.

You can specify initial values for the generated attributes. Open the desired association's standard specification, then select the Java A or Java B tab. Modify the InitialValue property to contain the initial value for the generated attribute.

Unidirectional Associations

As with bidirectional associations, Rose will generate attributes to support unidirectional associations. With a unidirectional association, however, an attribute is generated at only one end of the relationship. Let's look at the Passenger and FrequentFlyerAccount classes again, but this time with a unidirectional relationship.

For these classes, code similar to the following code for Passenger would be created:

```
//Source file: C:\\Passenger.java
```

```
public class Passenger
{
    private string FirstName;
    private string LastName;
    private string Address;
    private string City;
    private string State;
    private long Zip;
    private string Phone;
    public FrequentFlyerAccount theFrequentFlyerAccount;

    public Passenger()
    {
    }
}
```

This is the code for FrequentFlyerAccount:

```
//Source file: C:\\FrequentFlyerAccount.java


public class FrequentFlyerAccount
{
    private int AccountID;
    private int NumberOfMiles;
    private string DateEstablished;

    public FrequentFlyerAccount()
    {
    }

    /**
    @roseuid 394590F100A2
    */
    public boolean AddMiles(int Miles)
    {
    }

    /**
    @roseuid 394590FE0209
    */
    public boolean UseMiles(int Miles)
    {
    }

    /**
    @roseuid 394591060124
    */
    public int NewAccount()
```

```
      {
      }

      /**
      @roseuid 39459113021D
      */
      public boolean DeleteAccount(int AccountID)
      {
      }
   }
```

As you can see, Rose will generate an attribute for the relationship at only one end of the associa-tion. Specifically, it will generate an attribute in the client class, but not in the supplier class.

The code generated in the supplier class is the same as discussed in the previous section about bidirectional associations. With a bidirectional association, each class is given a new attribute, and the code discussed in the previous section is included in both classes. With a unidirectional association, the code is included only in the client class.

Again, note that the multiplicity here is one to one. Next let's take a look at how code is affected when the multiplicity settings are changed.

Associations with a Multiplicity of One to Many

In a one-to-one relationship, Rose can simply create the appropriate attributes to support the associ-ation. With a one-to-many relationship, however, one class must contain a set of the other class. Let's look at an example.

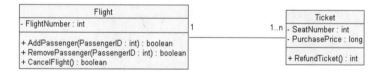

In this case, we have a one-to-many relationship. Each flight has many tickets, but each ticket is for only one flight. The code generated for this relationship is shown below in the code for Flight:

```
//Source file: C:\\Flight.java


public class Flight
{
   private int FlightNumber;
   public Ticket theTicket[];

   public Flight()
   {
   }
```

```java
/**
@roseuid 39446ECD011F
*/
public boolean AddPassenger(int PassengerID)
{
}

/**
@roseuid 39446ED40101
*/
public boolean RemovePassenger(int PassengerID)
{
}

/**
@roseuid 39446EDB03BE
*/
public boolean CancelFlight()
{
}
}
```

Following is the code for Ticket:

```java
//Source file: C:\\Ticket.java


public class Ticket
{
    private int SeatNumber;
    private long PurchasePrice;
    public Flight theFlight;

    public Ticket()
    {
    }

    /**
    @roseuid 3945946F0378
    */
    public int RefundTicket()
    {
    }
}
```

In this example, Ticket simply contains an attribute of type Flight because the multiplicity states that there is one instance of Flight for each instance of Ticket. However, the multiplicity also states that there are many instances of Ticket for each instance of Flight. Therefore, an array of Ticket objects is created inside Flight.

If you don't want to use an array, you can change the code-generation properties to use a different container class. In either the Java tab of the standard association specification window or the Field tab of the Java association specification window, set the ContainerClass code-generation property to the name of the container class you'd rather use.

In the following example, we created a class called TicketList, which is a collection of Tickets. The following code is generated for the above association, but with the container class as type TicketList.

Code for Flight:

```java
//Source file: C:\\Flight.java


public class Flight
{
    private int FlightNumber;
    public TicketList theTicket;

    public Flight()
    {
    }

    /**
    @roseuid 39446ECD011F
    */
    public boolean AddPassenger(int PassengerID)
    {
    }

    /**
    @roseuid 39446ED40101
    */
    public boolean RemovePassenger(int PassengerID)
    {
    }

    /**
    @roseuid 39446EDB03BE
    */
    public boolean CancelFlight()
    {
    }
}
```

Associations with a Multiplicity of Many to Many

The code generated here is similar to that created for a one-to-many relationship. With a many-to-many relationship, however, Rose will generate arrays on both ends of the relationship. Let's look at the code generated for the following relationship.

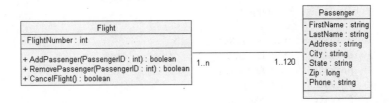

This is the code for Flight:

```
//Source file: C:\\Flight.java


public class Flight
{
    private int FlightNumber;
    public Passenger thePassenger[];

    public Flight()
    {
    }

    /**
    @roseuid 39446ECD011F
    */
    public boolean AddPassenger(int PassengerID)
    {
    }

    /**
    @roseuid 39446ED40101
    */
    public boolean RemovePassenger(int PassengerID)
    {
    }

    /**
    @roseuid 39446EDB03BE
    */
    public boolean CancelFlight()
    {
    }
}
```

This is the code for Passenger:

```
//Source file: C:\\Passenger.java
```

```
public class Passenger
{
    private string FirstName;
    private string LastName;
    private string Address;
    private string City;
    private string State;
    private long Zip;
    private string Phone;
    public Flight theFlight[];

    public Passenger()
    {
    }
}
```

In this situation, arrays are created at both ends of the relationship. An array is used by default, but as we mentioned earlier, you can change the container class that is used. To do so, use the relationship specification window for the association. On the Java A or Java B tab, change the Container-Class property to the name of the container class you wish to use.

To change the container class for all many-to-many association relationships, choose Tools ➤ Options from the menu. On the Java tab, select Role from the drop-down list box. Change the value of the ContainerClass code-generation property to the container class you wish to use.

Reflexive Associations

A reflexive association is treated much the same as an association between two classes. Let's look at the code generated for the following situation:

```
//Source file: C:\\EnginePart.java


public class EnginePart
{
    public EnginePart theEnginePart[];

    public EnginePart()
    {
    }
}
```

As with a regular association, an attribute is created inside the class to support the relationship. If the multiplicity is one, a simple attribute is created. If the multiplicity is more than one, an array is created as an attribute, as above.

Aggregations

There are two types of aggregation relationships: by-value and by-reference. With a by-value relationship, one class contains another. With a by-reference relationship, one class contains a reference to another. Code generated for either type of aggregation in Java is the same.

Here we have an aggregation relationship between a flight schedule and the flights on the schedule. Each schedule contains one or more flights, and each flight can be on zero or more schedules.

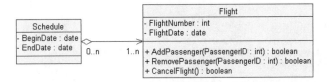

The code that is generated shows a Flight attribute inside Schedule. Because the multiplicity of the relationship is one or more, there is an array of Flights inside Schedule.

The following is the code for the Schedule class:

```
//Source file: C:\\Schedule.java


public class Schedule
{
    private date BeginDate;
    private date EndDate;
    public Flight theFlight[];

    public Schedule()
    {
    }
}
```

The following is the code for the Flight class:

```
//Source file: C:\\Flight.java


public class Flight
{
    private int FlightNumber;
    private date FlightDate;

    public Flight()
    {
    }
```

```
/**
@roseuid 39446ECD011F
*/
public boolean AddPassenger(int PassengerID)
{
}

/**
@roseuid 39446ED40101
*/
public boolean RemovePassenger(int PassengerID)
{
}

/**
@roseuid 39446EDB03BE
*/
public boolean CancelFlight()
{
}
}
```

Rose uses the value in the ContainerClass property when the multiplicity of the relationship is greater than one. If the ContainerClass contains no value, then Rose will use an array to contain the multiple objects.

Dependency Relationships

With a dependency relationship, no attributes are created. If there is a dependency between Class A and Class B, no attributes will be created in either Class A or Class B. Here we have a dependency between Flight and Passenger:

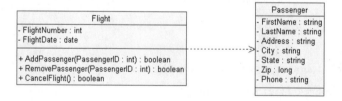

The code that is generated will look something like the following:

```
//Source file: C:\\Flight.java


public class Flight
{
    private int FlightNumber;
    private date FlightDate;
```

```java
    public Flight()
    {
    }

    /**
    @roseuid 39446ECD011F
    */
    public boolean AddPassenger(int PassengerID)
    {
    }

    /**
    @roseuid 39446ED40101
    */
    public boolean RemovePassenger(int PassengerID)
    {
    }

    /**
    @roseuid 39446EDB03BE
    */
    public boolean CancelFlight()
    {
    }
}
```

and

```java
//Source file: C:\\Passenger.java


public class Passenger
{
    private string FirstName;
    private string LastName;
    private string Address;
    private string City;
    private string State;
    private long Zip;
    private string Phone;

    public Passenger()
    {
    }
}
```

Rose will place no references to Flight inside Passenger or Passenger inside Flight. The dependency relationship does not generate any code for the relationship.

Generalization Relationships

A generalization relationship in UML becomes an inheritance relationship in Java. In your Rose model, an inheritance relationship is shown as follows:

For this type of relationship, Rose will generate something that looks like this:

```
//Source file: Parent.java

//Source file: C:\\Parent.java


public class Parent
{

    public Parent()
    {
    }
}
```

and

```
//Source file: C:\\Child.java


public class Child extends Parent
{

    public Child()
    {
    }
}
```

In the code for the parent class, there is no mention of the child class. This helps keep the parent generic; many classes can inherit from it without affecting its code. In the child class, the code is generated to support its inheritance from the parent class. The class declaration will look like this:

```
Public class Child extends Parent
```

Interfaces

In Rose, a Java interface is modeled as a class with a stereotype of Interface. It contains operation signatures, but does not contain any implementation for the operations. The implementation of the operations is contained in other classes. The interface is connected with a realization relationship to the class(es) that implement the interface:

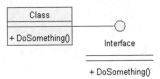

When you generate code, Rose will generate a Java interface. The code for the interface and implementation classes from the example above is shown here:

This is the code for the interface class:

```
//Source file: C:\\Interface.java


public interface Interface
{

    /**
    @roseuid 3945AB7201CA
    */
    public void DoSomething();
}
```

and for the implementation class:

```
//Source file: C:\\Class.java


public class Class implements Interface
{

    public Class()
    {
    }

    /**
    @roseuid 3945AC1B032C
    */
    public void DoSomething()
    {
    }
}
```

As you can see, Rose places the "implements" keyword in the implementation class to set the interface for that class. Once the code has been generated, you can program the DoSomething() operation in the implementation class.

Java Beans

You can model a Java Bean in Rose as an attribute. The attribute will have all of the standard specifications available in Rose, with three additional fields: the type of bean (Bound, Constrained, Simple, or Not a Bean); a Read/Write field, which controls the Get and Set operations generated; and a flag for change management. Figure 14.12 shows the Java attribute specification window, in which you can set these three properties.

FIGURE 14.12

Setting Java Bean properties

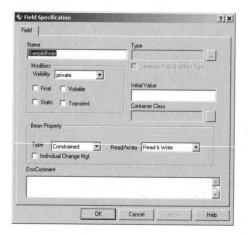

The Read/Write field controls whether a bean Get and/or bean Set operation will be generated. The Read & Write option will create both a Get and a Set operation. Read will create only a Get operation, and Write will create only a Set operation.

There are three types of beans available. A simple bean creates just a Get and Set method, depending on the value of the Read/Write field. In the above example, the code will look like this:

```
//Source file: C:\\SampleClass.java


public class SampleClass
{
   private int SampleBean;

   public SampleClass()
   {
   }

   /**
 * Access method for the SampleBean property.
 *
```

```
* @return    the current value of the SampleBean property
   @roseuid
   */
   public int getSampleBean()
   {
      return SampleBean;
      }

   /**
* Sets the value of the SampleBean property.
*
* @param aSampleBean the new value of the SampleBean property
   @roseuid
   */
   public void setSampleBean(int aSampleBean)
   {
      SampleBean = aSampleBean;
      }
}
```

With a bound bean, Rose will include an `import java.beans.*` statement in the generated code. In addition, it will generate a declaration, a Set operation, an optional Get operation (depending on the value of the Read/Write field), a PropertyChangeSupport attribute, an addPropertyChange-Listener operation, and a removePropertyChangeListener operation. The code will now look like this:

```
//Source file: C:\\SampleClass.java

import java.beans.*;

public class SampleClass
{
   private int SampleBean;

   /**
* common PropertyChangeSupport instance
   */
   protected PropertyChangeSupport commonPCS = new PropertyChangeSupport(this);

   public SampleClass()
   {
   }

   /**
* Access method for the SampleBean property.
*
* @return    the current value of the SampleBean property
   @roseuid
```

```
    */
    public int getSampleBean()
    {
        return SampleBean;
    }


    /**
 * Sets the value of the SampleBean property.
 *
 * @param aSampleBean the new value of the SampleBean property
    @roseuid
    */
    public void setSampleBean(int aSampleBean)
    {
        SampleBean = aSampleBean;
    }

    public void addPropertyChangeListener(PropertyChangeListener listener)
    {
        commonPCS.addPropertyChangeListener(listener);
        }

    public void removePropertyChangeListener(PropertyChangeListener listener)
    {
        commonPCS.removePropertyChangeListener(listener);
        }
}
```

Finally, with a constrained bean, Rose will include an `import java.beans.*` statement in the code. It will also create a declaration, a Set operation, an optional Get operation (depending on the value of the Read/Write field), a VetoableChangeSupport property, an addVetoableChangeListener operation, and a removeVetoableChangeListener operation. The code in this situation will look like this:

```
//Source file: C:\\SampleClass.java

import java.beans.*;

public class SampleClass
{
    private int SampleBean;

    /**
 * common VetoableChangeSupport instance
    */
    protected VetoableChangeSupport commonVCS = new VetoableChangeSupport(this);
```

```
   public SampleClass()
   {
   }


   /**
* Access method for the SampleBean property.
*
* @return   the current value of the SampleBean property
   @roseuid
   */
   public int getSampleBean()
   {
      return SampleBean;
   }


   /**
* Sets the value of the SampleBean property.
*
* @param aSampleBean the new value of the SampleBean property
   @roseuid
   */
   public void setSampleBean(int aSampleBean) throws PropertyVetoException
   {
      SampleBean = aSampleBean;
   }

   public void addVetoableChangeListener(VetoableChangeListener listener)
   {
      commonVCS.addVetoableChangeListener(listener);
      }

   public void removeVetoableChangeListener(VetoableChangeListener listener)
   {
      commonVCS.removeVetoableChangeListener(listener);
      }
}
/*
SampleClass.removePropertyChangeListener(PropertyChangeListener){
      commonPCS.removePropertyChangeListener(listener);
      }
 */
/*
SampleClass.addPropertyChangeListener(PropertyChangeListener){
      commonPCS.addPropertyChangeListener(listener);
      }
 */
```

Support for J2EE

The J2EE standard is a method for developing complex distributed applications without needing to focus on the details of transaction processing, database connectivity, or security. Instead, J2EE allows the developers to focus on the unique business logic of the application. J2EE elements—including EJBs, servlets, JAR files, and WAR files—are now supported in Rational Rose. In this section, we'll explore how to create each of these four types of elements in Rose.

EJBs

An Enterprise Java Bean, or EJB, is modeled in Rose as a class with an EJB stereotype. Depending upon the bean type (Entity or Session), the class will have a stereotype of EJBEntity or EJBSession. An entity EJB will have relationships to three other elements: the home interface, the remote interface, and the primary key. Each of these three is modeled in Rose as a class with stereotypes EJBHomeInterface, EJBRemoteInterface, and EJBPrimaryKey, respectively. Figure 14.13 shows an example of an entity EJB.

FIGURE 14.13

Entity EJB

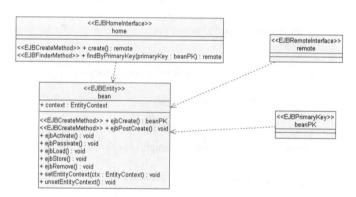

With a session EJB, the class will have relationships to two other classes: the home interface and the remote interface. These classes have stereotypes of EJBHomeInterface and EJBRemoteInterface, respectively.

To create an EJB, select Tools ➤ Java ➤ J2EE ➤ New EJB. Using the window shown in Figure 14.14, enter the type of EJB (Entity or Session), the name of the home interface, the name of the remote interface, and the name of the EJB.

If this is an entity bean, use the Bean-Managed or Container-Managed radio buttons to control whether the bean's persistence is managed by the container or within the bean itself.

If the bean is a session bean, use the Stateless or Stateful radio buttons to control whether the client maintains the bean's state between method calls.

FIGURE 14.14

Setting EJB
properties

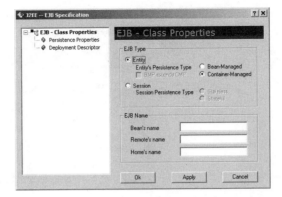

If this is an entity EJB, select the Persistence Properties option in the treeview on the left side of the window in Figure 14.14. The Persistence Properties window is shown in Figure 14.15. Using this window, you can set items such as the name of the primary key class and the ejbFinder's method, name, parameter, and parameter type.

FIGURE 14.15

Setting Persistence
properties

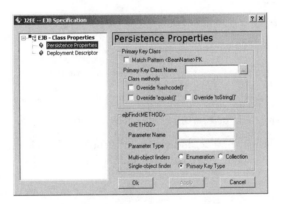

You can enter the name of the primary key in the Primary Key Class Name field, or check the Match Pattern check box. If Match Pattern is checked, the name of the primary key will be the bean name followed by the letters "PK."

In the Class Methods field, checking the hashcode(), equals(), or toString() check box(es) will cause Rose to generate the selected method(s) in the code.

In the ejbFind<Method> field, you enter the name of an ejbFinder method to create. In the Parameter Name field, enter the parameter(s) for the method. If there are multiple parameters, separate them with commas. In the Parameter Type field, enter the data type for each parameter. Enter the types, separated by commas, in the order in which the parameters are listed.

Select the Deployment Descriptor option in the treeview on the left side of the window to view the Deployment Descriptor window, as shown in Figure 14.16. Once these properties are set, Rose can generate the appropriate XML documents for the descriptor.

FIGURE 14.16

Setting Deployment
Descriptor
properties

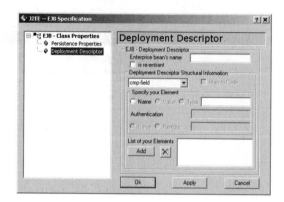

You have the option to enter a value in the Enterprise Bean's Name field. If you enter a name, this is the name that will be used in the `.jar` file. If not, Rose will use the implementation bean's name.

Next, check the Is Re-entrant box if more than one client will be able to access the bean's methods.

In the Deployment Descriptor Structural Information area, select one of the following from the drop-down list box:

◆ Cmp-field for a container-managed persistence entry

◆ Env-entry for a environment variable entry

◆ Resource-ref for a resource manager reference entry

◆ Ejb-ref for a reference to the home or remote interface of another EJB

◆ Security-role-ref for a security role reference entry

Then, enter the name, value, and type for the entry. For an ejb-ref entry, specify the home and remote interfaces. Click the Add button to add the entry to the list, and create other entries as needed.

Servlets

Like an EJB, a servlet is modeled in Rose as a class with a special stereotype. In this case, the stereotype is Http_Servlet. Using the servlet properties dialog boxes we will discuss in this section, you can control what methods and other properties are created for the servlet.

To create a new servlet, select Tools ➤ Java ➤ J2EE ➤ New Servlet. You will see the J2EE Servlet Specification window, as shown in Figure 14.17.

FIGURE 14.17

Servlet Specification
window

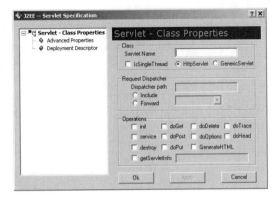

First, enter the name of the servlet. Then, check IsSingleThread if one thread of the servlet instance will execute at a time. Check HttpServlet or GenericServlet if the servlet extends either of these. In the Dispatcher Path field, enter the path to another servlet that will be used to receive requests or send requests to the current servlet. In the Operations area, check the method(s) that you would like Rose to generate for the servlet.

Select the Advanced Properties option on the left side of the window to display the Advanced Properties window, as shown in Figure 14.18.

FIGURE 14.18

Servlet Advanced
Properties window

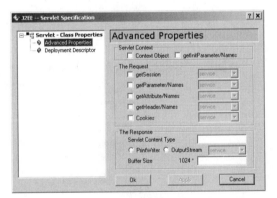

Select the Context Object check box to create a servlet context object. In the The Request section of the screen, select the method(s) the servlet will use to retrieve requests. In the Servlet Content Type field, enter the type that the servlet will use to respond to a client.

Select the Deployment Descriptor option on the left side of the window to display the deployment descriptor options for the servlet, as shown in Figure 14.19. These parameters will be used to create the WAR file for the servlet.

FIGURE 14.19

Servlet Deployment
Descriptor window

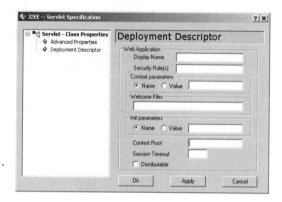

First, enter a descriptive name for the servlet in the Display Name field. Then, enter the security role(s) and the name and value of a context parameter, if any. Next, list the welcome files to include, enter the init parameter name and value, provide a session timeout value, and choose whether or not the servlet is distributable.

JAR and WAR Files

Java Archive (JAR) and Web Archive (WAR) files are used as containers for EJBs and servlets, respectively. To create a JAR file, select Tools ➢ Java ➢ J2EE ➢ New ejb-JAR file. To create a WAR file, select Tools ➢ Java ➢ J2EE ➢ New WAR file. The JAR or WAR specification window will appear. The JAR specification window is shown in Figure 14.20.

FIGURE 14.20

JAR Specification
window

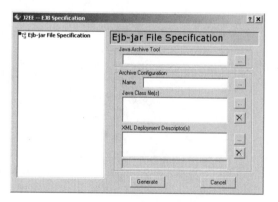

In the Java Archive Tool field, select the executable that will be used to create the JAR (if you are creating a WAR, select the executable that will be used to create the WAR). Enter the JAR or WAR name in the Name field. In the Java Class File(s) field, select the class(es) to include in the JAR or WAR. Finally, in the XML Deployment Descriptor(s) field, select the XML deployment descriptors to include.

Automated J2EE Deployment

In Rose 2001A, you can generate source code for Java classes. Deployment occurs manually after the generation. Rose 2002 automates the deployment of Java classes to WebLogic, WebSphere, and Sun Reference implementations. Follow the steps below to deploy Java classes.

1. Start the J2EE Deployment Wizard by selecting Tools ➤ J2EE Deploy ➤ Deploy from the menu.

2. Select the deployment target from the following list:

   WebLogic 5.1

   WebLogic 6.0

   WebLogic 6.1

   WebSphere 3.5

   Web Server (J2EE 1.2)

3. Select the working directory where temporary files will be stored.

4. Select the directory for the Java class files.

5. Check Edit XML Deployment Descriptors to customize XML deployment descriptor files prior to deployment.

   Rose will display a Properties window for the selected deployment target. Specific information on the Properties window is dependent on the deployment target.

6. Specify the property values, and then click Next.

7. Rose will display a window prompting for the model elements to deploy.

8. Select the model elements to deploy, and then click Next. Deployments to WebLogic and WebSphere can deploy EJBs and Java classes. Deployments to WebApplication can deploy web files, servlets, and Java classes.

   Rose will display a summary screen.

9. Review and make changes as needed prior to deployment.

   If the Edit XML Deployment Descriptors check box is checked, Rose will display an editor, which can be used to edit the XML deployment descriptors.

10. Click Save All to begin the deployment process.

    When Rose is finished, a summary screen will be displayed.

Reverse Engineering

When you reverse engineer Java code, Rose will read the classes, relationships, attributes, and operations from the code and generate the appropriate model elements.

In this section, we'll go through each of the steps needed to reverse engineer Java code. The information in your code will be imported directly into the Rose model that is currently open.

1. If you are using J2EE, JFC, or another Java foundation, create a new model and select the appropriate framework.

2. Select Tools ➤ Java ➤ Reverse Engineer Java. Rose will display the Java Reverse Engineer window, as shown in Figure 14.21. Using this window, you can select the files you want to reverse engineer.

   If you instead see a message that the ClassPath environment variable is not set, there is another step that you must take first. Create an environment variable called ClassPath, and set this variable to the directory or directories where the Java class files are stored.

FIGURE 14.21

Java Reverse
Engineer window

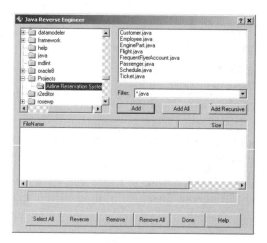

3. From the directory tree structure, select the directory that contains the files you want to reverse engineer. As you change directories, the available files will appear in the list box in the upper-right area of the window, as we saw in Figure 14.21.

4. Select the files you wish to reverse engineer and press Add. The files will now appear in the lower section of the window.

5. Once all needed files have been added to the bottom section of the window, click to select the files you wish to reverse engineer (or press the Select All button to reverse engineer them all) and then click the Reverse button. If there are any errors, they will be written to the log window.

You can reverse engineer .java files, .class files, .jar files, or .cab files. When Rose reverse engineers Java code, it places the new classes in the browser, but does not include them on any Class diagrams.

Java constructs are reverse engineered using the mapping discussed throughout this chapter. For example, interfaces are modeled as classes with a stereotype of Interface. Here, we will briefly review the mapping for reverse engineering.

Rose will look for classes in the source code, and will reverse engineer the attributes and operations of each class. For each operation, the operation code itself will not be included in the model, but the operation signature, including the parameters and return type, will be. Rose will also look for and model any "static," "final," "abstract," "native," or "synchronized" keywords for the operation. Finally, Rose will model the visibility of the operation as public, private, protected, or package.

Rose will also look for interfaces, and will reverse engineer them as classes with an Interface stereotype. It will establish a realize relationship between the implementation class and the interface.

If an attribute is a primitive data type, such as an integer or string, Rose will simply model it as an attribute of the reverse-engineered class. If, however, the attribute's type is another class in the Rose model, Rose will model it as a relationship between the two classes. For example, if the Flight class has an attribute called PassengerName, which has a type of Passenger, Rose will create an association between Flight and Passenger with a role called PassengerName.

For each attribute, Rose will examine any initial value, the attribute visibility (public, private, protected, or package), and any "static," "final," "volatile," or "transient" keywords for the attribute.

Summary

In this chapter, we took a look at how various Rose model elements are implemented in Java. Using the code-generation properties for classes, packages, attributes, operations, associations, aggregations, and other model elements, you have a great deal of control over what gets generated.

We examined the steps needed to generate code from a Rose model, and to reverse engineer Java code into a Rose model. Again, these are the steps you need to follow to generate code:

1. Create components.

2. Assign Java classes to components.

3. Set code-generation properties.

4. Select Tools ➤ Check Model.

5. Select Tools ➤ Java ➤ Syntax Check.

6. Select the class(es) or component(s) to generate.

7. Select Tools ➤ Java ➤ Code Generation.

The steps you'll need to reverse engineer Java code are:

1. Load the appropriate framework.

2. Select Tools ➤ Java ➤ Reverse Engineer Java.

3. Select the file(s) to reverse engineer, and press Reverse.

In the next chapter, we'll take a look at code generation and reverse engineering with Rose and Visual Basic. The Visual Basic add-in includes standard VB constructs such as class modules, forms, interfaces, and ADO objects. The wizard-driven user interface provides a quick and easy way to set your code-generation properties, generate VB code, and reverse engineer VB code. All of these features can help you build robust applications that stay consistent with the object model.

Chapter 15

Visual Basic Code Generation and Reverse Engineering

IN THIS CHAPTER, WE discuss how to generate Visual Basic code from your Rational Rose model and how to reverse engineer Visual Basic code into a Rose model.

To generate code, you will need to follow these steps:

1. Create components (see Chapter 10, "Component View").

2. Assign classes to components (see Chapter 10).

3. Set the code-generation properties.

4. Select a class or component to generate on a Class or Component diagram.

5. Select Tools ➤ Visual Basic ➤ Update Code to begin the Code-Generation Wizard.

6. Select Tools ➤ Visual Basic ➤ Browse Visual Basic Source to view the generated code.

We'll discuss the code-generation properties that can be set, and take a close look at how each Rose model element is implemented in the code.

Rose will use a lot of information in the model to generate code. For example, it will look at the multiplicity, role names, containment, and other details of each relationship. It will look at the attributes, operations, visibility, and other details of each class. From all of the information you enter using the specification windows for the various model elements, Rose will gather what it needs to generate code.

To reverse engineer code, you will need to follow these steps:

1. Create a component and assign a Visual Basic project to the component.

2. Select Tools ➤ Visual Basic ➤ Update Model from Code.

3. Select the component(s) and class(es) to update.

4. Select Finish to complete the process.

◆ Setting Visual Basic code-generation properties

◆ Generating Visual Basic code from your Rose model

◆ Mapping Rose elements to Visual Basic constructs

◆ Reverse engineering Visual Basic code into a Rose model

Starting a Visual Basic Project

Rather than start from scratch, you may want to import the standard Visual Basic classes into your Rose model. By doing so, you will have access to all of the standard classes and interfaces, and you can set up the appropriate relationships between your classes and the standard Visual Basic classes. This, in turn, will help in the code-generation and reverse-engineering processes.

Begin by creating a new Rose model. When the Framework Wizard appears, select Visual Basic Standard. The Visual Basic framework will be loaded, and the classes will show under the stdole Ver 2.0, VB Ver 6.0, VBA Ver 6.0, and VBRUN Ver 6.0 packages in the Logical view. Your Rose model will look like Figure 15.1.

FIGURE 15.1

Visual Basic framework

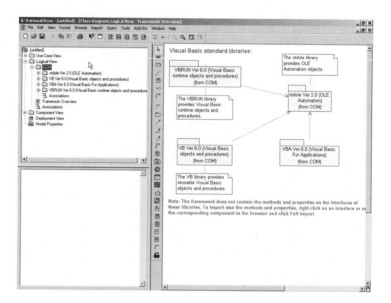

Each of these four packages contains a set of standard classes, interfaces, and relationships. Each package contains an overview diagram that presents the elements in the package and the relationships between them. You can familiarize yourself with the model elements in the packages and then set up the needed relationships between your classes and the standard ones.

Visual Basic Code-Generation Properties

Visual Basic code generation using Rational Rose is extremely flexible. You have full control over what gets generated and many of the details of how the generated code will look. For example, for each class, you can decide if initialization and termination routines will automatically be created. For each attribute, you control the visibility, name, and whether Get and Set operations should automatically be created. For each module, you control the filename. For each generalization, you control if the implements delegation is used.

All of these things are controlled through the code-generation properties. Rose provides property sets that deal with classes, attributes, operations, module specifications, associations, and generalizations.

You can see all of these properties by selecting Tools ➤ Options, then selecting the Visual Basic tab.

Anything you change using this window will set the default for all classes, attributes, operations, and so on.

You can also set the code-generation properties for a single class, attribute, operation, or other model element. To do so, open the specification window for the model element and select the Visual Basic tab. On this tab, you can change the properties that apply to that particular type of model element.

Finally, you can set the properties using the Visual Basic Model Assistant. The Model Assistant is a visual tool used to provide detailed information for a class or other model element. These details are then used in the code-generation and reverse-engineering processes.

In the following sections, we'll examine the code-generation properties for classes, operations, attributes, and modules. We'll look at how to set the properties using the specification window or the Model Assistant.

Class Properties

Class properties are the Visual Basic code-generation properties that apply to classes. These properties will let you change the class name and set other class-specific properties.

There are three places to set these properties. To set them for all classes, select Tools ➤ Options, then click the Visual Basic tab and select Class from the drop-down list box. To set them for only one class, select the Visual Basic tab on the class specification window and edit the properties there, or use the Model Assistant.

Table 15.1 lists the Visual Basic class properties, their purposes, and their default values.

TABLE 15.1: CLASS CODE-GENERATION PROPERTIES

PROPERTY	PURPOSE	DEFAULT
Update Code	Specifies if code can be updated for the class	True
Update Model	Specifies if the model can be updated for the class	True
OptionBase	Sets the base identifier for arrays (usually 0 or 1)	\<blank\>
OptionExplicit	Controls whether variable names must be explicitly declared	True
OptionCompare	Controls the method by which string comparisons are made	\<blank\>
Instancing	Determines how classes are exposed to other applications	MultiUse

Many of these class properties can be set using the Model Assistant. To open the Model Assistant, right-click the class and select Model Assistant. The window shown in Figure 15.2 will be displayed.

The Should Be Generated field corresponds to the Update Code property and determines whether the class will be reflected in the generated code. The Should Be Updated from Code field corresponds to the Update Model property, and the Instancing field corresponds to the Instancing property.

FIGURE 15.2

Using the Model
Assistant's Class
tab to set class
properties

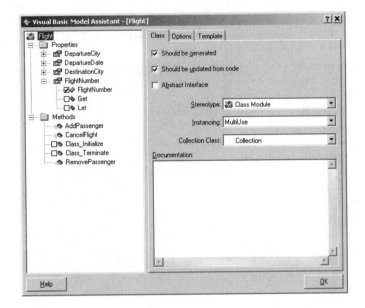

In addition to these fields, you can set the following information using this screen:

◆ The Abstract Interface field sets the class as abstract. No method bodies will be created for this class.

◆ The Stereotype field sets the type of class (class module, interface, form, collection, module, etc.). Select one of the standard Visual Basic stereotypes from the drop-down list box. The stereotype you select controls what type of class Rose will generate in Visual Basic.

◆ The Collection Class field is used to create a new, user-defined collection class. Rose will create the collection class and set up a dependency between the collection class and the current class:

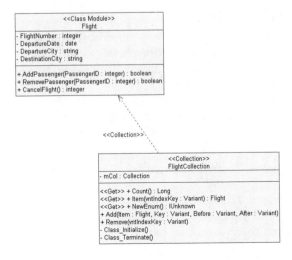

The Option Base, Option Explicit, and Option Compare properties can be set using the Options tab of the Model Assistant, as shown in Figure 15.3.

FIGURE 15.3

Using the Model Assistant's Options tab to set class properties

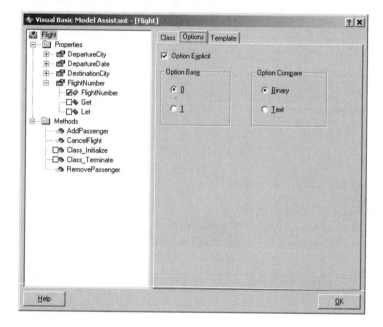

Using the Template tab, you can control whether debug code is added to the Initialize and Terminate events of the class, whether "Your code goes here..." comments are added to the class methods, and whether error-handling code is added to the class methods. By default, all of these are set to False. Some class stereotypes have additional fields that can be set using the Template tab. We will discuss those in the upcoming "Classes" section under "Generated Code."

Attribute Properties

Attribute properties are the Visual Basic properties that relate specifically to attributes. Using these properties, you can, for example, decide whether the attribute will be generated in the code, what the attribute name should be in the generated code, and whether Get, Set, or Let operations should be created for the attribute.

There are three places to set these properties. To set them for all attributes, select Tools ➤ Options, then click the Visual Basic tab and select Attribute from the drop-down list box. To set them for only one attribute, select the Visual Basic tab on the attribute specification window and edit the properties there, or use the Model Assistant.

Table 15.2 lists the attribute properties, their purposes, and their default values.

TABLE 15.2: ATTRIBUTE CODE-GENERATION PROPERTIES

PROPERTY	PURPOSE	DEFAULT
New	Controls if the attribute is generated with a new modifier	False
WithEvents	Controls if the attribute is generated with the With Events modifier	False
ProcedureID	Sets the Visual Basic procedure ID	\<blank\>
PropertyName	The name of the property to which the attribute belongs	\<blank\>
Subscript	Sets the array subscript to use when generating data members for the attribute	\<blank\>

As you can see in Figure 15.4, you can set the attribute visibility and data type using the Model Assistant. You can also set the New, WithEvents, and Subscript properties using this window.

FIGURE 15.4

Using the Model Assistant to set attribute properties

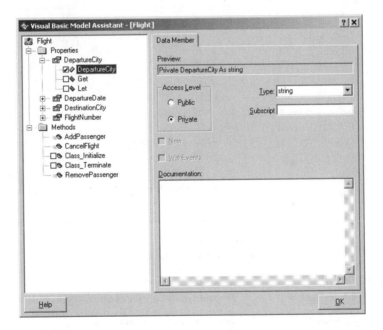

Underneath each attribute in the treeview section of the Model Assistant, you can see the Get and Let options. Selecting these will control whether Get and Let methods will be created for this particular attribute. After you select the methods you'd like to generate, you can set additional information for the methods using the Model Assistant. This information is discussed in the following section, "Operation Properties."

Operation Properties

The operation properties are the Visual Basic code-generation properties that are specific to operations. These properties will let you set the name of the operation, control whether the operation is static, and set other code-generation specifications for each operation.

There are three places to set these properties. To set them for all operations, select Tools ➤ Options, then click the Visual Basic tab and select Operation from the drop-down list box. To set them for only one operation, select the Visual Basic tab on the operation specification window and edit the properties there, or use the Model Assistant.

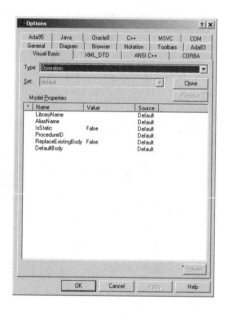

Table 15.3 lists the operation code-generation properties, their purposes, and their default values.

TABLE 15.3: OPERATION CODE-GENERATION PROPERTIES

PROPERTY	PURPOSE	DEFAULT
LibraryName	Sets the name of library in which to generate the operation	\<blank\>
AliasName	Sets the name of an operation alias	\<blank\>
IsStatic	Controls if the operation is static	False
ProcedureID	Sets the Visual Basic procedure ID	\<blank\>
ReplaceExistingBody	Specifies whether to overwrite existing body code with the default body code	False
DefaultBody	If ReplaceExistingBody is True, specifies the default text (code and comments) to include in the body	\<blank\>

Figure 15.5 shows the Model Assistant window for an operation.

FIGURE 15.5

Using the Model
Assistant to set
operations

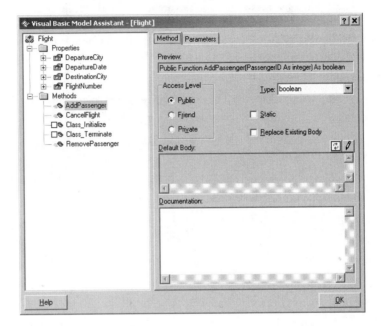

As noted earlier in this chapter, this window is used not only for operations you've defined, but for the generation of Get and Let methods for the attributes as well. Let's look at what can be set on this screen:

♦ Access Level field sets the visibility of the operation (public, private, or friend).

♦ Type field sets the return type of the operation.

♦ Static field corresponds to the IsStatic property.

♦ Replace Existing Body field corresponds to the ReplaceExistingBody property.

♦ DefaultBody field corresponds to the DefaultBody property. Note that for Get and Let operations, Rose provides code in this field for you.

Using the Parameters tab, you can add or remove parameters, and set the following for each parameter:

♦ Data type (Type field)

♦ Initial value (Initial Value field)

♦ Whether or not the parameter is optional (Optional field)

♦ Whether the parameter is passed by value or by reference (ByRef and ByVal fields)

♦ Whether an indefinite number of parameters may be passed for the operation (ParamArray field)

Each of these settings will affect the generated code.

Module Specification Properties

The module specification properties are related to the project files you will generate from Rose. There are three places to set these properties. To set them for all components, select Tools ➤ Options, then click the Visual Basic tab and select Module Specification from the drop-down list box. To set them for only one component, select the Visual Basic tab on the component specification window and edit the properties there, or use the Visual Basic Component Properties window.

Table 15.4 lists the code-generation properties for components, their purposes, and their default values.

TABLE 15.4: MODULE SPECIFICATION CODE-GENERATION PROPERTIES

PROPERTY	PURPOSE	DEFAULT
ProjectFile	Sets the name of the project file	<Set using the Code Generation Wizard>
UpdateCode	Specifies if code can be generated for this component	True
UpdateModel	Specifies if the model can be updated for this component	True
ImportReferences	Specifies whether to import ActiveX components	True
QuickImport	Specifies whether to import only ActiveX interface classes or all classes including methods and operations	True
ImportBinary	Determines whether Rose should import the type library for the component on the next reverse engineer	False

To open the Visual Basic Component Properties window, as shown in Figure 15.6, right-click the component and select Properties.

FIGURE 15.6

VB Component
Properties Window

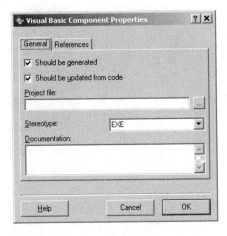

The Should Be Generated and Should Be Updated from Code fields correspond to the UpdateCode and UpdateModel properties, respectively. The Project File field corresponds to the ProjectFile property. Using the References tab, you can set the QuickImport, ImportBinary, and ImportReferences properties.

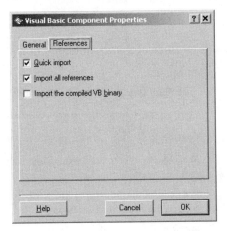

Role Properties

Role properties are the Visual Basic code-generation properties that affect the code generated for relationships. The role properties let you set the name of the attribute that is created; control the generation of Get, Set, and Let operations; and change other specific pieces of the generated code.

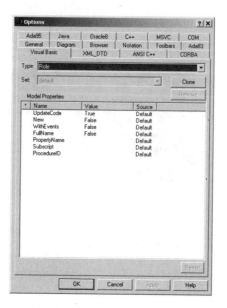

There are two places to set these properties. To set them for all associations, select Tools ➤ Options, then click the Visual Basic tab and select Role from the drop-down list box. To set them for only one operation, select the Visual Basic tab on the association specification window and edit the properties there. Table 15.5 lists the code-generation property for roles.

TABLE 15.5: ROLE CODE-GENERATION PROPERTIES

PROPERTY	PURPOSE	DEFAULT
UpdateCode	Specifies if code can be generated for this role	True
New	Controls if the association is generated with a new modifier	False
WithEvents	Controls if the association is generated with the With Events modifier	False
Fullname	Specifies whether to use the full name of the referenced class in the property declaration	False
PropertyName	The name of the property to which the attribute created to support the relationship belongs	<blank>
Subscript	Specifies the array subscript for an attribute	<blank>
ProcedureID	Sets the Visual Basic procedure ID	<blank>

Generalization Properties

Generalization properties are the Visual Basic code-generation properties that affect the code generated for generalization relationships. As Visual Basic does not support inheritance, there are only two properties for generalization relationships. The ImplementsDelegation property controls whether the generalization is realized by an implements delegation. The FullName property controls whether the full name of the class, including the component name, should be used in the implements statement.

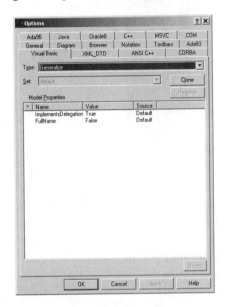

There are two places to set these properties. To set them for all generalizations, select Tools ➤ Options, then click the Visual Basic tab and select Generalize from the drop-down list box. To set them for only one generalization, select the Visual Basic tab on the generalization specification window and edit the properties there.

Using the Code-Generation Wizard

After you create classes and associations in the Rose model, you can use a Code-Generation Wizard to generate the Visual Basic code. To begin this process, select the objects to generate, then select Tools ➤ Visual Basic ➤ Update Code from the menu. You will see the screen shown in Figure 15.7.

FIGURE 15.7

Code-Generation
Wizard

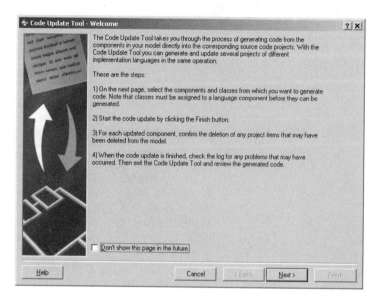

If you have not yet assigned the objects to components, you will see a window like the one in Figure 15.8. You have the option of assigning the classes to an existing component (in this example, there is a single component called Airline Reservation with a stereotype of Standard EXE). Alternatively, you can create a new component and assign classes to it.

FIGURE 15.8

Assigning
components and
classes

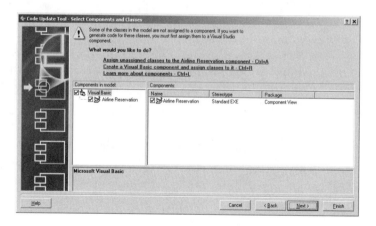

To assign classes to an existing component, right-click the component in the Code-Generation Wizard shown in Figure 15.8 and select Assign Classes. You will see a list of unassigned classes:

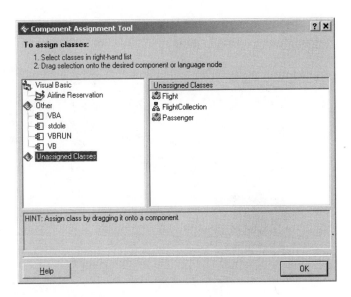

Drag and drop each class from the right side of the screen to the appropriate component on the left side. Once all classes are assigned, click OK.

To create a new component, select the Create a Visual Basic Component and Assign Classes to It option, as shown in Figure 15.8, or press Ctrl+R. You will be asked what type of component to create:

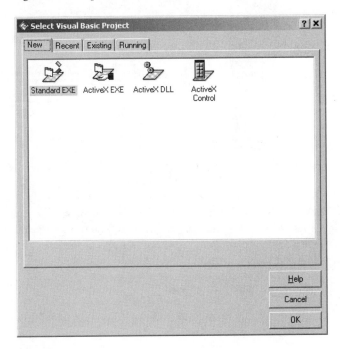

Select the appropriate type (in this example, we use a Standard EXE) and press OK. The component will be added, and all unassigned classes will be assigned to it:

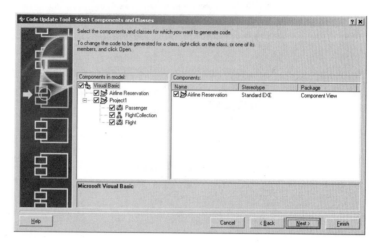

Check the box next to the components or classes you wish to update. Notice that if you click on a class, you can preview the code that will be generated for the attributes and operations of that class:

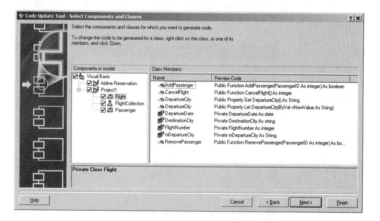

Right-click and select Open to view the properties for an object in the treeview. Rose will display the appropriate Model Assistant screen, and allow you to modify any code-generation properties before the final code is generated. For example, right-clicking the Flight class will display the screen shown in Figure 15.9.

FIGURE 15.9

Setting code-
generation properties
for the Flight class

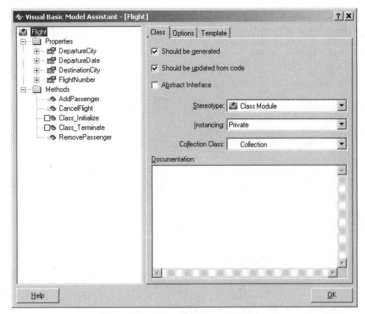

Once all classes have been assigned and all code-generation properties are set, click Next to complete the process. You will see a summary screen, as shown in Figure 15.10. Press Finish to generate
the code. If Visual Basic is not already running, Rose will launch it and create the appropriate project,
classes, and other elements.

FIGURE 15.10

Code-generation
summary screen

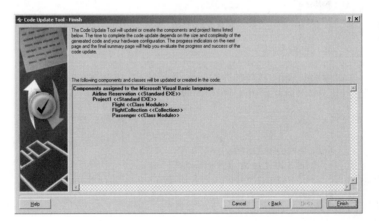

An example of the code generated for the Flight class follows below. In the remainder of this chapter, we will discuss the mapping between a Rose model and Visual Basic code.

```
Option Explicit

'##ModelId=3A818E9F01D0
Private DepartureCity As String

'##ModelId=3A818EAC02C9
Private DepartureDate As String

'##ModelId=3A818EB300CA
Private DestinationCity As String

'##ModelId=3A818EB70134
Private FlightNumber As String

'##ModelId=3A818ECE01A6
Private Function RemovePassenger(PassengerID As int) As boolean

End Function

'##ModelId=3A818EBF03B7
Public Function AddPassenger(PassengerID As int) As boolean

End Function

'##ModelId=3A818EC9007C
Public Function CancelFlight() As Boolean

End Function

'##ModelId=3A818F8303D7
Private Sub Class_Initialize()

End Sub

'##ModelId=3A818F84034C
Private Sub Class_Terminate()

End Sub
```

Generated Code

In the following sections, we'll take a look at the Visual Basic code generated for a class, an attribute, an operation, and for the different types of relationships between classes. In each of these sections, we include some sample code to give you an idea of what will be generated from your Rose model.

Rose uses the information in the specifications of the model elements when generating code. For example, it will look at the different specifications for a class (visibility, attributes, operations, and so on) when generating code for the class.

Let's begin by looking at the code generated for a typical class.

Classes

A class in the Rose model will be implemented as a class in Visual Basic. The type of class that is generated depends on the stereotype you assign the class in Rose. The default Visual Basic stereotype is Class Module. Classes with this stereotype will be implemented as a class module in Visual Basic. In our example, we have a Flight class:

<<Class Module>> Flight
- FlightNumber : integer - DepartureDate : date - mDepartureCity : String - DestinationCity : string
+ AddPassenger(PassengerID : integer) : boolean + RemovePassenger(PassengerID : integer) : boolean + CancelFlight() : integer <<Get>> + DepartureCity() : String <<Let>> + DepartureCity(vNewValue : String)

The following is the code generated for the Flight class:

```
Option Explicit

'##ModelId=395EA80B0088
Private FlightNumber As Integer

'##ModelId=395EA87C01A3
Private DepartureDate As Date

'##ModelId=395EA880036C
Private mDepartureCity As String

'##ModelId=395EA884028B
Private DestinationCity As String

'##ModelId=395EA88D0176
Public Function AddPassenger(PassengerID As Integer) As Boolean

End Function

'##ModelId=395EA8970383
Public Function RemovePassenger(PassengerID As Integer) As Boolean

End Function
```

```
'##ModelId=395EA8A1008E
Public Function CancelFlight() As Integer

End Function

'##ModelId=395EB1D202F5
Public Property Get DepartureCity() As String
    DepartureCity = mDepartureCity
End Property

'##ModelId=395EB2CA0201
Public Property Let DepartureCity(ByVal vNewValue As String)
    mDepartureCity = vNewValue
End Property
```

Notice that Rose generated all of the attributes, their data types, and their visibility; the operations with their parameters, data types, visibility, and return types; and the Get and Let operations for DepartureCity.

The Get and Let methods were created because we set the option to create them using the Model Assistant. While Rose generates just the method headers for any operations you've added, it will generate the actual code for Get and Let operations. This saves the programmers from the tedious task of generating and coding Get and Let operations for all of the attributes.

The Option Explicit line is included because the OptionExplicit class property for this class was set to True.

The ModelId lines were created to help synchronize Rose and Visual Basic during round-trip engineering. This feature allows you to change a method name, for example, in the Rose model or in the code, and still be able to synchronize the model with the code.

WARNING *Be careful not to change the ModelId numbers in the code.*

Much of the information in your Rose model will be used directly when generating code. For example, the attributes, operations, relationships, and class name will directly affect the code generated for each class. Other model properties, such as the documentation entered for the class, will not directly affect the code. These properties are created as comments in the generated code.

Table 15.6 lists properties of a class, and notes which of these properties will directly affect the code generated.

The Flight class has a stereotype of Class Module. Let's look at what is generated for some of the other stereotypes. Note that while many different types of classes can be generated in Visual Basic, the Visual Basic add-in will not generate parameterized classes.

TABLE 15.6: EFFECT OF CLASS PROPERTIES ON GENERATED CODE

PROPERTY	EFFECT ON CODE
Name	Name in model will become class name
Type	Directly affects the type of class created
Stereotype	Directly affects the type of module file created (Class Module, MDI Form, etc.)
Export Control	Does not affect generation
Documentation	Generated as a comment
Cardinality	Does not affect generation
Space	Does not affect generation
Persistence	Does not affect Visual Basic code generation, but does affect whether DDL can be generated for the class
Concurrency	Does not affect generation
Abstract	Does not affect generation
Formal Arguments	Formal arguments are included in the code for a parameterized class
Operations	Generated in code
Attributes	Generated in code
Relationships	Generated in code

FORM

The Form stereotype will create a Visual Basic form. Attributes become properties of the form. Operations become methods of the form.

Rose can generate the default Visual Basic methods—such as the Initialize, Load, and Unload methods—for the form. To decide which methods to generate, open the Model Assistant for the class and select the appropriate method(s) on the left side of the window.

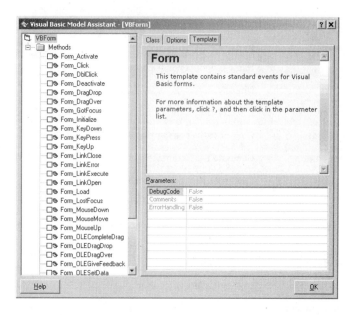

As you select these methods, you will be given the option to change the method visibility (public, friend, or private). You can check the Replace Existing Body check box so that when Rose generates the method, the code you've entered in the Default Body field will be generated:

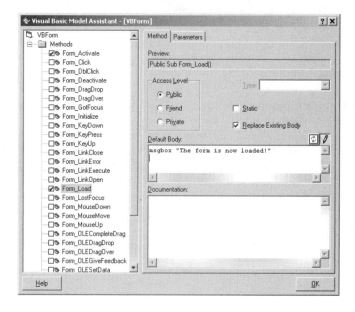

Using the Template tab of the Model Assistant, you can set the following options:

◆ DebugCode adds debug code to the Initialize and Terminate events. The default setting is False.

◆ Comments adds "Your code goes here…" comments to the methods of the class. The default setting is False.

◆ ErrorHandling adds error-handling code to the methods of the class. The default setting is False.

MDI FORM

The MDIForm stereotype will create a Visual Basic MDI form. Attributes become properties of the form. Operations become methods of the form.

As with a Form stereotype, Rose can generate many default methods in an MDI form class. Open the Model Assistant for the class and select the methods to generate. Then, enter the method visibility and the code to be generated for that method.

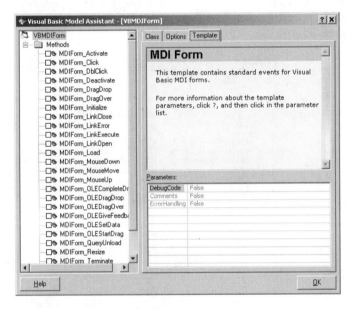

Using the Template tab of the Model Assistant, you can set the following options:

◆ DebugCode adds debug code to the Initialize and Terminate events. The default setting is False.

◆ Comments adds "Your code goes here…" comments to the methods of the class. The default setting is False.

◆ ErrorHandling adds error-handling code to the methods of the class. The default setting is False.

ADO CLASS

The ADOClass stereotype will create an ADO class in Visual Basic, which will exhibit some persistent behavior. Attributes of the class become properties of the ADO class. Operations become methods of the ADO class.

In addition, Rose can generate the following properties. Use the Model Assistant to select the properties to generate.

◆ BOF

◆ ConnectionString

◆ EOF

◆ Recordset

◆ mrs (generated by default)

Rose can generate a number of standard methods for the class, including the MoveFirst, MoveLast, MoveNext, MovePrevious, GetAll, and DeleteAll methods. Use the Model Assistant to select the operations to generate.

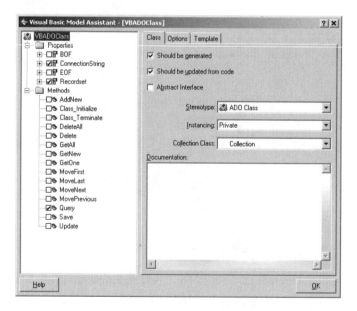

By default, Rose will generate the Query method, which creates and fills a recordset using a query passed in as a parameter.

The following code is an example of what is generated for an ADO class:

```
Option Explicit

'Private constant with database connection string. Default from
'template parameter ConnectionString (which defaults to an empty
```

```
'string).
'##ModelId=395EC4060255
Private Const ConnectionString As String = ""

'##ModelId=395EC406033B
Private mrs As Recordset

'Public Property Get to get a reference to the private ADO
'Recordset (mrs).
'##ModelId=395EC40602A5
Public Property Get Recordset() As Recordset
    Set Recordset = mrs
End Property

'Private Function to return ADO Recordset from query sent as SQL
'string input parameter. Creates a Connection and a Recordset.
'Connects Recordset to the Connection, queries the database (with
'the SQL string) which fills the recordset with the result.
'Disconnects the Recordset from the Connection and closes the
'Connection. Returns the created, queried and filled Recordset.
'Uses the module level constant ConnectionString as connection
'string on connection. Uses client side cursors on Connection.
'##ModelId=395EC40602E1
Private Function Query(ByVal SQL As String) As Recordset
    Dim aco As Connection
    Dim ars As Recordset

    ' Create objects
    Set aco = CreateObject("ADODB.Connection")
    Set ars = CreateObject("ADODB.Recordset")

    ' Open Connection
    aco.CursorLocation = adUseClient
    aco.ConnectionString = ConnectionString
    aco.Open

    ' Open Recordset
    ars.CursorType = adOpenKeyset
    ars.LockType = adLockBatchOptimistic
    ars.ActiveConnection = aco
    ars.Open SQL

    ' Return Recordset
    Set Query = ars

    ' Disconnect Recordset from Connection
    Set ars.ActiveConnection = Nothing
```

```
      ' Close Connection
      aco.Close
End Function
```

As with other stereotypes, you can set certain code-generation properties using the Template tab of the Model assistant. For an ADO class, the following options are available:

◆ DebugCode adds debug code to the Initialize and Terminate events. The default setting is False.

◆ Comments adds "Your code goes here…" comments to the methods of the class. The default setting is False.

◆ ErrorHandling adds error-handling code to the methods of the class. The default setting is False.

◆ MTSEnabled determines whether or not the class is MTS aware. If this option is set to True, Rose can generate a CreateInstance method and a Get method for the ObjectContext property.

◆ ConnectionString sets the database connection string to be used.

◆ TableName sets the name of the table corresponding to the class.

◆ PrimaryKeyFieldName sets the name of the primary key of the table corresponding to this class.

MTS CLASS

The MTS Class stereotype is used to model Microsoft Transaction Server (MTS) classes in Rose. Attributes you've defined in Rose become attributes of the class in Visual Basic. Operations you've defined in Rose become methods of the Visual Basic class.

By default, an MTS class is not ADO-enabled. However, you can change this setting by using the Model Assistant:

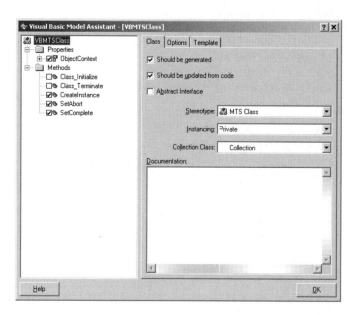

The following properties and methods are generated by default:

◆ ObjectContext property, which is the current MTS ObjectContext object

◆ CreateInstance, which creates a new instance of an object

◆ SetAbort, which provides rollback functionality

◆ SetComplete, which commits a transaction

The following is an example of the code generated for an MTS class:

```
Option Explicit

'Private Property Get to return the current ObjectContext object
'(assigned to the object by MTS). If the object is not running in
'MTS, the returned value will be Nothing.
'##ModelId=395EC3EA0395
Private Property Get ObjectContext() As ObjectContext
    ' Return current ObjectContext
    Set ObjectContext = GetObjectContext()
End Property


'Private Function to create a new instance of another object
'specified as an input parameter (which is a ProgID string).
'This method handles the creation of objects both running in
'and outside of MTS. If there is an ObjectContext object for
'the current object - i.e. it is running in MTS -
'the CreateInstance method of the ObjectContext is called.
'If not, the CreateObject API is called. This is the only
'way you should use to make instances of new objects from
'the class.
'##ModelId=395EC3EA03D1
Private Function CreateInstance(ByVal ProgID As String) As Variant
    ' Create object (inside MTS or not)
    If Not ObjectContext Is Nothing Then
        Set CreateInstance = ObjectContext.CreateInstance(ProgID)
    Else
        Set CreateInstance = CreateObject(ProgID)
    End If
End Function


'Calls the ObjectContext SetAbort method (if running in MTS) for
'transactional Rollback behavior.
'##ModelId=395EC3EB002F
Private Sub SetAbort()
    ' Set Abort status on current ObjectContext object
    If Not ObjectContext Is Nothing Then
        ObjectContext.SetAbort
    End If
```

```
End Sub

'Calls the ObjectContext SetComplete method (if running in MTS)
'for transactional Commit behavior.
'##ModelId=395EC3EB0057
Private Sub SetComplete()
    ' Set Complete status on current ObjectContext object
    If Not ObjectContext Is Nothing Then
        ObjectContext.SetComplete
    End If
End Sub
```

Using the Template tab of the Model Assistant, you can set the following code-generation options:

♦ DebugCode adds debug code to the Initialize and Terminate events. The default setting is False.

♦ Comments adds "Your code goes here…" comments to the methods of the class. The default setting is False.

♦ ErrorHandling adds error-handling code to the methods of the class. The default setting is False.

♦ ADOEnabled determines whether or not the class is ADO aware. If this option is set to True, Rose can generate GetAll, GetNew, GetOne, Query, Save, and Update operations.

♦ ConnectionString sets the database connection string to be used.

♦ TableName sets the name of the table corresponding to the class.

♦ PrimaryKeyFieldName sets the name of the primary key of the table corresponding to this class.

♦ MTSTransactionMode sets the MTS support level (Not an MTS Object, No Transactions, Requires Transaction, Uses Transaction, or Requires New Transaction).

MODULE

A Module stereotype becomes a Visual Basic module. Attributes become properties of the module. Operations become methods of the module.

Using the Template tab of the Model Assistant, you can set the following:

♦ DebugCode adds debug code to the Initialize and Terminate events. The default setting is False.

♦ Comments adds "Your code goes here…" comments to the methods of the class. The default setting is False.

♦ ErrorHandling adds error-handling code to the methods of the class. The default setting is False.

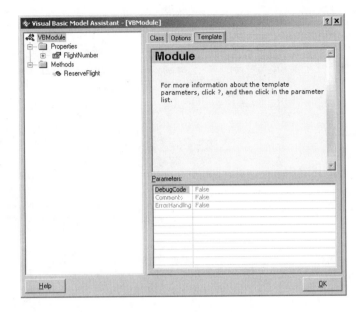

COLLECTION

A Collection stereotype becomes a Visual Basic collection. Attributes become properties of the collection. Operations become methods of the collection. In addition, Rose generates the following methods by default:

- Get Count, which returns the number of items in the collection. Rose will code this method for you

- Get Item, which returns an item from the collection. Rose will code this method for you

- Get Enum, which supports the enumeration of the collection for the For…Each syntax

- Add, which adds a new item to the collection

- Remove, which removes an item from the collection

- Initialize method, which creates an instance of the class in memory

- Terminate method, which does any "clean-up" work and removes an instance of the class from memory

You can determine which methods to generate by using the Model Assistant:

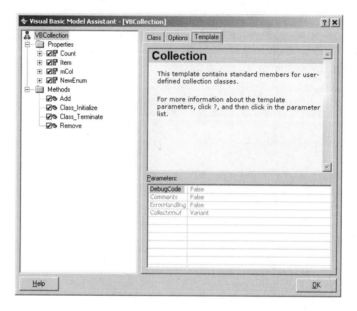

The following code is an example of what is created in Visual Basic for a class with a stereotype of Collection:

```
Option Explicit

'local variable to hold collection
'##ModelId=395EC3EC0320
Private mCol As New Collection

'used when retrieving the number of elements in the
'collection. Syntax: Debug.Print x.Count
'##ModelId=395EC3EB03BF
Public Property Get Count() As Long
    Count = mCol.Count
End Property

'used when referencing an element in the collection
'vntIndexKey contains either the Index or Key to the collection,
'this is why it is declared as a Variant
'Syntax: Set foo = x.Item(xyz) or Set foo = x.Item(5)
'##ModelId=395EC3EC0009
Public Property Get Item(vntIndexKey As Variant) As Variant
    Set Item = mCol(vntIndexKey)
End Property
```

```
'this property allows you to enumerate
'this collection with the For...Each syntax
'##ModelId=395EC3EC006D
Public Property Get NewEnum() As IUnknown
    Set NewEnum = mCol.[_NewEnum]
End Property

'used when adding a new item to the collection
'syntax: x.Add ayz
'##ModelId=395EC3EC00A9
Public Sub Add(Item As Variant, Optional Key As Variant, Optional Before As
Variant, Optional After As Variant)
    If Len(Key) = 0 Then
        mCol.Add Item
    Else
        mCol.Add Item, Key
    End If
End Sub

'used when removing an element from the collection
'vntIndexKey contains either the Index or Key, which is why
'it is declared as a Variant
'Syntax: x.Remove(xyz)
'##ModelId=395EC3EC018F
Public Sub Remove(vntIndexKey As Variant)
    mCol.Remove vntIndexKey
End Sub

'##ModelId=395EC3ED003C
Private Sub Class_Initialize()

End Sub

'##ModelId=395EC3ED0078
Private Sub Class_Terminate()

End Sub
```

Using the Template tab of the Model Assistant, you can set the following options for the collection:

◆ DebugCode adds debug code to the Initialize and Terminate events. The default setting is False.

◆ Comments adds "Your code goes here…" comments to the methods of the class. The default setting is False.

◆ ErrorHandling adds error-handling code to the methods of the class. The default setting is False.

◆ CollectionOf defines the class of which the collection is a grouping.

NOTE   When reverse engineering a collection, Rose will create a class with a stereotype of Class Module, not Collection.

USER CONTROL

The User Control stereotype will create a Visual Basic user control. Attributes become properties of the user control. Operations become methods of the user control. In addition to the operations you define in Rose, you can generate many default methods for the user control, including Click, Double-Click, KeyDown, Resize, and Show.

Using the Model Assistant, select the method(s) to be generated in Visual Basic for the user control.

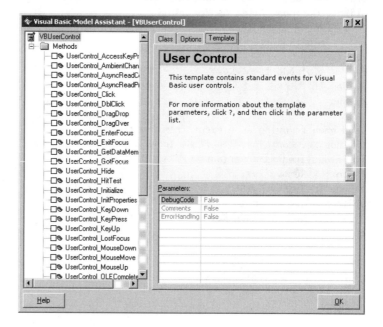

On the Template tab, you can set the following options:

◆ DebugCode adds debug code to the Initialize and Terminate events. The default setting is False.

◆ Comments adds "Your code goes here…" comments to the methods of the class. The default setting is False.

◆ ErrorHandling adds error-handling code to the methods of the class. The default setting is False.

PROPERTY PAGE

The PropertyPage stereotype will create a Visual Basic property page. Attributes become properties of the page. Operations become methods of the page. As with many other stereotypes, Rose can generate default methods for you through the Model Assistant:

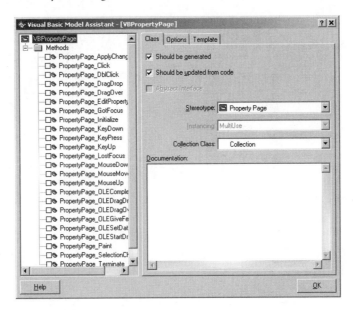

On the Template tab, you can set the following options:

◆ DebugCode adds debug code to the Initialize and Terminate events. The default setting is False.

◆ Comments adds "Your code goes here…" comments to the methods of the class. The default setting is False.

◆ ErrorHandling adds error-handling code to the methods of the class. The default setting is False.

DATA REPORT

A DataReport-stereotyped class is generated as a Visual Basic data report. Any attributes of the class become properties of the data report. Any operations become methods in the data report. In addition, Rose can generate standard methods for you:

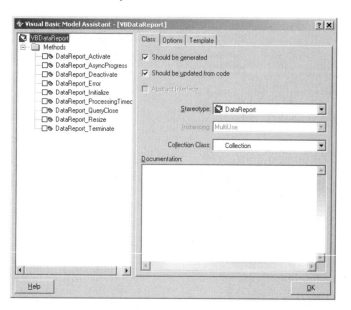

The following is an example of a data report generated from Rose:

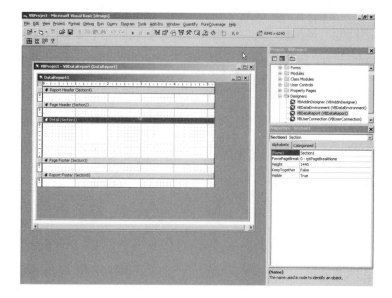

On the Template tab of the Model Assistant, you can set the following options for the data report:

◆ DebugCode adds debug code to the Initialize and Terminate events. The default setting is False.

◆ Comments adds "Your code goes here…" comments to the methods of the class. The default setting is False.

◆ ErrorHandling adds error-handling code to the methods of the class. The default setting is False.

DATA ENVIRONMENT

A class with a stereotype of Data Environment will create a DataEnvironment class in Visual Basic. As with other stereotypes, attributes and operations are implemented as properties and methods of the generated class.

When generating a data environment, Rose will add a connection object to the generated class. You can then set up the connection, including the connection type (ODBC, etc.) and data source using Visual Basic.

Rose can also generate Initialize and Terminate methods for the data environment. Use the Model Assistant to set which operations to generate:

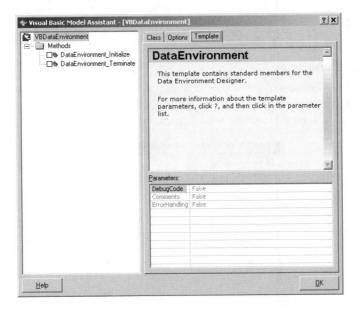

On the Template tab of the Model Assistant, you can set the following options:

◆ DebugCode adds debug code to the Initialize and Terminate events. The default setting is False.

◆ Comments adds "Your code goes here…" comments to the methods of the class. The default setting is False.

◆ ErrorHandling adds error-handling code to the methods of the class. The default setting is False.

The following is an example of the data environment created from Rose:

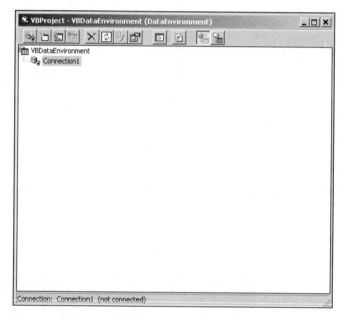

USER CONNECTION

The UserConnection stereotype will create a Visual Basic user connection. Attributes become properties of the connection. Operations become methods of the connection. You can set up Rose to generate default methods through the Model Assistant:

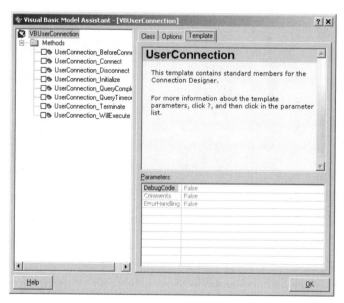

On the Template tab of the Model Assistant, you can set the following options:

♦ DebugCode adds debug code to the Initialize and Terminate events. The default setting is False.

♦ Comments adds "Your code goes here…" comments to the methods of the class. The default setting is False.

♦ ErrorHandling adds error-handling code to the methods of the class. The default setting is False.

Once the user connection has been created, you can use Visual Basic to set the connection details, add queries, and complete the code for the connection.

USER DOCUMENT

A User Document stereotype becomes a Visual Basic user document. Attributes become properties of the user document. Operations become methods of the user document. The Model Assistant will enable you to set the default methods to be generated.

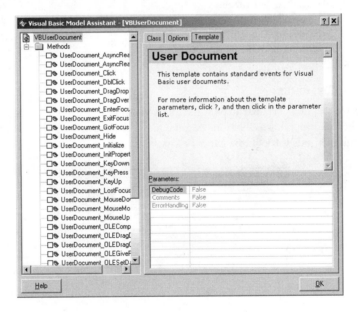

Using the Template tab of the Model Assistant, you can set the following:

♦ DebugCode adds debug code to the Initialize and Terminate events. The default setting is False.

♦ Comments adds "Your code goes here…" comments to the methods of the class. The default setting is False.

♦ ErrorHandling adds error-handling code to the methods of the class. The default setting is False.

NOTE *You cannot generate a user document that is assigned to a component with a Standard EXE stereotype. Map the user document to another component (ActiveX EXE, for example) before generating code.*

TYPE AND ENUM

A Type or Enum class must be modeled as a class nested within another class. To do this, open the specification of the nesting class and select the Nested tab. Right-click in the whitespace to add a new nested class, and set the stereotype of the nested class to Type or Enum.

Once you have added the nested class, double-click it to open the nested class specification. Click the Attributes tab to add one or more attributes to the nested class before generating code.

The following is an example of a Type and Enum class generated from Rose:

```
Option Explicit

'##ModelId=39600F880341
Public Enum VBEnum
    '##ModelId=3960106A01BF
    EnumAttribute = 4
End Enum

'##ModelId=39600FA10206
Public Type VBType
    '##ModelId=3960107A0245
    TypeAttribute As Boolean
End Type
```

ADD-IN DESIGNER

The Add-In Designer stereotype will create a Visual Basic add-in designer. Attributes become properties of the designer, while operations become methods of the designer. You can set up Rose to generate default methods through the Model Assistant:

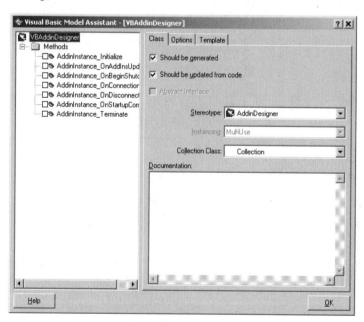

On the Template tab of the Model Assistant, you can set the following options:

◆ DebugCode adds debug code to the Initialize and Terminate events. The default setting is False.

◆ Comments adds "Your code goes here…" comments to the methods of the class. The default setting is False.

◆ ErrorHandling adds error-handling code to the methods of the class. The default setting is False.

Once the designer has been created, you can use Visual Basic to set the details. The following is an example of an add-in designer created from Rose:

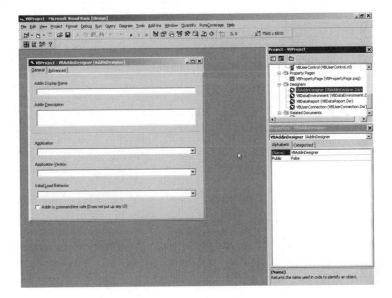

DHTML PAGE

A class with a stereotype of DHTMLPage will be implemented as a DHTML page in Visual Basic. As with other stereotypes, attributes and operations of the class in Rose become properties and methods of the Visual Basic class.

Using the Model Assistant, you can select the methods to be generated in the code:

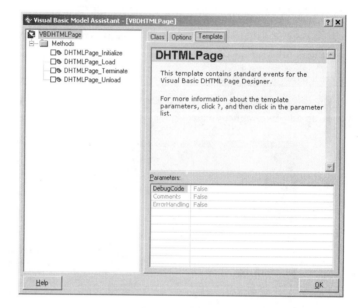

On the Template tab of the Model Assistant, you can set the following options:

◆ DebugCode adds debug code to the Initialize and Terminate events. The default setting is False.

◆ Comments adds "Your code goes here…" comments to the methods of the class. The default setting is False.

◆ ErrorHandling adds error-handling code to the methods of the class. The default setting is False.

NOTE   *You cannot generate a DHTML page that is assigned to a component with a Standard EXE stereotype. Map the DHTML page to another component (ActiveX EXE, for example) before generating code.*

Attributes

Aside from the class itself, Rose will generate the attributes for the class. For each attribute, Rose will include:

◆ Visibility (public or private only; protected visibility is not allowed)

◆ Data type

◆ Default value

◆ Get operation (optional)

◆ Set operation (optional)

◆ Let operation (optional)

For a given attribute, Rose will generate code similar to the following:

```
Option Explicit

'##ModelId=39601FD70178
Private mPrivateAttribute As Integer

'##ModelId=39602033026A
Public Property Get PrivateAttribute() As Integer
    PrivateAttribute = mPrivateAttribute
End Property

'##ModelId=396020340059
Public Property Let PrivateAttribute(ByVal vNewValue As Integer)
    mPrivateAttribute = vNewValue
End Property
```

You can control whether the Get, Let, and Set operations are generated by using the Model Assistant for the class. In the Properties portion of the treeview, find the appropriate attribute and check the Get, Let, or Set method check boxes under the property to generate those methods. You can also change the attribute visibility and data type using the Model Assistant.

An attribute with a stereotype of Const will be generated as a Visual Basic constant. Use the Initial Value field in the attribute specifications to set the value of the constant. In this example, we created a constant called DaysInWeek with an initial value of 7. The following line of code was generated:

```
Private Const DaysInWeek As Integer = 7
```

By default, Rose will prefix the attribute name with an "m" when generating code. To change the prefix used, select Tools ➤ Visual Basic ➤ Properties, and edit the Data Member Prefix field.

Operations

Rose generates code for each of the operations in the class. For each operation, the generated code includes the operation name, the parameters, the parameter data types, and the return type. Each operation will generate code similar to the following:

```
'This is documentation entered through Rose for the PublicOperation method.
'

'##ModelId=3960239403E1
Public Function PublicOperation(Argument1 As Integer) As Boolean

End Function
```

As you can see, the full operation signature is generated in the code. Any documentation you enter for the operation is also generated as a comment in the code. If you enter information for the operation protocol, qualifications, exceptions, time, space, preconditions, semantics, or postconditions, this information will *not* be included in the generated code. Once you have generated the code, you insert the implementation code for each operation.

As with other model elements, you can control the code generated for an operation by modifying its code-generation properties. For example, you can create static functions by modifying the IsStatic property. The code-generation properties for operations are listed earlier in this chapter, in Table 15.3, for your reference.

Bidirectional Associations

To support bidirectional associations, Rose will generate attributes in the code. Each of the classes in the relationship will contain an attribute to support the association. Unlike Visual C++, Rose Visual Basic does not require that you assign role names in order to generate attributes to support the relationship. However, if you do not assign role names, the attributes will be called NewProperty. If you do assign role names, Rose will use the role names as the names of the generated attributes. For example, let's look at the code generated for the following:

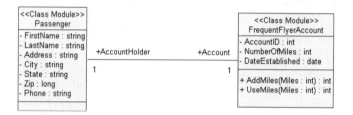

Here is the Visual Basic code generated for these two classes. First, let's look at the Passenger class:

```
Option Explicit

'##ModelId=39614F5402F7
Private FirstName As String

'##ModelId=39614F5702B5
Private LastName As String

'##ModelId=39614F5A01F1
Private Address As String

'##ModelId=39614F5D0250
Private City As String

'##ModelId=39614F5F01EE
Private State As String

'##ModelId=39614F610179
Private Zip As Long

'##ModelId=39614F6B00DD
Private Phone As String
```

```
'##ModelId=39614F990350
Public Account As FrequentFlyerAccount
```

Now let's look at the FrequentFlyerAccount class:

```
Option Explicit

'##ModelId=39614F7300C1
Private AccountID As int

'##ModelId=39614F7503A9
Private NumberOfMiles As int

'##ModelId=39614F7A02C0
Private DateEstablished As Date

'##ModelId=39614F99035A
Public AccountHolder As Passenger

'##ModelId=39614F8902FD
Public Function UseMiles(Miles As int) As int

End Function

'##ModelId=39614F840089
Public Function AddMiles(Miles As int) As int

End Function

'##ModelId=39614F7300C1
Private AccountID As int

'##ModelId=39614F7503A9
Private NumberOfMiles As int

'##ModelId=39614F8902FD
Public Function UseMiles(Miles As int) As int

End Function

'##ModelId=39614F840089
Public Function AddMiles(Miles As int) As int

End Function
```

As you can see, Rose will automatically generate attributes on both sides of the bidirectional association relationship. With the AccountHolder attribute, FrequentFlyerAccount can easily access Passenger. Using the Account attribute, Passenger can easily access FrequentFlyerAccount.

TIP   *Remember that if you supply no role names, the default (and less useful) attribute name NewProperty will be used. If you supply a role name, that role name will be used as the attribute name.*

In the Model Assistant, you can elect to generate Get and Set methods for the attribute generated to support the relationship:

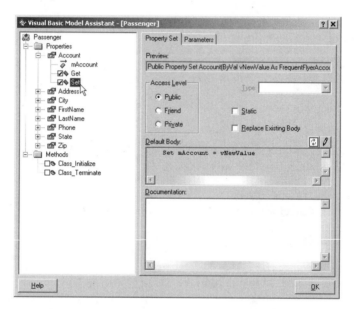

Rose will create the methods and then code them for you:

```
'##ModelId=396152BE0268
Public Property Get Account() As FrequentFlyerAccount
    Set Account = mAccount
End Property
```

```
'##ModelId=396152C00333
Public Property Set Account(ByVal vNewValue As FrequentFlyerAccount)
    Set mAccount = vNewValue
End Property
```

Note that this association has a multiplicity of one to one. See below for a discussion of how other multiplicity settings will affect code generation.

Unidirectional Associations

As with bidirectional associations, Rose will generate attributes to support unidirectional associations. With a unidirectional association, however, an attribute is generated only at one end of the relationship.

Again we have the Passenger and FrequentFlyerAccount classes, but this time the relationship is unidirectional. An attribute will be created inside Passenger, but not inside FrequentFlyerAccount. The following lines of code are from Passenger:

```
'##ModelId=39614F990350
Private Account As FrequentFlyerAccount
```

As you can see, Rose will generate a private attribute for the relationship at only one end of the association. Specifically, it will generate an attribute in the client class, but not in the supplier class.

The code generated in the supplier class includes all of the code lines discussed in the previous section about bidirectional associations. With a bidirectional association, each class is given a new attribute, and the code discussed in the previous section is included in both classes. With a unidirectional association, the code is included only in the client class.

Again, note that the multiplicity here is one to one. Let's take a look at how code is affected when the multiplicity settings are changed.

Associations with a Multiplicity of One to Many

In a one-to-one relationship, Rose can simply create the appropriate attributes to support the association. With a one-to-many relationship, however, one class must contain a set of the other class.

To begin, let's look at an example.

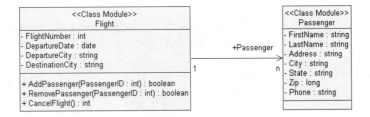

In this case, we have a one-to-many relationship. As we saw in the previous section, Flight can simply generate an attribute that is a reference to Passenger. However, a simple attribute in the Flight class won't be enough. Instead, the attribute generated in Flight must use a sort of container class or an array as its data type. (Rose will use a collection as the default.) The following code is generated in the Flight class:

```
'##ModelId=396154B0001F
Public Passenger As Collection
```

Rose provides you with the Collection type as a container class. If you would rather, you can use an array by specifying the Subscript role property. To do so, open the specification window for the relationship and select the Visual Basic A or Visual Basic B tab. Then specify a value for the Subscript code-generation property. Here, we use a subscript of 3:

```
'##ModelId=396154B0001F
Public Passenger(3) As Passenger
```

Associations with a Multiplicity of Many to Many

The code generated here is similar to that created for a one-to-many relationship. In this type of relationship, however, Rose will generate container classes on both ends of the relationship.

Let's look at the code generated for the following relationship:

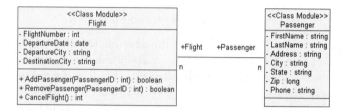

In this situation, container classes are used at both ends of the relationship. The code that is generated will look something like the following two classes.

First, the Flight class will contain:

```
'##ModelId=396154B0001F
Public Passenger As Collection
```

Next, the Passenger class will contain:

```
'##ModelId=396154B00021
Public Flight As Collection
```

Again, Rose uses a collection class as the default container, but you can change this to an array by modifying the Subscript code-generation property in the relationship specification window.

Reflexive Associations

A reflexive association is treated much the same as an association between two classes. For the following situation,

this code is generated:

```
'##ModelId=3961578B0369
Public NewProperty As Collection
```

As with a regular association, an attribute is created inside the class to support the relationship. If the multiplicity is one, a simple attribute is created. If the multiplicity is more than one, a container class is used.

As you can see, the code generated here is very similar to the code generated in a typical one-to-many relationship. In this situation, Class A contains an attribute of type Collection.

Aggregations

There are two types of aggregation relationships: by value and by reference. With a by-value relationship, one class contains another. With a by-reference relationship, one class contains a reference to another. Both of these types of relationships are generated identically in Rose Visual Basic.

The code generated for an aggregation relationship is the same as the code generated for an association relationship. Let's look at an example:

The aggregation relationship tells us that, conceptually, a fleet is made up of many aircraft. When we generate code, however, Rose doesn't care whether there is an association or an aggregation between the classes. The Fleet class will contain a collection of Airplanes:

```
'##ModelId=396159720233
Public NewProperty As Collection
```

Dependency Relationships

With a dependency relationship, no attributes are created. If there is a dependency between Class_A and Class_B, no attributes will be created in either Class_A or Class_B.

Generalization Relationships

A generalization relationship in UML becomes an inheritance relationship in object-oriented languages. However, Visual Basic does not support inheritance. Instead, a generalization can become an implements delegation in Visual Basic. In your Rose model, a generalization relationship is shown as follows:

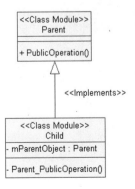

No special code will be inserted into the parent class. This allows it to be reusable and independent of the child class.

The child class contains three special areas of code. First, an Implements Parent statement is added. Second, an instance of the parent class is created inside the child class. Finally, copies of the parent's public methods are inserted into the child class.

```
Option Explicit

'##ModelId=39615A930379
Implements Parent

'##ModelId=39615AA50180
Private mParentObject As New Parent

'##ModelId=39615AA501C6
Private Sub Parent_PublicOperation()
    Call mParentObject.PublicOperation
End Sub
```

Reverse Engineering

As with code generation, reverse engineering with Visual Basic is done through a wizard. Rose Visual Basic includes a Model Update Wizard that will walk you through the steps of selecting the class(es) to reverse engineer and pulling them into your Rose model.

To begin the process, select Tools ➤ Visual Basic ➤ Update Model from Code. The reverse-engineering wizard will begin, as shown in Figure 15.11.

If you have already created some Visual Basic components, Rose will list them and give you the option to select the components to reverse engineer. If not, Rose will prompt you to create a component, as shown in Figure 15.12.

FIGURE 15.11

Visual Basic reverse-engineering wizard

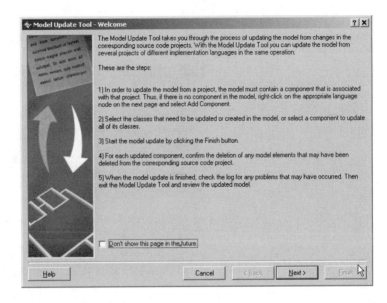

FIGURE 15.12

Creating a Visual Basic component

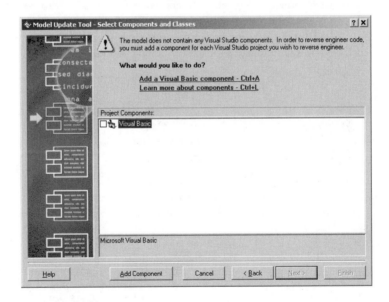

To create a component, select Add a Visual Basic Component, or press Ctrl+A. Then select the type of component to create (Standard EXE, ActiveX EXE, ActiveX DLL, or ActiveX Control) and press Add.

When you are returned to the Select Components and Classes window, right-click the new component and select Properties. In the Project File field, enter the Visual Basic project to reverse engineer:

Once you have added a component (or if you already had components added), Rose will prompt you to select the components to reverse engineer. Press Next to see a summary screen, and then press Finish to start the reverse-engineering process.

If you did not start the project by using the Visual Basic framework, Rose will first reverse engineer a COM package with subpackages containing the standard Visual Basic classes and types:

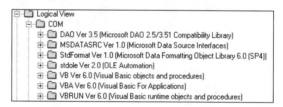

Rose will then, of course, reverse engineer the classes you selected using the wizard. In the following example, we reverse engineered some of the classes in our airline example.

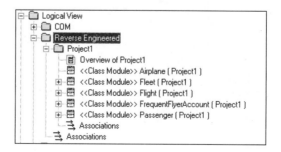

Each Visual Basic class is reverse engineered as a Rose class with the appropriate stereotype. Table 15.7 lists the Visual Basic class types and their corresponding Rose model stereotypes.

TABLE 15.7: VISUAL BASIC-TO-ROSE MAPPING

VISUAL BASIC CLASS	ROSE STEREOTYPE
Class Module	Class Module
Interface	Class Module with Public visibility
Form	Form
MDI Form	MDI Form
DHTML Page	DHTML Page
Property Page	Property Page
Interface	Class Module with Public visibility
Module	Module
User Connection	User Connection
User Control	User Control
User Document	User Document
Web Class	Web Class
Template Web Item	Template Web Item
Custom Web Item	Custom Web Item
Data Environment	Data Environment
Data Report	Data Report
Add-In Designer	Add-In Designer
Collection	Class Module

Summary

In this chapter, we took a look at how various Rose model elements are implemented in Visual Basic. Using the code-generation properties for classes, packages, attributes, operations, associations, aggregations, and other model elements, you have a great deal of control over what gets generated. Through the code-generation and reverse-engineering capabilities of Rose, you can keep your source code and Rose model synchronized.

Again, the steps needed to generate code are as follows:

1. Create components.

2. Assign classes to components.

3. Set the code-generation properties.

4. Select a class or component to generate on a Class or Component diagram.

5. Select Tools ➢ Visual Basic ➢ Update Code to start the Code Generation Wizard.

6. Select Tools ➢ Visual Basic ➢ Browse Source Code to view the generated code.

To reverse engineer a Visual Basic project, follow these steps:

1. Create a component and assign a Visual Basic project to the component.

2. Select Tools ➢ Visual Basic ➢ Update Model from Code.

3. Select the component(s) and class(es) to update.

4. Select Finish to complete the process.

In the next chapter, we will explore one of the newest features of Rational Rose: the XML DTD add-in. This new feature gives you the capability of modeling not only your application, but also the structure of your XML DTD files. You can use Rose to reverse engineer and visualize existing DTD structures or to model and generate new ones. As we will see in the next few chapters, Rose now has the ability to model your entire application: object model, XML DTD structure, database structure, and web components.

Chapter 16

XML DTD Code Generation and Reverse Engineering

WE KNOW THAT ROSE can be used to model the design of a software system. It can be used to model the database and the business surrounding the system. But there is one more piece in many software systems that we haven't addressed so far: the use of Extensible Markup Language (XML). To get a complete picture of the system, we need to be able to see all of the pieces, including XML.

In this chapter, we'll discuss one of the new add-ins available for Rose: the integration with XML DTD (document type definition). As XML gains popularity in the industry, this new tool gives a design team the ability to model a complete software solution, including the code in C++, Visual Basic, or Java and the XML DTD components.

In this chapter, we'll take a look at how Rose can be used to model DTD elements, how DTD can be generated from Rose, and how DTD can be reverse engineered into Rose. Sometimes, a DTD can be just as complex as a system design model. Keeping track of the elements in a DTD and ensuring that the correct syntax is used can be a challenge. Rose gives you a picture of the DTD structure, making it easier for you to design the DTD and validate the design. Rose also provides you with a syntax check, so you can be sure the syntax is correct before you generate code.

Although we use the term "code generation," it is important to note that XML is not source code as we would typically think of it. XML is not a programming language, but rather a standard that can be used to exchange data between applications. Like HTML, XML includes tags that provide the interpreter with information about the data contained within the document. Unlike HTML, however, XML can include custom-defined tags. You can create a new standard data format using these custom tags and exchange data with anyone else, as long as they know the format.

This is where a DTD file comes in. The DTD includes metadata, or data about the data. It outlines the structure used by the XML file. An XML parser then uses the DTD file in conjunction with the XML file itself to interpret the file.

◆ Setting XML DTD code-generation properties

◆ Generating DTD files from your Rose model

◆ Mapping Rose elements to DTD constructs

◆ Reverse engineering DTD files

Introduction to XML DTD

XML evolved as the need arose to structure data on the Web. HTML is very useful for displaying information, but it contains only a limited number of tags that you can use when creating a document. XML is much more flexible; you can create whatever tags you need to effectively describe the data in the document.

The tags are defined in the DTD file for the XML file. A DTD document is comprised of elements that define the types of data that can be included in the XML file.

Elements

An *element* is defined in three key pieces. The first is the ELEMENT keyword, which indicates that the text to follow defines an element. The second is the name of the element. Each element name must be unique. Further, XML does not allow an element to begin with the characters "xml" in upper or lower case. Finally, the *content model* defines the items that make up the element. For example, here we have an element called "book" that is made up of a title, table of contents, introduction, and section.

```
<!ELEMENT book (title, tableofcontents, introduction, section)>
```

The title, tableofcontents, introduction, and section make up the content model. An element can also contain text in its content model. We can indicate this by using the notation #PCDATA in the content model. For example:

```
<!ELEMENT title (#PCDATA)>
```

Here we have an element called title, which is simply a string of text. An element may contain other elements, text (PCDATA), or both in its content model.

This is useful, but it doesn't let us know whether the items in the content model are required or how many items can be contained within the element. There are three symbols we can use here to get more information:

- A plus sign (+) indicates that the item is required and that there may be more than one.

- An asterisk (*) indicates that the item is not required and that there may be more than one.

- A question mark (?) indicates that the item is not required and that there can be only one.

Using these symbols, we return to our example:

```
<!ELEMENT book (title+, tableofcontents?, introduction?, section+)>
```

Our example says that a book must have a title. It may or may not have a table of contents or introduction, and will never have more than one table of contents or introduction. It must have at least one section, but can have more than one.

As you can see, we can get a lot of information about the element by including these three symbols in the content model. They are included in the DTD to spell out the rules that apply to the elements and the items in their content models.

Notice that the items in the content model are separated by commas. Commas indicate that the items must appear in the order they are listed in the content model. Our book must first have a title, then a table of contents, then an introduction, and finally its sections.

In some situations, however, you may want to indicate that there is a choice involved. To show a choice, you can use a choice operator (|). The notation would then be:

```
<!ELEMENT A (B|C)>
```

This notation suggests that element A is comprised of B or C.

Attributes

An element may have one or more *attributes*. An attribute is simply a piece of information about the element. Like attributes in the object model, an entity's attribute has a name, data type, and optional default value.

An attribute is declared using the following notation:

```
<!ATTLIST ElementName AttributeName DataType DefaultValue>
```

For example:

```
<!ATTLIST Author Name CDATA>
<!ATTLIST Employee EmpID ID>
```

If an element has more than one attribute, they are listed as follows:

```
<!ATTLIST Employee Name CDATA Address CDATA Phone CDATA>
```

There are three additional keywords that can be added to an attribute. The keyword #REQUIRED indicates that the attribute is mandatory. The #IMPLIED keyword indicates that the attribute is not required. Finally, the #FIXED keyword indicates that the attribute's value cannot change. If the attribute is fixed, it must be given a default value.

To assign a default value to an attribute, enter the value at the end of the attribute declaration. For example:

```
<!ATTLIST book language CDATA "Spanish">
```

This declaration assigns the default value "Spanish" to a book's language.

Sometimes you want to set a list of valid values for an attribute. In our example, let's assume books must be in Spanish, English, or Japanese. We would specify this as follows:

```
<!ATTLIST book language CDATA (Spanish | English | Japanese) "Spanish">
```

Here, the language must be Spanish, English, or Japanese, and the default is Spanish.

Entities and Notations

An *entity* is used when you want to use a simple word to represent a more complex string. It is a way to enter a lot of information by simply typing the entity name. Entities help simplify documents and keep you from repetitive typing.

An entity may be internal or external. An internal entity is defined in the DTD. An external entity is defined outside the DTD and corresponding XML document (for example, in another XML document). The SYSTEM keyword indicates that the entity is an external entity. External entities may be parsed or unparsed.

Some examples of entities include text strings, external files, and special characters.

TEXT STRINGS

If there is a long text string that is repeated many times, an entity can be used to represent the string. For example, instead of typing "the quick brown fox jumps over the lazy dog," you can just type "&lazydog." The format of this type of entity looks like this:

```
<!ENTITY EntityName "entity text">
```

For example,

```
<!ENTITY lazydog "the quick brown fox jumps over the lazy dog">
```

We define the entity "lazydog" as the string "the quick brown fox jumps over the lazy dog." Now to use the entity, all we have to do is type an ampersand (&) followed by the entity name. Anywhere we type "&lazydog," the XML parser will replace "&lazydog" with the full phrase.

EXTERNAL FILES

An entity can be used to represent an external XML file. In this situation, we need to add the SYSTEM keyword. The entity declaration looks like this:

```
<!ENTITY EntityName SYSTEM "entity location">
```

For example, if you have the text from the Declaration of Independence in another file, you can define an entity and use that entity name rather than type all of the text. Our entity declaration would look like this:

```
<!ENTITY Independence SYSTEM "/independence.xml">
```

Now all we need to do is use the keyword &Independence wherever we want a reference to the external file.

SPECIAL CHARACTERS

When you need to use a special character, such as ®, you can define an entity that, when used, will be replaced by that special character. This saves you the headache of trying to remember the decimal value of the special character.

PARSED AND UNPARSED ENTITIES AND NOTATIONS

An entity may be parsed or unparsed. A parsed entity is one that follows the rules we described earlier in this section; when the XML parser encounters the entity, it replaces the entity name with the text or file the entity represents.

The XML parser will ignore an unparsed entity. So why use unparsed entities? They provide a way to include things such as graphics files, video, audio, or other files that are not in XML format. When the XML parser sees an unparsed entity, it will call an application that can process the entity. For example, it may call an application to run the video, which will have an entity declaration that looks like this:

```
<!ENTITY MyVideo SYSTEM "C:\Videos\Vacation.vid">
```

The XML parser knows which application to call on to process the entity because of a construct called a *notation*. A notation identifies the application to be used to process a particular entity, and provides the application location. A notation is documented as follows:

```
<!NOTATION NotationName SYSTEM "notation location">
```

For example:

```
<!NOTATION Video SYSTEM "C:\MyVideoPlayer.exe">
```

The picture is almost complete, but we're still missing one piece. How does the XML parser know that the Video notation applies to the MyVideo entity? We need to add one last piece to the entity declaration, to tie it to the Video notation. We use the NDATA keyword, followed by the notation name. So now our example contains the two lines:

```
<!ENTITY MyVideo SYSTEM "C:\Videos\Vacation.vid" NDATA Video>
<!NOTATION Video SYSTEM "C:\MyVideoPlayer.exe">
```

DTD-to-UML Mapping

When reverse engineering or generating DTD, Rose will map the different DTD constructs to classes with the appropriate stereotype. In the remainder of this chapter, we will discuss in detail how the DTD constructs map to Rose model elements. Table 16.1 lists the XML DTD constructs and their corresponding model elements.

TABLE 16.1: DTD-TO-ROSE MAPPING

DTD CONSTRUCT	ROSE ELEMENT
Element	Class with stereotype DTDElement
Attribute	Attribute of element class
Entity	Class with stereotype DTDEntity
Notation	Class with stereotype DTDNotation
Empty element type	Class with stereotype DTDElementEmpty
Any element type	Class with stereotype DTDElementAny
Parsed character element type	Class with stereotype DTDElementPCDATA
Content model with items separated by ","	Class with stereotype DTDSequenceGroup
Content model with items separated by "&"	Class with stereotype DTDSet
Content model with items separated by "|"	Class with stereotype DTDChoiceGroup

DTD Code-Generation Properties

Rose XML provides DTD specification windows for the classes in the model. You will see a slightly different window for each DTD stereotype supported by Rose. In this section, we'll look at the different properties you can set for classes with the various DTD stereotypes.

Regardless of the stereotype, to view the specification window, you right-click the class and select Open Specification.

You can set code-generation properties for the following items:

- ◆ Project
- ◆ Classes
- ◆ Attributes
- ◆ Roles
- ◆ Components

In this section, we will use the following DTD example to discuss the different code-generation properties. This is an example of a DTD file that defines a book:

```
<!–The following DTD defines a book–>
<!ELEMENT book (title,tableofcontents,introduction?,section+)>
<!ELEMENT chapter (title,paragraph+)>
<!ATTLIST chapter
ChapterNum ID #REQUIRED
Description CDATA #REQUIRED
NumPages CDATA #REQUIRED
>
<!ELEMENT introduction (paragraph+)>
<!ELEMENT section (title,chapter+,paragraph+)>
<!ELEMENT paragraph (#PCDATA)>
<!ELEMENT title (#PCDATA)>
<!ELEMENT tableofcontents (#PCDATA)>
```

Project Properties

The project specifications control the editor that will be used, and set the different code-generation options for the overall project. To view the project properties, select Tools ➤ XML_DTD ➤ Project Specification. The window shown in Figure 16.1 will appear.

FIGURE 16.1

XML Project Specification window

The XML project properties are listed in Table 16.2. The settings here will affect all classes, relationships, and other elements in the Rose model.

TABLE 16.2: XML PROJECT PROPERTIES

PROPERTY	PURPOSE	DEFAULT
Editor	Controls the editor, which uses, views, and edits a DTD. Select from Built-In (Rose editor) or Windows Shell, or type in the name of a third-party editor you would like to use.	Built-In
Stop On Error	Stops the code-generation process if an error is encountered.	True
Create Missing Directories	Create directories for the components in the model.	True

Class Properties

Rose XML provides different code-generation properties for the different types of classes you can create. Each type of class has its own stereotype, such as DTDElement or DTDEntity. In this section, we'll look at each of these stereotypes and examine the code-generation properties that can be set.

In the "Generated Code" section later in this chapter, we will take a closer look at each of these types of classes, discuss their purposes, and describe the UML notation used for the class.

Before you attempt to generate code, you should review the code-generation properties for your classes to help ensure that the code you get is the code you expected to get. Let's begin by looking at a class with a stereotype of DTDElement.

DTDELEMENT

A class with a stereotype of DTDElement corresponds to an ELEMENT declaration in a DTD file. To expand on our earlier example (see the "Elements" section), there are several elements: book, tableofcontents, introduction, section, chapter, paragraph, and title. Each of these is modeled as a class with a stereotype of DTDElement.

The code-generation properties for a DTD element include the element name, type, and comments. Figure 16.2 shows the Class Specification window for a DTD element.

You can change the name of the element in the Name field. The Type field sets the stereotype of the element. The stereotypes include:

◆ DTDEmpty, which is an empty element, suggesting that the element cannot contain text or other elements. However, these elements can still have attributes.

◆ DTDPCDATA, which is an element that can contain text.

◆ DTDAny, which is an element that can contain text or other elements.

Finally, you can enter a comment for the element in the DocComment field. Any comments you enter here will appear as comments in the generated DTD.

FIGURE 16.2

Class Specification
window for a
DTD element

DTDGROUP

The DTDGroup stereotype is used to show a collection of elements that make up the content model of another element. In the book example:

```
<!ELEMENT book (title,tableofcontents,introduction?,section+)>
```

a DTD group is used to show the grouping of the title, table of contents, introduction, and section in the content model for a book. Figure 16.3 shows the notation. We will discuss this notation in detail in the "Generated Code" section of this chapter.

FIGURE 16.3

DTD group example

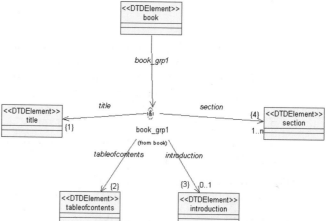

There are two code-generation properties on the specification window for a DTDGroup class. The first is the Grouping Type, which can be set to one of two settings:

- The Choice setting will generate code in the format ELEMENT A (B | C), suggesting that element A consists of either B or C.

◆ The Sequence setting will generate code in the format ELEMENT A (B,C), suggesting that element A consists of B and C, in that order.

The second code-generation property is set in the Occurrence field, which determines the multiplicity of the elements in the content model.

DTDENTITY

A DTD entity is used as a placeholder for a single character or a string of text. It can also be used as a placeholder for video, audio, or other types of information. You can set the code-generation properties for an entity by using the specification window shown in Figure 16.4.

FIGURE 16.4

Class Specification window for a DTD entity

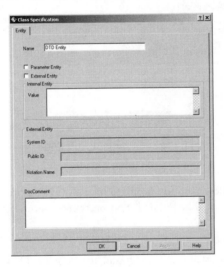

Table 16.3 lists the entity code-generation properties and the purpose of each.

TABLE 16.3: DTD ENTITY PROPERTIES

PROPERTY	PURPOSE
Parameter Entity	Determines whether this is a parameter entity.
External Entity	Determines whether this is an external entity, which refers to a file that is outside the XML DTD.
Internal Entity Value	Sets the character, string, or other entity to use in place of an internal entity.
External Entity System ID	Location (URL) of the external file.
External Entity Public ID	Alternate location of the external file.
External Entity Notation Name	Format of the external file. If this property is set, a notation must be created for the external entity (see the "DTDNotation" section on the next page).
Comments	Comments for the entity. Comments will be generated in the DTD.

DTDNOTATION

An external entity can be further described with a notation. The notation specifies the format (audio, video, word processor, etc.) for the external entity. The code-generation properties for a notation are set with the specification window for the class, as shown in Figure 16.5.

FIGURE 16.5

Class Specification window for a DTD notation

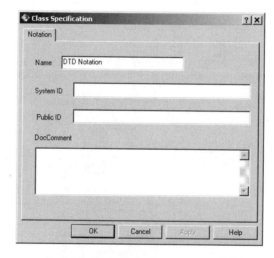

There are only two code-generation properties for a DTDNotation class. The System ID property sets the location of the entity. The Public ID property sets the alternate location.

Attribute Properties

There are several properties that can be set for an attribute in a DTD class. Figure 16.6 shows the different properties that can be set.

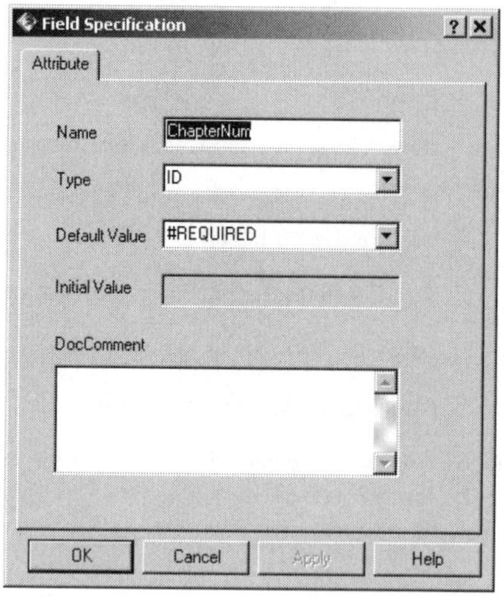

FIGURE 16.6

XML attribute properties

Table 16.4 lists the attribute properties, their purposes, and their default values.

TABLE 16.4: XML ATTRIBUTE PROPERTIES

PROPERTY	PURPOSE
Name	Sets the name of the attribute in the generated DTD.
Type	Sets the data type of the attribute. Valid values are CDATA (character data), ENTITIES (), and ENTITY().
Default Value	Determines whether the attribute is required or not.
Initial Value	Sets the default for the attribute.
DocComment	Comments to be generated for the attribute in the DTD.

Role Properties

Role properties are those properties that apply to the associations between the elements, entities, and other classes. These properties control the multiplicity between the elements, as well as the order of the elements in a content model. Figure 16.7 shows the Role Specification window.

FIGURE 16.7

XML role properties

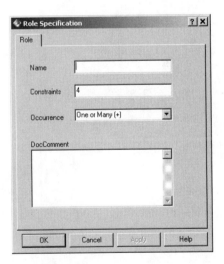

There are four properties that can be set. The Name field is used to set the name of the role. This will not affect the generated DTD.

The Constraints field is used to model the order in which the element appears in the content model. The example in Figure 16.7 is the relationship between a book and a section. The DTD reads as follows:

```
<!ELEMENT book (title,tableofcontents,introduction?,section+)>
```

In this example, the Constraints field on the relationship between book and section was set to "4" because section is the fourth item in the content model for a book.

The Occurrence field sets the multiplicity of the relationship. In this example, each book can have one or more sections. This is noted in the DTD by the plus sign (+) after the section in the content model for the book element. It is noted in the Rose model by setting the Occurrence field to One or Many (+). The possible values for the Occurrence field include:

◆ One

◆ Zero or one (?)

◆ Zero or Many (*)

◆ One or Many (+)

Finally, the DocComment field can be used to enter comments for the relationship. Unlike comments for an attribute, these comments will not be included in the generated DTD file.

Component Properties

In Rose, the DTD file itself is modeled as a component. The different elements contained in the DTD are mapped to the component in Rose. As with other model elements, code-generation properties are set through the specification window. Figure 16.8 shows the specification window for a DTD component.

FIGURE 16.8

XML Component Specification window

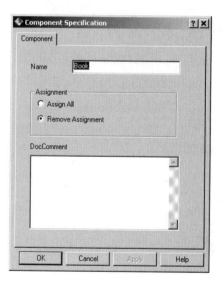

In this window, the Name field sets the name of the DTD file to be generated. The Assignment field controls how classes are mapped to a component. If Assign All is selected, all new and existing classes will automatically be mapped to the component. If Remove Assignment is selected, all classes will be removed from that component.

Generating Code

Once you have created the necessary elements, entities, and other Rose model items, you can generate a DTD file from the model. To do so, follow these steps:

1. Set the code-generation properties, as discussed throughout this chapter.

2. Select Tools ➢ XML_DTD ➢ Syntax Check. This will run a DTD-specific syntax check of your model, and let you know if there are any invalid items or other errors.

3. Create a component to represent the DTD file. This is an optional step, but if you do not create a component, Rose will create a separate DTD for each class.

4. Map the classes to the DTD component. You can do this using the Realizes tab on the standard component specification window. In the Realizes tab, right-click the classes to map to the component and select Assign.

5. Select the class(es) you wish to generate.

6. Select Tools ➢ XML_DTD ➢ Generate Code.

7. To view the generated DTD for a class, right-click the class on a diagram and select XML_DTD ➢ Browse DTD Source.

Generated Code

In the following sections, we'll take a look at the DTD generated for various types of model elements, including classes, attributes, and association relationships. In each of these sections, we'll include some sample code to give you an idea of what will be generated from your Rose model.

Let's begin by looking at the code generated for various types of classes.

Classes

Classes in the model will be translated into elements, entities, or content models of an element. The translation occurs based on the stereotype that the class was assigned. Let's start with element classes.

ELEMENTS

A DTD element is represented in the Rose model as a class with a stereotype of <<DTDElement>>.

Through association relationships, the element is connected to a group, which is then related to any other elements that are in the content model. Note that all elements in the content model must be contained in the Rose model in order for the DTD to be generated.

We'll get into the details of the content model shortly, but first let's look at the element stereotypes. You can further refine an element by changing its stereotype. The available element stereotypes include:

DTDElementAny: This stereotype suggests that the element's content model can contain text and other elements. The keyword ANY is included in the generated DTD. For the chapter element, the following is generated:

```
<!ELEMENT Chapter ANY>
```

DTDElementEmpty: This stereotype suggests that the element cannot contain text or other elements in its content model. The entity may, however, have attributes. In this case, the keyword EMPTY is included in the generated DTD. Our chapter element would now look like this:

```
<!ELEMENT Chapter EMPTY>
```

DTDElementPCDATA: This stereotype suggests that the element may contain text in its content model. With this stereotype, the chapter element would look like this:

```
<!ELEMENT Chapter (#PCDATA)>
```

To set the stereotype of an element, open its specification window. In the Type field, select the appropriate stereotype (ANY, EMPTY, or PCDATA), as shown in Figure 16.9.

FIGURE 16.9

Setting an element stereotype

Rose 2001A and 2002 include icons for each of the element types. You can use these icons by right-clicking a class and selecting Options ➤ Stereotype Display ➤ Icon. The following icons are used by Rose:

Element Any

ElementANY

Element Empty

< >

ElementEmpty

Element PCDATA

<a>

ElementPCData

CONTENT MODEL

As mentioned earlier, an element is connected to the elements in its content model through association relationships. Figure 16.10 is an example from our book model.

FIGURE 16.10

Content Model
in Rose

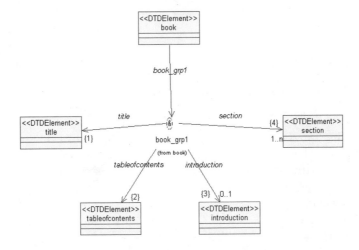

In this example, a book has a title, a table of contents, an introduction, and sections. A class with a stereotype of DTDGroup is used to collect the elements into the content model for the book. There are two types of groups, corresponding to the two ways the elements in a content model are separated.

In the DTD, the elements in the content model may be separated by commas, indicating that the elements must appear in the sequence in which they are listed. Alternately, the elements (or a subset of them) may separated by a choice operator (|), which implies the word "or." (For example, ELEMENT A (B|C) suggests that element A may contain B or C.)

This information is indicated by the type of DTDGroup class you are using. This notation represents one type:

```
<<DTDSequenceGroup>>
```

In Rose 2001A and 2002, a class with a stereotype of DTDSequenceGroup is displayed as an ampersand with a circle around it, as shown in Figure 16.11. This grouping suggests that the elements were separated by commas (i.e., there is a sequence to the elements).

FIGURE 16.11

An example of a sequence group

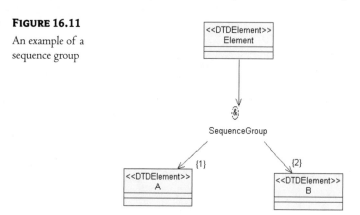

NOTE *In Rose 2001, a sequence group is displayed as a filled square.*

This notation represents another type:

<<DTDChoiceGroup>>

In Rose 2001A and 2002, a class with a stereotype of DTDChoiceGroup is displayed as an "or" symbol (choice operator) with a circle around it, as shown in Figure 16.12. This stereotype suggests that the elements are part of a choice in the content model.

FIGURE 16.12

An example of a choice group

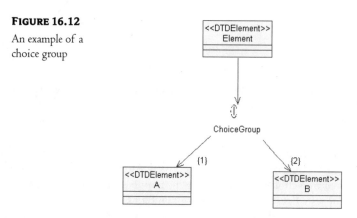

NOTE *In Rose 2001, a choice group is displayed as a hollow square.*

To create a sequence or choice group:

1. Right-click the element and select Open Standard Specification.

2. Select the Nested tab.

3. Right-click anywhere inside the white space and select Insert.

4. Enter the name of the sequence or choice group.

5. Press OK.

6. The new group will appear in the browser under the entity. Right-click the group and select Open Specification.

7. Set the stereotype to DTDGroup and press OK. The DTD Class Specification window for a group will appear.

8. Set the Grouping Type to Choice or Sequence.

9. Set the Occurrence field to the appropriate multiplicity.

10. Press OK.

Details on the association relationships tell us whether or not each element is required and the multiplicity for each element. Table 16.5 lists the association multiplicity notations and their DTD equivalents.

TABLE 16.5: CONTENT MODEL MULTIPLICITY

MULTIPLICITY IN ROSE	DTD SYMBOL	MEANING
0..1	?	Element is not required, but if it is present, there may be only one.
0..n	*	Element is not required, and there may be more than one.
1..n	+	Element is required, and there may be more than one.

Figure 16.13 includes examples of each multiplicity option, in Rose and in DTD.

The order of the elements in the content model is translated into the Rose model in the form of constraints. Each association relationship can have a constraint, which is shown in braces { }. In the example ELEMENT A (B, C, D), the association relationship between A and B would have a constraint of 1, the relationship between A and C would have a constraint of 2, and the relationship between A and D would have a constraint of 3. Figure 16.14 shows a Rose model and the corresponding DTD file. By examining the constraints, you can see the order the elements are listed in the content model.

FIGURE 16.13

Content model
multiplicity in
Rose and in DTD

FIGURE 16.14

Content model
element order in
Rose and in DTD

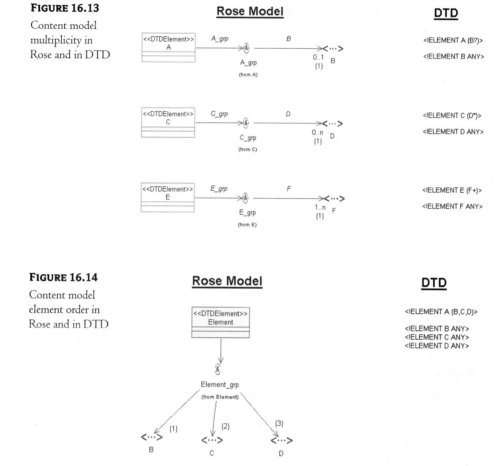

Elements may also contain attributes. See the "Attributes" section later in this chapter for a discussion of modeling attributes and the generation of attributes in a DTD file.

Next, let's examine how entities are modeled in Rose and translated into the DTD file.

ENTITIES

Like elements, entities are represented as classes in the Rose model. An entity is given the stereotype <<DTDEntity>>. Using the specification window shown in Figure 16.15, you can set the details of the entity that will be generated in the DTD.

If the entity is an internal entity, enter the entity value in the Value field in the specification window. The value will appear in the generated DTD, as follows:

```
<!ENTITY Company "ACME DTD Files, Inc.">
```

If the entity is an external entity, select the External Entity check box and fill in the System ID, Public ID, and Notation Name fields:

System ID　　Enter the location of the entity in this field. For example, **documentwithentity.xml**.

Public ID　　Enter an alternate address for the entity in this field.

Notation Name　　If the external entity has a notation, enter the name of the notation here. Rose will include the NDATA keyword in the generated DTD, similar to the following:

```
<!ENTITY MyVideo SYSTEM "C:\Videos\Vacation.vid" NDATA Video>
```

FIGURE 16.15

DTD entity specification window

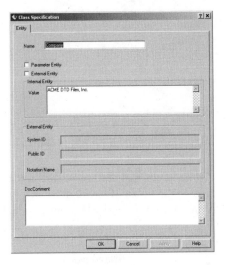

Whether the entity is internal or external, you can enter a comment into the DocComment field. Anything you enter in this field will appear as a comment in the generated DTD.

To create an entity:

1. Create a new class.

2. Assign the stereotype <<DTDEntity>> to the class.

3. Use the specification window to set the entity details as described above.

4. Create a notation if needed (see the following "Notations" section).

In Rose 2001A and 2002, you can use a special icon to represent an entity. Create an entity as described above. If the icon is not showing, right-click the class and select Options ➤ Stereotype Display ➤ Icon. The Entity icon looks like this:

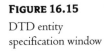

Entity

NOTATIONS

A notation is modeled as a class with a stereotype of <<DTDNotation>>. As with entities, the details for the notation are set using the specification window (see Figure 16.16).

FIGURE 16.16

DTD notation pecification window

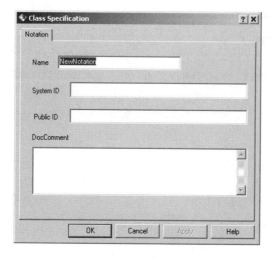

Using this window, you set the location of the application used to process the entity. You may also set an alternate location using the Public ID field.

The notation is linked to the appropriate entity by a bidirectional association relationship. For example:

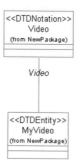

Here is the DTD generated for the classes shown above.

```
<!ENTITY MyVideo SYSTEM "C:\Videos\Vacation.vid" NDATA Video>
<!NOTATION Video SYSTEM "C:\MyVideoPlayer.exe">
```

NOTE *As long as the relationship exists, it does not matter what you enter in the Notation Name field on the entity specification window. If, for example, entity A is connected to notation N1 with an association relationship, and the Notation Name field on entity A's specification window refers to notation N2, notation N1 will still be used to generate the DTD.*

To create a notation:

1. Create a new class.

2. Assign the stereotype <<DTDNotation>> to the class.

3. Use the specification window to set the notation details as described above.

Rose 2001A and 2002 provide an icon that can be used for notations. The Notation icon looks like this:

Notation

Attributes

An element's attributes are modeled as attributes within the element class. Each attribute has a data type and optional default value. These can be set using the Field Specification window, as shown in Figure 16.17.

FIGURE 16.17

DTD Field
Specification
window

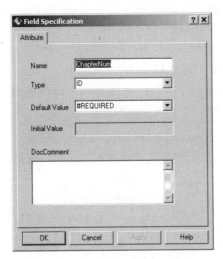

The Type property is used to document the data type of the attribute. There are several options for the Type property, including:

♦ CDATA, which means that the attribute is simple character data

♦ ENTITIES, which means that the attribute is a group of entities

♦ ENTITY, which means that the attribute is another entity

♦ ID, which means that the attribute is an element identifier

♦ IDREF, which means that the attribute is a reference to the ID of another element

- IDREFS, which means that the attribute is a group of IDREFs

- NMTOKEN, which means that the attribute is a name token attribute, which is a single word

- NMTOKENS, which means that the attribute is a collection of NMTOKENs

The Default Value and Initial Value fields determine whether or not the attribute is required and what the initial value in the attribute will be. Neither the initial value nor the default value is required. The possible settings include the following:

- The #REQUIRED default value suggests that the attribute is required to have a value on every occurrence of the element in the document. The initial value may or may not be entered if #REQUIRED is set. If an initial value is entered, it will be generated in the code as the initial value for the attribute.

- The #IMPLIED default value suggests that the attribute is not required and an initial value is not present.

- The #FIXED default value means that the attribute is not required, but if it is present, it must match the initial value.

- No default value means that an initial value should be entered. The attribute will not be required in the document, but if it is not present, the initial value will be assumed.

Reverse Engineering DTD

While generating a DTD can be useful, it may be even more valuable to reverse engineer existing DTD files into your Rose models. Many projects have a number of large and complex DTD structures, and Rose is an excellent way of visualizing these structures. This can be particularly useful when trying to analyze the structure of a complex DTD that you didn't create.

In this section, we'll discuss how to reverse engineer a DTD or group of DTD files into your Rose model.

1. To begin, create a new model or open an existing model.

2. Select Tools ➤ XML_DTD ➤ Reverse Engineer XML DTD.

3. Rose will display the XML/DTD Reverse Engineering dialog box, as shown in Figure 16.18.

4. Select the files you wish to reverse engineer in the upper-right portion of the screen, and press Add.

5. Select the files to reverse engineer from the list in the bottom portion of the screen, and press Reverse.

6. When finished, press Done.

Rose will create a folder in the Logical view called NewPackage. All reverse-engineered items will be placed in this folder.

FIGURE 16.18

XML/DTD
Reverse Engineering
dialog box

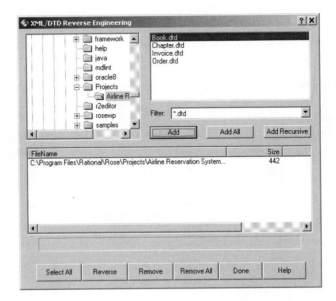

Summary

In this chapter, we discussed how Rose can be used to model and generate an XML DTD file. We examined how DTD elements, attributes, entities, and content models can be structured in Rose, and how Rose can create the DTD file. Finally, we discussed the reverse engineering of a DTD file into a Rose model.

To review, these steps should be followed to generate a DTD:

1. Set the code-generation properties.

2. Select Tools ➢ XML_DTD ➢ Syntax Check.

3. Create a component to represent the DTD file, and map the classes to the DTD component.

4. Select the class(es) you wish to generate.

5. Select Tools ➢ XML_DTD ➢ Generate Code.

6. To view the generated DTD for a class, right-click the class on a diagram and select XML_DTD ➢ Browse DTD Source.

The following steps should be followed to reverse engineer a DTD:

1. Select Tools ➢ XML_DTD ➢ Reverse Engineer XML DTD.

2. Select the files you wish to reverse engineer in the upper-right portion of the screen, and press Add.

3. Select the files to reverse engineer from the list in the bottom portion of the screen, and press Reverse.

4. When finished, press Done.

In the next chapter, we'll examine the creation and reverse engineering of CORBA elements using Rose. CORBA is an interface standard that helps components communicate, even if the components are programmed in different languages. Using Rose, you can design CORBA elements, set up relationships between the CORBA classes and classes in other languages, and generate the CORBA classes. Or, you can reverse engineer an application with CORBA elements to analyze the application architecture.

Chapter 17

CORBA/IDL Code Generation and Reverse Engineering

ROUNDING OUT THE POWERFUL code-generation abilities of Rose is the CORBA/IDL add-in. From your Rose model, you can forward engineer code through the Component diagrams. In order to create the code, however, Rose will examine the properties of the classes—including the code-generation properties, attributes, operations, relationships, and packages—in the Logical view.

◆ Setting IDL code-generation properties

◆ Generating IDL code from your Rose model

◆ Mapping Rose elements to IDL constructs

◆ Reverse engineering IDL source code

CORBA/IDL Code-Generation Properties

CORBA (Common Object Request Broker Architecture) is a specification that supports the use of distributed objects. Through the interface definition language (IDL), a developer can create language-independent interfaces for components. The developer can then create components in multiple languages, and use IDL to help the objects communicate. The CORBA/IDL that is generated from your Rose model is controlled by a series of code-generation property sets. Rose includes a property set for attributes, classes, dependencies, aggregations, module bodies, module specifications, operations, associations, subsystems, and for the overall project.

You can view and set all of these properties by selecting Tools ➤ Options, then selecting the CORBA tab.

Anything you change using this window will set the default for all classes, attributes, operations, and so on.

You can also set the code-generation properties for a single class, attribute, operation, or other model element. To do so, open the specification window for the model element and select the CORBA tab. On this tab, you can change the properties that apply to that particular type of model element. In the following sections, we'll examine the CORBA code-generation properties.

Project Properties

Project properties are the CORBA code-generation properties that apply to the whole project rather than to any specific model element, such as a class or relationship.

The options in this section include things like the default directory to use when generating code and the maximum number of errors that can occur during code generation. Each of the project properties is listed in Table 17.1 along with its purpose and default value.

TABLE 17.1: CORBA CODE-GENERATION PROJECT PROPERTIES

PROPERTY	PURPOSE	DEFAULT
CreateMissingDirectories	Controls whether Rose should create directories to mirror the packages when generating code.	True
Editor	Controls which editor to use to view and edit CORBA files.	Built-In (Uses a built-in CORBA editor)
IncludePath	Path used to resolve the location of .IDL files during code generation and reverse engineering.	Empty
StopOnError	Controls whether Rose will stop generating code if it encounters an error.	True
PathSeparator	Sets the character (such as the backslash) to separate path elements.	<blank> (uses the default for the operating system)

You can also set these properties through the Tools ➢ CORBA ➢ Project Specification menu item, as shown on the following page.

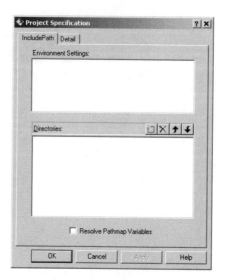

It does not matter whether you set the properties in the Tools ➤ Options area or through the Project Specification window. Changes you make in one area will be reflected in the other.

Class Properties

Class properties are the CORBA code-generation properties that apply specifically to classes. Most of the class properties are set through the Class Specification window. There are a few properties, however, that can also be set through the Tools ➤ Options area, as shown below:

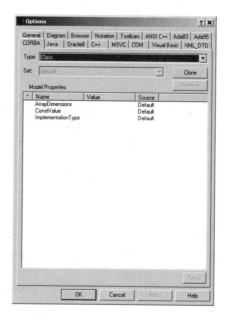

Table 17.2 lists the CORBA class properties on the Tools ➤ Options window, their purposes, and their default values.

TABLE 17.2: CORBA/IDL CODE-GENERATION CLASS PROPERTIES

PROPERTY	PURPOSE	DEFAULT
ArrayDimensions	Sets the dimensions of the array used in the class definition if the class is a typedef.	Empty
ImplementationType	This value has different uses based on the class's stereotype. If CORBA-Constant, then the value indicates the data type of the constant. If CORBATypeDef, then the value indicates the data type. If CORBAUnion, then the value is equivalent to the switch type.	Empty
ConstValue	If a CORBA constant is being generated, controls the value of the constant.	\<blank\>

The properties listed above apply to all types of CORBA classes. You can, however, set additional properties for the different CORBA stereotypes supported by Rose.

When you first create a class and try to open its specification window, Rose will prompt you for the type of class to create:

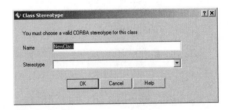

In the Stereotype field, select from the following: Interface, CORBAConstant, CORBAEnum, CORBA-Exception, CORBANative, CORBAStruct, CORBATypedef, CORBAUnion, CORBAValue, or CORBACusomValue. Once you have selected a stereotype, the appropriate specification window will appear.

INTERFACE SPECIFICATION

On the interface specification window, you can set the following:

◆ Inherits From to set the parent class

◆ Attribute/Role Ordering to set the order in which attributes and roles will be generated in the code

◆ DocComment for comments that will be generated in the code

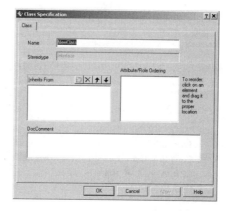

CORBACONSTANT SPECIFICATION

On the constant specification window, you can set the following:

◆ Implementation Type to set the data type of the generated constant

◆ Constant Value to set the value of the generated constant

◆ DocComment for comments that will be generated in the code

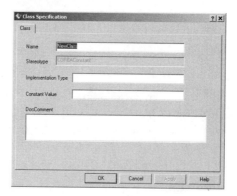

CORBANATIVE SPECIFICATION

On the CORBANative specification window, you can set only the DocComment field, which is for comments that will be generated in the code.

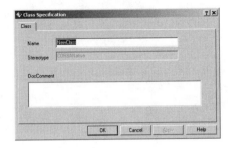

CORBATYPEDEF SPECIFICATION

On the typedef specification window, you can set the following:

◆ Implementation Type to set the data type of the generated typedef

◆ Array Dimensions to indicate that the typedef's declarator is an array and sets the dimensions of the array

◆ DocComment for comments that will be generated in the code

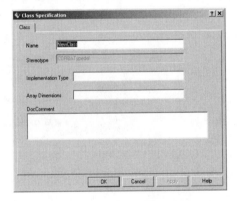

CORBAUNION SPECIFICATION

On the union specification window, you can set the following:

◆ Attribute/Role Ordering to set the order in which attributes and roles will be generated in the code

◆ Switch Type to set the switch type for case statements for the union

◆ DocComment for comments that will be generated in the code

CORBAVALUE/CORBACUSTOMVALUE

On the value specification window, you can set the following:

◆ Inherits From to set the parent class

◆ Attribute/Role Ordering to set the order in which attributes and roles will be generated in the code

◆ DocComment for comments that will be generated in the code

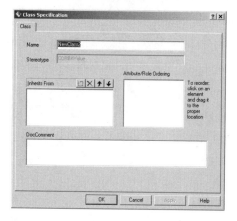

OTHER CORBA STEREOTYPES

On the specification window, you can set the following for other CORBA stereotypes (CORBA-Enum, CORBAException, and CORBAStruct):

◆ Attribute/Role Ordering to set the order in which attributes and roles will be generated in the code

◆ DocComment for comments that will be generated in the code

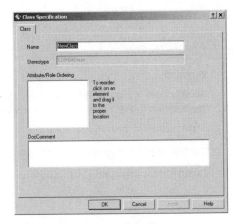

Attribute Properties

Attribute properties are the CORBA properties that relate specifically to attributes. Using these properties, you can control what is generated for each attribute in the model.

There are three places to set these properties. To set them for all attributes, select Tools ➤ Options, then click the CORBA tab and select Attribute from the drop-down list box. To set them for only one attribute, select the CORBA tab on the attribute standard specification window, or open the CORBA specification window and edit the properties there.

Table 17.3 lists the attribute properties, their purposes, and their default values.

TABLE 17.3: CORBA CODE-GENERATION ATTRIBUTE PROPERTIES

PROPERTY	PURPOSE	DEFAULT
ArrayDimensions	Sets the array dimensions used for an exception, struct, or union when the BoundedRoleType association property is set to Array	<blank>
CaseSpecifier	Sets the label of the case statement of a union	<blank>
IsReadOnly	Controls whether the generated attribute is read only	False
Order	Sets the order of generated attributes and roles	<blank>

As with classes, these attribute properties, as well as some additional properties, can be set using the CORBA specification windows. The following shows the specification window for a CORBA attribute:

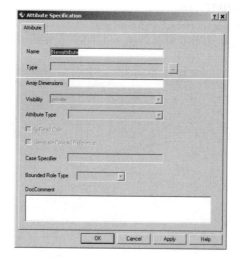

In the Name field, you can set or change the attribute's name. Whatever has been entered here will be used as the attribute name in the generated code. In the Type field, enter the data type (long, char, etc.) of the attribute. The Visibility field allows you to set whether the attribute is public or private. The Bounded Role Type field is used for an exception, struct, or union and determines whether to create an array or a sequence attribute to support a relationship with bounded multiplicity. The Array Dimensions, Case Specifier, and Is Read Only fields are identical to the ArrayDimensions, CaseSpecifier, and IsReadOnly properties described in Table 17.3. In the specification window, you can change either these fields or the properties.

Operation Properties

Operation properties are the CORBA code-generation properties that are specific to operations.

There are three places to set these properties. To set them for all operations, select Tools ➤ Options, then click the CORBA tab and select Operation from the drop-down list box. To set them for only one operation, select the CORBA tab on the operation's standard specification window, or open the CORBA specification window for the operation and edit the properties there.

Table 17.4 lists the operation code-generation properties, their purposes, and their default values.

TABLE 17.4: CORBA CODE-GENERATION OPERATION PROPERTIES

PROPERTY	PURPOSE	DEFAULT
OperationIsOneWay	Controls whether the one-way keyword will be generated for the operation	False
Context	Includes a context statement for the operation	\<blank\>

Additional properties can be set through the CORBA Operation Specification window, as shown on the following page.

The Name, Return, and Arguments fields are used to set the operation's signature, including its parameters. The Visibility field controls whether the operation is public or private and will be directly used in code generation. The Raises field is used to set an exception class that will deal with exceptions for the operation.

Module Properties

Module properties are the properties that are related to the components in your Rose model. There are three places to set these properties. To set them for all components, select Tools ➢ Options, then click the CORBA tab and select Module Specification from the drop-down list box. To set them for only one component, select the CORBA tab on the component's standard specification window, or open the CORBA specification window for the component and edit the properties there.

Table 17.5 lists the code-generation properties for components, their purposes, and their default values.

TABLE 17.5: CORBA CODE-GENERATION COMPONENT PROPERTIES

PROPERTY	PURPOSE	DEFAULT
AdditionalIncludes	Used to enter any additional #include statements you want to see in the code	\<blank\>
CmIdentification	Used to enter codes that your configuration management software can use	%X%%Q%%Z%%W%
CopyrightNotice	Used to enter a copyright in the file	\<blank\>
InclusionProtectionSymbol	Sets the symbol that will be used to prevent a file from being included more than once	Auto Generate

You can also set these values using the CORBA specification window for the component. To open the CORBA specification window, right-click the component and select Open Specification.

Association (Role) Properties

Role properties are the CORBA properties that deal with associations. Using these properties, you can control the code generated for the associations.

Because roles are implemented as attributes, many of the code-generation properties are identical for an attribute and a role. Two properties, however, are unique to roles: GenerateForwardReference and BoundedRoleType.

There are three places to set role properties. To set them for all associations, select Tools ➤ Options, then click the CORBA tab and select Role from the drop-down list box. To set them for only one association, select the CORBA tab on the association's standard specification window, or open the CORBA specification window for the association and edit the properties there.

Table 17.6 lists the code-generation properties for associations, their purposes, and their default values.

TABLE 17.6: CORBA CODE-GENERATION ASSOCIATION PROPERTIES

PROPERTY	PURPOSE	DEFAULT
ArrayDimensions	Sets the array dimensions used for an exception, struct, or union when the BoundedRoleType association property is set to Array	\<blank>
CaseSpecifier	Sets the label of the case statement of a union	\<blank>
GenerateForwardReference	Controls whether a referenced interface is included with an #include statement or a forward reference	#include (False)
IsReadOnly	Controls whether the generated attribute is read only	False
Order	Sets the order of attributes and roles generated	\<blank>
BoundedRoleType	If the relationship multiplicity is greater than one, controls whether an array or sequence is used for the generated attribute	Sequence

These properties can also be set using the CORBA Attribute Specification window:

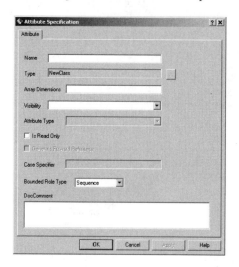

Dependency Properties

The dependency properties are the CORBA properties that control how dependency relationships are generated.

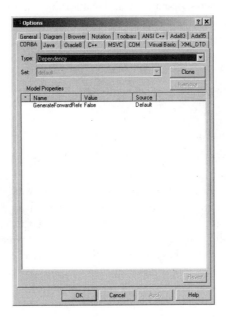

There are two places to set the dependency property. To set the property for all dependencies, select Tools ➤ Options, then click the CORBA tab and select Dependency from the drop-down list box. To set the property for only one dependency, select the CORBA tab on the dependency specification window and edit the properties there. There is only one dependency property, GenerateForwardReference, which controls whether a referenced interface is included with an #include statement or a forward reference. By default, a #include statement is used.

Generated Code

In the following sections, we'll examine the CORBA that is generated from the various types of model elements. Rose will use the information you entered in the specification windows for the various model elements when generating the CORBA/IDL.

Let's begin by looking at the code generated for a typical class.

Classes

A class in your object model will generate a single IDL file. The file that is generated will look something like the following:

```
Interface TheClass
{
};
```

A great deal of additional information, such as configuration management statements, copyright notices, and include statements, will also be generated in the code. We'll look at a complete file in the following section, "Standard Code Generation."

All of the attributes, operations, and relationships of the class will be reflected in the generated code. The major elements generated for each class include:

- Class name
- Attributes
- Operations
- Relationships
- Documentation

When generating code, Rose will use the package structure you established in the Component view of your model to generate the appropriate directories. A directory will be created for each package in the model. Within each of the directories Rose creates will be the files for the classes in that package.

Much of the information in your Rose model will be used directly when generating code. For example, the attributes, operations, relationships, and class name of each class will directly affect the code generated. Other model properties, such as the documentation entered for the class, will not directly affect the code. These properties are created as comments in the generated code.

Table 17.7 lists the properties available in the class specification window and notes which of these properties will directly affect the IDL that is generated.

TABLE 17.7: EFFECT OF CLASS SPECIFICATIONS ON IDL

PROPERTY	EFFECT ON CODE
Name	Name in model will become class name
Type	No effect
Stereotype	No effect
Export Control	No effect
Documentation	Comment
Cardinality	No effect
Space	No effect
Persistence	No effect
Concurrency	No effect
Abstract	No effect
Formal Arguments	No effect
Operations	Generated in code
Attributes	Generated in code
Relationships	Generated in code

STANDARD CODE GENERATION

Let's look at the code generated for the following class.

The following IDL file was generated for the SampleClass:

```
//Source file: C:/corba/SampleClass.idl

#ifndef __SAMPLECLASS_DEFINED
#define __SAMPLECLASS_DEFINED

/* CmIdentification
   %X% %Q% %Z% %W% */

#include "IncludedClass.idl"

interface SampleClass {
};

#endif
```

Let's examine each piece of this file, one at a time.

Module Section

The module section contains some basic information about the class being generated. It includes the following line:

```
//Source file: C:/corba/SampleClass.idl
```

This section includes comments that describe what class is being generated and where the IDL file is located.

Configuration Management Section

The configuration management section is provided to support integration with your configuration management software. It includes the following lines:

```
/* CmIdentification
   %X% %Q% %Z% %W% */
```

This section of the file includes information about your configuration management settings. The properties on the second line (%X% %Q% %Z% %W%) are the default configuration management settings. To change the configuration management settings, select Tools ➤ Options from the menu. In the CORBA tab, select Module Specification from the drop-down list box to display the module specification code-generation properties. You can use the CmIdentification property to change the default values on this second line. Using this property, you can set the Change Management settings to a string that your configuration management software will recognize.

Some sample values you can place in this setting include:

◆ $date, which inserts the date the code was generated

◆ $time, which inserts the time the code was generated

◆ $module, which inserts the component name

◆ $file, which inserts the component's file

Preprocessor Directives Section

The preprocessor directives include the following lines:

```
#ifndef __SAMPLECLASS_DEFINED
#define __SAMPLECLASS_DEFINED
```

These lines are inserted into the code to prevent the file from being included more than once.

Includes Section

The includes section is the area of the generated code that shows any entries you added in the AdditionalIncludes code-generation property for the component and any entries you added in the Includes section of the specification window for the component.

The includes section for the SampleClass is as follows:

```
#include "IncludedClass.idl"
```

In this example, only one other class, called IncludedClass, was included.

Class Definition Section

This section contains information about the class itself, including the class name, its attributes, its operations, and its relationships. For the class example above, the definition section includes the following:

```
interface SampleClass {
};
```

If you entered any documentation for the class using the documentation window or the documentation area of the class specification window, this documentation will be included as a comment in the code.

CODE GENERATED FOR DIFFERENT TYPES OF CORBA/IDL

The code that is generated depends directly upon the stereotype (interface, union, const, etc.) of the class. Let's examine the code generated for the following class, with each of the different CORBA/IDL stereotype options.

```
      SampleClass
- Attribute1 : string
- Attribute2 : string
```

TypeDef Generation

If the class stereotype is set to CORBATypeDef, an interface will not be generated for the class. Instead, a typedef will be created. In the Implementation Type property on the Class Specification window, enter the definition that this typedef will be aliasing. The code generated for the Sample-Class class looks like this:

```
//Source file: C:/corba/SampleClass.idl

#ifndef __SAMPLECLASS_DEFINED
#define __SAMPLECLASS_DEFINED

/* CmIdentification
  %X% %Q% %Z% %W% */

#include "IncludedClass.idl"

typedef long SampleClass;

#endif
```

Enumeration Generation

The second CORBA type you can generate is an enumeration. If you select this option, Rose will use the keyword "enum" in the generated file. The following is the code generated for the class above, but with the stereotype set to CORBAEnum.

```
//Source file: C:/corba/SampleClass.idl

#ifndef __SAMPLECLASS_DEFINED
#define __SAMPLECLASS_DEFINED

/* CmIdentification
  %X% %Q% %Z% %W% */

#include "IncludedClass.idl"
```

```
enum SampleClass {

   Attribute1,
   Attribute2
};


#endif
```

Constant Generation

The third CORBA type that you can generate is a constant. In this case, Rose will include the keyword "const" in the generated IDL. To generate a constant, set the class stereotype to CORBAConstant. In the Class Specification window, set the Implementation Type field to the data type you wish to use and the Constant Value field to the value of the constant.

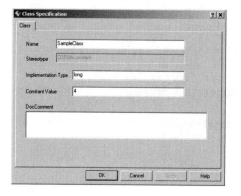

The following is the file generated for SampleClass.

```
//Source file: C:/corba/SampleClass.idl

#ifndef __SAMPLECLASS_DEFINED
#define __SAMPLECLASS_DEFINED

/* CmIdentification
   %X% %Q% %Z% %W% */

#include "IncludedClass.idl"

const long SampleClass = 4;

#endif
```

Exception Generation

The fourth CORBA type you can generate is an exception. If the class stereotype is set to CORBA-Exception, Rose will include the keyword "exception" in the code. Here is the file generated for SampleClass:

```
//Source file: C:/corba/SampleClass.idl

#ifndef __SAMPLECLASS_DEFINED
#define __SAMPLECLASS_DEFINED

/* CmIdentification
  %X% %Q% %Z% %W% */

#include "IncludedClass.idl"

exception SampleClass {
   string Attribute1;
   string Attribute2;
};

#endif
```

Structure Generation

Another CORBA type you can generate is a structure. Rose will include the "struct" keyword in the generated file if the stereotype of the class is set to CORBAStruct. The attributes of the class will appear as data members in the generated file. The code generated for SampleClass is:

```
//Source file: C:/corba/SampleClass.idl

#ifndef __SAMPLECLASS_DEFINED
#define __SAMPLECLASS_DEFINED

/* CmIdentification
  %X% %Q% %Z% %W% */

#include "IncludedClass.idl"

struct SampleClass {
   string Attribute1;
   string Attribute2;
};

#endif
```

ValueType Generation

By setting the stereotype to CORBAValue, you can generate a valuetype. Here is the code generated for the SampleClass class with a stereotype of CORBAValue:

```
//Source file: C:/corba/SampleClass.idl

#ifndef __SAMPLECLASS_DEFINED
#define __SAMPLECLASS_DEFINED

/* CmIdentification
  %X% %Q% %Z% %W% */

#include "IncludedClass.idl"

valuetype SampleClass {
   ;
   ;
};

#endif
```

Union Generation

Finally, you can generate a union in CORBA by setting the class stereotype to CORBAUnion. The generated code looks like this:

```
//Source file: C:/corba/SampleClass.idl

#ifndef __SAMPLECLASS_DEFINED
#define __SAMPLECLASS_DEFINED

/* CmIdentification
  %X% %Q% %Z% %W% */

#include "IncludedClass.idl"

union SampleClass switch(long) {
   case 1: string Attribute1;
   case 2: string Attribute2;
};

#endif
```

Before you can generate code, each of the attributes must have a case specifier. Open the specification window for each of the attributes, and enter a value in the Case Specifier property. The values you enter will control the case statements generated in the code. In the above example, the case specifier for Attribute1 is 1, and the specifier for Attribute2 is 2.

Attributes

As you may have noticed in the previous examples, attributes are generated in the code along with the class. This isn't true for all CORBA types, however. In this section, we'll examine the code generated for attributes for each of the types: interface, typedef, enumeration, constant, exception, structure, and union. For each of these types, we'll take a look at what is generated for the following class:

ATTRIBUTES GENERATED FOR AN INTERFACE

In an interface, all of the attributes of the class will appear in the generated code. For each attribute, Rose will include:

◆ Data type

◆ Documentation

This is the interface that is generated for the SampleClass class:

```
//Source file: C:/corba/SampleClass.idl

#ifndef __SAMPLECLASS_DEFINED
#define __SAMPLECLASS_DEFINED

/* CmIdentification
   %X% %Q% %Z% %W% */

#include "IncludedClass.idl"

interface SampleClass {
   attribute string Attribute1;
   attribute string Attribute2;
};

#endif
```

ATTRIBUTES GENERATED FOR A TYPEDEF

If the class stereotype is set to CORBATypeDef, attributes do not appear in the generated code.

ATTRIBUTES GENERATED FOR AN ENUMERATION

With an enumeration, Rose will place the attributes in the generated code. However, Rose will ignore the data types, default values, and other specifications of the attribute. Here is the enumeration generated for the SampleClass class:

```
//Source file: C:/corba/SampleClass.idl

#ifndef __SAMPLECLASS_DEFINED
#define __SAMPLECLASS_DEFINED

/* CmIdentification
   %X% %Q% %Z% %W% */

#include "IncludedClass.idl"

enum SampleClass {

   Attribute1,
   Attribute2
};

#endif
```

ATTRIBUTES GENERATED FOR A CONSTANT

If the class stereotype is set to CORBAConstant, attributes do not appear in the generated code.

ATTRIBUTES GENERATED FOR AN EXCEPTION

If the class stereotype is set to CORBAException, all attributes of the class will be included in the code. For each attribute, the code will include:

◆ Data type

◆ Documentation

Here is the code generated for SampleClass when the stereotype is set to CORBAException:

```
//Source file: C:/corba/SampleClass.idl

#ifndef __SAMPLECLASS_DEFINED
#define __SAMPLECLASS_DEFINED

/* CmIdentification
   %X% %Q% %Z% %W% */

#include "IncludedClass.idl"
```

```
exception SampleClass {
   string Attribute1;
   string Attribute2;
};

#endif
```

ATTRIBUTES GENERATED FOR A STRUCTURE

If the class stereotype is set to CORBAStruct, all attributes of the class will be included in the code. For each attribute, the code will include:

◆ Data type

◆ Documentation

Here is the code generated when the SampleClass stereotype is set to CORBAStruct:

```
//Source file: C:/corba/SampleClass.idl

#ifndef __SAMPLECLASS_DEFINED
#define __SAMPLECLASS_DEFINED

/* CmIdentification
   %X% %Q% %Z% %W% */

#include "IncludedClass.idl"

struct SampleClass {
   string Attribute1;
   string Attribute2;
};

#endif
```

ATTRIBUTES GENERATED FOR A UNION

If the class stereotype is set to CORBAUnion, the attributes of the class will appear as case statements in the union. Here is the code generated for SampleClass:

```
//Source file: C:/corba/SampleClass.idl

#ifndef __SAMPLECLASS_DEFINED
#define __SAMPLECLASS_DEFINED

/* CmIdentification
   %X% %Q% %Z% %W% */

#include "IncludedClass.idl"
```

```
union SampleClass switch(long) {
   case 1: string Attribute1;
   case 2: string Attribute2;
};
```

```
#endif
```

The values used in the case statements are set by the values you enter in the Case Specifier field in each attribute's specification window.

Operations

The operations you define in your Rose model will appear in the generated IDL. Like attributes, though, operations are included only for certain CORBA types. In this section, we'll take a look at the code generated for operations of the following class:

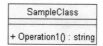

We'll examine how the code is generated as the stereotype of the class changes.

OPERATIONS GENERATED FOR AN INTERFACE

With an interface, all of the operations for the class will appear in the generated code, along with their parameters, parameter data types, and return type. For the SampleClass class, the following interface was generated:

```
//Source file: C:/corba/SampleClass.idl

#ifndef __SAMPLECLASS_DEFINED
#define __SAMPLECLASS_DEFINED

/* CmIdentification
   %X% %Q% %Z% %W% */

#include "IncludedClass.idl"

interface SampleClass {
   /*
   @roseuid 39B5C1A0006A */
   string Operation1 ();

};

#endif
```

Operations are shown in the generated IDL only for interfaces. If the class stereotype is a typedef, enumeration, const, exception, struct, or union, operations will not be generated in the code.

Bidirectional Associations

To support bidirectional associations, Rose will generate attributes in the code. Each of the classes in the relationship will contain an attribute to support the association. The names of the generated attributes will be controlled by the role names on the association relationship. You must enter role names before you can generate code.

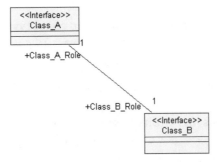

The code generated for the two classes shown above will resemble the following:

```
interface Class_A {
   attribute Class_B Class_B_Role;
};
```

and

```
interface Class_B {
   attribute Class_A Class_A_Role;
};
```

As you can see, Rose will automatically generate attributes on both sides of the bidirectional association relationship. With the Class_B_Role attribute, Class_A can easily access Class_B. Using the Class_A_Role attribute, Class_B can easily access Class_A.

The full code generated for Class_A is:

```
//Source file: C:/corba/Class_A.idl

#ifndef __CLASS_A_DEFINED
#define __CLASS_A_DEFINED
```

```
/* CmIdentification
   %X% %Q% %Z% %W% */

#include "Class_B.idl"

interface Class_A {
   attribute Class_B Class_B_Role;
};
```

As you can see, Class_A now includes an attribute of type Class_B. Class_B will also include an attribute of type Class_A. These two attributes support the relationship between Class_A and Class_B.

BIDIRECTIONAL ASSOCIATIONS GENERATED FOR A TYPEDEF

If the stereotype for Class_A is set to CORBATypeDef, a Class_B attribute will not be included in the code for Class_A. However, an #include statement will be added to the code in Class_A, as follows:

```
#include "Class_B.idl"
```

BIDIRECTIONAL ASSOCIATIONS GENERATED FOR AN ENUMERATION

If the stereotype of Class_A is set to CORBAEnum, an include statement for `Class_B.IDL` will be included in the code. An attribute will not, however, be generated in Class_A. The code for Class_A looks like this:

```
//Source file: C:/corba/Class_A.idl

#ifndef __CLASS_A_DEFINED
#define __CLASS_A_DEFINED

/* CmIdentification
   %X% %Q% %Z% %W% */

#include "Class_B.idl"

enum Class_A {

};

#endif
```

BIDIRECTIONAL ASSOCIATIONS GENERATED FOR A CONSTANT

If Class_A is a constant, it will have an include statement for Class_B, but will not have an attribute that supports the relationship. Here is the code generated for Class_A:

```
//Source file: C:/corba/Class_A.idl
```

```
#ifndef __CLASS_A_DEFINED
#define __CLASS_A_DEFINED

/* CmIdentification
   %X% %Q% %Z% %W% */

#include "Class_B.idl"

const long Class_A = 4;

#endif
```

BIDIRECTIONAL ASSOCIATIONS GENERATED FOR AN EXCEPTION

If Class_A is an exception, an attribute of type Class_B will be generated inside it. Here is the code generated for Class_A:

```
//Source file: C:/corba/Class_A.idl

#ifndef __CLASS_A_DEFINED
#define __CLASS_A_DEFINED

/* CmIdentification
   %X% %Q% %Z% %W% */

#include "Class_B.idl"

exception Class_A {
   Class_B Class_B_Role;
};

#endif
```

BIDIRECTIONAL ASSOCIATIONS GENERATED FOR A STRUCTURE

If the stereotype of Class_A is CORBAStruct, an attribute will be created inside Class_A when you generate the IDL.

The code for Class_A is as follows:

```
//Source file: C:/corba/Class_A.idl

#ifndef __CLASS_A_DEFINED
#define __CLASS_A_DEFINED

/* CmIdentification
   %X% %Q% %Z% %W% */

#include "Class_B.idl"
```

```
struct Class_A {
   Class_B Class_B_Role;
};

#endif
```

BIDIRECTIONAL ASSOCIATIONS GENERATED FOR A UNION

If the stereotype for Class_A is set to CORBAUnion, the generated code will have an include statement for Class_B, and will include an instance of Class_B within the switch statement. Here is the code generated for Class_A:

```
//Source file: C:/corba/Class_A.idl

#ifndef __CLASS_A_DEFINED
#define __CLASS_A_DEFINED

/* CmIdentification
  %X% %Q% %Z% %W% */

#include "Class_B.idl"

union Class_A switch() {
   case 1: Class_B Class_B_Role;
};

#endif
```

Note that the attribute generated from the association needs a case specifier, as do the other attributes of Class_A. The case specifier can be set using the Case Specifier Role code-generation property for the relationship.

Unidirectional Associations

As with bidirectional associations, Rose will generate attributes to support unidirectional associations. With a unidirectional association, however, an attribute is generated at only one end of the relationship.

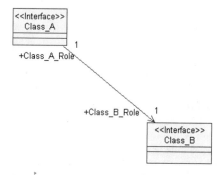

For the Class_A and Class_B classes above, code similar to the following would be created:

```
interface Class_A {
   attribute Class_B Class_B_Role;
};
```

and

```
Interface Class_B
{
};
```

As you can see, Rose will generate a private attribute for the relationship at only one end of the association. Specifically, it will generate an attribute in the client class, but not in the supplier class.

For each of the other CORBA types (typedef, enumeration, const, exception, struct, or union), Rose will generate code as shown in the bidirectional associations sections above. The only difference with a unidirectional association is that the attribute will be created on only one side of the relationship.

Note that the multiplicity here is one to one. Let's take a look at how code is affected when the multiplicity settings are changed.

Associations with a Multiplicity of One to Many

In a one-to-one relationship, Rose can simply create the appropriate attributes to support the association. With a one-to-many relationship, however, one class must contain a set of the other class.

To begin, let's look at an example.

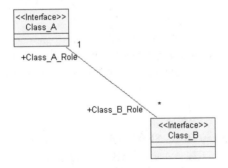

In this case, we have a one-to-many relationship. As we saw earlier, Class_B can generate an attribute that is simply a pointer to Class_A, but a simple pointer attribute in the Class_A class won't be enough. Instead, the attribute generated in Class_A must use some sort of container class as its data type. In IDL, there are two container classes you can use: a sequence or an array. By default, Rose will use a sequence.

For this example, Rose will generate code similar to the following:

```
interface Class_A {
   typedef sequence <Class_B> Class_B_Role_def;

   attribute Class_B_Role_def Class_B_Role;
};
```

and

```
interface Class_B {
   attribute Class_A Class_A_Role;
};
```

As you can see, Class_B includes a simple pointer to Class_A, as we saw earlier. However, a container class was used in Class_A when generating the Class_B attribute.

The full code generated for Class_A is:

```
//Source file: C:/corba/Class_A.idl

#ifndef __CLASS_A_DEFINED
#define __CLASS_A_DEFINED

/* CmIdentification
   %X% %Q% %Z% %W% */

#include "Class_B.idl"

interface Class_A {
   typedef sequence <Class_B> Class_B_Role_def;

   attribute Class_B_Role_def Class_B_Role;
};

#endif
```

Again, Rose will use a sequence as the default container class. To use an array instead, open the relationship specification and change the BoundedRoleType property to Array. To use an array for all relationships with a multiplicity greater than one, select Tools ➤ Options from the menu. On the CORBA tab, select Role from the drop-down list box and change the value in the BoundedRoleType property to Array.

ONE-TO-MANY ASSOCIATIONS GENERATED FOR A TYPEDEF

If the stereotype of Class_A is CORBATypeDef, an #include statement will be added to the code, but an attribute will not be generated in Class_A to support the relationship with Class_B. The code generated for Class_A is as follows:

```
//Source file: C:/corba/Class_A.idl

#ifndef __CLASS_A_DEFINED
#define __CLASS_A_DEFINED

/* CmIdentification
   %X% %Q% %Z% %W% */
```

```
#include "Class_B.idl"

typedef sequence <Class_B> Class_A;

#endif
```

ONE-TO-MANY ASSOCIATIONS GENERATED FOR AN ENUMERATION

As with a typedef, Rose will not generate attributes to support the relationship if Class_A is an enumeration. There will, however, be an #include statement in the code generated for Class_A. The code for Class_A is as follows:

```
//Source file: C:/corba/Class_A.idl

#ifndef __CLASS_A_DEFINED
#define __CLASS_A_DEFINED

/* CmIdentification
   %X% %Q% %Z% %W% */

#include "Class_B.idl"

enum Class_A {

};

#endif
```

ONE-TO-MANY ASSOCIATIONS GENERATED FOR A CONSTANT

If Class_A is a constant, it will have an #include statement for Class_B, but will not have an attribute for the relationship. The code for Class_A is shown below:

```
//Source file: C:/corba/Class_A.idl

#ifndef __CLASS_A_DEFINED
#define __CLASS_A_DEFINED

/* CmIdentification
   %X% %Q% %Z% %W% */

#include "Class_B.idl"

const long Class_A = 4;

#endif
```

ONE-TO-MANY ASSOCIATIONS GENERATED FOR AN EXCEPTION

If Class_A is an exception, an attribute will be created inside it to support the relationship to Class_B. In a one-to-many relationship, Rose will use a container class when generating this attribute. By default, as with one-to-many relationships between interfaces, Rose will use a sequence as a container. You can change the container class to use an array by changing the BoundedRoleType role property to Array.

The following code is generated for Class_A when its stereotype is set to CORBAException and Class_A has a one-to-many relationship with Class_B.

```
//Source file: C:/corba/Class_A.idl

#ifndef __CLASS_A_DEFINED
#define __CLASS_A_DEFINED

/* CmIdentification
  %X% %Q% %Z% %W% */

#include "Class_B.idl"

exception Class_A {
   sequence <Class_B> Class_B_Role;
};

#endif
```

ONE-TO-MANY ASSOCIATIONS GENERATED FOR A STRUCTURE

When the stereotype of Class_A is set to CORBAStruct, and Class_A has a one-to-many relation-ship with Class_B, an attribute will be created in Class_A to support that relationship. As with the other one-to-many relationships, Rose will use a container class when creating the attribute. By default, a sequence is used. To use an array instead, change the BoundedRoleType role property.

The following is the code generated for Class_A:

```
//Source file: C:/corba/Class_A.idl

#ifndef __CLASS_A_DEFINED
#define __CLASS_A_DEFINED

/* CmIdentification
  %X% %Q% %Z% %W% */

#include "Class_B.idl"

struct Class_A {
   sequence <Class_B> Class_B_Role;
};

#endif
```

ONE-TO-MANY ASSOCIATIONS GENERATED FOR A UNION

If Class_A is a union, both an #include statement and an attribute will be generated in Class_A to support the relationship with Class_B. The code for Class_A is as follows:

```
//Source file: C:/corba/Class_A.idl

#ifndef __CLASS_A_DEFINED
#define __CLASS_A_DEFINED

/* CmIdentification
   %X% %Q% %Z% %W% */

#include "Class_B.idl"

union Class_A switch() {
   case 1: sequence <Class_B> Class_B_Role;
};

#endif

#endif
```

Associations with a Multiplicity of Many to Many

The code generated here is similar to that created for a one-to-many relationship. With a many-to-many relationship, however, Rose will generate container classes on both ends of the relationship.

Let's look at the code generated for the following relationship:

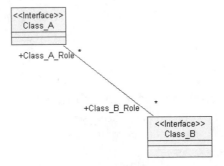

In this situation, container classes are used at both ends of the relationship. The code that is generated will look something like the following:

```
interface Class_A {
   typedef sequence <Class_B> Class_B_Role_def;

   attribute Class_B_Role_def Class_B_Role;
};
```

and

```
interface Class_B {
   typedef sequence <Class_A> Class_A_Role_def;

   attribute Class_A_Role_def Class_A_Role;
};
```

The complete code generated for Class_A will look exactly as it did in the previous section. The difference is that now the code for Class_B will also include an attribute with a container type. The code generated for Class_B is:

```
//Source file: C:/corba/Class_B.idl

#ifndef __CLASS_B_DEFINED
#define __CLASS_B_DEFINED

/* CmIdentification
   %X% %Q% %Z% %W% */

#include "Class_A.idl"

interface Class_B {
   typedef sequence <Class_A> Class_A_Role_def;
   attribute Class_A_Role_def Class_A_Role;
};

#endif
```

MANY-TO-MANY ASSOCIATIONS GENERATED FOR OTHER CORBA TYPES

The code generated for a many-to-many relationship with other CORBA types will look exactly like the code we examined in the previous section. The only difference is that Class_B will now contain an attribute of type Class_A.

Associations with Bounded Multiplicity

An association with bounded multiplicity is one that has a range of numbers at one end of the relationship. For example, the following relationship has bounded multiplicity:

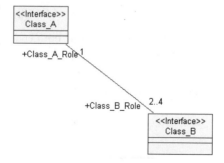

In this example, each instance of Class_A is related to 2–4 instances of Class_B.

The two types of bounded relationships we will examine are bounded associations and fixed associations. Bounded associations have a multiplicity range, like 2..4. Fixed associations have a single number in the multiplicity. For example, a multiplicity of 4 is fixed.

For the example above, Rose will generate something like this:

```
interface Class_A {
    typedef sequence <Class_B, 4> Class_B_Role_def;
    attribute Class_B_Role_def Class_B_Role;
};
```

and

```
interface Class_B {
    attribute Class_A Class_A_Role;
};
```

As with one-to-many and many-to-many relationships, Rose uses container classes when generating the attributes. By default, Rose will use a sequence, but you can change the container to an array. You make this change by selecting the CORBA A or CORBA B tab of the relationship specification and then changing the BoundedRoleType property to Array. To change the container class for all bounded relationships, select Tools ➤ Options from the menu. On the CORBA tab, select Role from the drop-down list box. Change the value in the BoundedRoleType property to Array.

BOUNDED ASSOCIATIONS GENERATED FOR AN EXCEPTION

If Class_A is an exception, the code generated will include an attribute to support the relationship to Class_B. In this case, a simplified version of the generated code will look something like this:

```
Exception Class_A
{
sequence <Class_B, 4> Class_B_Role;
};
```

As with other relationships where the multiplicity is greater than one, Rose will use a sequence as the default container class. To use an array, change the BoundedRoleType property to Array.

BOUNDED ASSOCIATIONS GENERATED FOR A STRUCTURE

The code generated for a structure will include an attribute to support the relationship between Class_A and Class_B. A simplified version of the code is as follows:

```
Struct Class_A
{
sequence <Class_B, 4> Class_B_Role;
};
```

Again, a sequence is the default container. To use an array instead, you can change the Bounded-RoleType role property to Array.

BOUNDED ASSOCIATIONS GENERATED FOR A UNION

If Class_A is a union and has a bounded association with Class_B, an attribute will be created in Class_A to support the relationship. By default, the container used in this attribute is a sequence. Here, we have a sequence length of 4.

```
union Class_A switch(int) {
case 3: sequence <Class_B, 4> Class_B_Role;
};
```

BOUNDED ASSOCIATIONS GENERATED FOR OTHER CORBA/IDL TYPES

If types other than interface, exception, structure, or union are used, no attributes will be generated to support the relationship. However, #include statements will be placed in both Class_A and Class_B.

Reflexive Associations

A reflexive association is treated much the same as an association between two classes. For the following situation:

code similar to this is generated:

```
interface Class_A {
    typedef sequence <Class_A> RoleA_def;
    attribute Class_A RoleB;
    attribute RoleA_def RoleA;
};
```

The first two lines support the 0..* end of the relationship. They include a container class that will support this multiplicity. The third line supports the end of the relationship with a multiplicity of one.

The full code generated for Class_A is as follows:

```
//Source file: C:/corba/Class_A.idl

#ifndef __CLASS_A_DEFINED
#define __CLASS_A_DEFINED

/* CmIdentification
   %X% %Q% %Z% %W% */
```

```
interface Class_A {
  typedef sequence <Class_A> RoleA_def;

  attribute Class_A RoleB;
  attribute RoleA_def RoleA;
};

#endif
```

REFLEXIVE ASSOCIATIONS GENERATED FOR AN EXCEPTION

If Class_A is stereotyped as an exception, only one attribute will be generated for the relationship. In this example, an attribute is generated to support the *one* end of the one-to-many relationship. The code for Class_A is shown below:

```
//Source file: C:/corba/Class_A.idl
#ifndef __CLASS_A_DEFINED
#define __CLASS_A_DEFINED
/* CmIdentification
   %X% %Q% %Z% %W% */
exception Class_A {
Class_A RoleB;
};
#endif
```

REFLEXIVE ASSOCIATIONS GENERATED FOR A STRUCTURE

If Class_A is a structure, an attribute will be created inside of it to support the reflexive relationship. If the relationship looks like the previous reflexive association, then the following code will be generated.

```
//Source file: C:/corba/Class_A.idl

#ifndef __CLASS_A_DEFINED
#define __CLASS_A_DEFINED

/* CmIdentification
   %X% %Q% %Z% %W% */

struct Class_A {
  Class_A RoleB;
};

#endif
```

REFLEXIVE ASSOCIATIONS GENERATED FOR A UNION

If Class_A is a union, a single attribute will be created inside the class to support the reflexive relationship. The following code is generated for Class_A:

```
//Source file: C:/corba/Class_A.idl

#ifndef __CLASS_A_DEFINED
#define __CLASS_A_DEFINED

/* CmIdentification
   %X% %Q% %Z% %W% */

union Class_A switch() {
   case 2: Class_A RoleB;
};

#endif
```

REFLEXIVE ASSOCIATIONS GENERATED FOR OTHER CORBA/IDL TYPES

Because attributes are not generated for a typedef, enumeration, or constant, reflexive associations with these types will not be reflected in the code.

Aggregations

When generating CORBA/IDL, associations and aggregations are treated the same. All of the considerations we've discussed so far (the multiplicity, whether the relationship is unidirectional or bidirectional, and whether or not the relationship is reflexive) apply the same to aggregations as they do to associations. This is true for any of the CORBA types (interface, typedef, enumeration, constant, exception, structure, or union).

For information about how unidirectional aggregations, aggregations with various multiplicity indicators, and reflexive aggregations are generated, please see the corresponding sections on associations.

Dependency Relationships

With a dependency relationship, attributes are not created. If there is a dependency between Class_A and Class_B, attributes will be created in neither Class_A nor Class_B.

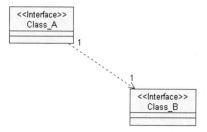

The code that is generated will look something like the following:

```
Interface Class_A
{
};
```

and

```
Interface Class_B
{
};
```

Rose will place only one reference to Class_B—an include statement for `Class_B.IDL`—inside of Class_A. Class_A will not be referenced in Class_B at all.

Because no attributes are generated for a dependency, an attribute will not be created for any of the CORBA types (interface, typedef, enumeration, constant, exception, structure, or union).

Generalization Relationships

A generalization relationship in UML becomes an inheritance relationship in IDL. In your Rose model, an inheritance relationship is shown as follows:

For this type of relationship, Rose will generate something that looks like this:

```
Interface Parent
{
};
```

and

```
Interface Child : Parent
{
};
```

Let's look at the actual code that is generated. In the code for the parent class, there is no mention of the child class. This helps keep the parent generic; many classes can therefore inherit from it without affecting its code.

In the child class, the code is generated to support its inheritance from the parent class. The code for the child class is as follows:

```
//Source file: C:/corba/Child.idl

#ifndef __CHILD_DEFINED
#define __CHILD_DEFINED

/* CmIdentification
  %X% %Q% %Z% %W% */

#include "Parent.idl"

interface Child : Parent {
};

#endif
```

GENERALIZATIONS GENERATED FOR A TYPEDEF

If the child class is a typedef, an #include statement will appear in the generated code for the child, but an inheritance relationship will not be shown in the code. The IDL for the child class is as follows:

```
//Source file: C:/corba/Child.idl

#ifndef __CHILD_DEFINED
#define __CHILD_DEFINED

/* CmIdentification
  %X% %Q% %Z% %W% */

#include "Parent.idl"

typedef  Child;

#endif
```

GENERALIZATIONS GENERATED FOR AN ENUMERATION

The same is true for an enumeration. Although an #include statement is generated, the inheritance relationship itself is not represented in the code. In this case, the generated code looks like this:

```
//Source file: C:/corba/Child.idl

#ifndef __CHILD_DEFINED
#define __CHILD_DEFINED

/* CmIdentification
  %X% %Q% %Z% %W% */
```

```
#include "Parent.idl"

enum Child {

};

#endif
```

GENERALIZATIONS GENERATED FOR A CONSTANT

As with a typedef or enumeration, a generalization relationship will not be directly implemented in code with a constant. An #include statement will be generated to reference the parent. The code for this example looks like this:

```
//Source file: C:/corba/Child.idl

#ifndef __CHILD_DEFINED
#define __CHILD_DEFINED

/* CmIdentification
   %X% %Q% %Z% %W% */

#include "Parent.idl"

const long Child = 4;

#endif
```

GENERALIZATIONS GENERATED FOR AN EXCEPTION

Inheritance is not supported with an exception. Therefore, as in the other cases, an #include statement will be generated, but the generalization itself will not be reflected in the code. The IDL for this situation looks like this:

```
//Source file: C:/corba/Child.idl

#ifndef __CHILD_DEFINED
#define __CHILD_DEFINED

/* CmIdentification
   %X% %Q% %Z% %W% */

#include "Parent.idl"

exception Child {
};

#endif
```

GENERALIZATIONS GENERATED FOR A STRUCTURE

As with the other CORBA types, inheritance is not supported with a structure. An #include statement will be included to reference the parent, but the inheritance relationship will not be reflected in the code. The IDL generated for a generalization with a structure is as follows:

```
//Source file: C:/corba/Child.idl

#ifndef __CHILD_DEFINED
#define __CHILD_DEFINED

/* CmIdentification
   %X% %Q% %Z% %W% */

#include "Parent.idl"

struct Child {
};

#endif
```

GENERALIZATIONS GENERATED FOR A UNION

A generalization with a union is much the same as a generalization with all other CORBA types, except interface. Because generalizations are not supported with a union, they will not appear in the generated code. The only reference to the parent in the generated code is an #include statement. The code looks like this:

```
//Source file: C:/corba/Child.idl

#ifndef __CHILD_DEFINED
#define __CHILD_DEFINED

/* CmIdentification
   %X% %Q% %Z% %W% */

#include "Parent.idl"

union Child switch() {
};

#endif
```

Reverse Engineering CORBA Source Code

You can reverse engineer CORBA source code into your Rose model. Each .idl file that you reverse engineer will be modeled as a component in Rose. The classes, relationships, and other elements in the file will appear in the Logical view.

To begin the process, first select Tools ➤ CORBA ➤ Project Specification. In the Directories field, select the directories that contain the source code you wish to reverse engineer.

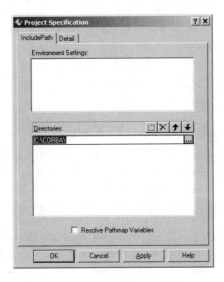

Once you complete this step, select Tools ➤ CORBA ➤ Reverse Engineer CORBA. In the reverse-engineering window, select the file(s) you wish to reverse engineer and press Add. Once all files have been added to the lower window, select the file(s) in the lower window to reverse engineer and press Reverse. If any errors occur during the reverse-engineering process, a note will be entered in the log window.

Elements in the .idl files will be mapped to Rose elements using the mapping described throughout this chapter.

Summary

In this chapter, we examined how the different types of elements in your Rose model are generated in CORBA /IDL. We looked at the different code-generation properties for classes, packages, attributes, operations, associations, aggregations, and other model elements, and discussed how these properties affect the generated code.

Again, the steps needed to generate code are:

1. Set the CORBA/IDL code-generation properties.

2. Select the class(es) or component(s) to generate on a Class or Component diagram.

3. Select Tools ➢ CORBA ➢ Generate CORBA.

Once these steps are complete, you will have CORBA/IDL files that were generated from your model. To reverse engineer CORBA source code, select Tools ➢ CORBA ➢ Reverse Engineer CORBA. Select the files to reverse engineer, and Rose will load information from the code into the model.

So far, we've examined how Rose can be used to model an application. An important aspect of many applications, however, is the database. In the next chapter, we'll take a look at how Rose can be used for data modeling. Through the powerful Data Modeler feature within Rose, you can model your database as well as your application, and ensure that your data model and object model are consistent with one another.

Chapter 18

Rose Data Modeler

So far, we've focused on modeling the application itself—creating the Use Case diagrams, Interaction diagrams, Class diagrams, and other artifacts needed to really understand how the system works. An essential element to nearly every system, however, is some form of persistent storage, typically a database.

Using Rose, you can model not only the application, but also the database or databases that support the application. Rose 2001, 2001A, and 2002 support the data-modeling notation that has been incorporated into UML.

- ◆ Comparing object models and data models

- ◆ Creating a data model

- ◆ Adding logic to a data model

- ◆ Modeling databases, schemas, tables, fields, stored procedures, triggers, and more

- ◆ Modeling primary keys, foreign keys, and entity relationships

- ◆ Modeling views

- ◆ Generating an object model from a data model

- ◆ Generating a data model from an object model

- ◆ Creating the database from a data model

- ◆ Reverse engineering a database into a data model

Object Models and Data Models

An object model is used for all of the pieces of the application that we have discussed so far—the classes, attributes, operations, relationships, components, and other constructs—*except* for the data. The primary emphasis of an object model is on memory—what objects will be created in memory, how will these objects communicate, and what is each object responsible for doing? The focus of the data model is, as the name implies, the database rather than the application.

While object modeling is concerned with memory efficiency, data modeling is more concerned with database efficiency. Table 18.1 lists some of the differences in perspective between the data model and the object model.

TABLE 18.1: CONCERNS IN DATA MODELING AND OBJECT MODELING

OBJECT MODEL	DATA MODEL
How can I design the classes to be memory efficient?	How can I design the database to be storage efficient?
What objects need relationships in the object model?	What tables need relationships in the data model?
How can I structure the data on the user interface to make the most sense to the end user?	How can I structure the data to speed access times?
How can I package the data with behavior to create classes?	How can I normalize the data?
What data will be used throughout the application, and what data will be used in only one area?	What data will be retrieved frequently?
How can I use generalizations or other design strategies to reuse code?	How can I incorporate the concept of inheritance into my data model if my DBMS doesn't directly support inheritance?

There is a definite disparity between the data model and the object model. The primary reason for this is the nature of the models themselves; objects are, by definition, focused on behavior *and* data, while the data model is focused on data. The object model, in most languages, supports inheritance, while the data model does not. Data types in programming languages and database management system (DBMS) packages are different. Join tables do not need to be included in the object model as a general rule (although association classes are sometimes needed). Two classes need to have a relationship if one needs to access attributes or operations of the other; two tables need to have a relationship if there is a logical connection between the data in the two tables. Two entity classes may have a relationship in the object model, but their tables may not be related in the data model.

To account for these natural differences, Rose supports the creation of both an object model and a separate data model. You can create both of these models in a single Rose file so that you have a complete understanding of your application and its database in one place.

So, which comes first: the data model or the object model? In many cases, the two models are developed concurrently. In the Inception phase, the team can develop both a rough data model and a rough object model, or a domain model. As Elaboration and Construction progress, the team can fill in the details of both models. Many of the entity classes from the Class diagrams will become database tables. There is not, however, a one-to-one correspondence. Because of the differences in perspective between the two models, a single entity class may become two or more database tables. Conversely, a single database table may be supported by two or more classes in the application.

Many projects, especially maintenance projects, begin with some sort of existing data model. Using Rose, you can reverse engineer the existing data model, and you can even automatically generate an object model from it. If you have an object model but no data model, you can automatically generate a data model from your object model.

Creating a Data Model

In Rose, the Data Model includes constructs in both the Logical view and the Component view. In the Logical view, you can create schemas, which in turn contain stored procedures. You can also create tables, which contain fields, constraints, triggers, primary keys, indexes, and relationships. Finally, you can create domains and domain packages.

In the Component view, you can model the databases themselves. Each database is modeled as a component with a <<database>> stereotype. Rose 2001A and 2002 support DB2, SQL Server, Sybase, Oracle, or ANSI SQL.

The primary steps in the creation of a data model are:

1. Create a database.

2. Add a schema to hold the data model and assign the schema to the database.

3. Create domain packages and domains.

4. Add tables to each schema.

5. Add details to the tables (fields, constraints, triggers, indexes, primary key).

6. Add relationships between the tables and add foreign keys.

7. Create views.

8. Create an object model from your data model.

9. Generate the database.

10. Keep the database synchronized with the model through the Update feature.

It isn't necessary to follow all of the steps in this order, but creating the database and schema first sets the DBMS that will be used. When you create tables, fields, and other data-modeling elements, the appropriate data types will then be available. In the remainder of this chapter, we will discuss each of these steps. Before we do, however, let's look at what logic might be incorporated into the data model.

Logic in a Data Model

Database-management systems are becoming more sophisticated every year. It's becoming easier to add logic to the database—so much so that it can be easy to become confused about what logic should go in the database and what logic should go in the application.

There is no simple way to determine what logic should go where, and a complete analysis of database design principles is outside the scope of this book, but here are some points to consider:

◆ General object-oriented practices suggest keeping at least some of the business logic in an application layer rather than in the database.

◆ In general, only logic related to the data itself should be housed in the database. This would include items such as required fields, valid values for fields, and field lengths.

◆ Many business rules can be enforced directly in the database through the use of constraints. Although the database is an appropriate location for this type of logic, the application must gather information from the end user, pass it through the business layer, and then across a network connection, which may be slow, before the data is validated. Keeping this logic in the business layer can sometimes help reduce unnecessary network traffic.

However, if a number of areas within the application, or even a number of different applications, need to use the same constraint, placing the logic in the database can help ensure that the rule is applied consistently.

◆ Some of the system logic can be carried out directly in the database through the use of stored procedures. There are advantages to this approach; functionality that is very data-intensive might be more appropriate as a stored procedure. If the functionality is strictly data manipulation, programming it as a stored procedure might be significantly faster than loading all the records into memory, having the application do the processing, and then storing the results back to the database.

However, there are some disadvantages to this strategy as well. Using stored procedures to implement any business logic inherently divides the business logic across at least two layers: the business logic layer and the database layer. When business logic changes, you may need to update both of these layers. You also run the risk of duplicate logic across the layers or, even worse, contradictory business logic across the two layers.

Too many stored procedures can also cause difficulties in migrating from one DBMS to another. Many database management packages have slightly different syntax, and migrating from one to another may necessitate rewriting of the stored procedures.

Again, there isn't necessarily an easy way to distinguish between the logic that should reside in the database and the logic that should reside in the application. Once you have decided to place logic in the database, you can model that logic by modeling stored procedures, constraints, and triggers in Rose. First, however, you must create a database and schema.

Adding a Database

A database is modeled in Rose as a stereotyped component. It is given a unique name, and assigned to a specific DBMS. At the time of this writing, Rose supports the following DBMS products:

◆ ANSI SQL 92

◆ IBM DB2 5.*x*

◆ IBM DB2 6.*x*

◆ IBM DB2 7.*x*

◆ IBM DB2 OS390 5.*x*

◆ IBM DB2 OS390 6.*x*

- Microsoft SQL Server 6.*x*
- Microsoft SQL Server 7.*x*
- Microsoft SQL Server 2000.*x*
- Oracle 7.*x*
- Oracle 8.*x*
- Sybase Adaptive Server 12.*x*

You can set the DBMS for a database using the Database Specification window. To add a database:

1. Right-click the Component View entry in the browser.
2. Select Data Modeler ➢ New ➢ Database.
3. Type the name of the database.
4. Right-click the new database in the browser and select Open Specification.
5. In the Target field, select the appropriate DBMS.

Adding Tablespaces

When using DB2, Oracle, or SQL server, you can add tablespaces to your database. A *tablespace* is a logical unit of storage for your tables. Within each tablespace are one or more containers, where a container is a physical storage device such as a hard drive. Each container is divided into smaller units called *extents*. Tables in the tablespace are evenly distributed across the containers within the tablespace.

NOTE *In Microsoft SQL Server, tablespaces are called filegroups, and containers are called files. In Oracle, containers are known as data files.*

Each tablespace has an initial size, in KB. Once that space has been used, the DBMS can automatically increase the size of the tablespace in preset increments. The size of the increments (in KB) can be set in Rose. Even when increments are set, the container cannot grow beyond its maximum size, which can also be set in Rose. Once tablespaces are established, you can assign tables to them.

To add a tablespace (SQL Server):

1. Right-click the database in the browser.
2. Select Data Modeler ➢ New ➢ Tablespace.
3. Type the name of the tablespace.
4. Right-click the new tablespace in the browser and select Open Specification. The namespace specification window will appear:

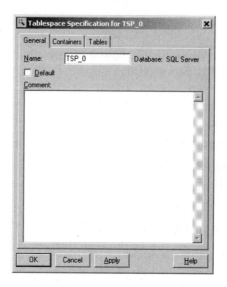

5. Check the Default field if you want this to be the default tablespace. Any tables that are not assigned to another tablespace will be assigned to the default tablespace.

To add a tablespace (Oracle):

1. Right-click the database in the browser.

2. Select Data Modeler ➤ New ➤ Tablespace.

3. Type the name of the tablespace.

4. Right-click the new tablespace in the browser and select Open Specification. The namespace specification window will appear:

5. Set the tablespace type to Permanent or Temporary. A temporary tablespace will allocate space for only the duration of the current database session. A permanent tablespace will remain in existence even after the end of the database session.

To add a tablespace (DB2):

1. Right-click the database in the browser.

2. Select Data Modeler ➤ New ➤ Tablespace.

3. Type the name of the tablespace.

4. Right-click the new tablespace in the browser and select Open Specification. The namespace specification window will appear.

5. Set the tablespace type to Regular or Temporary. A temporary tablespace will allocate space only for the duration of the current database session. A regular tablespace will remain in existence even after the end of the database session.

6. Set whether the tablespace is managed by the DBMS or by the operating system. If it is managed by the operating system, you cannot add new containers after creating the tablespace, but the existing tablespaces can be expanded. If it is managed by the DBMS, the existing tablespaces cannot be expanded, but you can add new containers.

To set up containers within a tablespace (SQL Server):

1. Right-click the tablespace in the browser and select Open Specification.

2. Select the Containers tab on the specification window.

3. Right-click anywhere in the white space, and select New.

4. Enter the tablespace filename, initial size, maximum size, and file growth (increment amount).

To set up containers within a tablespace (Oracle):

1. Right-click the tablespace in the browser and select Open Specification.

2. Select the Containers tab on the specification window.

3. Right-click anywhere in the white space, and select New.

4. Enter the tablespace filename, initial size, maximum size, and extent size (increment amount).

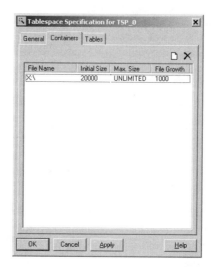

To set up containers within a tablespace (DB2):

1. Right-click the tablespace in the browser and select Open Specification.

2. Select the Containers tab on the specification window.

3. Right-click anywhere in the white space, and select New.

4. Enter the tablespace extent size, prefetch size in pages, page size, and buffer pool name.

   The extent size is the tablespace increment amount in number of pages. A prefetch can speed up a query by fetching more pages than are currently being read by the query. The Prefetch Size field shows the number of pages to be prefetched. The page size is the amount of space (in KB) per page. Finally, the buffer pool is a memory buffer that can be used to hold the prefetched pages.

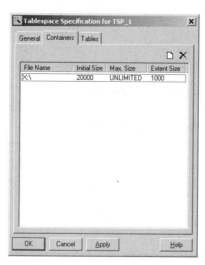

To view the tables that have been assigned to a tablespace:

1. Right-click the tablespace in the browser and select Open Specification.

2. Select the Containers tab on the specification window.

3. Select the Tables tab to view a list of tables in the tablespace.

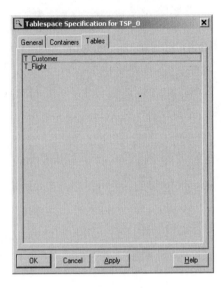

See the upcoming "Adding Tables" section for information about assigning a table to a tablespace.

Adding a Schema

A *schema* is a container for your data model. All of the tables, fields, triggers, constraints, and other data-modeling elements are contained within a schema. The two exceptions are domains, which are contained within domain packages, and the database itself, which is modeled in the Component view.

In the Logical view, there is a package called Schemas. All of the schemas you create for a project are located within this package. Each schema is modeled as a stereotyped package:

Each schema must be mapped to a database in the model. Each database may contain one or more schemas. The DBMS assigned to a schema will be the same as the DBMS assigned to the schema's database.

To create a schema:

1. Right-click the Logical View entry in the browser or the Schemas folder within the Logical view.

2. Select Data Modeler ➤ New ➤ Schema.

3. Right-click the new schema in the browser, and select Open Specification.

4. Select the appropriate database in the Database drop-down list box. The database's DBMS will automatically be filled into the Target field.

Creating a Data Model Diagram

Once the schema has been created, you can create a Data Model diagram within it. A Data Model diagram is used to add, edit, or view tables and other elements within the data model; it serves a similar purpose as the Class diagram in the object model. Although you can add data-modeling elements directly into the browser, the Data Model diagram is a good way to graphically depict the elements and their relationships. You can create as many Data Model diagrams as you need for each schema.

To create a Data Model diagram:

1. Right-click the schema in the browser.

2. Select Data Modeler ➤ New ➤ Data Model Diagram.

3. Type the name of the new diagram.

4. Double-click the diagram to open it.

As with other diagrams in Rose, the Data Model diagram has a specialized toolbar that you can use to add tables, relationships, and other data-modeling elements. Table 18.2 lists the buttons available on this toolbar.

TABLE 18.2: Icons in the Data Model Diagram Toolbar

Icon	Button	Purpose
	Selects or Deselects an Item	Returns the cursor to an arrow to select an item.
	Text Box	Adds a text box to the diagram.
	Note	Adds a note to the diagram.
	Anchor Note to Item	Connects a note to an item in the diagram.
	Table	Adds a new table to the diagram.
	Non-identifying Relationship	Draws a non-identifying relationship between two tables.
	Identifying Relationship	Draws an identifying relationship between two tables.
	View	Adds a new view to the diagram.
	Dependency	Draws a dependency between two tables.

Creating Domain Packages and Domains

A domain can be used to enforce business rules such as required fields, valid values for the fields, and default values for the fields. A *domain* is a pattern that, once established, can be applied to one or more fields in the database. For example, assume you are working with a system that stores many types of phone numbers. You can set up a domain called Phone that would include all of the business rules that apply to all types of phone numbers. In the details of the domain, you can set the data type to Long, set the default value to 0, and indicate that a value is required. Once the domain is set up, you can apply it to various fields in the database: Home_Phone, Work_Phone, Fax_Number, and so on. Each of these fields will now have a data type of Long, a default value of 0, and will be required.

Using domains is entirely optional, but two of the benefits of using domains are consistency and maintenance. Applying domains helps you ensure that the business rules are consistent across many fields—in this case, across all fields related to phone numbers. Domains also centralize the business rules, which can make them easier to change. If, for example, the business rules change and phone numbers are no longer required, you could change the domain and re-create the tables, rather going into each table individually and making the change.

In Rose, domains are located inside a domain package. Each domain package is assigned to a specific DBMS, and all of the domains within it must use the data types provided by that DBMS. If you are working with more than one DBMS in a given project, create separate domain packages for each. A domain is not, however, specific to a schema; a single domain can be used across multiple schemas.

To create a domain package:

1. Right-click the Logical View in the browser.

2. Select Data Modeler ➤ New ➤ Domain Package.

3. Right-click the new package and select Open Specification.

4. Select the DBMS to use for that domain package.

NOTE *Once you have set a DBMS for a domain package, it cannot be changed.*

To create a domain:

1. Right-click the domain package in the browser.

2. Select Data Modeler ➤ New ➤ Domain.

3. Right-click the new domain and select Open Specification.

4. On the General tab, enter the name of the domain.

5. Select Generate on Server to generate a server-based or distinct data type.

6. Select the domain's data type. The choices available in this list box will depend upon the DBMS of the domain package.

7. Enter the field length for the domain. Not all data types require a field length.

8. Enter the precision and scale for the domain. Precision is the number of digits allowed in a numeric field. Scale is the number of digits to the right of the decimal point in the number. Not all data types require a precision or scale.

9. Select Unique Constraint if fields that use the domain must have a unique value. A constraint will be generated in the database if this field is checked. Note that not all data types will allow a unique constraint.

10. Select Not Null if fields that use this domain must contain a value.

11. Select For Bit Data (DB2 only) if the domain should support ForBitData.

12. Enter a default value, or select a value from the list box if fields that use this domain should have a default.

On the Check Constraints tab of the specification window, you can set constraints for the domain. A *constraint* is an expression that must be true before data can be altered in the database. For example, you may want to enforce a business rule that requires all transactions in an accounting system to have a transaction number greater than 1000. You can create a domain called Transaction, and add a constraint that checks the value of the field and returns False if the value is less than 1000.

Constraints can also be added to individual tables; we will discuss this in the next section, "Adding Tables." A domain constraint appears in the browser below the domain, and has the stereotype <<Check>>.

On the Check Constraints tab, select New to add a new constraint. Rose will automatically create a constraint name for you and populate the Name field. In the Expression field, enter the SQL statement for the constraint. To edit an existing constraint, select the constraint from the drop-down list box in the Name field.

You can drag and drop a domain onto a Data Model diagram. Rose will use the following symbols if the stereotype display is set to Decoration or Icon, respectively.

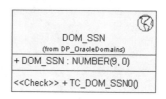

Adding Tables

Once you have established a schema, you can create tables in it. Each table in a database is modeled as a persistent class in Rose with a stereotype of Table. The tables within a schema must have unique names. In Rose, a table is modeled using the following symbols, when the stereotype display option is set to Decoration or Icon, respectively:

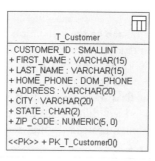

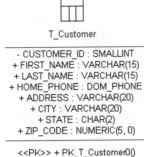

T_Customer

- CUSTOMER_ID : SMALLINT
+ FIRST_NAME : VARCHAR(15)
+ LAST_NAME : VARCHAR(15)
+ HOME_PHONE : DOM_PHONE
+ ADDRESS : VARCHAR(20)
+ CITY : VARCHAR(20)
+ STATE : CHAR(2)
+ ZIP_CODE : NUMERIC(5, 0)

<<PK>> + PK_T_Customer0()

The DBMS for the table is set by the DBMS of the schema containing it. In other words, all tables within a schema use the same DBMS.

To add a table:

1. Open a Data Model diagram.

2. Select the Table button from the toolbar.

3. Click anywhere inside the diagram to create the table.

4. Type the name of the new table.

OR

1. Right-click the schema in the Logical view.

2. Select Data Modeler ➤ New ➤ Table.

3. Type the name of the new table.

The next step in the process is to add details to the tables: fields, keys, indexes, constraints, and triggers.

Adding Columns

Each field, or column, in the database is modeled as an attribute in the Logical view under the table that contains it.

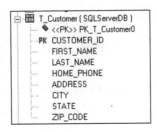

There are two types of columns: data columns and computed columns. A computed column uses a SQL statement to calculate its value from one or more other columns. For example, a company might have a retirement fund set up, and each employee is able to place a maximum of 4 percent of their annual salary into this fund. The table Employee would include the two columns: AnnualSalary and MaxRetirementContribution. The value in MaxRetirementContribution would be equal to 4 percent of the value in AnnualSalary. MaxRetirementContribution, therefore, is a computed column. A data column is any column that does not contain a calculated value.

Microsoft SQL Server also supports the concept of an identity column, which is a column with a system-generated value. For example, an identity column with a data type of Integer would assign the values 1, 2, 3, 4, and so on to the rows in the table.

To add a column:

1. Right-click the table and select Open Specification.

2. Select the Columns tab of the specification window.

3. Right-click anywhere in the white space and select Insert.

4. Double-click the new column. This will open the Column Specification window.

5. Enter the name of the new column.

6. Select the Type tab:

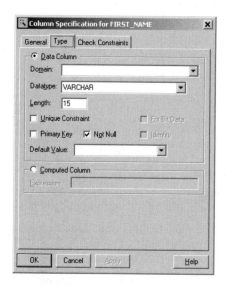

7. Select the Data Column or Computed Column radio button (SQL Server only).

8. If the column is a data column, enter the following:

   ◆ Domain, if you have created a domain and wish to apply it to this column. If you use a domain, you will not need to enter any of the following fields other than Unique Constraint or Primary Key. The domain definition will cause the other fields to be automatically filled in for you.

♦ Data Type for the column. The choices available in this drop-down list box will depend on the DBMS for this table.

♦ Length, which is the number of characters allowed in the column. This value cannot be set for all data types.

♦ Precision, which is the number of digits allowed in a numeric column. This value cannot be set for all data types.

♦ Scale, which is the number of digits to the right of the decimal point in a numeric column. This value cannot be set for all data types.

♦ Unique Constraint, if the values in the column must be unique.

♦ Primary Key, if this is the identifying column for the table. You can create a composite primary key by selecting this option for more than one column. When a column is a primary key, it has a red "PK" to the left of it in the browser.

♦ Not Null, if the column will not allow null values. If you set the Primary Key option, the Not Null option must also be set.

♦ Identity (SQL Server only), if this is an identity column. SQL Server will automatically generate values for an identity column. Note that the data type must be a numeric type to allow this option.

♦ For Bit Data (DB2 only), if the column supports ForBitData.

9. If the column is a computed column (SQL Server only), enter the SQL statement that will be used to calculate the column value.

10. Select the Check Constraints tab and add constraints if necessary. See the upcoming section, "Adding Constraints."

OR

1. Right-click the table in the Logical view.

2. Select Data Modeler ➤ New ➤ Column.

3. Type the name of the new column.

4. Double-click the new column to open the Column Specification window. Complete the column specifications as described above.

Setting a Primary Key

If a column is marked as a primary key, it is the identifying column for the table. In other words, it contains the unique values that distinguish the rows from each other. For example, the primary key in an Employee table might be the Social Security number.

To set the primary key for a table:

1. Right-click the column in the Logical view, and select Open Specification.

2. Select the Type tab in the Column Specification window.

3. Select the Primary Key option.

Note that if you set a column as the primary key, the Not Null field is automatically checked and cannot be deselected. Primary keys cannot contain null values.

Adding Constraints

A constraint is a conditional statement that must be true in order for a table to be updated. You can add a constraint either to a domain, as described above, or to a table. Constraints are a way to enforce business rules. An example of using constraints might be checking that the value in a Birth_date field is prior to the current date. You can check that the value in a State field is a valid state abbreviation or that the value in a Gender field is M or F.

KEY CONSTRAINTS

There are three types of key constraints: primary key constraints, unique constraints, and indexes. A *primary key constraint* ensures that the value entered into a primary key field is not null and is unique. Rose automatically creates a primary key constraint for you when you create a primary key for a table.

A *unique constraint* ensures that the value entered into a column is unique. Rose automatically creates a unique constraint for you when you select the Unique Constraint check box for a field on the Column Specification window.

An *index* provides quick access to records by searching only through a list of key columns when searching for rows in the table.

To add a key constraint:

1. Open the table or Column Specification window.

2. Select the Key Constraints tab.

3. Click New.

4. Select the type: Primary Key Constraint, Unique Constraint, or Index.

5. In the Columns list box, select the column(s) to which the constraint applies. Use the Add button to move the selected columns to the Key Columns list box.

6. Select the Deferrable check box (Oracle and SQL 92 only) if you want to make the constraint deferred. A nondeferred constraint will run at the end of a statement. A deferred, initially immediate constraint will run at the beginning of a transaction. A deferred, initially deferred constraint will run at the end of a transaction.

7. Select the Unique check box (index constraint) if the index is unique.

8. Select the Clustered check box if you want to make an index clustered.

9. In the Fill Factor/PCT Threshold/PCTFree field, optionally enter the free percentage (1–100) of the index. Each DBMS has a different name for this field.

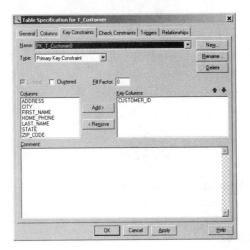

CHECK CONSTRAINTS

A *check constraint* is any constraint other than a primary key, unique, or index constraint. In other words, it is any constraint other than a key constraint. Check constraints are added on the specification window of either a field or table. The constraints themselves are linked to the table, but you can enter them in either location.

To add a check constraint:

1. Open the table or Column Specification window.

2. Select the Check Constraints tab.

3. Click New.

4. In the Expression field, enter the SQL statement for the constraint.

5. If you are using Oracle or SQL 92, you can select the Deferrable option. Nondeferrable constraints are evaluated at the end of the SQL statement. For example, a nondeferrable constraint might be evaluated at the end of an insert statement. Deferrable constraints can be Initially Immediate, in which case they are evaluated at the beginning of the statement. Deferrable constraints can also be Initially Deferred, in which case they are evaluated at the end of the transaction.

Once a check constraint has been added, it appears in the browser underneath the table, and has a stereotype of <<Check>>.

Adding Triggers

A *trigger* is a SQL procedure that runs upon a specific event. For example, you can set up a trigger to run every time a record is inserted into a specific table. Triggers can be set up to run when a row is inserted, changed, or deleted.

The specifications for a trigger will vary with the DBMS you are using. A trigger will be modeled in the Logical view, under the table to which it applies, and will have the stereotype <<Trigger>>.

To add a trigger:

1. Open the Table Specification window.

2. Select the Triggers tab.

3. Click New.

4. Set the Trigger Event:

   ◆ Select Insert if the trigger should run when a row is inserted.

   ◆ Select Delete if the trigger should run when a row is removed.

   ◆ Select Update if the trigger should run when a row is changed. If you select Update, enter the column that should be updated for the trigger to run.

5. Set the Trigger Type:

   ◆ Before will run the trigger before the trigger event.

   ◆ After will run the trigger after the trigger event.

◆ Instead Of will run a view trigger instead of a table trigger. The Instead Of option is available only when creating a trigger for a SQL Server 2000 or Oracle view.

6. Set the Granularity (Oracle and DB2 only) to Row if the trigger should run after each row is inserted, updated, or deleted; set it to Statement if the trigger should run after the statement has executed.

7. Set the Referencing check box if you want to set up references in the trigger. Enter the name of the Old Row, which is the name of the row before the trigger executes, and the New Row, which is the name of the row after the trigger executes. In DB2, you can also enter Old Table, which is the name of the table before the trigger executes, and New Table, which is the name of the table after the trigger executes.

8. Enter a value in the When Clause field if you wish to further refine when the trigger executes. The When Clause is a condition that must be true for the trigger to execute.

9. Enter the SQL statement for the trigger in the Action Body field.

Adding Indexes

An *index* is modeled as a key constraint in a table. An index is a structure that allows for quick searches of a table. One or more columns are used for an index; when a search is performed, only those columns are searched.

To add an index:

1. Open the table or Column Specification window.

2. Select the Key Constraints tab.

3. Click New.

4. Set the Type to Index.

5. In the Columns list box, select the column(s) that will be used in the index. Use the Add button to move the selected columns to the Key Columns list box.

6. Select the Deferrable check box (Oracle and SQL 92 only) if you want to make the constraint deferred. A nondeferred constraint will run at the end of a statement. A deferred, initially immediate constraint will run at the beginning of a transaction. A deferred, initially deferred constraint will run at the end of a transaction.

7. Select the Unique check box (Index constraint) if the index is unique.

8. In the Fill Factor field (or PCT Threshold field for Oracle), optionally enter the free percentage (1–100) of the index.

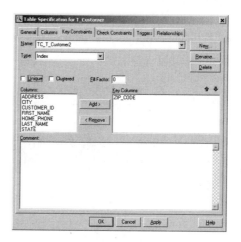

Adding Stored Procedures

Like a trigger, a *stored procedure* is a piece of functionality in the database. It is essentially a small program that can be invoked directly by the application or by a trigger. It can accept input parameters and return one or more values, called output parameters.

Some DBMS packages support two types of stored procedures: regular stored procedures and functions. A function returns a value, while a stored procedure does not. A stored procedure can, however, return an output parameter.

In Rose, a stored procedure is modeled as an operation with the stereotype <<SP>>. It is created within a special class with a stereotype of <<SP Container>>. A stored procedure is not specific to a table, and is therefore created underneath the schema rather than underneath a table.

To add a stored procedure:

1. Right-click the schema in the browser.

2. Select Data Modeler ➤ New ➤ Stored Procedure.

3. Rose will create a stored procedure container and place the new stored procedure in it. To create a stored procedure inside an existing container, right-click the existing container and select New ➤ Stored Procedure.

4. Right-click the new stored procedure and select Open Specification.

5. On the General tab, enter the following:

- In the Name field, enter the name of the stored procedure.

- In the Language field, enter the language for the stored procedure. In most cases, the language will be SQL. Some DBMS packages also support other languages, such as C, Java, or COBOL.

- In the External Name field, enter the path or library for the procedure. This field is not needed if the language is set to SQL.

- In the Type field, enter the type (procedure or function) of stored procedure. A function returns a value while a stored procedure does not. Not all DBMS packages support functions.

- In the Return Type field, enter the data type of the value returned from a function. This field is not needed unless the stored procedure is a function.

- In the Length field, enter the number of characters in the return value. This field is not needed for all data types.

- In the Precision field, enter the number of digits to the right of the decimal point in the return value. This field is not needed for all data types.

- In the Scale field, enter the number of digits in the return value. This field is not needed for all data types.

- The Null Input Action (DB2) field controls what should happen if the function receives a null parameter. Return Null will return a null value from the function. Call Procedure will cause the function to run even with a null parameter.

- The Parameter Style (DB2) field sets the way parameters should be sent to and received from a stored procedure.

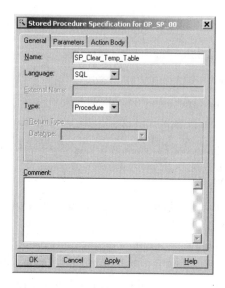

6. On the Parameters tab, enter any needed parameters. Right-click the white space and select Insert to add a new parameter. Enter the following:

◆ Parameter data type.

◆ Length, precision, and scale, if necessary.

◆ Direction: In is used for an input parameter. Out is used for an output parameter, which is similar to a return value. In Out is used for an input parameter that may be changed by the stored procedure and is then output to the calling application or trigger.

◆ Default value, if needed.

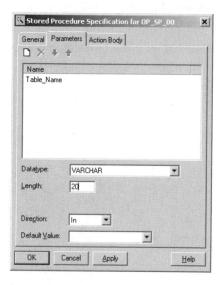

7. On the Action Body tab, enter the SQL for the stored procedure.

Adding Relationships

A relationship in the data model is similar to a relationship in the object model. Where a relationship in the object model joins two classes, a relationship in the data model joins two tables. There are two primary types of relationships supported by Rose: identifying relationships and non-identifying relationships.

In either case, a foreign key is added to the child table to support the relationship. With an identifying relationship, the foreign key becomes part of the primary key of the child table. In this situation, a record cannot exist in the child table without being linked to a record in the parent table. An identifying relationship is modeled as a composite aggregation:

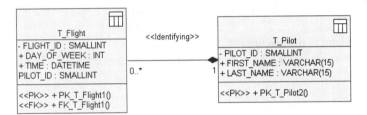

A non-identifying relationship will still create a foreign key in the child table, but the foreign key field will not become part of the primary key of the child table. In a non-identifying relationship, the relationship cardinality (multiplicity) controls whether a record in the child table can exist without a link to a record in the parent table. If the cardinality is 1, a parent record must exist. If the cardinality is 0..1, the parent record does not need to exist. A non-identifying relationship is modeled as an association:

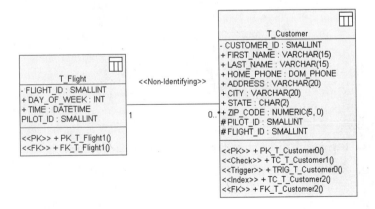

To add an identifying relationship:

1. Select the Identifying Relationship toolbar button.

2. Drag and drop from the parent table to the child table.

3. Rose will automatically add a primary key constraint and a foreign key constraint to the child table.

To add a non-identifying relationship:

1. Select the Non-identifying Relationship toolbar button.

2. Drag and drop from the parent table to the child table.

3. Rose will automatically add a foreign key constraint to the child table.

Cardinality defines the number of rows in one table related to a single row in another table. Cardinality in the data model has much the same meaning as cardinality in the object model. You set cardinality options on both ends of the relationship. The cardinality at the end of the relationship nearest the parent can be set to 1 if the relationship is mandatory, or set to 0..1 if the relationship is optional. The cardinality nearest the child table controls how many records in the child table can be created for each record in the parent table.

A many-to-many relationship is modeled through the use of a join table:

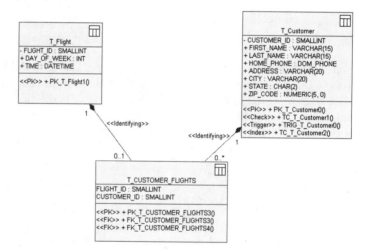

To set cardinality and other relationship specifications:

1. Right-click the relationship and select Open Specification.

2. Select the General tab.

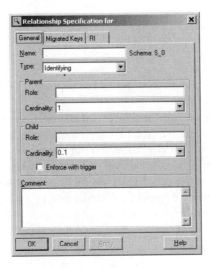

3. Enter the name of the relationship if desired.

4. Select the type of relationship (Identifying or Non-identifying).

5. Assign roles to the parent and child tables (optional).

6. Set the cardinality for both sides of the relationship.

7. Select the Enforce with Trigger check box to automatically generate a trigger that will enforce the cardinality rules you just established.

8. Select the Migrated Keys tab.

9. The names of the fields in the child and parent table that participate in the relationship are listed. You can change the field names here if needed.

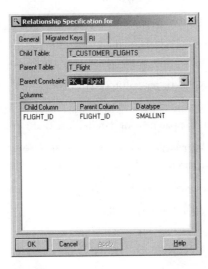

Adding Referential Integrity Rules

Referential integrity establishes a set of rules that help keep the data consistent. For John Doe, for example, you may have an employee record in the employee table and two address records (one for his home address and one for his work address) in the address table. If the John Doe record in the employee table is deleted, the address records will be "orphaned" (that is, they will no longer have an employee to refer to).

Referential integrity helps avoid these situations by specifying what should happen when the parent record is updated or deleted. You have several options. One option is for the child record(s) to be automatically updated or deleted. Or, you can prevent the parent from being updated or deleted at all. Or, you can run a trigger when updating or deleting the parent record. Once you choose your option, you enter this information on the relationship specification in Rose.

There are two primary types of referential integrity: trigger or declarative. Trigger-enforced referential integrity will run a trigger when the parent is updated or deleted. Declarative referential integrity includes the constraint as part of the foreign key clause. The following options are available when setting referential integrity:

- Cascade determines that when the parent is updated or deleted, all child records are updated or deleted.

- Restrict prevents the parent from being updated or deleted.

- Set Null sets the foreign keys in the child record to Null if the parent record is updated or deleted.

- No Action does not enforce referential integrity at all.

- Set Default sets the foreign keys in the child record to a default value if the parent record is updated or deleted.

To set referential integrity for a relationship:

1. Right-click the relationship and select Open Specification.

2. Select the RI (referential integrity) tab.

3. Select either the Triggers or the Declarative Referential Integrity radio button to control whether a trigger-enforced or declarative referential integrity rule will be used.

4. If you selected a trigger-enforced rule, enter the following:

   - Parent Update sets the option (Cascade, Restrict, Set Null, No Action, Set Default) to use when the parent is updated. Note that not all options are supported by each DBMS.

   - Parent Delete sets the option (Cascade, Restrict, Set Null, No Action, Set Default) to use when the parent is deleted. Note that not all options are supported by each DBMS.

   - Child Restrict, if checked, will prevent orphan child records from being created.

5. If you selected a declarative rule, enter the following:

◆ Parent Update sets the option (Cascade, Restrict, Set Null, No Action, Set Default) to use when the parent is updated. Note that not all options are supported by each DBMS.

◆ Parent Delete sets the option (Cascade, Restrict, Set Null, No Action, Set Default) to use when the parent is deleted. Note that not all options are supported by each DBMS.

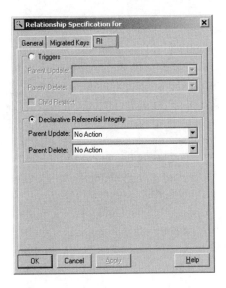

Working with Views

A *view* is a way of looking at the data a little differently than it is structured in the database. You can create a "virtual" table using a view that will contain data from one or more tables in the database. Views help secure the database; you can give a group of users read-only access to a view in order to prevent accidental modifications of the underlying data.

In Rose, a view is modeled using the following symbol:

On the Data Model diagram, a dependency is drawn between the view and the table or tables that are the source of its data, as shown in Figure 18.1.

FIGURE 18.1

Modeling a view

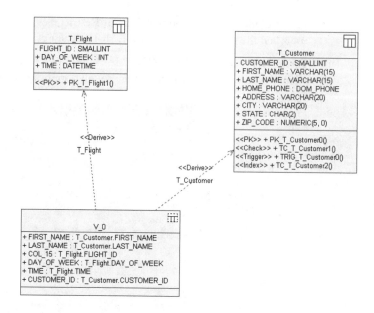

To create a view:

1. Right-click the schema in the browser.

2. Select Data Modeler ➣ New ➣ View.

3. Name the new view.

4. Right-click the new view and select Open Specification.

5. On the General tab, enter the following:

   ◆ Name is used to name or rename the view. Each view within a schema must have a unique name.

   ◆ Schema displays the name of the schema that contains the view. This field cannot be changed.

   ◆ Updateable controls whether a user can modify data using the view. This field can be set only when using Oracle, DB2, or SQL 92.

   ◆ Distinct determines that, if this is set, only unique rows will be included in the view.

   ◆ Materialized (Oracle) means that, if this option is set, the view will be populated when it is forward engineered from Rose. If this option is not set, the view will still be created, but will not be populated with data.

   ◆ Check Option controls what constraints will be applied to the view. The None option will prevent constraints from being enforced on the view. The Local option will enforce any constraints you have set up for the view or for any views dependent on this view. The Cascade option will enforce any constraints you have set up for the view, constraints for dependent views, and constraints for the tables that contain the source data.

6. On the From tab, enter the following:

◆ Select the table(s) and/or view(s) from the Available Members list box that you would like to use in the view. Press Add to move the selected tables or views to the View Members list box.

◆ The Correlation Name field sets the alias that will be used for the table or view in the current view's SQL statement.

◆ In the Where Clause field, enter a SQL where clause, order by, or group by statement that will be included in the view. Be sure to include the phrase "WHERE," "ORDER BY," or "GROUP BY."

7. On the Columns tab, enter the following:

   ♦ View Columns lists the columns that will be included in the view. To add a new column, select the Import Columns button. A list of all available columns will be displayed. To remove a column, select it and press the Delete toolbar button.

   ♦ Alias shows the alias name of the column.

8. On the SQL tab, you can see the SQL statement that was built as you selected tables and columns on the other tabs. You can also enter a SQL statement directly into this window, or change the SQL statement Rose has generated for you. As you change the SQL statement, Rose will update the table and column selections on the other tabs.

Generating an Object Model from a Data Model

One of the new features of Rose is the ability to automatically generate an object model from a data model. This feature is particularly useful when you are working on a project to re-engineer an existing application and database. You can reverse engineer an existing database, and then generate the object model from it. Of course, this feature is useful in other types of projects as well. Any time you want to be sure that the object model and data model are consistent, or you want to reverse engineer information from an existing database or data model, the object model generation is helpful.

Not all of the constructs in the data model have meaning in an object model. Indexes, stored procedure, and other database elements are not mapped to the object model. Table 18.3 lists the data model elements and the corresponding object model elements.

TABLE 18.3: DATA MODEL AND OBJECT MODEL ELEMENTS

DATA MODEL ELEMENT	OBJECT MODEL ELEMENT
Schema	Package
Table	Class
Column	Attribute
Trigger	None
Stored procedure	None
Intersection table with only primary/foreign key columns	Many-to-many association
Intersection table with columns other than primary/foreign key	Many-to-many association with association class
Identifying relationship	Composite aggregation
Non-identifying relationship	Association
Cardinality	Cardinality
Index	None
Database	None
Constraint	None
Domain	None

To create an object model from a data model:

1. Right-click the schema and select Data Modeler ➤ Transform to Object Model.

2. Enter the destination package name. The destination package is the name of a package that will be created in the Logical view to hold the new objects.

3. Enter the prefix. The prefix will be added to the name of each table to create the classes in the object model.

4. Select the Include Primary Keys check box to create attributes for the primary key columns as well as for the other columns. If this check box is not selected, Rose will generate attributes for the non-primary key columns, but not for the primary key columns.

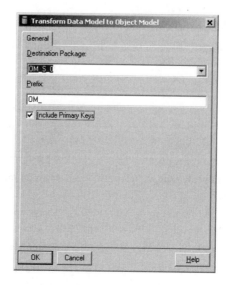

Generating a Data Model from an Object Model

Just as you can generate an object model from a data model, you can generate a data model from an object model. As the project progresses and you have discovered more entity classes, generating the data model will give you a good start to your database design.

When generating the data model, Rose will look for classes with the persistent attribute marked as True. You can set a class to Persistent or Transient in the standard class specification window on the Detail tab. If you want to generate a table for the class, set it to Persistent.

A package of classes in the Logical view will become a schema in the data model. If there is an existing schema of the same name, Rose will add any new classes as tables in the schema. It will not, however, change the tables in the schema if classes in the object model change. Instead, it will note the changes in a log so that you can apply them to the schema if you wish.

Table 18.4 lists object model elements and their corresponding data model elements.

TABLE 18.4: OBJECT MODEL AND DATA MODEL ELEMENTS

OBJECT MODEL ELEMENT	DATA MODEL ELEMENT
Package	Schema
Persistent class	Table
Attribute	Column
Operation	None
Many-to-many association	Intersection table

Continued on next page

TABLE 18.4: Object Model and Data Model Elements *(continued)*

OBJECT MODEL ELEMENT	DATA MODEL ELEMENT
Composite aggregation	Identifying relationship
Association or non-composite aggregation	Non-identifying relationship
Cardinality	Cardinality
Association class	Intersection table

To create a data model from an object model:

1. Create a database in the Component view.

2. Right-click any attribute in the classes that you wish to become a primary key in the generated tables. Select Data Modeler Part of Object Identity. If you do not select a primary key attribute, Rose will create a primary key for you by creating a column called "<table name>ID."

3. Right-click a package in the Logical view and select Data Modeler ➤ Transform to Data Model.

4. Enter the destination schema name, which is the name of a schema that will be created to hold the new data elements.

5. Enter the target database, which is the name of an existing database in the Component view.

6. Enter a prefix that will be added to each class name to create the table names.

7. Select the Create Indexes for Foreign Keys check box to automatically create index constraints for foreign keys.

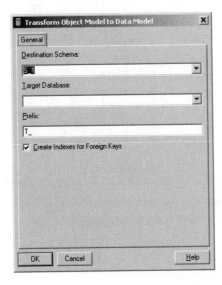

Generating a Database from a Data Model

At any point during the project, you can generate the database or DDL script from the data model. Rose gives you the choice of simply generating the DDL or running the DDL to create the database.

Rose includes a wizard that walks you through the steps of creating the database. To begin, right-click a schema to generate and select Data Modeler ➤ Forward Engineer. After the welcome screen, select the elements you wish to generate:

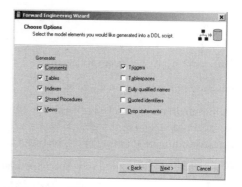

Next, enter the name of the DDL file to create. If you want to create the DDL, but not run it, click Next. If you want to run the new DDL against a database, select the Execute check box. Enter the connection information for your DBMS and press the Test Connection button to be sure that the connection is working properly.

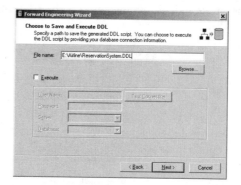

Press Finish to complete the process. Rose will generate the DDL and optionally run it against the database. If any errors are encountered, Rose will add them to the log.

All of the tables, columns, and relationships in the schema will be generated in the DDL or database. The following example shows a table in the Rose model.

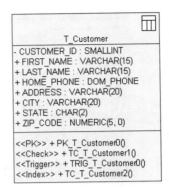

The following is the corresponding DDL:

```
CREATE TABLE T_Customer (
    CUSTOMER_ID SMALLINT IDENTITY NOT NULL,
    FIRST_NAME VARCHAR ( 15 ) NOT NULL,
    LAST_NAME VARCHAR ( 15 ) NOT NULL,
    HOME_PHONE NUMERIC ( 10 ) NOT NULL,
    ADDRESS VARCHAR ( 20 ) NOT NULL,
    CITY VARCHAR ( 20 ) NOT NULL,
    STATE CHAR ( 2 ) NOT NULL,
    ZIP_CODE NUMERIC ( 5 ) NOT NULL,
    CONSTRAINT PK_T_Customer0 PRIMARY KEY NONCLUSTERED (CUSTOMER_ID),
    CONSTRAINT TC_T_Customer1 CHECK (CUSTOMER_ID > 1000)
    ) ON TSP_0
GO

CREATE INDEX TC_T_Customer2 ON T_Customer (ZIP_CODE)
GO
```

Updating an Existing Database

Once a database has been created, you may make changes to either the data model in Rose or the database itself. Frequently, the two get out of synchronization, which can cause difficulties when trying to further modify the database design or maintain the application later.

Rose includes a compare-and-synchronize feature to address this problem. The feature includes a graphical, side-by-side representation of the database and data model. Using this feature, you can select the changes to be made to the data model or database to synchronize the two again.

To begin the synchronization, right-click a schema and select Data Modeler ➤ Compare and Sync. You will be given the option to synchronize with either a DDL script or a database. If you select DDL script, you will be prompted for the name of the script. If you select database, you will be prompted for the database connection information.

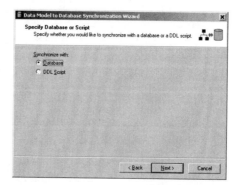

Next, select the options you would like to synchronize. Rose will always synchronize tables and constraints, but you can also synchronize indexes, triggers, and other elements.

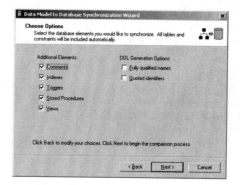

Rose will then display the differences between the model and the database, as shown in Figure 18.2. Select a difference in the table, and then select one of the following four options from the toolbar:

◆ Import, which will import the change from the database into the data model

◆ Export, which will export the change from the data model to the database

◆ Delete, which will remove the change from both the data model and the database

◆ Ignore, which will ignore the change

Once you finish the changes, select Next. Rose will allow you to preview the changes to be made. When you are satisfied with the list of changes, press Next to commit the changes.

FIGURE 18.2

Model and database compare-and-synchronize feature

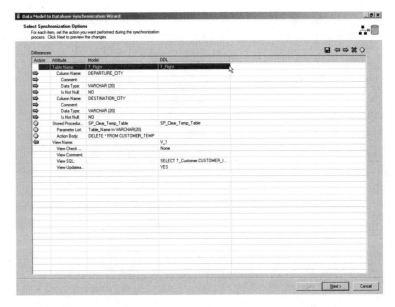

Reverse Engineering a Database

You can reverse engineer a database into a data model in Rose. When you reverse engineer the database, Rose will create the database component in the Component view and the tables and other database elements in a schema in the Logical view. Once you have reverse engineered the database, you can generate an object model or perform a synchronization using the methods described earlier in this chapter.

To begin the process, select Tools ➤ Data Modeler ➤ Reverse Engineer. After the welcome screen, you will be asked whether to reverse engineer from a DDL script or a database. If you select DDL, you will be prompted for the target DBMS and the name of the file. If you select database, you will be prompted for the database connection information.

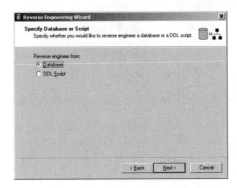

Next, select the item(s) to reverse engineer. Tables and constraints will always be imported, but you can select other elements to reverse engineer.

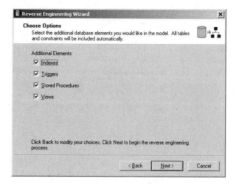

When you have finished, click Next. Rose will create a schema in the Logical view. Within this schema will be the tables, constraints, and other model elements from your database. If Rose encounters any problems during the reverse-engineering process, these will be noted in the log. Rose will also create a new component in the Component view. This component represents the database itself.

Summary

In this chapter, we examined the data-modeling capabilities of Rose. Combining the object model and data model into a single tool helps the team gain a more complete understanding of the system structure and organization. The forward- and reverse-engineering capabilities help you ensure that your object model, data model, and database stay synchronized.

In this chapter, we specifically discussed the following:

◆ The differences between an object model and a data model

◆ How to create a data model

◆ How to add data-modeling elements

◆ How to generate an object model from a data model

◆ How to generate a data model from an object model

◆ How to generate and reverse engineer a database

◆ How to keep your object model, data model, and database synchronized

In the next chapter, we'll focus on web development, looking at the different stereotypes and tools Rose provides to model an Internet or intranet application. With these tools, you can model ASP, JSP, HTML pages, and other web objects. Using Class diagrams, you can see the relationships between these objects and analyze your application architecture. The Rose Web Modeler add-in is an excellent way to visualize existing applications or to design new ones.

Chapter 19

Web Modeling

IN THIS WORLD OF e-business, e-commerce, and e-government, no discussion of UML would be complete without a discussion of web modeling. Although similar to traditional client/server applications, web applications have their own unique benefits and challenges, which naturally affect their design.

Rose 2001, 2001A, and 2002 include an add-in that supports the code generation and reverse engineering of web applications. You can model and generate HTML pages, ASP pages, JSP pages, and other types of web classes using Rose.

◆ Modeling a web application

◆ Reverse engineering a web application

◆ Generating code for a web application

Modeling a Web Application

Whether you are creating a new web application from scratch, or reverse engineering and modifying an existing application (see "Reverse Engineering a Web Application" later in this chapter), it is necessary to first gain an understanding of the different web stereotypes and relationships. Before we look at these, however, let's take a look at web architecture in general.

In many ways, a web application is similar to a traditional distributed application. The logic is divided into two or more areas, or tiers. At a minimum, the presentation logic is separated into the presentation layer, and the business logic is separated into a server logic layer. The presentation layer runs on the client, while the business logic runs on the server. In many cases, the business logic is separated into two or more layers of its own. For example, the logic dealing with the connection to the database may be separated from the rest of the business logic.

One of the primary differences between a web application and a traditional distributed system is in the persistency of the connection between the two (or more) layers. In a distributed system, once objects have been instantiated on the client and the server, they can communicate with each other only when needed. A web application, on the other hand, is stateless—once the communication between the client and the server ends, the server loses all information about the client. It no longer knows who was logged in or what they were doing. One way to manage this challenge is through the use of cookies. A *cookie* is a file that resides on the client and can store state information about the client so that the next time a connection is established with the server, the contents of the cookie can be used to give the server state information.

Another difference lies in the deployment environment. An advantage of the Web, of course, is the ability to reach thousands of users without needing to worry about setting up each machine. The disadvantage is the ability to reach thousands of machines, many of which may have slightly different configurations. Different browsers, operating systems, connection speed, processor, memory configuration, and other factors can complicate web deployment. Not all components will run with all browsers, so the designer has extra work to do if the application must run on several different types of browsers.

There are two primary patterns to a web architecture: thin client and thick client. In a thin client architecture, very little logic is placed on the client side. Few, if any, ActiveX controls, applets, or other components are downloaded to the client browser and run on the client machine. Two of the advantages of this approach are speed and portability. Downloading components to the client can be very slow, so minimizing the number of downloads helps to increase the speed of the application. A thin client architecture can also be more portable, because not every component will work on every type of browser. Minimizing the number of different component technologies needed for your application can help ensure that the application will work in different browsers. The disadvantage to the thin client approach is that the user interface can't necessarily have a lot of bells and whistles; client-side components may be needed to provide an enhanced user interface.

The second approach to a web application is to use a thick client architecture. In a thick client, more logic is run on the client. When a component is needed on the client, it will be automatically downloaded from the server. This approach gives the team the option of including more sophisticated controls on the user interface. The team can also build applets or other components to run some logic on the client. The advantage of this approach is the ability to create more robust user interfaces. The disadvantages are speed and portability. The downloads take time, and there is no guarantee that the different browsers will support the application if too many different types of components are downloaded.

The process of modeling a web application begins just like the process of modeling a client/server application—with analysis. The team defines the use cases, gathers and documents the requirements, and writes the flow of events for the use cases. We won't discuss this in detail here; see Chapter 4, "Use Cases and Actors," for information about use cases and actors.

Once the flow of events has been written for a use case and its requirements have been documented, the design process can begin for that use case. This involves the creation of Sequence diagrams, Collaboration diagrams, Class diagrams, Statechart diagrams, Component diagrams, and Deployment diagrams.

As in a client/server application, Sequence and Collaboration diagrams show the objects that participate in a use case scenario. As the designers are building and reviewing the Sequence diagrams, however, they must keep the web architecture in mind. There are a few primary considerations. First, because the application is stateless, the designers cannot assume that once an object is instantiated, it can be accessed indefinitely by the other objects. As soon as the connection between the client and server is broken, objects on one layer cannot access objects on the other, and the server loses all information about the state of the client. The designers can, however, use cookies and session objects to store state information. A cookie is a small file on the client machine that can be used to store state information, while a session object is created on the server and holds information about a particular client through the life of the client's session. After a period of time, say 30 minutes, the server assumes that the client has timed out, and the session object will be released.

If the team uses session objects, they will appear in the Sequence and Collaboration diagrams, just as any other objects. One very useful tool in Rose 2001A and 2002 is the ability to place destruction marks on the Sequence diagrams. This notation can make it easier for the team to remember which objects are available in memory at which point in time.

A second consideration in web modeling is that client pages should not have access to server resources. The designers should ensure that none of the pages, applets, or other client-side components can directly access the server. Instead, they should access a server page, which can then access the server-side components. If the application is a thin client, the designers should minimize the number of components downloaded to the client machine. As they are building the Sequence and Collaboration diagrams, therefore, the team should not use many client-side components.

Before you begin modeling, you will need an area in Rose to create your classes. You will work in the Logical view, but you must first set up a virtual directory. A *virtual directory* is a stereotyped package in Rose that represents a physical directory on your network. Any classes in the virtual directory will be generated into the physical directory.

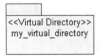

To create the virtual directory:

1. Right-click the Logical view in the browser.

2. Select Web Modeler ➤ New ➤ Virtual Directory.

3. Right-click the new virtual directory. The specification window will appear:

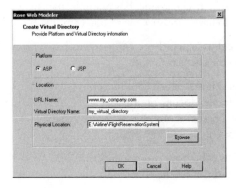

4. Select the platform (ASP or JSP) you will use for this application.

5. Enter the URL of your web application. Rose requires the URL to generate code or to reverse engineer web classes into the model.

6. Enter the virtual directory name. This is the name of the virtual directory package that will appear in the Logical view in Rose. All of the classes for this web application will be placed in this package.

7. Enter the physical location. All classes in this web application will be generated into this location and reverse engineered from this location.

Once you have created the virtual directory, you can create web objects inside it.

Web Class Stereotypes

To model your web application, you will need to create classes to represent your client pages, server pages, and HTML pages. To complete the picture, you can then add relationships between these model elements. When Rose generates code, it will examine both the classes and the relationships.

There are three different types of class stereotypes that can be generated or reverse engineered in Rose: client pages, server pages, and HTML pages.

CLIENT PAGES

Client pages are HTML-formatted pages that run on the client. These contain some functionality, but typically do not include intensive business logic. Logic on the client pages is usually related to presentation of the data. Client pages do not directly access business objects on the server; this is the role of a server page. In Rose, a client page has the following notation:

Client Page

The functionality in a client page can be programmed in either VBScript or JavaScript. Any scripting here is strictly client-side. For example, the client page may format some text on the screen. Client pages do have access to any resources available on the client. These resources could include:

◆ ActiveX controls, which are components based on the Microsoft COM model, that are downloaded to the client machine.

◆ JavaScript objects, which could be objects provided by the document object model, such as window, frame, document, image, etc. These could also be custom objects defined by the programmer. These custom objects can be assigned their own attributes and operations, but are not reverse engineered into Rose.

◆ Java applets, which are components that, like ActiveX controls, are downloaded to the client machine and run on the client.

Typically, you use these three types of components to add complex functionality to the client. HTML will give you some flexibility, but it is frequently not sophisticated enough to program complex client-side behavior.

ActiveX controls and applets can be modeled in Rose as classes or components with the stereotype of <<ActiveX>> or <<Applet>>. Because a component may consist of several classes, you can simply model an ActiveX control or applet in the Component view. If you want to model the classes within a component or show the relationships between your classes and the component, you can model the control or applet as a class in the Logical view as well.

To add a client page:

1. Right-click the virtual directory in the Logical view.

2. Select Web Modeler ➤ New ➤ Client Page.

3. Enter the name of the new page.

OR

Create a server page using the method described in the following section, "Server Pages." A client page will automatically be created for each server page you create using this method.

In the specification for the client page, you can set detailed attributes for the client page. Table 19.1 lists the attributes and their meanings:

TABLE 19.1: CLIENT PAGE ATTRIBUTES

ATTRIBUTE	SPECIFICATION WINDOW TAB	MEANING
Alink	General	Link color
Background	General	URI to background image
BgColor	General	Background color
BottomMargin	General	Bottom margin in pixels
Class	General	Class name for element
Dir	General	Text direction for element
ID	General	Element name
Lang	General	Language of element's content
LeftMargin	General	Left margin in pixels
Link	General	Text color of links
MarginHeight	General	Frame margin height in pixels
MarginWidth	General	Frame margin width in pixels
RightMargin	General	Right margin in pixels
Style	General	Style information for element
Text	General	Text color
Title	General	Additional element information

Continued on next page

TABLE 19.1: CLIENT PAGE ATTRIBUTES *(continued)*

ATTRIBUTE	SPECIFICATION WINDOW TAB	MEANING
TopMargin	General	Top margin in pixels
Vlink	General	Link color for visited links
OnLoad	Events	Process to run on loading the page
OnUnload	Events	Process to run when unloading the page
FileName	RTE Options	Name of physical file for page (ASP, JSP, HTML)
RTESynchronization	RTE Options	Whether or not to generate code for this page

SERVER PAGES

Server pages are objects that have access to the resources available on the server. For example, if some security processing needs to take place, a server page would communicate with various components on the server to perform that processing. Separating the application into client pages and server pages helps to separate the presentation logic from the business logic, which aids in both maintenance and reuse. In Rose, a server page has the following notation:

ServerPage

Unlike a client page, a server page has full access to the server's resources. It can communicate with the objects on the server to carry out business functionality, and then build client pages to show the results of the processing to the end user. One server page can also redirect control to another, allowing the second server page to take over processing.

To create a server page:

1. Right-click the virtual directory in the Logical view.

2. Select Web Modeler ➤ New ➤ Server Page.

3. Enter the name of the new page.

Rose will create the server page, and will also automatically create a client page for you. The client page handles the client-side functionality, such as display logic. The server page handles the business processing and builds the client page. Rose will also automatically add a build relationship between the server page and the client page. We will discuss relationships shortly.

In the specification window for the server page, you can set the following two values:

◆ File Name is the physical name of the page (ASP, JSP, or HTML).

◆ RTE Synchronization controls whether the page will be generated or not.

FORMS

Forms are simple HTML pages that contain text boxes, list boxes, and other data input controls. The purpose of a form is simply to receive information from the end user and to display information to the end user. Business logic is not included on a form.

A client page may contain one or more forms. Each form on a client page is associated with that page using an aggregation relationship. Fields on the form are modeled as attributes of the form, and are given the stereotype HTML Input. In Rose, the following symbol is used to represent a form:

Form

(from ServerPage_Client)

To create an HTML form:

1. Right-click the client page on which the form is to be located.

2. Select Web Modeler ➤ New ➤ HTML Form.

3. Enter the name of the new form.

Like client pages and server pages, forms have detailed specifications that will be used during the code-generation process. Any values that you set on the General tab will appear in the generated HTML. Table 19.2 lists the specifications for the HTML Form stereotype, and the purpose of each specification.

TABLE 19.2: HTML FORM ATTRIBUTES

ATTRIBUTE	SPECIFICATION WINDOW TAB	MEANING
Action	General	Form-processing agent
Class	General	Class name for element
Enctype	General	Content type used to encode the form's data
ID	General	Element name
Lang	General	Language of element's content
Method	General	HTTP method to submit form's data
Style	General	Cascading style sheet for element
Target	General	Name of frame target
Onblur	Events	Process to run when element loses focus
Onclick	Events	Process to run on mouse click
Ondblclick	Events	Process to run on mouse double-click

Continued on next page

TABLE 19.2: HTML FORM ATTRIBUTES *(continued)*

ATTRIBUTE	SPECIFICATION WINDOW TAB	MEANING
Onfocus	Events	Process to run when element gains focus
Onkeydown	Events	Process to run when a key is pressed down
Onkeypress	Events	Process to run when an alphanumeric key is pressed
Onkeyup	Events	Process to run when a key is released
Onmousedown	Events	Process to run when the mouse button is pressed
Onmousemove	Events	Process to run when the mouse moves
Onmouseout	Events	Process to run when the mouse cursor is moved off of the element
Onmouseover	Events	Process to run when the mouse cursor is placed on the element
Onmouseup	Events	Process to run when the mouse button is released
Onreset	Events	Process to run when the form is reset
Onsubmit	Events	Process to run when the form is submitted
RTE Synchronization	RTE Options	Whether or not to generate the element
Resolve Relative Paths Dynamically	RTE Options	Automatically resolve paths in referenced files (Note: Setting this field to Default will set it to True/False, depending upon what is set in Tools ➤ Web Modeler ➤ User Preferences.)

An HTML form is really just a collection of input fields. Rose supports three types of input fields: an HTML Input, an HTML Select, or an HTML TextArea. Once you have added a form, you can add more input fields using Web Modeler.

An HTML Input is a field on the form. It can have one of these types: text, password, check box, radio, submit, reset, file, hidden, image, or button. The HTML input will be modeled as an attribute of the form.

To add a new HTML Input field:

1. Right-click the HTML form.

2. Select Web Modeler ➤ New ➤ HTML Input.

3. Select the type of input (text, checkbox, etc.).

4. Enter the name, ID, and value of the input.

5. Select OK to create the new input.

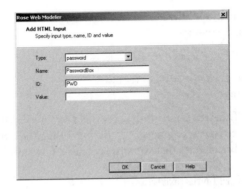

6. Right-click the new input.

7. Edit the input specifications, event handlers, and round-trip engineering options on the specification window.

This HTML input will be generated in the code as follows:

```
<input ID="PWD" Name="PasswordBox" Type="password">
```

An HTML Select is a select box field. The select box has a list of values, and allows the user to select one or more of the values in the list.

To add a new HTML Select field:

1. Right-click the HTML form.

2. Select Web Modeler ➤ New ➤ HTML Select.

3. Enter the name and ID of the field.

4. Select OK to create the new field.

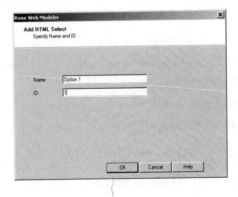

5. Right-click the new field.

6. Edit the field specifications, event handlers, and round-trip engineering options on the specification window.

The field will be generated in the code as follows:

```
<select ID="1" Name="HTMLSelect">
    </select>
```

An HTML TextArea is a multi-line text field on an HTML form. These fields can be used any time the user needs to enter long strings of text. Using the attributes associated with the field, you can set the number of lines that will display on the text area, whether the text area is editable, the tab index for the control, and other properties.

To add a new HTML TextArea field:

1. Right-click the HTML form.

2. Select Web Modeler ➤ New ➤ HTML TextArea.

3. Enter the name and ID of the field.

4. Select OK to create the new field.

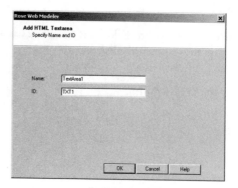

5. Right-click the new field.

6. Edit the field specifications, event handlers, and round-trip engineering options on the specification window.

The field will be generated in the code as follows:

```
<textarea ID="TXT1" Name="TextArea1" Rows="4">
```

All of these types of fields (Input, Select, or TextArea) will appear as attributes of the form on which they are displayed. When code is generated, Rose will examine both the fields and their properties to determine what HTML to generate.

Form
(from ServerPage_Client)

<<HTML Input>> + OK : button
<<HTML Input>> + PasswordBox : password
<<HTML Select>> + HTMLSelect1 : Select
<<HTML Textarea>> + TextArea1

Relationships

Now that we have classes in the model, the next step is to add relationships. There are four primary types of relationships between web elements: link relationships, build relationships, redirect relationships, and submit relationships.

A *link relationship* is used to represent a hypertext link between two client pages or between a client page and a server page. The link is drawn as an association relationship between two classes, with a stereotype of <<Link>>.

Client Page 1   Client Page 2

To set the detailed specifications for the link, right-click the association and select Open Specification. Table 19.3 lists the properties of a link association.

TABLE 19.3: LINK RELATIONSHIP ATTRIBUTES

ATTRIBUTE	SPECIFICATION WINDOW TAB	MEANING
AccessKey	General	Key that will set focus to the element
Class	General	Class name for element
Dir	General	Directional orientation
HREF	General	Link location
ID	General	Element name
Lang	General	Language of element's content
Name	General	Link destination
Style	General	Cascading style sheet for element
TabIndex	General	Tab order of the element
Target	General	Where the link displays in the browser

Continued on next page

TABLE 19.3: LINK RELATIONSHIP ATTRIBUTES *(continued)*

ATTRIBUTE	SPECIFICATION WINDOW TAB	MEANING
Title	General	Document referenced by HREF attribute
Onblur	Events	Process to run when element loses focus
Onclick	Events	Process to run on mouse click
Ondblclick	Events	Process to run on mouse double-click
Onfocus	Events	Process to run when element gains focus
Onkeydown	Events	Process to run when a key is pressed down
Onkeypress	Events	Process to run when an alphanumeric key is pressed
Onkeyup	Events	Process to run when a key is released
Onmousedown	Events	Process to run when the mouse button is pressed
Onmousemove	Events	Process to run when the mouse moves
Onmouseout of the element	Events	Process to run when the mouse cursor is moved off
Onmouseover the element	Events	Process to run when the mouse cursor is placed on
Onmouseup	Events	Process to run when the mouse button is released
RTE Synchronization	RTE Options	Whether or not to generate the element
Resolve Relative Paths Dynamically	RTE Options	Automatically resolve paths in referenced files (Note: Setting this field to Default will set it to True/False, depending upon what is set in Tools ➤ Web Modeler ➤ User Preferences.)

A *build relationship* is used to show that a server page builds a client page. Like a link relationship, a build relationship is modeled as a stereotyped association.

ServerPage   <<Build>>   ServerPage_Client
(from ServerPage)

When you create a server page, Rose will automatically create a client page for you and link the client page to the server page with a build relationship, and the client page will be modeled as a nested page within the server page. Each client page can be built by only one server page. However, a single server page may build several client pages. To create additional client pages for a server page, right-click the server page and select New ➤ Nested Class. Give the new client page a name, and assign it a stereotype of "Client Class." Finally, create a build relationship between the server page and the new client page.

A *redirect* or *forward relationship* is used when control is passed from one server page to another. A redirect relationship is used in an ASP application, and a forward relationship is used in a JSP application. In this example, ServerPage1 is redirecting control to ServerPage2.

Once you have generated code, a line similar to the following will be inserted. The following line appears in `ServerPage1.asp`:

```
<% Response.Redirect("ServerPage2.asp") %>
```

A redirect or forward relationship has three attributes in its specification window. The Page attribute is used to set the destination page name. The RTE Synchronization property is used to control whether or not the relationship will be generated. Finally, the Resolve Relative Paths attribute controls whether paths will be automatically resolved.

A *submit relationship* is used when a form submits information to a server page. At that point, the user has finished entering information onto the form, and the information is ready for processing. The web server can then begin to process the information. A submit relationship is also shown as a stereotyped association:

Reverse Engineering a Web Application

In many situations, your team will be undertaking an effort to modify an existing application. In these cases, the best place to start is reverse engineering the existing application. Once that has been done, the team can examine the current system architecture, make any needed additions or modifications to the design, and generate the code.

Rose supports the reverse engineering of ASP, JSP, and HTML pages. It assigns the appropriate stereotypes to the classes and creates relationships between them.

Begin the reverse-engineering process by selecting Tools ➤ Web Modeler ➤ Reverse Engineer a New Web Application. After the welcome screen, you will be prompted for the location of your application.

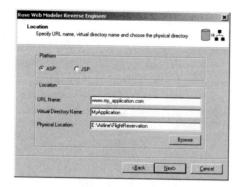

First, select the platform—either ASP or JSP—that is used by your application. In the URL Name field, enter the URL of the application. In the Virtual Directory Name field, enter the name of a package to create in Rose. During the reverse-engineering process, Rose will create a package in the Logical view with this name. All reverse-engineered classes and relationships will be placed inside this package. Finally, in the Physical Location field, enter the path to the application files.

Next, you will see a treeview with all available ASP, JSP, and HTML pages to reverse engineer. By default, all pages will be selected. Select the page(s) you wish to reverse engineer and press Next.

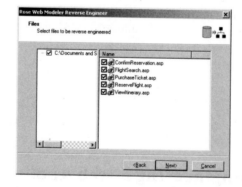

Rose will examine each of the files and reverse engineer them into the model. If any errors occur, Rose will enter them into the log.

An ASP page is reverse engineered as a class with the stereotype <<Server Page>> and an associated class with the stereotype <<Client Page>>. The server page and the client page are linked with a build relationship. The VBScript or Java on the ASP or JSP server page is modeled as an operation on that page.

The form(s) on the client page are modeled as separate classes in Rose, with a stereotype of <<Form>>. Any controls on the form are reverse engineered as attributes of the form.

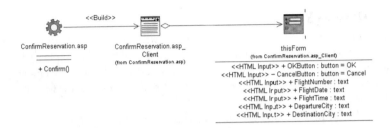

Generating Code for a Web Application

After you have reverse engineered and modified a web application or modeled a web application from scratch, Rose will generate code for you. Rose will create the HTML, ASP, and JSP files from the model.

Rose will generate code for the following:

- Server pages
- Client pages
- Forms
- Form input fields
- Form select fields
- Form text area fields
- Redirect or forward relationships
- Link relationships

When you generate code, Rose will first look for an existing file with the same name as the class you are generating. If a file is found, Rose will update it. Otherwise, a new file is created. The stereotype of the class, coupled with the platform of the virtual directory, controls what type of file will be created. The files created for server pages will be either ASP or JSP files. A client page with no relationship to a server page will generate an HTML file.

To generate code from your model:

1. Right-click the virtual directory.

2. Select Web Modeler ➢ Generate Code.

3. Rose will generate code, and then log any errors to the log window.

Summary

In this chapter, we examined the modeling of web applications with UML and Rose. To a certain extent, modeling web applications is similar to modeling other applications. We still create use cases and the flow of events. We still create Sequence and Collaboration diagrams that show how the objects interact with each other. And we still create Class diagrams to show what classes are needed and how they relate.

A chief difference is in the kinds of classes and relationships that are used in web modeling. By stereotyping our classes as client pages, server pages, or forms, we can be sure that Rose will generate the appropriate source code. Where client/server applications have standard association relationships, web applications have a few types of associations: build relationships, link relationships, submit relationships, and redirect relationships.

Once you have modeled your web application, Rose can generate code for you. You can use the round-trip engineering capabilities of Rose to update your code, update the model, and keep the model and code consistent.

Like the rest of UML, the web notation will continue to evolve as new web languages and technologies are introduced. Rose will evolve along with the notation, providing support for these new concepts and helping organizations design both client/server and web applications more effectively.

Appendix:

Getting Started with UML

UML is made up of a number of different types of diagrams. Each gives the reader a slightly different perspective of the system's design. Some are high-level and intended to give you an understanding of the functionality in the system. Others are very detailed and include the specific classes and components that will be built to implement the system. Still others are midway between these two levels: They provide design details but from a higher-level perspective.

The set of diagrams gives you a complete picture of the system design. Different members of the team create different types of diagrams, and each is used by a different set of people. While building the system, the developers will refer to the diagrams to understand what classes and components need to be built. Later, when a team is maintaining the system, they can refer to the diagrams to understand the system structure, analyze the impact of a potential change, and document any design changes that were made.

UML is constantly being refined to incorporate new ideas and technologies. For example, it can now be used to model an XML DTD. As the object-oriented world changes, UML can change along with it. At the same time, though, it is a standard, and modifications to it are centrally managed. UML is controlled by the Object Management Group, which has members from large and small companies around the world.

Rational Software has developed a systems development lifecycle titled the Rational Unified Process (RUP). RUP complements UML by providing specific process steps, roles, responsibilities, guidelines, workflows, and templates that can be used to develop software. Although RUP complements UML, you may use UML without using RUP.

UML includes many different diagram types. Business Use Case diagrams are used to model the organization. Business workflow (activity) diagrams are used to show the processes within the organization. Use Case diagrams show the functionality to be provided by the system and the people and entities that interact with the system. Activity diagrams show the flow of logic through a use case. Sequence and Collaboration diagrams show the objects that are needed to implement the functionality of a use case, and include the messages between the objects. Statechart diagrams are used to model dynamic behavior, and are frequently used in real-time systems. Component diagrams show the components that will be created for the system and the relationships between them. Finally, Deployment diagrams are used to show the network structure and where the system will be deployed on the network.

Building a Business Use Case Diagram

A Business Use Case diagram is a mechanism for modeling the work done by the organization itself. The diagram contains *business use cases*, which are functions performed by the organization; *business actors*, which are entities outside the organization that interact with it; and *business workers*, which are roles within the organization.

The Business Use Case diagram gives someone an understanding of what the organization does and who interacts with it. It is supplemented by activity diagrams, which detail the workflows within the organization.

A business process team or a business analysis team typically creates the diagram. It is nontechnical, and can be used by any member of the organization to gain a better understanding of the organization.

To create a new Business Use Case diagram, follow these steps:

1. Right-click a package in the Use Case view.

2. Select New ➤ Use Case Diagram.

3. Right-click the toolbar and select Customize.

4. Add buttons for business actor, business use case, business worker, business entity, and organizational unit.

A *Business Use Case diagram* shows a subset of the business use cases, business workers, and business actors of the organization.

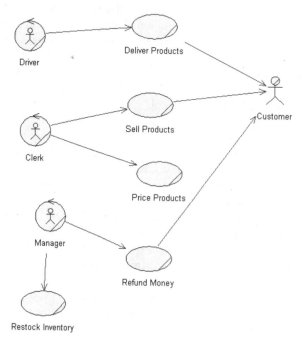

Follow these steps to add business actors to your diagram:

1. Determine the business actors.

2. Select the Business Actor toolbar button.

3. Click in the Use Case diagram to add the actor.

4. Name the actor.

A business actor is an individual, group, company, or other entity outside of the organization that directly interacts with the organization.

Use these steps to add business workers to the diagram:

1. Determine the business workers.

2. Select the Business Worker toolbar button.

3. Click in the Use Case diagram to add the worker.

4. Name the worker.

A business worker is a role within the organization.

Follow these steps to add relationships between the business actors and business use cases:

1. Select the Unidirectional Association toolbar button.

2. Drag an arrow from the actor or business worker to the use case.

A *communicates relationship* between a business actor and a business use case shows how a business actor or business worker interacts with the organization.

Follow these steps to group the business actors, business workers, and business use cases into organization units.

1. Select the Organization Unit toolbar button.

2. Click inside a Business Use Case diagram to place the organization unit.

3. In the browser, drag and drop business actors, business workers, business use cases, Business Use Case diagrams, and activity diagrams into the new organization unit.

An *organization unit* is used to group together business modeling elements such as business actors and business use cases. These units can help to organize the model and show how the company itself is organized.

Building a Workflow (Activity) Diagram

Activity diagrams are commonly used in two situations. In business modeling, they can be used to document the workflow of a process within the organization. In systems modeling, they can be used to document the flow of logic through a use case.

An activity diagram that focuses on workflow shows you the people or groups within the workflow, the steps in the process, decision points in the process, areas where steps in the process can occur in parallel, objects affected by the workflow, states of the objects, and transitions between steps in the process. UML contains notation for all of these items.

To create a new activity diagram:

1. Right-click a use case or package in the Use Case view.

2. Select New ➤ Activity Diagram.

An *activity diagram* models a process in the organization. It can be used to analyze either existing or new processes. These types of diagrams are frequently used in business process re-engineering efforts or in any situation where the workflow is complex or undocumented.

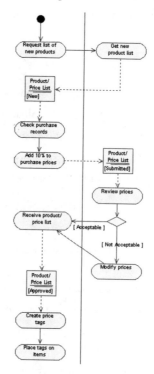

To partition your diagram into sections for each actor or worker's responsibilities, follow these steps:

1. Determine the participants in the workflow.

2. Select the Swimlane toolbar button.

3. Click in the diagram to add the swimlane.

4. Name the swimlane with the name of the role or group in the workflow.

A *swimlane* is a vertical section of the diagram that will contain all of the workflow steps that a particular person or group performs. You divide the diagram into many swimlanes, one for each person or group in the process.

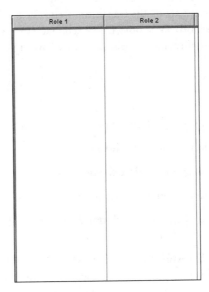

To add detailed steps to the diagram:

1. Select the Activity toolbar button.

2. Click in the diagram to add the activity.

3. Name the activity.

An *activity* is a step in the workflow. It can contain actions, which are steps within the activity. The activity is placed in the swimlane of the individual or group that performs the activity.

Follow these steps to set the sequence of the activities:

1. Select the Transition toolbar button.

2. Drag an arrow from one activity to the next.

3. Right-click the transition arrow and select Open Specification.

4. Optionally add an event and event arguments on the General tab.

5. Optionally add a guard condition, action, send event, send event arguments, and send target on the Detail tab.

A *transition* shows how the process moves from one step (activity) to the next. An event triggers the movement from one activity to another. An event can have arguments. A guard condition controls when the transition can or cannot occur; the guard condition must be true for the transition to occur. An action occurs while the process is transitioning from one activity to another. It is typically a quick process that occurs as part of the transition itself. The send target suggests that, as part of the transition, a message is sent to some object. The send target is the object receiving the message. The send event is a message sent to another object. It may have arguments.

Follow these steps to add decision points to the logic:

1. Select the Decision toolbar button.

2. Click in the diagram to place the decision.

3. Draw transitions from the decision to the activities that may occur after the decision.

4. Place guard conditions on each transition arrow. The guard conditions will control which path is taken after the decision.

A *decision point* in the workflow indicates when the workflow can take two or more different paths. Transition arrows leading from the decision to activities show the different paths that the workflow can follow. Guard conditions on the transitions indicate under which conditions each path will be followed. Guard conditions must be mutually exclusive.

To add objects to the workflow:

1. Select the Object toolbar button.

2. Click inside the diagram to place the object.

3. Select the Object Flow toolbar button.

4. Drag an arrow from an activity to the object it affects or from the object to the activity that uses the object as input.

An *object* is an entity affected by the workflow. It can serve as input into a process step, in which case a dashed object flow arrow is drawn from the object to the process step. Or, it can be affected by a process step, in which case an object flow arrow is drawn from the step to the object.

Object

Follow these steps to add synchronizations to the workflow:

1. Select the Synchronization toolbar button.

2. Click in the diagram to place the synchronization bar.

3. Draw a transition arrow from an activity to the synchronization bar, indicating that the parallel processing begins after that activity.

4. Draw transition arrows from the synchronization bar to the activities that can occur in parallel.

5. Create another synchronization bar to indicate the end of the parallel processing.

6. Draw transition arrows from the synchronous activities to the final synchronization bar to indicate that the parallel processing stops once all of those activities are complete.

A *synchronization* indicates that two or more steps in the workflow may be completed in parallel. A synchronization bar is used to show where two or more activities may occur simultaneously. These can be very effective in analyzing the efficiency of a workflow; examining the amount of parallel activity can help to optimize a workflow.

Building a Use Case Diagram

A Use Case diagram is a graphical representation of the high-level system scope. It includes *use cases*, which are pieces of functionality the system will provide, and *actors*, who are the users of the system. Looking at a Use Case diagram, you should easily be able to tell what the system will do and who will interact with it.

You can create one or more Use Case diagrams for a single system. If you create more than one, each will show a subset of the actors and/or use cases in the system. You can also group the use cases and actors into packages to help organize the model.

The Use Case diagram can be helpful in communicating with the end users of the system. It is designed to be straightforward and nontechnical so that everyone on the team can come to a common understanding of the system scope. It is usually created by the technical team, but in conjunction with an end user representative.

To create a new Use Case diagram:

1. Right-click a package in the Use Case view.

2. Select New ➣ Use Case Diagram.

A *Use Case diagram* shows a subset of the use cases and actors in the system. You can create as many Use Case diagrams as you need to fully document the system scope.

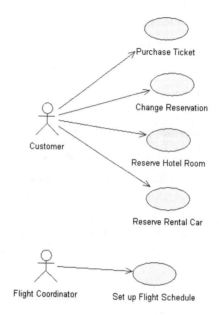

Follow these steps to add actors to the diagram:

1. Determine the actors for your system.

2. Select the Actor toolbar button.

3. Click in the Use Case diagram to add the actor.

4. Name the actor.

An actor is a person, system, piece of hardware, or other thing that interacts with your system.

Follow these steps to add use cases to the diagram:

1. Add the use cases to the diagram.

2. Select the Use Case toolbar button.

3. Click in the Use Case diagram to add the use case.

4. Give the use case a name.

A use case is a piece of functionality the system will provide. It is usually named in the format <verb><noun>, such as "Deposit Check" or "Withdraw Cash." Use cases are high-level and implementation-independent.

To add relationships between the actors and use cases:

1. Select the Unidirectional Association toolbar button.

2. Drag an arrow from the actor to the use case.

A *communicates relationship* between an actor and a use case indicates that the actor initiates the use case. An actor may initiate one or more use cases.

To add includes relationships between appropriate use cases:

1. Select the Include Use Case toolbar button.

2. Drag an arrow from a use case to the use case it includes.

An *includes relationship* suggests that one use case must include another. In other words, running one use case means that the other must be run as well. One use case may be included by one or more other use cases.

To add extends relationships between appropriate use cases:

1. Select the Extend Use Case toolbar button.

2. Drag an arrow from the extending use case to the use case it extends.

An *extends relationship* is used when one use case optionally extends the functionality provided by another. In other words, if one use case runs, an extending use case may or may not run.

Follow these steps to group the use cases, actors, and other elements into packages:

1. Right-click the Use Case view or another package and select New ➤ Package.

2. Name the new package.

3. In the browser, drag and drop use cases, actors, Use Case diagrams, or other modeling elements into the new package.

A *package* is a UML mechanism used to group items together. Grouping can help to organize the model, and can also help in managing any changes in the model elements. You may nest one package inside another to further organize the model.

To add generalization relationships between appropriate use cases:

1. Select the Generalization toolbar button.

2. Drag an arrow from the child use case to the parent use case.

A *generalization relationship* between two use cases indicates that one use case (the child) inherits all of the functionality provided by the other use case (the parent).

To add generalization relationships between appropriate actors:

1. Select the Generalization toolbar button.

2. Drag an arrow from the child actor to the parent actor.

A generalization relationship between actors indicates that one actor (the child) inherits the characteristics of another actor (the parent). The child actor may initiate all of the use cases that the parent can initiate.

Building an Interaction Diagram

An Interaction diagram is a graphical representation of how the objects and actors in a system interact with one another to achieve the desired goal of the system. There are two types of Interaction diagrams, *Sequence diagrams* and *Collaboration diagrams*. Sequence diagrams illustrate the interactions of objects along a timeline. Collaboration diagrams show the interactions, but without the timeline. These two diagrams display the same information, just in different ways.

You can create multiple Interaction diagrams for each use case in a system. More than one is typically created to illustrate the interaction given different scenarios.

Sequence diagrams are usually created to show the flow of functionality and control throughout the objects in the system. Collaboration diagrams are typically used to illustrate which objects communicate with other objects. Sequence diagrams answer questions about how the system will work. Collaboration diagrams answer questions about the soundness of the structure of the system.

To create a new Sequence diagram:

1. Right-click a use case in the Use Case view.

2. Select New ➤ Sequence Diagram.

Once you have created the Sequence diagram, you next need to determine which actors and objects to place on it. One method is to drag all actors involved in the use case to the Sequence diagram, then walk through the functionality, adding objects to facilitate that functionality as needed.

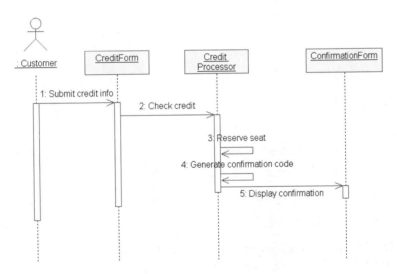

To add actors and objects to the Sequence diagram:

1. Select any actors involved in the use case and drag them into the new Sequence diagram.

2. Select the Object toolbar button.

3. Click in the Sequence diagram to add an object.

4. Name the object.

5. Add additional objects as needed.

At this point, the objects and actors are on the Sequence diagram, but Interaction diagrams would be fairly useless without showing the interactions. Messages are used to accomplish this. A message is simply some form of communication between one object or actor and another.

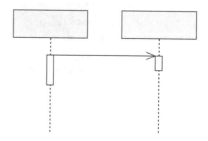

Messages can also be *reflexive*, meaning that the object communicates some information to itself.

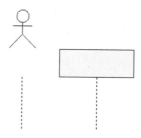

Follow these steps to add messages to the diagram:

1. Select the Message toolbar button.

2. Click on the actor or object to initiate the message.

3. Drag the message to the actor or object to receive the message.

4. Name the message.

TIP *Pressing F5 on a Sequence diagram will create the corresponding Collaboration diagram. You can also use F5 to toggle between a Sequence diagram and its Collaboration diagram.*

Collaboration diagrams are not time-based, but show the interactions of the objects as a whole. This is useful for pointing out potential bottlenecks (objects that individually communicate with a large number of objects). Sequencing of messages is shown on a Collaboration diagram by numbering the messages.

To create a new Collaboration diagram:

1. Right-click a use case in the Use Case view.

2. Select New ➤ Collaboration Diagram.

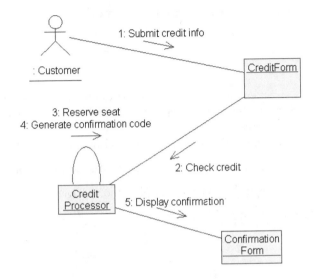

Once you have created the Collaboration diagram, you then need to determine which actors and objects to place on it. One method is to drag all actors involved in the use case to the Collaboration diagram, then walk through the functionality, adding objects as needed to facilitate that functionality.

To add actors and objects to a Collaboration diagram:

1. Select any actors involved in the use case and drag them into the new Collaboration diagram.

2. Select the Object toolbar button.

3. Click in the Collaboration diagram to add an object.

4. Name the object.

5. Add additional objects as needed.

Before adding messages, we must link the objects or actors that will communicate. This is done by adding an object link using the toolbar. Once the object link is established, messages can be added. On Collaboration diagrams, the messages are either *link* messages or *links to self*. A link message is analogous to a message in a Sequence diagram. A link to self is analogous to a reflexive message in a Sequence diagram.

To add object links to the Collaboration diagram:

1. Select the Object Link toolbar button.

2. Click on one actor or object to be linked.

3. Drag the object link to the actor or object to be linked.

After the object link is established, messages can be created. Link messages are created either using the Link Message toolbar button or the Reverse Link Message toolbar button, depending on the direction of the message.

Follow these steps to add messages to the Collaboration diagram:

1. Select the Link Message or Reverse Link Message toolbar button.

2. Click the object link on which to place the message.

3. Name the message.

To add reflexive links to a Collaboration diagram:

1. Select the Link to Self toolbar button.

2. Click on the object to be linked.

3. Name the reflexive link.

TIP   *Pressing F5 on a Collaboration diagram will create the corresponding Sequence diagram.*

Building a Class Diagram

A Class diagram is used to show a subset of the classes, interfaces, packages of classes, and relationships in the system. A typical system will have many different Class diagrams.

In Rose, different icons are used to represent different kinds of classes on a Class diagram. For example, Rose contains icons for interfaces, client pages, session EJBs, COM objects, and many other types of classes. Rose also contains icons that distinguish analysis classes from design classes. An *analysis class* is an implementation-independent view of the system, intended to be an initial sketch of the system design. *Design classes* are implementation-specific and correlate to the classes that will eventually be created in the source code.

Rose can generate code that will include the class name, attribute types, default values, operation signatures, and class relationships. Developers use the Class diagrams to see the system structure and to know what operations to create for a given class.

Follow these steps to create a new Class diagram:

1. Right-click a package in the Logical view.

2. Select New ➤ Class Diagram.

A *Class diagram* includes a subset of the classes, attributes, operations, relationships, and packages of classes in the system. You can create as many Class diagrams as you need to fully document the system design.

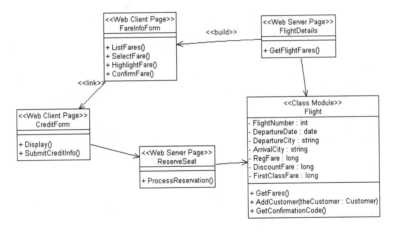

To add analysis classes to the model:

1. Select the Boundary, Entity, or Control class button from the toolbar.

2. Click in the diagram to add the class.

3. Name the class.

An analysis class is an implementation-independent class. The analysis classes are used to document some of the concepts within the system and to create a conceptual view of the system design.

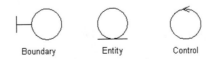

To add design classes to the model:

1. Create an additional Class diagram.

2. Add design classes to the model.

3. Select the Class button from the toolbar.

4. Click in the diagram to add the class.

5. Give the class a name.

A design class is an implementation-specific class within the model. It will correspond to a class in the source code.

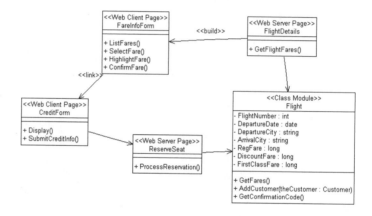

To add interface classes:

1. Select the Interface button from the toolbar.

2. Click in the diagram to add the interface.

3. Name the interface.

An *interface* is used to expose the public operations of a class without exposing the implementation. An interface contains method signatures, but no implementation.

Interface

Follow these steps to add attributes to the classes:

1. Right-click a class on the diagram.

2. Select New ➤ Attribute.

3. Type the attribute name, followed by a colon, and then the attribute's data type (i.e., **Address:String**).

4. Optionally enter a default value for the attribute, by following the data type with an equals sign and then the default value (i.e., **Address:String = 123 Main St.**).

5. Right-click the attribute in the browser window and select Open Specification.

6. Set the attribute visibility (public, private, protected).

An *attribute* is a piece of information associated with a class. All objects in a given class will share the same attributes, but each object may have its own attribute values.

```
┌─────────────────────┐
│        Class        │
├─────────────────────┤
│ - Attribute1 : string│
│ - Attribute2 : int   │
├─────────────────────┤
│                     │
└─────────────────────┘
```

Follow these steps to add operations to the classes:

1. Right-click a class on the diagram.

2. Select New ➤ Operation.

3. Enter the operation signature, including parameters and a return type. Use the format OpName(Parm1:Parm1DataType, Parm2:Parm2DataType):ReturnType (for example, **AddNumbers(X:Int, Y:Int): Long**).

4. Right-click the operation in the browser window and select Open Specification.

5. Set the operation visibility (public, private, protected).

An *operation* is a method within the class. In Rose, you can define the operation name, parameters, visibility, return type, and parameter data types. Certain operations, such as Get() and Set() methods for attributes, can be automatically generated by Rose.

```
┌────────────────────────────────────┐
│               Class                │
├────────────────────────────────────┤
│ - Attribute1 : string              │
│ - Attribute2 : int                 │
├────────────────────────────────────┤
│ + Operation1(parm : string) : int  │
│ + Operation2(parm2 : int) : boolean│
└────────────────────────────────────┘
```

Web Modeling

Thanks to the recent work of people such as Jim Conallen, UML is now being used more and more frequently to model web applications. Rose includes a number of class stereotypes for web modeling, such as client pages, server pages, and HTML forms.

These web classes are placed on a Class diagram and, like traditional classes, can include attributes, operations, and relationships. Using Class diagrams, you can view the web classes and their interrelationships, and also see how the web classes interact with the other classes in the system.

Before following any of these procedures, select Tools ➤ Options. On the Diagram tab, set the default language to Web Modeler.

To add server pages to the model:

1. Select the Server Page class button from the toolbar.

2. Click in the diagram to add the class.

3. Name the class.

A *server page* contains logic that runs on the server, and uses server resources such as database connections, security services, or file services.

Server Page

To add client pages to the model:

1. Select the Client Page class button from the toolbar.

2. Click in the diagram to add the class.

3. Name the class.

A *client page* contains logic that runs on the client machine.

Client Page

Follow these steps to add HTML forms to the model:

1. Select the HTML Form class button from the toolbar.

2. Click in the diagram to add the class.

3. Name the class.

An *HTML form* represents a simple HTML page and the fields contained within that page.

Form

To add applets to the model:

1. Select the Applet class button from the toolbar.

2. Click in the diagram to add the class.

3. Name the class.

An *applet* is a small application that is downloaded to the client machine and runs on the client.

To add a web application object to the model:

1. Select the Web Application class button from the toolbar.

2. Click in the diagram to add the class.

3. Name the class.

An *application* is an object that is used to maintain state information, and is shared among all users of an application.

Follow these steps to add session objects to the model:

1. Select the Web Session class button from the toolbar.

2. Click in the diagram to add the class.

3. Name the class.

A *session object* is an object that is used to maintain state information, and is specific to a single client and the current session.

Follow these steps to add COM objects to the model:

1. Select the COM Object class button from the toolbar.

2. Click in the diagram to add the class.

3. Name the class.

A *COM object* is an object such as an ActiveX control that uses Microsoft's Component Object Model.

COM Object

Adding Class Relationships

There are many different types of relationships between classes. An *association relationship* indicates that one class needs to communicate with another. Associations may be unidirectional or bidirectional. An *aggregation relationship* suggests a whole/part relationship between two classes. A *generalization relationship* indicates a parent/child inheritance relationship between two classes. Finally, a *dependency relationship* is a weaker form of association, suggesting that a change to one class may affect another.

Association names can be added to a relationship to clarify the relationship's purpose. Role names can also be used that show what role each class plays in the relationship. Multiplicity settings show how many instances of one object are related to a single instance of the other object.

Relationships are drawn on Class diagrams as arrows between the two related classes. Different types of arrows are used to indicate different types of relationships.

Follow these steps to add association relationships between the classes:

1. Select the Unidirectional Association or the Bidirectional Association toolbar button.

2. Drag an arrow from one class to the other.

3. Type an association name, if needed.

An association relationship is a semantic connection between classes. It indicates that one class needs to communicate with another (for example, one class needs to send a message to the other). Unidirectional associations suggest that the messages can be sent in only one direction, while bidirectional associations suggest that messages can be sent in both directions (i.e., each class can call a method of the other).

To add aggregation relationships:

1. Select the Aggregation toolbar button.

2. Drag an arrow from the "whole" class to the "part" class.

3. Type an association name, if needed.

An aggregation relationship is used to denote a whole/part relationship between classes. In this situation, one class logically contains another. Association and aggregation relationships are created identically during code generation.

To add generalization relationships:

1. Select the Generalization toolbar button.

2. Drag an arrow from the child class to the parent class.

A generalization relationship is used to show an inheritance relationship between two classes. The child class inherits all attributes, operations, and relationships of the parent.

To add dependency relationships:

1. Select the Dependency toolbar button.

2. Drag an arrow from one class to the other.

A dependency relationship is a weaker form of an association relationship. While one class still needs to communicate with the other, neither class is responsible for instantiating, destroying, or otherwise managing the other. When generating code for an association relationship, a reference to one class is created inside the other through a new attribute. With a dependency relationship, no attributes are created to support the relationship. Dependency relationships must be unidirectional.

Follow these steps to add multiplicity to the relationships:

1. Right-click one end of the relationship.

2. Select Multiplicity and then the appropriate multiplicity setting for that end of the relationship.

3. Right-click the other end of the relationship and set its multiplicity.

Multiplicity shows how many instances of one class are related to a single instance of another class. Multiplicity indicators are placed at both ends of a relationship to show the number of instances in both directions. Multiplicity is not included on a generalization relationship.

To add role names to the relationships:

1. Right-click one end of the relationship.

2. Select Role Name.

3. Type the role name on the diagram.

4. Select the other end of the relationship and set its role name.

Role names indicate what role a class plays in a relationship. For example, in the relationship between Person and Company, a Person could play the role of Employee. Role names are used in the code-generation process; when an attribute is created to support a relationship, the attribute is named with the role name.

Building a Statechart Diagram

A Statechart diagram is used to show the dynamic behavior of an object. It shows the various states in which an object can exist, what state an object is in when it is created, what state an object is in when it is destroyed, how an object moves from one state to another, and what an object does when it is in various states. All of this information helps a developer get a complete picture of how a particular object should behave.

Using Rose, you can create one or more Statechart diagrams for a class, and include all of the information listed above. Statechart diagrams do not need to be created for every class in a model. Classes with significant dynamic behavior, complex behavior, or behavior that is not well understood among the development team are good candidates for Statechart diagrams.

Follow these steps to create a Statechart diagram:

1. Right-click a class in the browser.

2. Select New ➤ Statechart Diagram.

3. Name the new diagram.

A *Statechart diagram* includes the various states, transitions, activities, and actions for an object in a particular class. Each class can have a single state/activity model, with one or more Statechart diagrams within it.

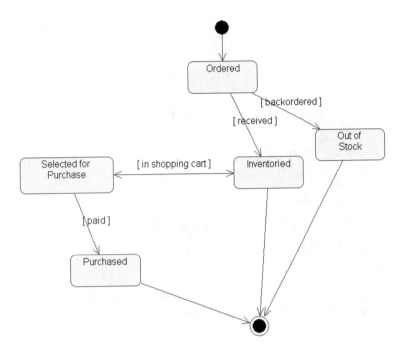

To add states to the diagram:

1. Select the Client Page class button from the toolbar.

2. Click in the diagram to add the class.

3. Name the class.

A *state* is a condition in which an object can exist. For example, an invoice can be New, Paid, Delinquent, or Canceled. Each of these represents a different state.

To add start and end states:

1. Select the Start State or End State button from the toolbar.

2. Click in the diagram to place the start state or end state.

A *start state* shows the state an object is in when it is first instantiated. A Statechart diagram has one, and only one, start state. A start state is shown as a black dot on the diagram. An *end state* shows what state an object is in right before it is removed from memory. A Statechart diagram may have zero, one, or more end states. An end state is shown as a bull's-eye on the diagram.

Start State

End State

To add activities to the states:

1. Right-click the state and select Open Specification.

2. Select the Actions tab.

3. Right-click in the white space and select Insert.

4. Double-click the new activity (the word "Entry/" in the list) to open the activity specification.

5. Enter the activity details.

An *activity* is some bit of processing that occurs while the object is in a particular state. Activities can occur upon entry into the state, while exiting the state, while in the state, or upon a particular event.

To add transitions between the states:

1. Select the State Transition button from the toolbar.

2. Drag from one state to another.

3. Right-click the transition.

4. Select Open Specification.

5. Add transition details, such as an event or guard condition.

A *transition* indicates how an object can move from one state to another. It may include an *event*, which triggers the transition, or a guard condition. An event may also be sent to another object during the transition. A *guard condition*, which is enclosed in square brackets, controls when the transition may or may not occur. An *action* on the transition is a small piece of processing that occurs during the transition itself. The format for these items on a transition line is:

```
Event(Arguments) [Guard] /Action ^SendEventTarget.SendEvent(Arguments)
```

Building a Component Diagram

A Component diagram is used to model the physical components in your system: source code files, executable files, DLL files, ActiveX objects, and so on. Using a Component diagram, the team can specify what components exist and what their relationships are to each other.

This exercise is especially helpful in optimizing the design and planning for deployment. By mapping each component to its appropriate architectural layer (database, business logic, presentation, etc.), the team can see the interaction between the layers themselves. The team can analyze and optimize the communication between the layers before coding is complete.

Rose supports a number of different component stereotypes, such as the ones mentioned above. To create a new Component diagram:

1. Right-click a package in the Component view of the browser.

2. Select New ➤ Component Diagram.

3. Name the new diagram.

A *Component diagram* is used to show a subset of the components or packages of components in the system and their relationships.

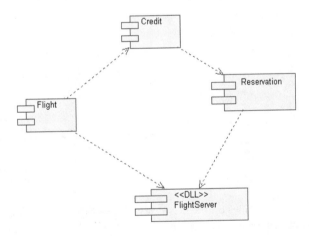

Follow these steps to add components to the model:

1. Select the Component button from the toolbar.

2. Click in the diagram to add the component.

3. Name the component.

4. Right-click the component.

5. Select Open Specification.

6. Set the component stereotype and language.

7. Select the Realizes tab.

8. Right-click each class that will be contained within the component, and select Assign. You may also drag the classes in the browser from the Logical view to the appropriate component in the Component view.

A *component* is one of the physical files that make up a system. Source code components will realize many of the various classes contained within the model.

Building a Deployment Diagram

Deployment diagrams illustrate the physical distribution of a system. A given project has one, and only one, Deployment diagram. These diagrams show the processors, devices, connections, and processes involved in the system.

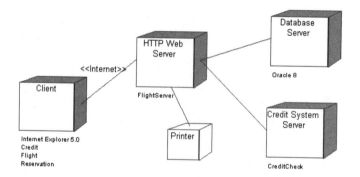

Processors are machines on the network with processing power, including servers and workstations. They do not include printers and other such devices. Processors run processes (executable code).

Follow these steps to create the Deployment diagram:

1. Double-click the Deployment view.

2. Select the Processor toolbar button.

3. Click the Deployment diagram to place the processor.

4. Name the processor.

5. Right-click on the processor and select New ➤ Process from the menu.

6. Name the process.

Devices are the other machines on the network. They include printers, scanners, dumb terminals, and backup devices.

To add devices to the diagram:

1. Select the Device toolbar button.

2. Click the Deployment diagram to place the device.

3. Name the device.

Connections are physical links between processors and other processors, devices and other devices, or processors and devices. Connections can be physical network connections or virtual connections—across the Internet, for example.

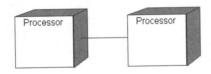

To add connections to the diagram:

1. Select the Connection toolbar button.

2. Click on one processor or device to be connected.

3. Drag the connection to the other processor or device to be connected.

4. Name the connection.

Index

Note to the reader: Throughout this index **boldfaced** page numbers indicate primary discussions of a topic. *Italicized* page numbers indicate illustrations.

TELL US WHAT YOU THINK!

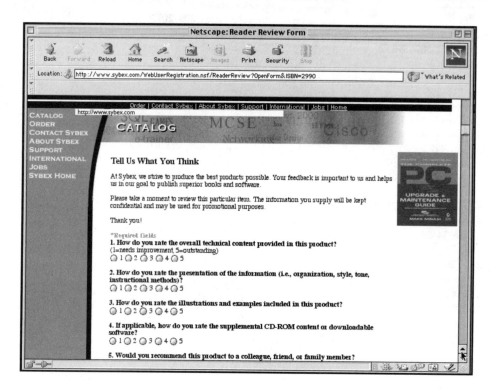

Your feedback is critical to our efforts to provide you with the best books and software on the market. Tell us what you think about the products you've purchased. It's simple:

1. Visit the Sybex website
2. Go to the product page
3. Click on **Submit a Review**
4. Fill out the questionnaire and comments
5. Click **Submit**

With your feedback, we can continue to publish the highest quality computer books and software products that today's busy IT professionals deserve.

www.sybex.com

SYBEX Inc. • 1151 Marina Village Parkway, Alameda, CA 94501 • 510-523-8233

 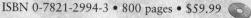